THE PASSIONATE BUREAUCRAT

THE PASSIONATE BUREAUCRAT

Lessons for the 21st Century from 4,500 Years of Public Service Reform

Max Everest-Phillips
UNDP Global Centre for Public Service Excellence, Singapore

NEW JERSEY · LONDON · SINGAPORE · BEIJING · SHANGHAI · HONG KONG · TAIPEI · CHENNAI · TOKYO

Published by

World Scientific Publishing Co. Pte. Ltd.
5 Toh Tuck Link, Singapore 596224
USA office: 27 Warren Street, Suite 401-402, Hackensack, NJ 07601
UK office: 57 Shelton Street, Covent Garden, London WC2H 9HE

Library of Congress Cataloging-in-Publication Data
Names: Everest-Phillips, Max, author.
Title: The passionate bureaucrat : lessons for the 21st century from 4,500 years of
 public service reform / Max Everest-Phillips.
Description: New Jersey : World Scientific, 2018. | Includes bibliographical references and index.
Identifiers: LCCN 2018014014 | ISBN 9789813234826
Subjects: LCSH: Public administration--History. | Bureaucracy. | Lagash (Extinct city)--
 Kings and rulers. | Urukagina--Influence. | Iraq--Civilization--To 634.
Classification: LCC JF1351 .E925 2018 | DDC 351--dc23
LC record available at https://lccn.loc.gov/2018014014

British Library Cataloguing-in-Publication Data
A catalogue record for this book is available from the British Library.

This book is written by the Director of the UNDP Global Centre for Public Service Excellence (GCPSE) in Singapore. The views expressed in this publication are those of the author and do not necessarily represent those of the Government of Singapore or the United Nations, including UNDP or any UN Member states.

Copyright © 2018 by Max Everest-Phillips

All rights reserved.

For any available supplementary material, please visit
https://www.worldscientific.com/worldscibooks/10.1142/10843#t=suppl

Desk Editor: Shreya Gopi

Typeset by Stallion Press
Email: enquiries@stallionpress.com

Printed in Singapore

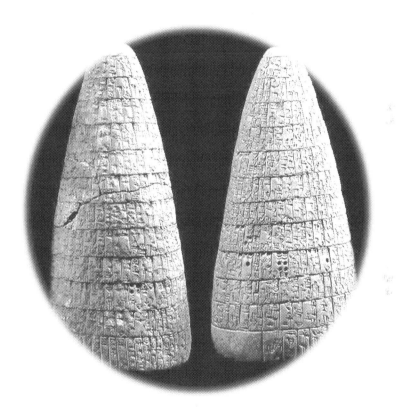

The two best preserved cone-shaped clay tablets that describe Urukagina's reforms of public administration in the Mesopotamian city-state of Lagash around 2350 BC.

Bliss it was in that dawn to be alive
But to be young was very heaven! Oh! Times
In which the meagre, stale, forbidding ways
Of custom, law, and statute, took at once
The attraction of a country in romance!

from

The French Revolution as it Appeared to Enthusiasts at its Commencement

by

William Wordsworth (1770–1850)

Dedication

To my wonderful daughters

Emily and Claudia

Years ago I first tried to explain to you why public administration is interesting. You both looked at me bemused, and together declared: 'That sounds dull'.

This is my second attempt.

With all my love.

30-cm high Lagash sculpture from the pre-Sargonic era: British Museum (Creative Commons license).

Foreword: Look Back to See Ahead

I am delighted to offer a few introductory remarks to this fascinating book on the first 4500 years of public sector reform. At the dawn of civilisation, the ruler of a Sumerian city-state had a radical idea. For the first time in recorded history, Urukagina of Lagash condemned systemic corruption in the civil service and proposed that public officials should work in the interest of citizens, rather than of their leaders and themselves. This ambitious concept remains with us: fulfilled in some places, but still to be achieved in others.

Three great — and inter-related — inventions of early civilisation were agriculture, public works and public administration. The bureaucrat fostered the planning, record-keeping and numeracy needed for the other two to develop. That remarkable achievement is a reminder of the power of public service to transform any economy and society — just as today officials are called upon to achieve the Sustainable Development Goals (SDGs) by 2030.

This book is a fascinating read and unashamedly innovative. It demonstrates that the first known reform of public administration, at Lagash in Mesopotamia some 4400 years ago, still has much to teach us. Perhaps more unexpectedly, it also argues that *plus ça change, plus c'est la même chose*: a good grounding in public sector reforms of the 21st century is useful for interpreting the tantalisingly limited evidence from ancient cuneiform tablets about those Sumerian reforms.

In so doing, this monograph draws parallels between the uncertainty in one of the world's most ancient civilisations and in the current context.

The intellectual interest in looking for principles guiding public administrative reform based on common principles and shared human values across such different times and contexts is to assist today's pursuit of public service excellence.

History, in explaining who we are and why we are the way we are, offers an invaluable anchor in the turbulent waters of our era. Humanity navigates Janus-like, looking both to the past and to the future for guidance and inspiration. In the present turmoil of 'fake news' and 'post-fact truth', the historian provides a glimpse of objective reflection on effective government.

In this thoroughly researched tome, Max takes us back to the dawn of civilisation. The world's first attempt to create a motivated and empowered public service offers lessons for modern times for developing countries. With typical imagination and flair, Max shows us that a new 'Bureaucratic Revolution' is underway. He argues that this will combine old skills of rational decision-making with new skills of passion and empathy. The despised bureaucrat of the late 20th century is the key competitive advantage of the 21st century.

The Global Centre for Public Service Excellence in Singapore has long been a key partner of the Astana Civil Service Hub. This is because, under the inspiring leadership of Max Everest-Phillips, his Centre has helped the UNDP to develop or adapt new thinking on building effective, accountable and transparent institutions in the public sector.

This book fizzes with important ideas, not least why an appreciation of history becomes more important as the future becomes more uncertain. Through Urukagina, we are reminded that the past is humanity's invaluable guide towards a better future. This study will help any reformer consider the challenges ahead while ensuring that public administration of the past will never again seem dull!

Alikhan Baimenov
Chairman
The Astana Civil Service Hub
Kazakhstan

Acknowledgments

Livet må forstås baglæns, men må leves forlæns.
(Life can only be understood backwards, but must be lived forwards).

Soren Kierkegaard

Why is the public service so evidently important yet so routinely derided, so easy to alter yet so infuriatingly difficult to improve? Gaining a grasp on the mercurial ectoplasm of public administration has taken me over 40 years, and I am still not certain that what we know is worth knowing.

Nevertheless, a new era in public service, the '4th Bureaucratic Revolution', is taking shape. This revolution is being driven by the heady cocktail of political turbulence and disruptive technology. As states jostle to keep up with globalisation while keeping the parochial interests of their citizens satisfied, the bureaucrat of the late 20th century, despised as inferior to her private sector counterpart, becomes a key competitive advantage of the 21st century. This is an unashamedly self-serving observation. Having been one of those faceless functionaries for much of the last four decades, it may perhaps be wishful thinking. I hope, however, the reader will see merit in the argument.

I am shameless in painting a 'big picture' view of government and public administration. More than enough, in my opinion, has already been turgidly written on the dull but worthy technical aspects of public service reform such as human resource management, digitalisation or policy formulation. These fields aim to encourage efficiency in departmental methods, by such steps as refining policies and procedures in recruitment, performance management, training and system design. But history suggests that ideas and politics prevent technocratic 'solutions' from working 'scientifically'. Understanding the past will grow more important as the future grows more uncertain.

This book will have achieved its aim if it gives pause for reformers to gather their thoughts and to overcome some predictable problems, while avoiding being bamboozled by sharp-suited consultants peddling a seductively simple patter of quick fixes. Reform of the public service around the world too often has been driven more by personal ambitions than by desired results, achieved little for citizens, while undermining the commitment and morale of the very same public officials on whose motivation the implementation of national and international development goals largely depends.

My reflections on government began in 1977, when I won an open scholarship to study modern history at the Queen's College, Oxford University. On my first day there, my don asked: 'What is feudalism?' ('modern', at Oxford, being delightfully defined as anything after the Fall of Rome in the year 410; 409 AD and before was ancient history. The New Year's Eve parties that year must have been spectacular, as people celebrated becoming 'modern' for the first time! My grandmother, who prided herself on having been a modern working woman in the 1920s, was always amused).

Ever since, while working in UK government ministries (the Foreign and Commonwealth Office, and the Department for International Development) and inter-governmental organisations (the Commonwealth Secretariat and the United Nations), I have been puzzling over many variations of the complex answers to such deceptively simple questions about the nature of governance and the characteristics of government in all its fascinating forms around the world.

When I joined the British Diplomatic Service in 1981, the UK civil service had a timeless quality. Ironically, that was precisely the moment when public officialdom was entering into sharp decline. That tumultuous decade witnessed the rise to dominance of an ideology around the private sector, marked by the coming to power of Margaret Thatcher in the United Kingdom and Ronald Reagan in the United States.

Acknowledgments

As one makes the inevitable and, in many ways surprisingly agreeable transition from young Turk to old fart, each generation snapping at the heels of their predecessors and seeking to dodge the sharp fangs of their successors, the self-absorbed quest for practicality fades and the more intriguing quest for ideas grows.

Most proposals to fine tune the engine of government overlook or take for granted the human dimensions of public bureaucracy. The importance of understanding the perspective of public officials, whose interests and incentives are crucial for the success or failure of reform and of development, is pressing. Yet they are all too often ignored.

Altering the civil service is a profoundly ideological task. The desirable characteristics of public servants and the ideal balance between equity, efficiency and effectiveness in government depend on political philosophy more than evidence. To date, however, the political leadership in almost every country has been painfully lacking in articulating a credible vision of the civil service needed for our times.

I have set myself the challenge of rectifying that gap. To do that, I venture to 'co-create' the future of public administration with its first known reformer. Building on the limited evidence for Urukagina's pioneering attempt to reform the public service 4400 years ago, I do not offer a blueprint for public service 'best practice'. Indeed the underlying message in the pages that follow is that, while 'best principles' exist, there is no magic formula for generating good government. My purpose, therefore, is to encourage anyone interested or involved in public sector reform to think more deeply about the topic, its history and politics — and to challenge normative 'solutions'.

In this endeavour, as with other idiosyncratic ideas I have developed in recent years, I am deeply indebted to the encouragement of the Chairman of the Astana Civil Service Hub in Astana. Alikhan Baimenov has always been an invaluable colleague, reliable friend and kindred spirit — indeed a Central Asian 'twin brother', as we were born just a few days apart. Professor Guy Peters, a renowned international expert in the field of public administration yet a delightfully approachable, modest and helpful academic good-heartedly encouraged this eccentric project. Professor Margaret Kobia, Minister of Public Service in Kenya, inspired the effort by her passion for progress and commitment to improving her country's civil servants.

For the last five years, I have had the good fortune to be the Director of the Global Centre for Public Service Excellence (GCPSE) in Singapore. Generously funded by the 'little red dot' of a country, the Centre collaborated closely with Singaporean public institutions. The achievements of Singaporean public servants inspire their counterparts everywhere. This book's most accurate title might be 'Notes on What I Learnt at GCPSE'. The Centre has highlighted the importance of excellence in public service for the 'Singapore Story' of this country's extraordinary success since independence in 1965.[1] Drawing out the lessons for today's developing countries is a significant contribution by the Government of Singapore to the UN's 2030 Agenda of SDGs. Many serving and retired officials of the country's public service have kindly supported our work. The full list is too long to note here, but particular thanks and recognition must go to the former and current members of the Centre's Board. I would like to extend my special gratitude to our independent board member, Professor Anastase Shyaka of the Rwandan Governance Academy.

I was fortunate to work in the UK's Diplomatic Service, where I encountered excellence and eccentricity in equal measure. As senior governance advisor at the Department for International Development, I benefited greatly from the expertise and experiences of many committed and thoughtful colleagues: Roger Wilson, Chief Governance Adviser when I joined; his successor, the late Sue Unsworth, who inspired many in the international development profession with a ground-breaking pamphlet 'Upside-Down Governance'; Peter Owen, until he took early retirement to bicycle to Bangkok; Roger Nellist, an enthusiast in equal measure for Competition Policy economics and the idiosyncrasies of the Commonwealth; and Graham Teskey, now with Abt Associates, who always inspired by his magician's knack for pulling rabbity clarity out of the battered top hat of bureaucratic confusion.

Responsible at one time for UK funding of governance research, I had the pleasure of working closely with the late Adrian Leftwich at York University, Mushtaq Khan at SOAS and Mick Moore at the Institute of Development Studies, all of them hugely inspiring and good-humoured

---

[1] The Singapore-UNDP publication of 2011, *Virtuous Cycles: The Singapore Public Service and National Development,* laid out the argument.

academics. The Secretary-General of the Commonwealth when I worked at the Commonwealth Secretariat, Kamalesh Sharma, was deeply impressive.

Filip Vukosavović, Chief Curator of the National Maritime Museum at Haifa, kindly shared his impressive PhD thesis, 'Reforms of Uruinimgina', that he submitted to the Senate of the Hebrew University in 2009. Karma Tshiteem, Head of the Royal Public Service Commission of Bhutan, happily taught me about Gross National Happiness and we wrote a paper together on the topic.[2] Thi Ngoc Bich Lu encouraged me to think more deeply. Henry Kippin, Director of Public Service Reform for the West Midlands, with whom I had wanted to write this book, offered positive and perceptive advice. Alan Whaites, Head of Profession for Governance at the UK's National School of Government International, combined quiet humour with deep expertise and admirable passion for development. Ryan Orange, former Deputy State Services Commissioner in New Zealand, provided practical insight from a country that has been reforming its public service for four decades. Panos Liverakos generously spent his 2017 Christmas holidays editing my text into a chapter for the ACSH/GCPSE 2018 joint publication. Shimani Aishath of the Maldives, formerly of GCPSE, proffered her usual effective support. Devadas Krishnadas, historian, writer, ex-bureaucrat and successful entrepreneur, offered gentlemanly wit and amiable demeanour, at critical moments restoring my faith in Singapore.

At the UNDP, I am grateful to many helpful colleagues, including Pedro Conceicao, Patrick Keuleers, Nigel Goh, Aziza Umarova, Kelvin Chai, Sky Tan and last but certainly not least, Arndt Husar, my deputy at the Global Centre in Singapore. Samuel Henry, a thoughtful intern from Sciences Po Bordeaux, kindly checked the references and conscientiously edited the text.

Many other friends, family members and colleagues variously helped in the research and writing of this work. The failings of this book, however, are entirely my own.

---

[2] Tshiteem, K. and Everest-Phillips, M. 2016. Public Service Happiness and Morale in the Context of Development: The Case of Bhutan. *Asia Pacific Journal of Public Administration*, 38, 168–185.

Contents

Dedication ix
Foreword xi
Acknowledgments xiii

Part A   Urukagina's Cones   **1**
Chapter 1   A Manifesto for Public Service in the Age of Anxiety   3
Chapter 2   Begin at the Beginning   23
Chapter 3   The Cones of Civilisation   49
Chapter 4   Urukagina's Reform Manifesto   63
Chapter 5   Revolutionary or Reactionary? Urukagina
             in the 20th Century   77
Chapter 6   Lugalzagesi and the Legitimacy of 'Reform'   99
Chapter 7   What Can Urukagina Teach the 21st Century?   113

Part B   Discontent and Failure   **123**
Chapter 8   Discontent With Bureaucracy   125
Chapter 9   The Failure of Technocratic Tinkering   137

Part C   Rethinking Public Service   **159**
Chapter 10   From Lagash to Liberia   161
Chapter 11   Plumbers or Psychotherapists?   181

Chapter 12 *Pour Encourager Les Autres*	219
Chapter 13 That Shrinking Feeling	241
Part D The Passionate Bureaucrats of the 21st Century	**259**
Chapter 14 The Fourth Bureaucratic Revolution	261
Chapter 15 Pen-Pushers With Passion?	281
Chapter 16 The Digital Developmental State	305
Chapter 17 'Something Must be Done!'	319
Conclusion: The 21st Century Race for a Creative State	335
Index	341

Part A
Urukagina's Cones

Chapter 1

A Manifesto for Public Service in the Age of Anxiety

When things go well in government, public officials rarely get any credit. Attention-seeking politicians, focused on the next election, are only too happy to hog the limelight. When government fails, political leaders are usually more than eager to blame their officials. Yet, whether ignored or derided, public service is critical to sustaining and improving the quality of life for nations around the world. A trusted, responsive and dynamic civil service underpins the ability of a state to deliver on the needs and aspirations of its citizens. Civil services ensure that governments now and in the future can be catalysts for progress.

As the second decade of the 21st century draws to an end, it is clear that the world faces an unparalleled range of existential challenges. From tackling terrorism to halting climate change, the problems are daunting. The ability to harness new technologies will be essential.

Every state in the coming years will require a high-performing public service dedicated to promoting shared, collective interests. Whatever the merits of the private sector and civil society, the future of this planet cannot be left to social movements or profit-maximising ambitions driven by personal enrichment and selfish individualism. A new generation of dynamic public servants is urgently needed. Their key attribute for success must be the ability to find solutions that build the legitimacy of the state in the eyes of its citizens. This will require prioritising the capacity of officials to win the trust of the population. That core objective demands enhanced skills and attributes in the public service. It will need to articulate eternal objectives — building a good society, defending human dignity, preserving the national interests, including being the stewards of the long-term future. This will put a premium on not only professionalism of the 'bureau-craft', measurable attributes of efficiency and effectiveness, but also such qualitative skills as empathy, emotional intelligence and ethics. The 'passionate bureaucrat', professional, evidence-focused, politically savvy and motivated by high ideals, must emerge to tackle the needs of a new and troubled era.

Our Age of Anxiety

We live at a time of deep concern over the unprecedented pace of change. The new phenomenon we are confronting is a complex mix of factors. These include sharply growing inequality, the 4th industrial revolution, advances in life sciences, the Internet of things, the digital economy,[1] rapid advances in communications, the rise of social media, shifts in energy supplies and 3D printing — and still the list goes on. In addition, jobless growth, the rise of China, unprecedented levels of migration, the demographics of ageing in the developed world and a youth bulge in many developing countries, with the world's population adding one billion over the last 12 years and set to grow by 2.9 billion — equal to another China and India — by 2050, are the backdrop.[2] Millions die of hunger whilst a third of all global food production is wasted. The first person to live up to 150 years has already been born.

This 'Age of Anxiety' may create both exaggerated expectations and excessive disillusionment over the '4th Industrial Revolution'. Sharply growing inequality around the world is increasing social tensions. Faced by the magnitude and complexity of change that is rapidly redefining human potential, reshaping industries and changing societies, political

---

[1] For example, every 10 percentage point increase in the penetration of broadband services is associated with an increase in per capita GDP of 1.38 percentage points; Internet and mobile phone penetration with a 1.12 and 0.81 percentage point increase, respectively: Minges, M. 2015. Exploring the relationship between broadband and economic growth. *World Development Report*, p. 3.
[2] UN. 2017. *World Population Prospects: The 2017 Revision*. New York.

leaders seem unable to articulate a convincing vision for getting through the current upheavals to reach a brighter future.

Instead, politics in many parts of the world is mired in rising populism and resurgent nationalism, post-fact politics, post-truth journalism and false and deliberately faked news. Social media are seen to act as society's conscience, but also create political 'echo chambers' in which the Internet plays a polarising post-fact role, including spreading fake news. The problem is exacerbated by a decline in the quality of journalism and concern over the distorting influence of lobbyists in some countries like the United States. Not unsurprisingly, the result is a new era, the 'Age of Anxiety'.

Change, complexity and global interdependence are creating new realities, unique opportunities and serious challenges for development that are profoundly different from those of the past. Emerging economies are rapidly industrialising; new technologies are coming quickly into use; and a growing web of interconnectedness is transforming geopolitics, international competitiveness and sustainability.

This '4th Industrial Revolution' is just the beginning, but the evidence for its future impact is already clear. For example, in South Africa, as a result of new technologies, 39% of core occupational skills will have altered by 2020; 47% of jobs in the United States will be automated by 2040.[3] By the end of 2016, around two-thirds of the world's population had access to a mobile phone. Mobile phone users include nearly everyone in the developed world and already 62% of the population in low and middle-income countries.[4] Potential new uses for artificial intelligence (AI) and cognitive computing are emerging. Already the annual R&D budget of the dominant Internet search engine Google is more than twice the combined R&D expenditure of the five biggest defence companies in the United States, an extraordinary change from the Cold War era that ended barely a generation ago.[5]

The 'great disruptive forces' of the 21st century are not of themselves new: climate change, industrial revolution, urbanisation (with more people living in cities today than were alive on the whole planet in 1970) and globalisation (in the global flow and networks of trade, finance and

---

[3] World Economic Forum. 2017. *The Future of Jobs and Skills in Africa*. Geneva.
[4] World Bank. 2016. *World Development Report: Digital Dividends*. Washington, DC.
[5] Letendre, L. 2017. Google … It Ain't Ford. *The Air Force Law Review*, 77, 51–64.

people) are familiar themes. For the first time in human history, more people live in cities and towns than in rural areas. By 2050, 67% of the world's population is projected to be urban. The contribution of cities to the global economy and human development will therefore increase. Cities are already engines of economic growth, accounting for 70% of global GDP and, while the world's largest 150 metropolitan areas represent only 13.5% of the global population, they account for over 40% of global GDP.[6]

Wicked Ostriches, Perfect Swans and Black Elephants

What is new in the 21st century, however, is the accelerating pace of these phenomena, their impact upon each other and the unknown new realities that in combination they will create. Their interdependence and complexity is also responsible for the increase of low-probability shocks and high-impact crises that suddenly seem to appear out of nowhere. A massive amount of unpredicted change of unforeseen nature and scale is inevitable. This will be a new era, featuring 'perfect storms',[7] 'wild cards'[8] and 'wicked problems'.[9] Chaos is becoming the 'new normal'. We may act like ostriches by sticking our heads in the sand when we see a black swan[10] heading in our direction, while 'black elephants' in the room may trample all under foot if ignored.

Such 'known unknowns' are combining with the ever-greater depths of uncertainty created by the VUCA world.[11] We are already aware of our bounded rationality and cognitive biases. Hyperbolic discounting,[12] the

---

[6] UN. 2014. *World Urbanization Prospects: The 2014 Revision.* New York.
[7] An event where a rare combination of circumstances aggravates a situation drastically.
[8] An uncontrolled or unpredictable factor.
[9] A difficult or impossible problem to solve because of incomplete, contradictory and changing requirements that are often difficult to recognize.
[10] An unpredictable or unforeseen event, typically with extreme consequences.
[11] US military acronym: 'Volatile, Uncertain, Complex and Ambiguous'. See also http://thinkunthinkable.org/downloads/Thinking-The-Unthinkable-Report.pdf. This also benefitted from the NTU Conference December 2016.
[12] The tendency for people to have a stronger preference for more immediate payoffs relative to later payoffs, making choices inconsistent over time — people make choices today that their future selves would prefer not to have made, despite using the same reasoning.

gambler's fallacy[13] and the information bias[14] are all only too familiar, but the list of humanity's known cognitive blind-spots and shortcomings seems to go on and on.

The wisdom of crowds quickly turns into mass hysteria and 'Extraordinary Popular Delusions'. Group-think, risk aversion and cognitive dissonance shade off into bubbles of false hope and collective denial in which no-one is guilty but everyone is to blame. We have no time to worry about all the other unexpectedly strange and scary 'unknown unknowns', doubtless too many for Wikipedia to list, but probably just waiting to happen.

A new disruptive age of digital public empowerment, big data and metadata challenges the human capacity to cope with the unprecedented scale of 'wicked problems'. Existing comfort zones are crumbling under the speed and nature of fundamental change. Disruption and discontinuity will become the new normal.

The New Era: Complexity in a Complex World

In the deep complexity of such complex systems that we cannot hope to control but only influence, there are no easy answers. Taking action to prevent or pre-empt seems ever more problematic and unlikely. These uncertainties will require public administrations to be prepared to 'Think the Unthinkable' or at least, 'Ponder the Unpalatable'. Yet Political leaders and their officials are still struggling to learn and build on lessons from the continuing fall-out after the 2008 Global Financial Crisis, the ever-accelerating pace of technological change and digital transformation, and delivering effectively in an unexpected climate of escalating geo-political instability.

As the tidal waves of ever-faster, less predictable change crash over our heads, the unelectable political maverick morphs into a popular ideological visionary. The silent majority is no longer silent. Old assumptions

---

[13] Tendency to think that future probabilities are altered by past events, when in reality they are unchanged. The fallacy arises from an erroneous conceptualization of the law of large numbers. For example, 'I've flipped heads with this coin five times consecutively, so the chance of tails coming out on the sixth flip is much greater than heads'.

[14] The tendency to seek information even when it cannot affect action.

for government decisions are washed away in the fast-moving current of the new public information age. Reaction time for those in authority has shrunk from 24 hours to something closer to 24 minutes, as policymaking by tweet takes hold in the White House.

The World Economic Forum's 2016 *Global Risks Report* highlighted three 'wicked problems': climate change, mass migration and cyber warfare. The opportunities and challenges for achieving economic growth, quality education, healthy and fulfilling lives for the coming years will be fundamentally different from those of the past. The past provides limited insight and guidance to shape the 'World We Want'. The sheer ambition of the United Nations' Sustainable Development Goals (SDGs) and the volatile new reality of the 21st century call for innovative approaches to turn good policies into results for citizens. Simplistic nationalist, isolationist, protectionist, xenophobic and populist narratives are challenging governments, as stewards for the future of their nation, to sharpen their ability to look towards the future to realise the grand vision inherent in 2030 Agenda.

In this new environment, the quarter of a century from the end of the Cold War with the Fall of the Berlin Wall now seems, in retrospect, to have been an era of relative certainty and abnormal stability. Who could declare the 'End of History' with Donald Trump in the White House? The new era is more like war than peace in the number and numbing pace of events that are being unleashed; or perhaps more like the lead up to war in the late 1930s, when democratic values crumbled at the Munich Conference of September 1938. Then economic uncertainty and political instability fed off each other.

The same is true today. The dynamic of recent years — exceptionally high rewards for those at the top, a hollowing out of the middle class, and the expansion of low-paid insecure jobs at the bottom — seems set not just to continue but to become more pronounced. In the longer term, it is estimated that two-thirds of children that are today in primary school will enter the world of work by taking jobs that have not yet been invented.

The result, globally, is a pervading mood of fear for managing in choppy seas surrounded by new, uncharted and turbulent waters. Public expectations of government are rising faster than public institutions can deliver.

Yet it is only too easy to forget that huge strides have been made. Real progress is happening, sometimes at an incredible pace: Rwandans today can expect to live 32 years longer than they did in 1990 and spend twice as long at school.[15] Furthermore, in almost every country, a more educated population with stronger professional organisations has fostered a vibrant civil society (and, some fear, a culture of narcissism).[16] New technology creates forums for openness and citizen feedback that challenge governments' ability to respond. As of December 2016, heads of states and governments in 173 countries are using Twitter for engaging with citizens. Facebook comes in close second with 169 governments having set up official pages on the social media platform.

The result, in many instances, is growing pressure to govern better. This means better regulation, less corruption and higher ethical standards in the conduct of public affairs. More and more, governments are responding to these pressures, demands and changes. Leaders realise that they cannot afford to lag behind in a world of increasingly dynamic and competitive markets, as well as pluralistic, diversified societies where higher expectations give birth to new, progressively more complex challenges.

All this uncertainty explains why it is important to strengthen public service. The challenges facing political and administrative leadership everywhere are already daunting and still growing.

Seven Attacks

In recent decades, efforts to undermine the motivation and morale of effective and efficient public officials working for the common good have advanced on seven fronts.

The first is ideological. This is encapsulated in the assertion, regardless of evidence and repeated often enough to have become regarded by many as a truism, that any public service is, by its very nature, inherently incompetent, indolent and unresponsive. Of course, if this were true, it would reflect the decisions of political leaders to allow it.

---

[15] UNDP. 2015. *Human Development Report 2015*. New York. Available online: http://hdr.undp.org/sites/default/files/2015_human_development_report.pdf.
[16] Twenge, J. 2010. *The Narcissism Epidemic: Living in the Age of Entitlement*. New York.

Consider post-independence Singapore, where political determination for building a highly disciplined and motivated public service has transformed the city-state.

The second is intellectual — and a 'Catch 22' conundrum. Public Choice Theory posits that Public Service is inherently self-serving and needs to be constrained, and New Public Management (NPM) propagates that it is inherently apathetic and needs to be incentivised into being effective.

The third is commercial — big profits are generated for consultants and the private sector by fostering the ideas of NPM: running government like a business, outsourcing services and promoting public–private partnerships.

The fourth is political — blaming the public service for failure offers a tempting scapegoat for politicians to deflect criticism of their own inadequate leadership and direction.

The fifth is financial — pay levels for professional posts in public service have lagged behind those of the private sector that either many high-skilled vacancies could not be filled or special pay arrangements were required.

The sixth is institutional — there has been selective truth in portraying obstructive public service unions and unhelpful 'street-level bureaucrats' to obscure much more positive images of devotion to public good, as famously demonstrated by the unstinting self-sacrifice of the New York Fire officers on and after 9/11.

And the seventh is organisational — both elected leaders and senior administrators benefit from creating a 'permanent revolution' of ceaseless reforms and reorganisation of public service. Despite mounting evidence over the years that many reforms achieve almost no lasting improvements, but greatly demoralise staff, the temptation to appear to be shaking up supposedly lazy and incompetent bureaucrats is all too great. This is aggravated by the fact that in some cases senior managers themselves lack the knowledge and skills, and sometimes the willingness, to use resources efficiently.

Tackling all seven of these causes is essential if an impartial and merit-based public service is to evolve in many countries. Such public administration is essential both in itself and for the legitimacy of the state.

But development is hampered by the lack of a credible theory of change to explain how or why an 'impartial, ethical, fair and meritocratic public service' emerges, and how it can be promoted and fostered. Is public service excellence the result of efforts to make government more accountable and responsive, closer to citizens, or more efficient?

Unfortunately, civil service reform has often failed. Three key reasons for this are: (i) excessive focus on cost-cutting irrespective of the consequences; (ii) inadequate attention to the politics; and (iii) applying 'best practice' rather than 'best fit'.

Getting to Helsinki?

Given the central role governments play in facilitating development, including providing public goods, addressing externalities, and laying the foundation for private property and private enterprise, improvement in public administration is essential for progress. Of course, 'good' governance is desirable everywhere: poverty reduction, growth, development, peace and security, free markets, transparency, property rights, the rule of law, the absence of corruption, a free media, free and fair elections, independent judiciaries, vibrant civil society and effective public services. If, in this vision, where all good things come together, why is every country not like Finland, where I served for three happy years as a young diplomat in the 1980s — well-run, honest and peaceful?

What are the priorities? If it is necessary — even a prerequisite — for all good things to be achieved together, the task becomes overwhelming. But fortunately, history shows that that is not the case. Rather, as countries get wealthy they can in the process develop 'good' government. The 21st century rich world (broadly speaking, OECD countries) did not first establish liberal democracy, free markets and merit-based public services and then achieve prosperity.

But in all instances of successful development, an effective public service has always been essential. Governments cannot otherwise get things done, and done well. The nature of the state varies (from democratic to autocratic, from liberal to authoritarian), the role of public administration remains the same: an effective civil service promotes the public good efficiently and fairly. Improving the competence of the state can and should better the lives of its people. If, then, the challenges of reform and enhancing civil service performance are universal, every reform addresses its own context. Yet, even if the specifics to a particular environment of time and place are unique, many principles (including strengthening accountability and responsiveness), issues (such as consolidating the intrinsic motivation of civil servants) and problems (e.g. politicisation, corruption, performance measuring) are shared.

So public sector reform seems to be the answer, offering a temptingly simple 'quick win': whatever the problem might be, cuts and reorganisation seem self-evidently to be the solution. Politicians, voters, citizens and taxpayers 'know' with passionate certainty, regardless of the evidence that 'bureaucrats' waste money, are slow and incompetent. Political leaders, in echoing that, often also feel the administrative leadership is thwarting their ambitions and chances of re-election.

The role which only the public service can play is being reinvented. While the details may be debated, the general trajectory is becoming increasingly clear. This will require civil servants to be much more creative in handling political ambiguity, advising government ministers on policy tensions and contradictions, and delivering services to the public.

For the state to thrive in the coming era, it will need to work simultaneously on achieving five outcomes: (i) unlocking the creativity and collaborative spirit needed to solve complex problems; (ii) overcoming the fallacy that the private sector is inherently more innovative and efficient than the public service; (iii) creating societies that are perceived by their citizens as fair; (iv) fostering the trust of citizens in their governments; and (v) bolstering the legitimacy of the state.

These daunting and interconnected aims will result in a new phenomenon: the public recognition by political leaders and citizens that future prosperity, environmental sustainability and social cohesion are dependent on committed and creative civil servants passionate about promoting the long-term national interest. This is a vision of public service that is a manifesto for state-building in our era for developed and developing countries alike.

Trusted by politicians and the people to tackle the great challenges that humanity faces in the 21st century, public service will be rejuvenated by this vision — to 'make a difference'. The world is changing fast, and the time has come to appreciate the contribution that bureaucratic expertise must make. Yet there are, at present, probably few more unpopular tasks than praising government bureaucracy. As we will see in the following chapters, literally ever since recorded history began, with the 1st Bureaucratic Revolution, the public official has been a derided figure. This phenomenon grew in the 2nd and 3rd Bureaucratic Revolutions, as the range and reach of the state expanded. In the Soviet Union in the 1930s, the government's own posters depicted crude caricatures of inefficient bureaucrats sleeping at their desks surrounded by piles of paper. Any failings of the state could conveniently be blamed on public officials. The nation was exhorted with slogans such as: *Fight the Bureaucrats who Hinder the Workers' Efforts!* Many officials ended up in Stalin's gulags.

Yet, without committed public bureaucrats, states and markets would not function, freedoms would not be upheld, and the poor, vulnerable and oppressed would suffer more. Their role in holding the state together is rarely noted. But in 2017, although it was never written down or given a codename, France's top officials had a detailed plan to 'protect the Republic' if far right leader Marine Le Pen was elected president. An unnamed senior official told the media: 'The philosophy, and the absolute imperative, was to keep the peace, while also respecting our constitutional rules'.[17] In the after-life, bureaucrats also play an important role. The Hindu God Chitragupta keeps a file on every person, recording their good and bad actions, in order to assign them to heaven or hell.

The end of the Cold War nearly 30 years ago released a preposterous arrogance in the West. This was symbolised by the infamous claim that history had come to an end. This woeful a historicism was personified by the disastrously self-serving Harvard economists sent in the early 1990s to assist Russia. There they applied theory without regard for context. They shamelessly profited personally from privatisation while doing enormous damage to the country and its relations with the West.[18] Clio,

---

[17] https://www.theguardian.com/world/2017/may/18/secret-plans-protect-le-pen-french-republic-emerge.
[18] http://www.institutionalinvestor.com/Article/1020662/How-Harvard-lost-Russia.html#.WNhHV4VOLsY.

the muse of history, was far from dead. Her influence weighs heavily on public administration.

Yet, while 'Administration is Policy', public policy and public administration have become disconnected from each other. The academic discipline of public administration has lost relevance by failing to generate new ideas on how to govern effectively, efficiently and equitably, in the totality of public purpose.[19] The current malaise in public administration research means that, only too often, writing in this field is either so theoretical as to be surreal, or so bogged down in practical detail as to lack adequate conceptual underpinning and a readily applicable theory of change. All too often, research results are frustratingly ambiguous. One finding, however, is incontrovertible: investment in fair and effective public administration always reaps enormous long-term dividends.

The civil service plays many functions. As the backbone of the state, it is a system of management, striving for effectiveness of the process of governing. At the same time, it provides a mechanism to impose political values, by enforcing or ignoring legislation. From that it follows that it can also be an organisation to promote trust between citizens and 'the state', by being just and fair to all — or not. It offers a practical way to represent the people in governance if officials broadly hire their personnel to reflect the diversity of the population. Public officials can be the 'human face' of efficiency, being seen to be trustworthy with public resources. Public service is the mechanism for ensuring inter-generational stewardship of the future. Bureaucratic quality has been shown to have a prominent impact on corruption[20] and on economic growth.[21]

---

[19] See Bourgon, J. 2017. *The New Synthesis of Public Administration Fieldbook*. Copenhagen. Dansk Psykologisk Forlag. Chapter 2 provides a trenchant critique. See also Kettl, D. F. 2015. The Job of Government: Interweaving Public Functions and Private Hands. *Public Administration Review, 75*, 219–229; Peters, B. G. and Pierre, J. 2016. *Comparative Governance: Rediscovering the Functional Dimension of Governing*. Cambridge. Cambridge University Press.

[20] Hall, R. E. and Jones, C. I. 1999. Why Do Some Countries Produce So Much More Output Per Worker Than Others? *The Quarterly Journal of Economics, 114*(1), 83–116; Treisman, D. 2000. The Causes of Corruption: A Cross-National Study. *Journal of Public Economics, 76*(3), 399–457.

[21] Evans, P. and Rauch, J. E. 1999. Bureaucracy and Growth: A Cross-National Analysis of the Effects of 'Weberian' State Structures on Economic Growth. *American Sociological*

The success of the civil service in these roles much depends on what sort of state is imagined by leaders and expected by citizens. Contrasting visions of the public sector may focus on increasing efficiency with minimal hold on society and provide a minimum of efficient public services: the 'night watchman state' that simply protects widows and orphans against the depredations of the powerful, rather than colluding with the powerful to prey on the weak and vulnerable. Another aspires to increasing civic participation and 'developmental democracy' by pursuing a positive role of empowering citizens.

One problem is that 'the state, that is, the functioning of executive branches and their bureaucracies, has received relatively little attention in contemporary political science... the overwhelming emphasis in comparative politics has been on democracy, transitions to democracy, human rights, transitional justice, and the like'.[22] Economists recognise 'government failure', in the sense of suboptimal policy choices, but, unlike the concept of market failure, there is no agreed definition of government failure. The term is often used, but rarely defined.

Grumbling about public service and public services has been a popular pastime for a very long time; trying to reform them a challenge to political leadership for almost as long. That the first recorded reform of public administration ended in catastrophic failure is surely worthy of analysis to find out why — especially since so many subsequent reforms have also failed. Widespread public sector reforms in recent decades have often proved disappointing.[23] The expected improvements in performance, accountability, transparency, quality of service and value for money have rarely materialised in the public sector. Externally imposed reforms restrict the space for home-grown solutions.[24]

Review, 64(5), 748–765. Rauch, J. E. and Evans, P. B. 2000. Bureaucratic Structure and Bureaucratic Performance in Less Developed Countries. *Journal of Public Economics,* 75, 49–71.

[22] Fukuyama, F. 2013. What Is Governance?. *Governance,* 26, 347–368.

[23] De Vries, M. and Nemec, J. 2013. Public Sector Reform: An Overview of Recent Literature and Research on NPM and Alternative Paths. *International Journal of Public Sector Management,* 26(1), 4–16.

[24] Fryer, K., Antony, J., and Ogden, S. 2009. Performance Management in the Public Sector. *International Journal of Public Sector Management,* 22(6), 478–498.

The Northcote-Trevelyan Report of 1854, famous for promoting meritocracy in Britain, actually set extraordinarily low expectations. The stated aim for its reforms was merely to remove only the 'decidedly incompetent, or incurably indolent'.

Lee Kuan Yew in Singapore, by contrast, is credited with a much more extraordinary long-term vision by which a small, fledgling republic with no natural resources was moulded into one of the best run countries in the world. At the core of this success was his understanding of the need for good public administration and that that required the creation of a 'clean, efficient, effective and indeed exceptional' public service ethos.[25]

The changes looming in the public sector of the 21st century present an opportunity to renew that ethos.[26] In past times and still in a few countries today, 'bureaucratic' implies professional in manner, being reasoned, rational, sensibly cautious, fair and impartial, working for the welfare of all.

This book is not a manual for achieving that 'reversal of fortune'. It offers no blueprint, provides no 'best practice' toolkit, nor suggests any reassuring answers. Simple certainties are eschewed, progress is not guaranteed and the rigid logic of project documents will not be found here. Quick fixes, 'silver bullets' and easy remedies are the 'Holy Grail' in a field where the difficulty lies not in identifying technical solutions, but in finding reform proposals that are politically feasible. Routes to development are nowadays recognised to be complex, non-linear and uncertain. Yet the implications of that conclusion are almost universally ignored. The simple reassurance of the certainty of logframes and modernisation theory remains the hidden paradigm.

The aim, therefore, should be more modest — yet hopefully more ambitious. The most important innovation will be in changing mindsets: one that puts public officials centre stage.

The challenge, however, is certainly not for the faint-hearted. But those countries, governments, peoples and businesses that think they can

---

[25] Ong, P. 2015. Head of Civil Service, Singapore Government. Available online at: https://www.psd.gov.sg/heartofpublicservice/.

[26] Parker, R. and Bradley, L. 2000. Organisational Culture in the Public Sector: Evidence from Six Organisations. *International Journal of Public Sector Management, 13*(2), 125–141.

undermine the morale of the public service and still enjoy well-run governments, sensibly balanced freedoms, carefully regulated markets and honest, impartial legal frameworks, have a nasty shock in store. 'The visible role of the State had been operating well before the invisible hand of the market could take on a role'.[27]

Why then, if the problem is clear, does reforming public service prove so difficult?

Note on Terminology

Public service, the civil service, the public sector and public administration have slightly different meanings. I have, however, used these terms usually interchangeably. The *Civil* or *Public Service* (or *public administration*, an older term implying less citizen-focus) is responsible for formulating, directing and co-ordinating the overall national policy in relation to the public service; providing leadership on matters pertaining to the public service including development of a positive image of the public service, high integrity and morale; and developing specific public service goals and priorities, to be achieved within the short, medium and long term. This is the main focus of the book.

Public sector covers all public employees, such as in state-owned enterprises. *Public services* differ from the *public service* in being the public goods (e.g. regulation and policy, as well as security, health, education, water and sanitation) and the organisations by which they are supplied at either central or lower levels of government. *Public service excellence* is displayed by a motivated, merit-based, innovative and adaptive public administration able to fulfil its duties effectively, efficiently and equitably. *Civil servants* are ministry personnel on the government payroll. This always includes the staff of central government departments, the focus here. Teachers, doctors and policemen, for example, may be paid by central government and so would be *public servants*; if paid by particular ministries and working under their employment contracts, are *civil servants*.

---

[27] Bourgon, *Op. cit.*, p. 151.

41mm high sculpture, from Urukagina's era (New York Metropolitan Museum).

Note on Urukagina

Much about Urukagina is uncertain — including the pronunciation of his name. Various alternative spellings have been proposed, including 'Irikagina' and 'Uruinimgina'. In the absence of decisive evidence for its transliteration, I have used 'Urukagina' as the first version in general use.

A Quick Introduction to Sumer

Before considering Urukagina and his cones, it may be helpful to know something about their context.

Agriculture began in Mesopotamia in the 10th millennium BC, after artificial irrigation had been invented. That process of bringing water through a network of canals required co-ordinated and disciplined effort.

4000–3000 BC. Across Mesopotamia, Sumer and other cities, including Eridu and Uruk (also known as Erech — vying to be the oldest and the location for the Tower of Babel) develop around monumental mud-brick temples set on high platforms.

An increasingly complex economy and stratified society generates new administrative skills with the development of cuneiform writing uses a reed stylus to incise and later impress signs on clay tablets.[28]

3000–2350 BC. The Early Dynastic period, 'Palaces' are built throughout Mesopotamia giving emphasis to royal authority in controlling the city-states. At Uruk, 'the first city in world history', large temple estates developed accounting records on clay tablets. The city was ruled by a 'priest-king' (the balance between political and sacerdotal authority, and the relevance of such a divide, remains contested — as is the nature of 'kingship') overseeing a highly hierarchical society.

One of the earliest written texts from Uruk provides a list of 120 officials. So which came first: writing or ranking? Recent research suggests that the emergence of the state and civilisation was not a natural evolution from the technological revolutions in producing food, one that is purported to have led to the accumulation of surpluses that 'freed' people from the subsistence economies of hunter-gatherers, but the other way around. It was the creation of the state as an institution (a ruler, having monopoly power over violence and taxation, walls delimiting territory, specialised functions to manage the administration of the state) that enabled the systematic mobilisation of the labour required (most of which was forced, and used not only for agriculture, but to build city walls and monuments) to make the small and independent towns that existed scattered since 5000 BC grow into larger cities and, ultimately, civilisations.[29]

---

[28] It is important to bear in mind that a semasiographic system of communication, unlike glottographic writing, can encode meanings directly without the imposition of language: Lambert, A. 2014. The Role of Rock Art in Early State Formation. *Rock Art Research, 31*(2), 205–224.

[29] Scott, J. 2017. *Against the Grain: A Deep History of the Earliest States.* Yale.

Uruk is the setting for the Epic of Gilgamesh (c. 2700 BC, but first recorded c. 2100 BC). This tale relates the legendary adventures of the eponymous hero in search of everlasting fame. Finally, he comprehends that it lay not in eternal life but in his accomplishments on behalf of both his people and his God. At the city of Ur, trade is revealed in spectacular graves containing objects made of imported gold, silver and lapis lazuli.

The Pre-Sargonic period (namely the time before Sargon of Akkad unified Mesopotamia around the year 2370 BC) during the Early Bronze Age (3300–2100 BC) is called by archaeologists the Early Dynastic (ED) era. This is divided into three phases: ED I lasted from c. 2900 to 2750 BC; ED II, from c. 2750 to 2650 BC; ED IIIa from c. 2650 to 2500 BC; and ED IIIb from c. 2500 to 2350 BC. This last phase covers nine rulers of Lagash:

1. Ur-Nanshe c. 2500–2475 BC: cuneiform tablets from his rule are relatively plentiful, perhaps indicating a long reign.
2. Akurgal c. 2475–2465 BC: few tablets, perhaps a sign of a short reign.
3. Eannatum c. 2465–2435 BC: relatively many tablets may indicate a long reign. Erected the 'Stele of the Vultures' in Girsu to mark victory in war against Umma.
4. Enanatum I c. 2435–2425 BC: younger brother of Eanatum.
5. Enmetena c. 2425–2400 BC: third son of Enanatum I. 'Brotherhood Pact' with Uruk.
6. Enanatum II c. 2400–2395 BC: son of Enmetena. Few surviving tablets may signal a short reign.
7. Enentarzi c. 2395–2390 BC: previously was *saga* priest.
8. Lugalanda c. 2390–2383 BC: son of Enentarzi.
9. Urukagina c. 2383–2370 BC.

Then, after Lugalzagesi, came a turning point in the history. For the first time, an empire arose. It was called after the city of Akkad, which its ruler Sargon chose for his capital (it has not yet been identified but was presumably located on the upper stretches of the Euphrates, between Sippar and Kish).

Ur-Nanshe was the founder of what is known as the 1st Dynasty of Lagash, nine reigns that lasted some 150 years, roughly from 2500 to 2350 BC. The inauguration of the dynasty by Ur-Nanshe was marked by the construction of many buildings, both civil — ramparts and canals — and religious. Temples were erected in honour of each of the country's high Gods.

For generations, Lagash and its bitter rival, the neighbouring city-state of Umma, some 20 miles away, had been inconclusively feuding over the border region, Gu-Edin (or Gu'edena). Enakalli, the *ensi* (king/ruler) of Umma, purposely destroyed the irrigation works there to create a desolate border zone. But Lagash, then at its zenith under Eannatum, had defeated Enakalli and forced Umma to pay an annual tribute in corn. Under Enakalli's son Urlumma, Umma invaded again but was routed by En-metena who captured Umma and killed Urlumma.

Under Urukagina, however, Lagash suffered catastrophic defeat. Umma's new king, Lugalzagesi, later also king of Uruk, was the son of the previous king Bubu, and served as priest for Goddess Nissaba (as his

Gudea of Lagash c. 2144–2124 BC (New York Metropolitan Museum, CC).

father had also done) before ascending the throne. Invading Lagash at least three times, the Umma forces under Lugalzagesi drove Urukagina out of his capital city. Urukagina retreated to Girsu, and then possibly allied with Sargon to defeat Lugalzagesi.

c. 2350 BC Sargon, from Akkad, a site yet to be identified, unified much of Mesopotamia by conquest, creating the world's first empire. Akkadian, a Semitic language related to modern Arabic and Hebrew, becomes the language of public administration.

The Akkadian Empire collapsed after two centuries. The independent city-states in southern Mesopotamia re-emerged. Lagash flourished under the rule of Gudea (c. 2150–2125 BC) and his son Ur-Ningirsu (c. 2125–2100 BC) who rebuilt its great temples installing statues of themselves in the shrines. The city of Assur arose c. 2000 BC, so technically Assyriology begins only then. By the Middle Assyrian period 1500–1000 BC, a wealth of archives of cuneiform tablets offers a detailed picture of government and public administration, and by the 13th century BC a strong ethos of written accountability had become institutionalised.[30]

---

[30] Postgate, N. 2014. *Bronze Age Bureaucracy*. Cambridge, p. 427.

Chapter 2

Begin at the Beginning

The 'Reform' Cones AO 3278 and AO 3149 on display in the Musée de Louvre (Creative Commons license).

An effective, efficient and equitable public administration is essential for a modern state to be able to deliver on its obligations to citizens and the international community. But how can a country improve its public service?

The problem is familiar. A new government is elected with a mandate to 'modernise the state' by tackling poor performance and low productivity in the public service. On the crest of electoral triumph, political enthusiasm for change is high. After years of the previous increasingly corrupt regime, the need for progress is great. International partners like the World Bank and IMF rush to back the media-savvy minister chosen to lead the reforms, heralding her as a 'champion of change'. US-trained experts fly in, offering international 'best practice'. Workshops generate much excitement for streamlining the formal structures of the civil service. Detailed projects with linear logical plans for implementation are enthusiastically signed, outlining the new legislation to be drafted and procurement processes involved. Sceptics declaring 'we've seen all this before' and warning that 'it's different here' are ignored.

Quick wins and 'low hanging fruit' are rapidly harvested but long holidays intervene. Committees start to grasp the complexity of the task. Powerful vested interests prove more stubborn and intransigent than had at first been assumed. Overt and, more dangerously, covert resistance is fierce (and comes from unexpected and surprisingly influential quarters). The minister in charge is suddenly promoted and transferred to a more important portfolio, following the sacking of a Cabinet colleague in an unrelated scandal.

Gradually, it becomes clear that the pace of reform has slackened. Serious flooding in the south-west of the country and a terrorist incident in the capital mean that the Prime Minister no longer has time to engage with the reform. The energetic and enthusiastic official responsible for guiding the detailed workplan is transferred back to the finance ministry to plug an unforeseen sizeable hole in tax revenues. Vocal union opposition to proposed changes to the pay and job grading system and threats of violent protests by some militant groups lead ministers to worry that the reform is haemorrhaging the government's political capital. The impetus for modernisation fades into implementing the less contentious activities of the reform plan. Renewed cynicism sets among increasingly demotivated public officials. At the next election, the incumbents are portrayed as the corrupt establishment.

Another scenario might see a package of comprehensive reforms attempted with an unpredicted worsening of results, a problem due to the disastrously opinioned or woefully ignorant views of key reformers. For example, one study of the Fulton committee on civil service reform in the United Kingdom between 1966 and 1968 concluded that it 'all too often displayed a lack of imagination in making its proposals, and when it did demonstrate that quality, realism was frequently absent'.[1] In the United States in 1973, a Congressional survey found 65% of citizens and 57% of elected congressmen believed that bureaucrats 'really run the country'; while 80% of congressmen and 73% of citizens agreed that 'government has become too bureaucratic'.[2]

If the best place to begin is at the beginning, there can be no better place to reflect on how states reform their public administration than in Room 1 of the Louvre in Paris. In that enormous museum, this cavernous area on the ground floor of the Richelieu wing is dedicated to *la Mésopotamie du Néolithique à l'époque des Dynasties archaïques de Sumer*. This part of the museum houses artefacts from the birthplace of human history, ancient Mesopotamia.

This name, the 'Land between the Two Rivers', refers to the flat valley of the southern Tigris and Euphrates rivers, home to the ancient culture of Sumer that flourished during the fourth and third millennium BC. Sumerology examines its history and archaeology, while Assyriology investigates the Assyrian culture that succeeded the Sumerian world. Both cultures were long lumped together with later 'Babylonia', familiar from the evocative tales in the Bible of its triumphs and vanities.

Tucked away among the monumental richness of Near Eastern antiquities and overshadowed by the museum's vastness, stands a small display case. Slightly forlorn in appearance, it contains two cone-shaped clay tablets.[3] These objects, each measuring some 27 cm in height and 15 cm in diameter at the base, rarely draw more than, at best, a swift glance from the passing armies of tourists. In that nearest equivalent in modern times to the tower of Babel, the Louvre museum, tourists jabbering in alomost every tongue on earth have no time to waste.

---

[1] Fry, G. 1969. *Statesmen in Disguise: The Changing Role of the Administrative Class of the British Home Civil Service 1853–1966*. London, p. 426.
[2] US Congress. Congressional Record 1973, part II, 115, III, 61.
[3] Cooper, J. 1985. Medium and Message: INSCRIBED CLAY Cones and Vessels from Pre-Sargonic Sumer. *Revue D'Assyriologie Et D'archéologie Orientale*, 79(2), 97–114.

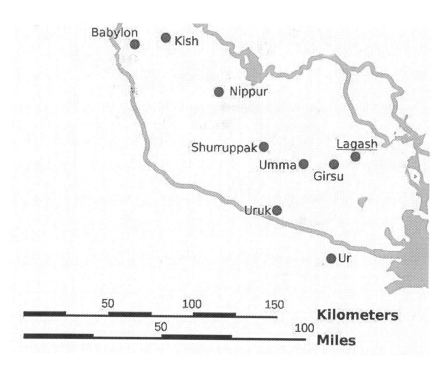

Map of ancient Sumer in southern Mesopotamia.

The rush to tick *La Joconde* off the list of cultural masterpieces to be photographed obscuring before one dies allows no time for distractions. Armed with guidebooks and cameras, nearly 30,000 foot soldiers invade this citadel of culture every day, marauding its 70,000 m^2 of world heritage in order to conquer human history in the two hours allotted by their tour guides before rushing on to the Eiffel Tower and Versailles.

Among the 35,000 masterpieces of paintings, drawings, sculptures, *objets d'art* and archaeological finds on display in Paris, Sumerian tablets appear dwarfed and insignificant. Made of clay, these ancient objects lack the size or sparkle of more eye-catching exhibits on display. Written in cuneiform in a long-dead language, few visitors can read their texts.

Lisa del Giocondo's smile has a good local reason to be fetchingly enigmatic. For those apparently dull clay tablets not only predate the original tower of Babel but also deserve as profound a grip on the human imagination as the creativity of Leonardo da Vinci. The tablets indicate the challenges in public administration over the last 4000 years or so, highlight shared common characteristics and therefore offer insights for the future.

An effective public service is central to a civilised society.[4] That was understood 4500 years ago. It matters all the more today, as the 21st century confronts enormous change. But even as civilisation was just emerging into history, citizens already believed that public institutions had long been mismanaged. To correct this, in around the year 2375 BC, Urukagina, the new ruler of the Sumerian city-state of Lagash in southern Mesopotamia, took dramatic steps to tackle corruption and correct the mismanagement that had arisen apparently within every branch of government. Urukagina swiftly implemented the first recorded reform of public administration.

The various surviving versions of Urukagina's reform of the public service in the city-state of Lagash are conveyed by the cone-shaped tablets, fragments of others and a few other cuneiform writings.

This first recorded analysis of bad governance springs out from the early pages of history in an already remarkably coherent form. Written in the Sumerian language in about 2375–2350 BC, recorded in cuneiform script and preserved on whole or shattered clay cone-shaped tablets, the texts have miraculously survived in various states of completeness and legibility. Collectively, the cones list some 41 corrupt practices, corrective reforms and general policies adopted in the 'cradle of civilisation' at a very early stage in recorded history.

The only complete, although damaged, surviving text of the 'Reforms' was labelled 'Cone C' when dug up, catalogued as 'AO 03149' in the inventory of the Louvre, classified as 'Ukg. 5' by academic listing, and 'P222608' in the international database of the Cuneiform Digital Library Initiative.

Its narrative has four distinct parts. The introduction, dedicated to the God Ningirsu, offers a brief description of the king's achievements in

---

[4] An extrapolation from the famous aphorism carved over the entrance to the IRS in Washington DC: *Taxes are the price we pay for a civilized society.*

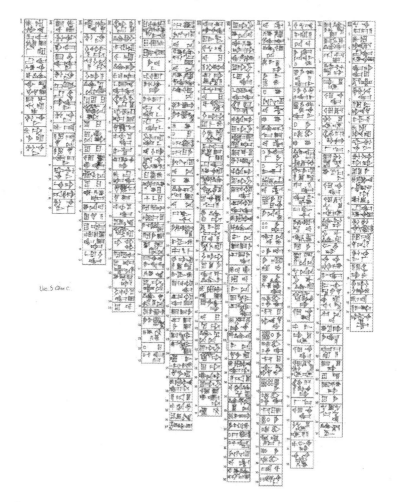

Cone C as transcribed by the French archaeologists who dug it up at the end of the 19th century.

public works. The second section lists the *abuses* of power committed by the former royal family, *their* officials or priests. The third part outlines *the* reforms enacted to end these *abuses*. The concluding section announces an amnesty for imprisoned citizens, the protection of widows and orphans, and the construction of a canal.

The arguments and evidence justifying reform emerge from the narrative. This presents the reform process in two roughly equal halves: first the background, and then Urukagina's actions. One impressive feature of the text is its bureaucratic accuracy and neatness evident in the clear *logic* between the 'abuses' described and the 'reforms' proposed.

His modernisation strategy had four elements. First, he claimed to be acting in accordance with the commandment of the state tutelary deity: his reforms were divinely sanctioned. Second, he ruthlessly sacked corrupt and poorly performing top officials:

> From the boats the chief of the boatmen he removed, from the donkeys and from the sheep their head herdsmen he removed, from the fish stores the fisheries inspector he removed, from (control over) the grain taxes of the lustration priests [and] the granary supervisor he removed, for the [payment of bribes] instead of sheep and lambs the officers (responsible) for it he removed, and as for the taxes which the temple administrators to the palace had delivered, the officials (responsible) for them he removed.

Third, Urukagina made a binding performance contract with the God to protect the weak (orphans and widows) from exploitation by the powerful. And last, he introduced progressive social reforms.

Linking this together with all the other versions offering slightly different detail, the composite narrative can be divided up into 12 short chapters. These chapters present three components: the background context of the mal-administration of Lagash; the practical measures taken by Urukagina to correct the situation; and the justification for his actions.

The ruler of Lagash paints a sorry picture of the public service which he inherited when he took power in the city-state. Corruption, he alleges, had engulfed every level and all ranks of officialdom, including temple administrators and the sacerdotal class.

According to Urukagina, this decay in the probity of public administration was not a recent phenomenon. He argues that 'since time immemorial', government officials in Lagash had abused their positions of authority unlawfully to seize key assets including boats, donkeys, sheep and fish. Officials bribed their superiors, stole firewood from the poor and vulnerable, oppressed the weak such as orphans and widows, and exploited funerals and other public rituals for personal gain. Senior officials abused their authority to steal from their subordinates and compelled ordinary people to work for them in their private estates and irrigation channels without compensation — not even giving these conscripted labourers any water to drink.[5]

Just like every outside challenger for political power ever since, Urukagina and his propagandists claim that under his predecessor, the rot in government had reached the very top. The former 'king' of Lagash and his family had seized the farmlands of the Gods and had then used temple oxen to plough the royal fields. The previous ruler and his top officials had profited from their public duty to dispense justice by taking bribes.

In recognising that many abuses were of long-standing, Urukagina was acknowledging systemic failures too. In tackling these problems, he set out his ambition to be a 'righteous ruler'. His vision for good governance included protecting the most vulnerable members of society, curbing the identified abuses of the rich and powerful, and enforcing the probity of political leaders and government officials. He also devised new social policies. Urukagina declared a general amnesty for prisoners, claimed theft had been eliminated, required wives to respect their husbands and abolished polyandry (or polygamy).

To date, interpretations of the reforms have overwhelmingly focused on their significance for the evolution of politics and the origins of legal institutions. Political scientists have traced key concepts, not least 'freedom', back to Urukagina.[6] His reforms have also been placed at the start of the development of codified law. They predate by six centuries the Code of Hammurabi, the sixth king of Babylon who set out 'an eye for an eye, a tooth for a tooth'.[7]

---

[5] Biggs, R. D.1987. *The Organization of Power. Aspects of Bureaucracy in the Ancient Near East*. Studies in Ancient Oriental Civilization, vol. 46. Chicago.

[6] Professor Kramer, a great enthusiast for the topic, wrote a book *History Begins at Sumer* of 1961 tracing almost every important human innovation back to the Sumerians (Kramer, 1961. *History Begins at Sumer*. Ch. 7, pp. 89–94).

[7] Hammurabi emphasised just and competent government, stipulating that any judge who reached an incorrect decision was to be fined and removed from the bench permanently. The Code of Hammurabi contains 280 judgments, or 'paragraphs', on civil and criminal law, concerning *awīlum* (freeholders), *muškēnum* (tenants) or *wardum* (slaves). A segment of the population could be conscripted to do public works, or war. This is usually portrayed

Viewed as literature, the reforms have been placed in the Babylonian tradition of 'praise poems'. These outrageously immodest works of propaganda, similar in our era to the obsequious glorification heaped on the rulers of North Korea, lauded the benevolent character of a ruler in formulaic terms. No action was apparently implied (just as Pyongyang's deification of Kim Il-Sung and Kim Jong-Il).[8] For example, Ur-Nammu, ruler of Ur c. 2100 BC congratulates himself for helping the disadvantaged:

> I have freed the sons of the poor from their duty of going to fetch firewood.

The later ruler of Lagash, Gudea (2144–2124 BC), is praised for enforcing the justice required by the Gods Nanše and Ninĝirsu:

> He provided protection for the orphan against the rich, and provided protection for the widow against the powerful.

But even if Urukagina's texts are presenting a literary motif rather than a substantive reform effort, the importance of his arguments for reforming public administration has never been adequately explored.

These 'Reforms' present a remarkably modern approach to reinventing government and improving public bureaucracy. They focus on obligations and entitlements of citizens.[9] The state was more than the household of the ruler. Officials were clearly meant to be working for the common good. Almost all the story relates to the actions and behaviours of state officials — that is, it is concerned about public administration. The 'Reforms' present well-developed ideas about the failings of public service and how to rectify them.

---

as an obligation like the *corvée* in medieval Europe, but could perhaps have more resembled the Maharashtra Employment Guarantee Scheme in the 1980s when the indigent sought the opportunity to work.

[8] The regime asserts that 'the Great Leader' wrote some 1,500 books while studying at university and, after graduating, penned six operas 'all of which are better than any in the history of music'.

[9] Moore, M. 2006. *How Does Taxation Affect the Quality of Governance?* IDS.

This theme of reform for improving governance is as important today as 4500 years ago. Flagrant abuse of public office, widespread corruption and institutionalised injustice existed in Sumer, the world's first civilisation, apparently in forms that seem still distressingly familiar in far too many countries of our own era.[10]

So what do the reform texts actually say? Combining the different versions, a coherent narrative emerges. The story divides up into 12 sections. Six sections present the context and need for reform (Part A). This is followed by Part B, the six sections that elaborate on the actions that Urukagina took to address the problems he had outlined.

Part A: Background

Political triumph: Public works completed

> Urukagina, king of Lagash, built the palace of Tirash and the Antasura (temple) for (the God) Ningirsu, the hero of Enlil. For (the Goddess) Bau he built the temple, the pantry to house regular provisions, and the sheep-shearing shed of the Holy City. For Nanshe, he dug the canal, her beloved canal, to Nigin, and extended its outlet into the centre of the sea. He built the wall of Girsu for Ningirsu.[11]

The reform narrative starts and ends with itemising Urukagina's policy on infrastructure, through major construction projects. These included enlarging the temples of Antasura and Bau,[12] and building the palace of Tirash, a warehouse to store regular provisions, the sheep-shearing shed, the canal to Nigin, and the wall around Girsu, the second

---

[10] E.g. at the time of writing (January 2018), the President of South Africa Jacob Zuma faces 768 charges of corruption.

[11] Enlil was the chief deity in the Sumerian pantheon. He was the father of Ningirsu, God of war, farming and scribes. Bau (or Baba), wife of Ningirsu, was the Goddess of healing. Nanshe, daughter of Enki (God of wisdom and fresh water) and Ninhursag (Goddess of Earth), was Goddess of social justice, prophecy, fertility, and fishing.

[12] Other records of his temple-building can be found at P431155 (Ukg.1), P431159 (Ukg.10) and P431160 (Ukg.11).

city of the Lagash state as its religious capital (and its political and administrative centre too after the city of Lagash was captured).

Such programmes of public works were clearly expected of kingship, for they are a standard feature of Sumerian royal tablets. Building initiatives assuaged the Gods, promoted the status of the ruler, secured the support of the priesthood, boosted economic activity and employment, improved communications and strengthened defences. Indeed, building the city wall around the administrative capital of Girsu was to prove critical for the survival of Urukagina's regime later in the last years of his reign.

The bad old days: Bribery and corruption was endemic

From distant times [or, from time immemorial], from when the seed (of life first) came forth, in those days boats were seized by the chief of the boatmen, donkeys were seized by the head herdsman, sheep were seized by the head herdsman, fish stores were seized by the fisheries inspector. The lustration priests at Ambar demanded {excessive} grain taxes.

The shepherds of wool-bearing sheep, instead of paying in kind with a healthy sheep, paid a bribe with silver.

The surveyor, the chief lamentation singer, the steward, the brewer, and all the foremen instead of a young lamb put silver.

The oxen of the Gods ploughed the garlic plots of the ruler, and in the best fields of the Gods were where the garlic plots and cucumber plots of the ruler were located.

Team donkeys and unblemished oxen were harnessed for the temple administrators, and the barley of the temple administrators was distributed to the teams of the ruler.

The temple administrators delivered (to the palace) a mongoose-ear garment, a ... -holding garment, an outer (?) garment, a draped (?) linen ..., unprocessed (?) flax, flax tied with cord, a bronze helmet, a bronze arrowhead, a bronze ..., gleaming leather, wings (feathers?) of a yellow crow, cumin, ..., a goat with its fleece, (as payment) for the il-tax.

The narrative then turns to corruption. At this point, Urukagina's argument holds that corruption was rampant and entrenched. One tablet (P222607) emphatically asserts that rampant corruption in public administration had always existed in Lagash: *From distant times, from when the seed (of life first) came forth.* Until Urukagina took office, public officials were shameless in exploiting their positions of authority for personal gain: the chief of the boatmen appropriated boats, the head herdsman seized donkeys and sheep, while the fisheries inspector purloined the fish stores. The priests at Ambar imposed excessive grain taxes.

Citizens connived in bribery: shepherds, the surveyor, the chief lamentation singer, the steward, the brewer and all the foremen, instead of paying the taxes they owed, all instead paid a bribe to the public officials.

How did this impact on the 'fiscal social contract' in Lagash? It is difficult to raise tax efficiently without a political process of bargaining with citizens and building up their trust in government.[13] This is a familiar story in the modern world. Citizens as voter-taxpayers, acting collectively, can play a key part in the oversight of the executive. This not only shaped the political evolution of all OECD countries[14] but also in developing countries.[15] In the years immediately before the 1994 military coup in the Gambia, lost revenues rose to 9% of GDP and income tax evasion expanded to 70% of total revenue due.[16] In Pakistan, the legitimacy of the state collapsed from the early 1970s. In a climate of on-going political turmoil and military rule, tax evasion more than trebled, and the tax/GDP ratio fell from 13.2% in 1998 to 10.6% in 2006.[17] In contrast, where governments finance themselves by persuading rather than coercing their citizens, they are more likely to rule democratically and to provide

---

[13] An increase in the trust in government by one degree increases tax morale by over 5%. Torgler, B. 2001. What Do We Know about Tax Morale and Tax Compliance? International Review of Economics and Business, 48, 395–419.

[14] North, D. 1990. *Institutions, Institutional Change, and Economic Performance*. Cambridge. High-income countries have high tax 'take' that pays for public services and 'public goods' such as effective legal systems that help to generate and maintain the state's high legitimacy.

[15] For example, Clapham, C. 2000. *War and State formation in Ethiopia and Eritrea*; Fjeldstad, O.-H. 2004. *To Pay Or Not to Pay? Citizens Views on Taxation in Local Authorities in Tanzania*; Hlophe, D., et al. 2002. *... And their Hearts and Minds Will Follow? Tax Collection, Authority and Legitimacy in Democratic South Africa*.

[16] Dia, M. 1993. *A Governance Approach to Civil Service Reform in Sub-Saharan Africa*. World Bank Technical Paper. 225. Washington, DC: World Bank.

[17] Saeed, K. 1996. Principle of Taxation: Taxation System of Pakistan. *Pakistan Journal of Public Administration*, January–June 1996.

services to citizens.[18] In the words of the Kenyan Revenue Authority, 'Pay your taxes and set your country free'.[19]

Ill-treatment of the poor

> The ... administrator cut down trees in the orchard of the poor and tied (the wood) up with reed twine.

The poor particularly suffered, but from whom? Some Sumerologists have translated this passage as clerical abuse of power against vulnerable women: the *sanga* (the steward of the temple estates) cut down the trees of indigent mothers;[20] others have interpreted this as indicating secular abuse of power once the concern of the temple for the well-being of the people had been dissipated.

The high cost of living: Burials

> For a corpse being brought to the grave, the undertaker took away seven jugs of beer, and 420 loaves of bread. The person(s) of ... took away two barig (72 l.) of hazi-barley, one woollen garment, one lead goat, and one bed, and one barig (36 l.) of barley. When a person was brought (for burial) into the reeds of Enki, his beer was seven jugs and his bread 420 loaves. The undertaker took away two barig of barley, one woollen garment, one bed, and one chair. The person(s) of ... took away one barig of barley. The craftsmen {ferry boatmen} in pairs received the fee for the ferry to the main gate (of the netherworld).

At Lagash under Urukagina, a complex barter economy flourished. Wool, barley and fish were major export products, bartered for imports such as copper.[21]

---

[18] Ross, M. 2004. Does Taxation Lead to Representation? *The British Journal of Political Science*, 34, 229–249.
[19] Kenyan Revenue Authority slogan, 2007.
[20] Kramer, N. 1963. *The Sumerians. Their History, Culture and Character.* University of Chicago Press.
[21] Prentice, R. 2010. *The Exchange of Goods and Services in Pre-Sargonic Lagash.* Münster: Ugarit-Verlag.

In the absence of coinage, one of the major costs faced by every family, funeral fees, were paid in kind. As death could not easily be predicted and therefore saving for such an eventuality difficult, the costs of a funeral would have been a major economic shock for ordinary people. This problem was worsened by the lack of progressivity in the cost: rich and poor paid the same. Priests demanded exorbitant fees to conduct funerals: seven jugs of beer, and 420 loaves of bread; while the undertaker was paid two barig (72 l.) of hazi-barley, one woollen garment, a goat, a bed, and one chair. The exploitation by the clergy seems to undermine the argument made in regard to the previous part of the narrative that the temples were 'pro-poor'.

Urukagina's predecessor, Lugalanda, appropriated land in the name of his wife and children

> The household of the ruler and the fields of the ruler, the household of the Woman's House and the fields of the Woman's House, and the household of the (royal) children and the fields of the children were consolidated.

Here Urukagina is accusing the previous ruler of Lagash of a reform that consolidated revenues not only of the *ensi* but also of the Woman's House, the temple devoted to the Goddess Bau.

Blaming one's predecessor is a standard ploy in politics and work, but this is risky if the post enjoys legitimacy of tradition.

A bloated and corrupt bureaucracy entrenched

> Public officials were present across the whole country, from the border territory of Ningirsu to the waters of the sea.
> When a senior official built a well and irrigation system across his land, he conscripted blind workers (to do the work).
> As the traditions were, it was.

The presence of public officials across the country is presented as a criticism, not as the sign of an effective state well embedded in the community. Therefore, some historians who argue for the importance of the reforms suggest 'public officials' here specifically means tax collectors.[22]

In developing countries today this relationship between the citizen as taxpayer or as voter remains difficult since most voters do not pay direct taxes. In Bangladesh, for example, less than 1% of the population fall within the tax net, with 4% of taxpayers (or less than 0.04% of the population) paying 40% of the tax revenue while 50% of taxpayers (less than 0.5% of the population) pay less than 1% of the total tax revenue.[23] The same 'social contract' is needed with the private sector. The informal sector is a major part of the economy in many developing countries in part because of low 'tax morale' (intrinsic willingness to pay taxes based on acceptance of the legitimacy and effectiveness of the state).[24]

Abuse of office by senior officials was rampant and ruthless. The 'blind'[25] were pressed into building wells and the irrigation channels for the private benefit of officialdom.

The first half of the narrative ends in fatalism: *As the traditions were, it was.* From time immemorial, mis-management of Lagash had been systematic and tolerated.

Overall, therefore, Urukagina could claim that he had acted in defence of the common people. In seizing power, if that is what he did, Urukagina could justify his *coup d'état*. Public officials were taking the boats, sheep and fish stores, cutting down the fruit trees for firewood and forcing powerless people to work for them. Furthermore, the ruler and top officials of the previous regime had used the temple lands, donkeys and oxen for their own ends. Urukagina sought to blame his predecessor. Lugalanda had allegedly appropriated land in the name of his wife and children and had grabbed the best farmland for himself and used the sacred oxen from the temples to plough his own fields.

---

[22] Kramer, *op. cit.*
[23] Sarker, T. and Kitamura, Y. 2006. *Technical Assistance in Fiscal Policy and Tax Administration in Developing Countries: The State of Nature in Bangladesh.* Keio University Tokyo.
[24] Torgler, B. and Schneider, F. 2007. *Shadow Economy, Tax Morale, Governance and Institutional Quality: Panel Data.* IZA Discussion Paper No. 2563.
[25] According to Cooper (p. 73), a non-free worker, of lower status than the shublugal.

While the former ruler is roundly condemned, the whole system was to blame: these abuses had been going on since time immemorial. The temple officials who formed or colluded with the state bureaucracy were all greedy and corrupt. They too used the temple oxen to plough their own fields and bribed their superiors to ignore this abuse. Temple administrators ruthlessly extracted taxation in kind (such as a 'mongoose-ear garment', linen, flax tied with cord, a bronze helmet, a bronze arrowhead, leather, cumin, a goat with its fleece) from the people.

The cones then repeat the argument that, from time immemorial, a bloated and corrupt bureaucracy was present across the whole country. Until Urukagina took political leadership to correct the problem, this state of affairs had been accepted with fatalism: *As the traditions were, it was.*

Such a forthright condemnation is quite extraordinary. It seems to damn all the great rulers of Lagash and to undermine the institution of kingship. Arguing for the rights of the people and claiming to defend their interests seems to challenge powerful vested interests.

The misappropriation of temple property, and particularly that of the city-God, allowed Urukagina to present himself as Ningirsu's champion, and by restoring the sacred lands which had been seized by the palace, he proved his own disinterestedness and afforded his subjects an example which he could insist upon their following.

The reforms of public administration seem to reveal, beneath the official decorum of Sumerian government, a society built on oppression, the existence of which would not be suspected from the pious foundation inscriptions and votive texts of the period.

The conquests achieved by Lagash during the epoch of the great patesis had undoubtedly added considerably to the wealth of the city and had given her, at least for a time, the hegemony in southern Babylonia. Eannatum, the most militarily successful ruler of the first dynasty of Lagash, conducted many campaigns abroad, including against the southern cities of Ur and Uruk, as well as against states to the north such as Kish, and was able to claim the title 'King of Kish', a title associated with the unity of the Mesopotamia under a single ruler.

Some historians see in this the beginning of class identity and repression. With the growth of the power of the state, the communitarian values on which earlier successes were achieved were lost. The simplicity of

Detail of AO 3278 (Creative Commons license).

ruler and temples had gradually evolved into luxurious palaces and sumptuous temples for the Gods. This put a considerable strain upon the resources of the state. The population was forced to contribute. New taxes were levied, and, to ensure their collection, tax inspectors were everywhere. Denmark had degenerated into North Korea.[26]

Part B: Public Service Reform

In the second half of the narrative, Urukagina details the actions he took to rectify the abuses itemised in the first half of the reform texts. He issued a general amnesty, releasing from prison not only debtors, but also swindlers, thieves, and murderers. He stopped exploitation of the poor or powerless and swore to protect the weak and vulnerable ('orphan or widow'), prefiguring the famous dictum of the Babylonian king Hammurabi some 600 years later (c. 1754 B.C.), in promulgating his law Code: 'so that the strong might not oppress the weak'.[27]

---

[26] Denmark is held up as a model state in development economics and for citizen wellbeing. See also Wiking, M. 2017. *The Little Book of Lykke: Secrets of the World's Happiest People.* Harper Collins Publishers.

[27] Mieroop, M. 2004. *King Hammurabi of Babylon: A Biography.* Cambridge.

Divine sanction for power

> When Ningirsu, the hero of Enlil, bestowed on Urukagina the kingship of Lagash, and Urukagina had been welcomed by the populace, he rectified the abuses of former times and carried out the commandments which his master Ningirsu had ordered.

In the second half of the narrative, Urukagina lays out his decisive actions to end this state of affairs. He first asserts both a divine mandate from Ningirsu, the God of the Lagash state,[28] to clean up corruption, with the support of the people. Soviet historians, however, argued that Urukagina was elected by a popular assembly, perhaps a little like the way in which Lenin had used, and then dissolved the Constituent Assembly in 1918.[29] An assembly and city hall have been identified in the second-millennium-BC city of Assur.

The divine mandate made it politically difficult to challenge the legitimacy and absolute authority of the ruler. The Stele of the Vultures, for example, erected about a 100 years before Urukagina's reign by one of his predecessors, Eannatum, to glorify his military triumphs, describes how Ningirsu visited Eannatum in a dream and instructed him to make war on Umma. This motif of divine commandment also continued after Urukagina. The cylinder inscriptions of the later king Gudea tell how Ningirsu ordered the rebuilding of his E-ninnu temple.

Although ruler by divine right, the acclamation of the people also mattered. Reference to popular support implies that Urukagina was concerned to strengthen his legitimacy and promote inclusive politics. His intuition has been validated in the intervening 4500 years. Over the long term, states and societies with more open and inclusive institutions, both political and economic, are more resilient and tend to be better governed. When inclusion goes beyond elites to encompass the population as a whole, states tend to be more legitimate, wealthier and less unequal.

Urukagina not only records the restoration of all the property which had formerly belonged to the temples dedicated to the God Ningirsu and his family, but also reaffirms the legitimacy of the city-God. The ruler only

---

[28] Urukagina's personal God was Ninshubur.
[29] For example, Diakonoff, I. 2013. *Early Antiquity*. University of Chicago Press, p. 82.

received the throne as a trust to be administered in the interest of the God. Royal fields and possessions were not his own property but were held on behalf of Ningirsu.

Decisive and visible action to tackle corruption

> Urukagina sacked the chief of the boatmen, the head herdsmen and the fisheries inspector. He also dismissed the granary supervisor from (control over) the grain taxes of the lustration priests, the tax officials responsible for taking bribes instead of healthy sheep and lambs, and the corrupt temple administrators who delivered these bribes to the palace.

Urukagina took decisive action. He removed many senior officials, including the tax collectors. He dismissed the priests and the temple administrators who had demanded and taken bribes. He dismissed corrupt officials, the chief boatmen, head herdsmen and fishery inspectors who had seized private property.

This sweeping action reflects the difficult trade-off in the civil service between delegation of authority to improve the flexibility, and the sense of loyalty, shared values and mutual trust relations among civil servants is a big challenge. There are no easy answers as to how to balance fragmentation and integration, individualisation and shared identity, market pressure and cultural cohesion.

One of the texts of the reforms, the Oval Plaque (Ukg. 6), adds other corrupt practices of public office to the list already recorded on the other tablets. One such abuse of public authority had been that a man could obtain a divorce just by paying a bribe to the ruler as head of the judiciary and his top official. Urukagina's reforms, if they do indeed include the measures listed on Ukg. 6 (recent scholarship has suggested it might predate Urukagina[30]), therefore curtailed his potential sources of income and that of his chief minister.

Their predecessors had enriched themselves by enforcing heavy and unjust fees for divorce. It is possible that, upon their first introduction,

---

[30] Vukosavović, F. 2009. *Reforms of Uruinimgina*. Unpublished PhD thesis, Hebrew University of Jerusalem.

these fees were defended as being a deterrent to divorce. But in practice they had the contrary effect. Divorce could be obtained on no grounds whatever by the payment of what was practically a bribe to the officials, with the result that the obligations of the marriage tie were not respected. The wives in earlier times had possessed two husbands. On the other hand, he inflicted severe punishment for infidelity on the part of the wife.

Reforming the state

> Urukagina recognised the God Ningirsu as master over the household of the ruler and the fields of the ruler, and the Goddess Bau as mistress over the household of the Woman's House, and the fields of the Woman's House. The God Shul Shaggana (son of Ningirsu and Bau) was the master over the household of the children and over the fields of the children.
>
> Across the entire country from the border territory of Ningirsu to the waters of the sea, no {corrupt?} persons shall serve as public officials.

Urukagina places the property of the ruler under the God, but whether he puts it under the jurisdiction of the temples and how independent the temples were from the royal household is unclear. Urukagina recognised the authority of the divine family — Ningirsu, Bau and Shul Shaggana. That could mean that Urukagina placed the property of the ruler under the jurisdiction of the 'Sumerian temple state' of which he was the vice-regent. Another explanation is that he 'nationalised' the priesthood and unified political and sacerdotal power.

The second paragraph echoes the earlier criticism that *Public officials were present across the whole country, from the border territory of Ningirsu to the waters of the sea.* An alternative translation, suggests all public officials, or at least all tax collectors, were sacked.[31] It seems improbable that all officials were dismissed, but even sacking the most outrageous perpetrators of corrupt practices probably gravely weakened his regime.

---

[31] Kramer, S. 1961. *History Begins at Sumer*. Ch. 7, pp. 89–94.

The Oval Plaque suggests that the shepherds of wool-bearing sheep were meant to pay taxation in kind, but bought their way out of their tax burden by paying a bribe in silver.[32] Officials did the same — the surveyor, the chief lamentation singer, the steward, the brewer, and the foremen also all reduced their tax burden by paying a bribe.

Was this the world's first white-collar crime? It is estimated that nowadays globally bribery amounts to $1 trillion every year;[33] corruption can on average amount to 25% of the cost of procurement contracts in many countries.[34] As a result, public-sector corruption undermines service delivery, with disproportionate impacts on the poor, women and girls;[35] and public funds lost to corruption are estimated to be 10 times the amount of official development assistance.[36]

Another text[37] adds further detail about the corruption in government before Urukagina and his corrective actions.

The oxen of the Gods ploughed the garlic plot of the ruler, and the best fields of the Gods became the garlic and cucumber plots of the ruler. In other words, his predecessor had used temple oxen to plough his own fields and had also sequestered the temple fields. *If a poor person made a fish-pond, someone would steal the fish:* again, the poor suffered. *If a man divorced his wife, the ruler took five shekels of silver and the chancellor*

---

[32] Foxvog, D. 1994. A New Lagaš Text Bearing on Uruinimgina's Reforms. *Journal of Cuneiform Studies*, 46, 11–15.

[33] ONE Campaign, *The Trillion-Dollar Scandal*, September 2014, http://www.one.org/international/blog/exposed-the-trillion-dollar-scandal/; World Bank, 2004, Costs of Corruption, http://web.worldbank.org/WBSITE/EXTERNAL/NEWS/0,,contentMDK:20190187~menuPK:34457~pagePK:34370~piPK:34424~theSitePK:4607,00.html.

[34] Centre for Global Development. 2014. *Publishing Government Contracts: Addressing Concerns and Easing Implementation*. Washington DC; Olken, B. A. and Pande, R. (2012). *Corruption in Developing Countries*. Abdul Latif Jameel Poverty Action Lab's Governance Initiative. MIT.

[35] Nawaz, F. 2009. State of Research on Gender and Corruption. U4. http://www.u4.no/publications/state-of-research-on-gender-andcorruption/downloadasset/403.

[36] UNDP. 2011. Fighting Corruption in the Water Sector: Methods, Tools and Good Practices. www.undp.org/content/undp/en/home/librarypage/democratic-governance/anti-corruption/fighting_corruptioninthewatersector.html.

[37] P431156: The oval plaque (Ukg. 6).

took one shekel of silver. *If a man smeared kohl*[38] *on the head (of someone else), the ruler took five shekels of silver, the chancellor took one shekel of silver, and the sage took one shekel of silver.* His predecessor and his top officials had not provided justice by due process, but had sought to profit from their offices.

After Urukagina became ruler, however, all this changed: *The ruler, the chancellor and the sage no longer take silver. If a poor man makes a fish pond, no one makes off with its fish.* He (Urukagina) abolished the crime of theft.

Then the tablet records one of the most quoted but least understood passages in cuneiform: *If a woman speaks ... disrespectfully to a man, that woman's mouth is crushed with a fired brick... Women of former times each married two men, but women of today have been made to give up that crime.*

The apparently progressive treatment of criminals noted earlier confronts apparently oppressive treatment of women. The polyandry of earlier times is intriguing.

Urukagina regulates fair burial costs

> For a corpse being brought to the grave, his beer will be three jugs and his bread eighty loaves. The undertaker shall receive one bed and one lead goat, and the person(s) of ... shall receive three ban (18 l.) of barley. When a person has been brought to the reeds of Enki, his beer will be 4 jugs and his bread 420 loaves. The undertaker shall receive one barig (36 l.) of barley, and the person(s) of ... shall receive three ban of barley. The high priestess shall be paid one woman's head band (?), and one sila (1 l.) of princely fragrance. 420 loaves of bread that have sat are the bread duty, forty loaves of hot bread are for eating, and ten loaves of hot bread are the bread of the table. Five loaves of bread are for the persons (in charge) of the levy, two pottery vessels and one sadug vessel of beer of Girsu. 490 loaves of bread, two pottery vessels and one sadug vessel of beer are for the lamentation singers of Lagash. 406 loaves of bread, one pottery vessel and one sadug vessel of beer are for the (other) lamentation singers.

---

[38] Black eye mascara.

This section is a reminder of the important role of the state in ensuring fairness. The new regulations seem, overall, to have cut the costs by about half: from seven jugs of beer to three, and from 420 loaves of bread to 80 or, when a person was buried in the reeds of Enki, the amount of beer owed was cut from seven jugs to four, and two barig of barley was reduced to one.

Social welfare measures

> 250 loaves of bread and one pottery vessel of beer are for the old wailing women. 180 loaves of bread and one pottery vessel of beer are for the old men of Nigin. The blind one who in ... stands, his bread for eating is one loaf, five loaves are his bread at midnight, one loaf is his bread at midday, and six loaves are his bread at evening.
>
> Sixty loaves of bread, one pottery vessel of beer, and three ban of barley are for the person who is to perform as the sagbur-priest.
>
> He eliminated the ferry toll and the craftsmen's bread for the Raised Hand (religious ritual).
>
> He stopped the administrator of ... from taking [wood] from the orchard of the poor.
>
> When a senior official seeks to purchase a donkey from a junior official, saying: 'I want to buy it!' the decision to sell is the right of the owner and he cannot be compelled to accept.
>
> When a nobleman seeks to purchase a house from a social inferior, saying: 'I want to buy it!' the decision to sell is the right of the owner and he cannot be compelled to accept.
>
> Urukagina issued a general amnesty, releasing from prison debtors, swindlers, thieves, and murderers, and cancelling their obligations.
>
> Urukagina made a binding covenant with Ningirsu that the weak and vulnerable ('orphan or widow') would be protected from the powerful.

This penultimate part of the narrative lists the further actions that Urukagina took. These steps included fixing a 'living wage' for the elderly and disabled, and for people performing religious rituals. The poor and minor officials are protected from misappropriation by powerful public functionaries.

The promulgation of a general amnesty for most types of prisoner — debtors, swindlers, thieves, and murderers — seems remarkably progressive.[39] This penultimate section ends by foreshadowing the famous dictum by which the Babylonian king Hammurabi justified the promulgation of his code of laws 600 years later: 'so that the strong might not oppress the weak'. The code of Ur-Nammu c. 2050 BC, founder of the third dynasty of Ur, similarly declares that he sacked corrupt officials and protected orphans and widows.

These measures all suggest a 'modern' understanding that government's role is to transform people into citizens, not just achieve satisfaction with public service delivery. Although Urukagina preserves his political independence by affirming that his 'performance contract' as being with the God, Ningirsu, not direct with the people, since the God had ordered him to protect the people, the ruler would be judged by the effectiveness of his public admiration on behalf of the citizens of Lagash.

Public works completed

> In that year Urukagina dug the little canal to Girsu in honour of the God Ningirsu, named it in his honour with authority from Nippur and extended the canal to Nigin.

The opening literary convention on public works that opened the narrative is picked up to close the narrative and indicates sacerdotal diplomacy with the main temple of Ningirsu at Nippur.

The background to this pioneering reform of public service was clearly a bitter struggle for power. But where power lay in Lagash is unclear. Most historians have suggested that this had arisen between the temple and the palace — the 'church' and the 'state', although differing interpretations have been presented as to the cause. Perhaps Urukagina's predecessor Lugalanda was an autocratic ruler had sought to suppress basic political, social and economic rights. Popular resistance to the

---

[39] For a discussion of this point, see: Steinkeller, P. 1992. The Reforms of UruKAgina and an Early Sumerian. Term for 'Prison'. *Aula Orientalis 9*, 227–233.

growing megalomania of the throne, state terror and bloodthirsty despotism resulted in the last king of the 1st Lagash dynasty, Urukagina being swept to power by collective political action against royal oppression, with 'the citizens of Lagash taking the side of the temple';[40] or 'Urukagina's reform centred mainly around the excesses of the priesthood'.[41] Another view suggests that the 'clergy' and public officials had both profited from the abuses of his predecessor's regime.

Urukagina immediately took action to end oppression and rectify animosity between church and state. Long-standing institutional weaknesses in the governance system were corrected. The public service became accountable. Then there were more complex corrupt practices involving bribery: the lustration (purification) priests, shepherds, the surveyor, the chief lamentation singer, the steward, the brewer, and all the foremen and the temple administrators were in collusion to profit from public office. Urukagina was certainly right to tackle this problem. Empirical evidence suggests that countries that improve governance also improve control over corruption, and better development outcomes are strongly and positively correlated with increased transparency, accountability and integrity.[42] Implementing those qualities must have required a significant change in mindset. Excellence in public service needs committed officials.

Urukagina's reforms have been described as the first legal code, although that is clearly hyperbole. The Reforms of Urukagina 'attempted to take steps to deal with the abuses which had arisen … and lists the

---

[40] Kramer, 1963, *op. cit.*, p. 79.

[41] Mercer, S. 1922. Divine Service in Early Lagash. *Journal of the American Oriental Society, 42*, 91–104, 97.

[42] UNDP Brief, Building on Evidence: Corruption a Major Bottleneck to MDG Achievements http://www.undp.org/content/dam/aplaws/publication/en/publications/democratic-governance/dg-publications-for-website/protecting-the-public-purse-anti-corruption-for-mdgs/MDGs%20and%20Anti-Corruption.pdf; Organisation for Economic Co-operation and Development, *The Rationale for Fighting Corruption*, Brief, CleanGovBiz, 2013, http://www.oecd.org/cleangovbiz/49693613.pdf; Transparency International. 2010. *The Anti-corruption Catalyst: Realizing the MDGs by 2015.* Transparency International, Germany.

reforms carried out to reduce the exorbitant nature of the taxes and the victimization of the economically weak'.[43] Tax burden was reduced.[44]

The cuneiform clay tablets in the shape of cones that record his pioneering efforts at public sector reform supposedly contain the first recorded use of the word 'freedom'. As a result, these 'Reform cones' have been described as forming:

> ... one of the most precious and revealing documents in the history of man and his perennial and unrelenting struggle for freedom from tyranny and oppression.[45]

This is the general narrative. Or, as a journalist summed it up:

> Matters were at low ebb in Lagash until, at last, a good man — Urukagina by name — came to power, an honest, God-fearing ruler who threw out the corrupt administrators, righted wrongs, ended unjust treatment of the poor, and rid the city of thieves, usurers and murderers.[46]

Archaeologists, historians and epigraphologists (readers of old texts) can and do quibble about the detail. But the big picture, developed over the last 100 or so years since the 'Reform cones' first came to light (dug up, and bought), still stands: that Urukagina was a good, progressive ruler who curbed corruption, righted wrongs, ended unjust treatment of the poor, protected the vulnerable, reduced taxation, re-established the separation of state and religion, offered criminals a second chance through a general amnesty, and above all, gave his people freedom.

But is it that simple? How far is this reputation justified? Well, perhaps not. It is time to consider the broader evidence.

---

[43] Saggs, H. W. F. 1969. *The Greatness That Was Babylon: A Survey of the Ancient Civilization of the Tigris-Euphrates Valley.* New York: Praeger, p. 65.
[44] Kramer, S. N. 1979. The First Case of Tax Reduction. *Challenge,* 22(1), 3–9.
[45] Kramer, N. 1963. *The Sumerians. Their History, Culture and Character.* University of Chicago Press.
[46] Wood, M. 1979. *Kramer of Sumer,* paraphrasing Kramer 1961, p. 93. http://archive.aramcoworld.com/issue/197905/kramer.of.sumer.htm.

Chapter 3

The Cones of Civilisation

Along with perhaps the other main text (Ukg. 6, the oval plaque), the two cone tablets form the core texts of our exploration of the first public administration 'reform' in history. Cones A/Ukg.1, Aa/Ukg.2/AO 4598a, Ab/Ukg.3/AO 4598b, AO 27621 and four fragments, MNB 1390, AO 12181, AO 12782 and clay tablet Crozer 005 (Cone D, in the collection of the Crozer Theological Seminary, Rochester, New York, USA)[1] are fragments, confirming the narrative around the elimination of corrupt practices of state officials. They provide a later version of the 'reforms', when Urukagina had been reduced to 'the king of Girsu' but more on that later.

Urukagina describes a number of practices of his society from long ago that he sets out to reform. Many of these relate to the privileges of the ensi over the temple establishment or of work supervisors over their domain of authority (e.g. Ukg. 04 B III 6–IV 25). Others deal with required burial provisions for the dead or payments for temple officials (e.g. Ukg. 04 B V 25–VI 18). Urukagina altered these provisions, reducing the power of the overseers, lowering provisions to officials, and

---

[1] FAOS 05/1, Ukg. 04, C; CIRPL Ukg. 60 cone D. Another fragment of a related 'reform' cone was discovered in 2007 lying unnoticed in a US collection: Vukosavović, F. 2008. A New 'Reform Text' of Uruinimgina: UKG. 63. *Revue d'assyriologie et d'archéologie orientale*, 1/2008 (vol. 102), pp. 5–8. Also central to understanding the reign of Urukagina are P431157 on attacks by Umma; P431158, 'the Lagash Lament'; P431155, P431159, P431160, P431161, P431162 and P431163 listing his public works. P431164 evokes Bau on his behalf. P431166 records a donation to Ningirsu.

extended protection to small-scale equity and property owners (see e.g. Ukg. 04 B X 20–32). He also states that he transferred control over the ensi's house and field (along with those of his wife and children) to the Gods of Lagash, Ningirsu, Baba and Shulshaga, as well as that he restored conditions of the state (ama-gi4), declaring the cancellation of debt and other penalties. He concludes by saying that he would not give over the orphan and the widow to the strong (Ukg. 04 B XI 30–31).

Usually referred to as the 'Reforms' of Urukagina, the collective narrative has been popularised as the earliest 'Reform Edicts', 'Declaration of Liberty' or 'Legal Code'. Together, the texts have often been described as forming one of the most important and dramatic records in the history of humanity: the first revolution in governance, the earliest known reform to public administration and the first steps in social development.[2] The archaeologists and museum curators who found and conserved these artefacts from Mesopotamia have done a good job in marketing their significance to a wider audience. These important cuneiform clay tablets are blessed with a memorable, agreed title.

Around the turn of the fourth to third millennium BC, the Sumerians had invented the first system of writing in the Middle East. Writing on clay tablets was cheap and easy, allowing a sophisticated bureaucracy to develop — or perhaps vice versa. The archives of cuneiform tablets structured the nature and ethos of government, and organised city life required public administration through the existence of inscribed tablets. The earliest tablets contain list items and measurements, as well as personal names and, occasionally, probably professions. This shows the purely practical origins of writing in Mesopotamia for administration.

The organising ability to administer huge estates was impressive. Under the third dynasty of Ur, for example, it was not unusual to prepare accounts for thousands of cattle or tens of thousands of bundles of reeds. Similar figures are attested at Ebla, three centuries earlier.

Detailed history from c. 2500 BC about the city-state of Lagash, its religious-administrative capital of Girsu and its relations with its

---

[2] The transliterations and translation are in: Frayne, D. R. 2008. *Pre-Sargonic Period (2700–2350 BC)*. Also see Sollberger, Geneva 1956, p. 48 ff.; Deimel, P. 1920. 'Die Reform texte Urukaginas', Or 2.

neighbour and rival, Umma, can be pieced together from an extensive corpus of inscriptions relating to nine rulers of its first dynasty. The archive of some 1200 tablets from the temple of Baba, the city Goddess of Girsu, date from the period of Lugalanda and Urukagina (first half of the 24th century).

The tablets were all dug up at the end of the 19th century — either by European archaeologists in search of Sumer, or by local treasure-hunters looking for tablets and other artefacts to sell to them.[3] The Louvre had established a Department of Oriental Antiquities in 1881 when the French vice-consul at Basra, Ernest de Sarzec, began to send back to Paris enormous quantities of Sumerian antiquities excavated from Telloh in Lower Mesopotamia.[4] The site was originally thought to be Lagash but turned out to be its second city and religious centre, Girsu. In archaeological digs lasting until 1933, its ruins yielded some 50,000 clay tablets. Then, 20 years later and some 15 miles away, archaeologists from the Metropolitan Museum New York discovered Lagash, at Tell Al-Hiba.[5]

As a result of these and a few other sites, more than 100,000 of such Sumerian clay tablets are now stored in the basements of the world's great

---

[3] Toscanne, P. 1903. *Les cônes d'Urukagina*. Louvre. Old Assyrian tablets were discovered shortly before 1880 by local villagers. When these so-called 'Cappadocian tablets' proved to interest collectors and to yield money, the inhabitants kept happily selling them to dealers and travellers over the next 60 years. Large numbers were obtained by the museums of Berlin, London, Paris, Yale, Geneva, Giessen, Heidelberg, Jena, Leiden, Liverpool, Moscow, New York, Oxford, Philadelphia, and St. Petersburg.

[4] He was director of the dig from 1877 to 1900, and wrote up his discoveries in a series *Découvertes en Chaldée* published between 1884 and 1912. Volume 2 (1894) published the 'reform' tablets for the first time: Cone A, B and C, and the oval plaque on plates L, LI, LII and L (see illustrations).

[5] Al-Hiba (ancient Lagash), one of the largest mounds in southern Iraq, was first investigated in 1887 by the German archaeologist Robert Koldewey. In 1968, the Metropolitan Museum of Art initiated excavations at a small part of the site, revealing occupation during the Early Dynastic period, c. 2900–2350 B.C., when al-Hiba, along with Telloh (ancient Girsu), were the two most important cities of the state of Lagash. A number of structures, including two temples, were investigated. A temple was located at the highest point on the western side of the mound dedicated to Ningirsu, the patron God of Lagash, where beer was prepared for the ritual feeding of the deity. The site was largely abandoned after the Early Dynastic period, although religious buildings continued to be constructed at the site into the second millennium B.C.

museums.[6] The clay tablets are written with a stylus shaped as a wedge ('cuneus') in columns and panels in mankind's oldest form of writing, the straight-line cuneiform script. The system of writing evolved, just as Chinese was to do slightly later, from simple pictographs for physical objects into a system capable of also capturing abstract meaning and rendering phonetic sounds.

Cuneiform flourished for some 3500 years, from c. 3500 BC, making it not only the oldest but also the longest surviving method of writing to date — but then died out. It was rediscovered in the early 19th century and painstakingly deciphered by scholars.

It is estimated that around 90% are administrative records. For instance, the temple archives of Nippur kept detail files about an impressively wide range of economic activities: legal transactions over slaves, the sale of a palm grove, loans of silver and promissory notes; records of transactions over corn, wheat and vegetables; receipts for different kinds of beans, dates, and figs; statements of grain shipments delivered, and of garments in store; expenditure on tilling the fields including wages and fodder for the oxen; renting of land to different people, along with details about the fields, their measurements, condition, etc.; inventories of implements, weapons, bronze and silver; expenditure on porphyry stone to make a couch for the deities, and on wool, sesame, straw, and grain for temple offerings; and wage bills to pay officials, employees, artisans and labourers and their sustenance in grain, vegetables, fish and drink.[7]

There they lie, mostly unread, for knowledge of cuneiform is a rare skill. But at least these tablets are safe. It is a sad reflection on humanity that many archaeological sites from the dawn of civilisation have suffered waves of looting and sporadic destruction, most recently since the invasion of Iraq in 2003.[8]

---

[6] There are large collections scattered around in the British Museum, the Louvre, the Vorderasiatisches Museum in Berlin, the Hermitage, and in Harvard, and the University of Pennsylvania museum.

[7] Clay, A. 1906. *Documents from the Temple Archives of Nippur*, vols. xiv, xv of the Publications of the Babylonian Expedition of the University of Pennsylvania (Philadelphia, University of Pennsylvania, 1906).

[8] https://www.britishmuseum.org/PDF/Iraq%20Report_with%20images.pdf.

Urukagina reduced the power of the state (e.g. Ukg. 04 B III 6–IV 25), dismissed top officials and alienated officials (e.g. Ukg. 04 B V 25–VI 18) and established secure property rights (e.g. Ukg. 04 B X 20–32) such as for orphans and widows (Ukg. 04 B XI 30–31), but fatally weakened the capacity of the state on which the upholding of such rights depended.

In the Oval Plaque, earlier military success in Lagash's border wars with Umma are invoked, apparently to remind the reader that what goes around comes around.

Texts from the Lagash rulers show a rapid and marked increase in text length and variety of objects inscribed, most still dedications of temple construction and ornamentation, but some providing much more information, the most famous of which being an account of the inter-generational border conflict (P222532) between the city-states of Lagash and Umma during the reigns of Eannatum and Enmetena.

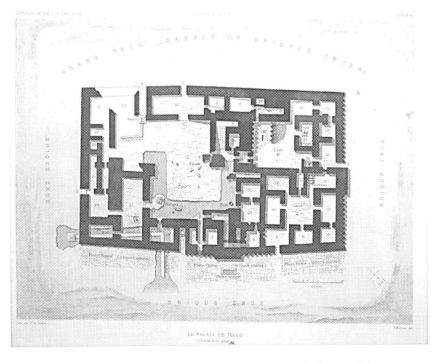

Sarzec's map of the 'Palais de Tello' (adapted from Ernest de Sarzec: Découvertes en Chaldée (Paris: Didier, 1884–1912)).

Information is decidedly thin about the emergence of public administration in the pre-Sargonic period. The first governments in the world developed when the first cities appeared in the fourth millennium BC. This occurred around Mesopotamia in the lands made fertile by the Ur and Euphrates rivers, augmented by human ingenuity in building irrigation systems. At places such as Uruk, Nippur and Kish, the development of bureaucracy documented the creation of states, class society and religion, the beginnings of commerce, and the building of palaces, temples and public works. Sumerian civilisation already included many aspects of modern life: writing, arithmetic, geometry, architecture, irrigation systems for large-scale mono-crop farming, sanitation, schools and professional armies.

Bureaucracy, by creating the past and inventing the future, made civilisation possible. Little is known about the system of government in the early city-states, before 2350 BC. That a complex hierarchy of ranks in public office already existed in the cities of Sumer as early as the fourth millennium is clear from the lexical lists of Uruk which record many official titles for posts in the city, temple and palace administration. Besides canal inspectors, heralds and bailiffs, there were rotating city magistrates at Shuruppak (Fara) in the early Early Dynastic (ED) III period.

The relationship between temple administrators and palace functionaries, their administration and detailed records is also unclear. Earlier ideas about the temple-state or the palace-totalitarian state: it seems likely that Mesopotamian bureaucracy developed in the temples, but that may be a projection from elsewhere: perhaps an effective state emerged to run the temples too? The evidence at Lagash, both in Pre-Sargonic times and from the Ur III period, suggests that a strong ruler could find ways of subsuming the traditional temple economy and its administration under the state with the central administration using writing to control the process and extend the remit of posts from origin in the internal administration of the palace household to the country as a whole. But perhaps a distinction between political and sacerdotal authority is an anachronism in the third millennium BC?

State–citizen relations have always been complex. No sooner had 'civilisation' (literally, 'city living') been invented, that the disgruntled 'never-satisfied' citizen emerged. Just at the same time as humanity made its greatest leap forward, complaining also began: one Sumerian tablet grumpily protests about 'the city, where the tumult of man is'. In other words, urban living had barely got under way than the hustle and bustle of town life was already an irritant to some people. Grumbling about life in general, and government in particular, is as old as the written record.

As a result, rules and regulations were needed for 'citizens' or at least city-dwellers to get on with each other. Along with civilisation and kill-joys, therefore, the Sumerians invented public administration — or perhaps its invention made civilised society possible. Clearly Urukagina inherited a sophisticated civil service, with many Weberian attributes — hierarchy, differentiated roles and record-keeping.

The reign of Urukagina, the last of the first dynasty of Lagash, is also the one for which the greatest number of cuneiform documents survive from that era. These clay tablets come from Girsu, where they were preserved in the Archives of the temple of local Goddess Bau and power base of the wife of Urukagina, Sasag. The archives conjure up a detailed picture of the political economy of Lagash. There the fields of the 'King', the 'Queen' and 'crown prince' were notionally the property of the Gods and Goddesses. The members of the Royal family were their representatives on Earth, perceived as divine bureaucrats and functionaries with the titles and hierarchy to match, of Doorkeeper, Butler, Chamberlain Coachman, Goatherd — and so acquired the legitimacy of the deities.[9] No distinction had been made between the royal household and the public interest: the two remained synonymous for thousands of years.

Even the self-serving officialdom at the heart of Public Choice Theory was anticipated by 4000 years. One Sumerian proverb warns: 'in a city without watchdogs, the fox is the overseer'. The legitimacy of the state was challenged before it was consolidated, and the genie of the bureaucratic reputation for self-serving, irresponsible profligacy and petty-minded time-wasting was out of the bottle. The honourable qualities of public service — trust, solidarity, mutual dependence, integrity — had apparently already been subverted even at the dawn of the history of public administration.

---

[9] Asiat. VI, 1905, pp. 551–558, de La Fuye described a tablet of Urukagina's reign, listing 130 officials and their wages.

How had that happened, when public administration had lost no time in developing the key characteristics of effective and efficient bureaucracy: detailed record-keeping, rigid hierarchy and the somnambulant but essential professional skills of law and accountancy?

Some clues emerge from the remaining 10% of the Sumerian tablets that are literary texts, royal inscriptions, legal documents and government correspondence.[10] Indeed the 'Sumerian Question' challenges whether 'Sumerian' refers to an ethnicity, culture or language.

The danger of reading too much from the present in the past is matched by the risk of not seeing enough similarity in shared human attributes.

State capacity is an important determinant of development. The effectiveness, efficiency and fairness of public administration depend on political context. Interpretation of that relationship between politics and good governance depends on the historian's ideology or 'theory of change'. In Mesopotamian studies, just as in international development, that has rarely been made clear or explicitly acknowledged.

Those non-descript clay tablets written in cuneiform at the birthplace of human history, ancient Sumer, and now lurking in the Louvre in Paris, and elsewhere present the first recorded major reform of the state as emerging with remarkably developed characteristics around the responsibilities of government.

The history of Urukagina's reforms and his reign at the end of the first dynasty of Lagaš can be anchored in the fragmentary knowledge of his predecessors and the well-documented long-standing Lagaš-Umma conflict.[11] Yet it appears in a near vacuum. This allows almost any

---

[10] The most frequently quoted literary text, written during the 22nd century of the 3rd millennium BC, perhaps 200 years after Urukagina's reign, is known as the 'Cylinders of Gudea'. Inscribed on two clay cylindrical tablets, it is the longest Sumerian literary composition (1,363 lines long) and relates how Gudea, ruler of the city-state Lagash c. 2144–2124 B.C., rebuilt the temple of Ningirsu.

[11] e.g. Frayne, D. 2008. *Royal Inscriptions of Mesopotamia: Pre-Sargonic Period 2700–2350 BC*; Cooper, J. S. 1983. Reconstructing History from Ancient Inscriptions: The Lagash-Umma Border Conflict. *SANE* 2/1, Malibu; Lambert, M. 1961. Recherches sur la vie ouvrière: les ateliers de tissage de Lagash au temps de Lugalanda et d'Urukagina. *ArOr*, 29, 422–443; 1963. La guerre entre Lugal-zaggesi et Urukagina: ses incidences sur

possible interpretation. So this is a study in historicity. How much can causality be understood and descriptions of events be taken at face value when the survival of sources is so haphazard? When 'imaginary reality' resembles fiction, structured around a morality for the plot that guides the coherence of the story from beginning to a satisfactory conclusion? Is there an alternative other than 'one damned thing after another'? What did 'kingship' mean — for secular, sacerdotal or apotropaic power, ritual and pageantry — in a small state along the Tigris and the Euphrates rivers 45 centuries ago?

Sargon of Agade became deified and achieved cult status among future generations — how did that affect the image of Urukagina, defeated by Lugalzagesi of Uruk who was in turn defeated by 'Sargon the Great'?

Chronographic historiography (i.e. seeing the past as a chronicle of facts, 'one damned thing after another') does little to bring Lagash to life. Rulers have always sought to create a glorious image for contemporaries and survival through immortality in posterity, but for texts apparently deliberately buried in the foundations of buildings, who was the intended audience? What message was a 'Reforms' text designed to convey?

In the absence of detailed knowledge, the temptation in joining together fragments is reconstruction guided by falling back on supposed historical parallels, preconceptions and hidden bias. The overt or subliminal aim is to create a familiar narrative out of the unknown in ways that are difficult to avoid. Was Urukagina a Mesopotamian precursor to the Holy Roman Emperor Henry IV, who famously or infamously submitted temporal power to the spiritual authority of the Papacy in 1077? Was Urukagina tackling corruption in order to revive faith, while restoring lands taken by his predecessor to temple control? If he is depicted as the Henry VIII of the Sumerian cities, he was exploiting the political frailty of the clergy to strengthen the state.

While some see the 'reforms' as 'freedom', other interpretations suggest the reform texts capture an early stage in the origins of political repression, social injustice and economic inequality. Feminists have pointed to the reforms as marking the beginning of the oppression of

---

l'économie de Lagash. A Summary, *Iraq,* 25(1963), 192–193, and 1966. La guerre entre Urukagina et Lugalzagesi. *RSO, 41,* 29–66.

women: 'When a woman against a man says: "¼", that woman's mouth will be crushed with a baked brick, (and) that baked brick will hang on the city gate' (Ukg. 6).

Worryingly, it sometimes seems that the esoteric world of Sumerology has been guilty of sins both of commission and omission. Challenging theories such as the feminist critique have simply been ignored,[12] while dubious anachronisms have too often gone unchallenged.

The prolific outpouring of articles in the 1920s by the German Jesuit Anton Deimel argued that mid-third millennium Sumer had witnessed harmonious 'temple-states' commanding the faith of rulers and peoples, dominating the economy of southern Mesopotamia. This was threatened when a temple-palace divide, triggered by priests who had been abusing their prerogatives by demanding exorbitant pay for their services at funerals, pitched the institutions of religion against the institutions of state in a struggle for power.

Deimel suggested that Urukagina had seen this risk in his predecessor's actions, and had sought to reverse it. The lands and people of the city belonged to the temples and the ruler and his family were merely the representatives of the divine family. Urukagina was. correcting the subversion by his predecessor of this precursor to the papal supremacy principle.

That view dominated until challenged in the 1950s by the 'Leningrad School' of Sumerologists in the former USSR. Diakonoff rejected Deimel's claim that Urukagina was revoking the palace's usurpation of temple lands.[13] The communist interpretation cast him as a reactionary opposed to primitive democracy and a stooge of the clergy. Religion was already an opiate of the people. The institution of royalty at Lagash claimed to be the earthly manifestation of divine will. In the 'reforms', the king articulates the first expression of the contract theory of public authority, declaring that he had been appointed by the Gods to be a 'good shepherd' of his people, responsible for fostering fairness and prosperity in the realm. But as 'patesi' literally meaning 'servant', was the ruler serving the Gods or the people? Were the temples using Urukagina to reverse his

---

[12] Van De Mieroop, M. 1999. *Cuneiform Texts and the Writing of History*. London.

[13] 1958. Some Remarks on the 'Reforms' of Urukagina. *RA, 52*, 1–15.

predecessor's policy of state control over the clergy by levying taxes on them or putting temple lands under the authority of the palace?

Meanwhile in the United States, Samuel Kramer saw Lagash as a land of liberty resembling the United States, ruled by a bicameral congress, remarkably similar to that on Capitol Hill in Washington.

Later scholars have pointed out that changing the 'House of the Woman' to the 'House/Temple of the Goddess Baba' still left control of temple lands in the hands of the royal family, and indeed questioned whether drawing a distinction between 'high priest' and 'king' was not anachronistic.

Translation of the texts is unquestionably difficult. Problems arise because Cuneiform is a system of. syllabic writing in which sign can have several readings, compounded by the idiosyncrasies of the Sumerian language and the specifics of the writing genre and location. The result is that the Sumerologist's theory or ideology influences the translation, and the translated text then appears to validate the argument. As Steinkeller warns, the texts remain 'an obstinately difficult source'.[14] Key words, lines or sentences have been translated in surprisingly different, sometimes contradictory ways. For example, Ukg. 6 contains the sentence apparently condemning polyandry: 'The women of before had two men, (but) today's women avoid this crime But if the final word is translated as 'debt slavery' instead of 'crime', this could simply be referring to the *obligations* of a woman enslaved by debt.

Overall, however, it is hard not to conclude that, with regard to deepening our broad understanding of the reforms, Sumerologists have made limited progress. As a result, Paul Kriwaczek, in a recent well-reviewed overview history, *Babylon: Mesopotamia and the Birth of Civilization* concluded on the 'reforms' that 'Urukagina wanted to be approved of, even loved by, his people'.[15] This seems less insightful than one of the earliest interpretations over a century earlier that outlined how Urukagina 'based his government on the support he secured from the people'.[16]

---

[14] Steinkeller, P. 1991. The Reforms of UruKAgina and an Early Sumerian Term for 'Prison'. *Aula Orientalis, 9,* 227–233.

[15] Kriwaczek, P. 2014. *Babylon: Mesopotamia And The Birth Of Civilization*. Atlantic Books.

[16] King, *op. cit.*, p. 173.

Musée du Louvre, clay cone fragments AO 05498a and b (Creative Commons license).

Much still remains ambiguous. It seems likely that Urukagina did not implement a revolution in government on the ambitious scale suggested by the full amalgamated text, but doubtless Urukagina undertook some reforms during his reign.

Urukagina, however, was not the first ruler in the first dynasty of Lagaš who claimed to be a 'reformer'. According to other royal inscriptions, Entemena carried out two different reforms (Ent 35 and 79), using phraseology similar to that deployed by Urukagina, 'returning the child to the mother and mother to son', and voiding interest loans related to grain. Probably other kings also claimed to instigate reforms of public administration and the justice system.

Urukagina also invented another 'first': historicity, by claiming that he was tackling abuses which had existed 'since time immemorial' — yet which nevertheless were in contradiction of the original divinely ordained way of life. Was Urukagina indeed himself the first historian? Did he trigger a shift to a historicised mode of writing during the Old Babylonian period, with the ruler placed in historical context? Was this due to the 'Reforms', which betray a new socio-political situation that warranted this?[17]

The elites — priests, administrators, powerful men, and the former ensi ('governor') and family — were all guilty of acting in their own interests, seizing property and debtors by colluding with corrupt judges. This is also the first use of a contract theory of government to explain the purpose of public authority. He may have usurped power for, in contrast to practically all of his predecessors, his documents never list his genealogy. If he was a usurper, in implementing reforms on the grounds of his 'covenant' with Ningirsu, patron God of Lagash, he was simply carrying out divine orders.

In addition, for posterity and to and contain possible opposition, he claimed the moral high ground. If he had come to power through a *coup d'etat.* It enjoyed divine sanction. The 'God-fearing' Urukagina was chosen by Ningirsu, the tutelary deity of the city, out of the whole multitude of Lagash citizens and enjoined to re-establish the 'divine laws'. Urukagina was therefore claiming that the right to power was not absolute but provisional, dependent on performance in delivering good governance. He was appointed by divine authority with a performance contract to tackle maladministration and corruption. He had legitimately deposed his predecessor Lugalanda (or Urtarsirsira), on the grounds that the God Ningirsu had bestowed the kingship of Lagash on him. Urukagina asserted that the divine will was that abuse of public office needed to be rectified.

Furthermore, a person named Urukagina is several times mentioned on the Obelisk of Manishtushu, grandson of Sargon. If this is indeed a reference to the former ruler of Lagash, now in political exile at Akkad, he was also the world's first recorded political asylum-seeker or refugee, possibly having invited Sargon to the south to attack Umma, Uruk and Ur.[18]

---

[17] Sallaberger, in Porter, B. (ed.). 2005. *Ritual and Politics in Ancient Mesopotamia.* American Oriental Series, vol. 88. New Haven.
[18] Powell, M. 1996. The Sin of Lugalzagesi. *Wiener Zeitschrift Für Die Kunde Des Morgenlandes, 86,* 307–314.

But the most important aspect of the reforms has so far been overlooked — in public administration. Its core tenet, the distinction between *public* and *private* realms dates back to Urukagina. The concept of the public and general interest, civil servants prioritise their duty to all citizens over personal considerations, is attributed to the Age of Reason and to Jean-Jacques Rousseau.

No wonder that when these inscriptions were deciphered and debated, the usually calm world of Sumerology and Assyriology was transfixed.[19] A new hero of social development, here was the world's first recorded enlightened ruler. He was clearly motivated to alleviate poverty, tackle social injustice, provide welfare to the sick, elderly and vulnerable, and institute the first tax reduction. Yet enthusiasm for such enlightened rule seems to blur reflection, as no commentator has ever attempted to explain how Urukagina managed the economics of increasing allocation to welfare while cutting the fiscal burden. Such throwaway comments as 'Urukagina dispensed with tax collectors' makes one wonder how those optimists think the state functions.[20]

---

[19] Deimel, P. 1920. Die Reformtexte Urukaginas. *Orientalia, 2,* 3–31; Lambert, M. 1956. *Revue d'Assyriologie et d'archéologie orientale, 50*(4), 169–184.

[20] World Press Freedom Committee — http://www.wpfc.org/site/docs/pdf/Publications/PressFreedomInOurGenes.pdf.

Chapter 4

Urukagina's Reform Manifesto

The texts of the clay tablets, and meaning of the narrative that they relate, are opaque and obscure. So few agreed 'facts' exist about the life of Urukagina, the socio-economic structure of the city of Lagash or even the chronology of the 'Early Dynastic IIIb period' (see 'A Quick Introduction to Sumerology' above) to which his reign belongs that almost any interpretation about his 'Reforms' is possible, if not always plausible.[1]

The history of Urukagina's 'Reform' often seems to reveal more about the 20th century than it does about Ancient Sumeria. The beguiling story — of liberty for all, social justice for the poor and power struggles between church and state in the third millennium BC — is little more than ill-substantiated personal opinion extrapolated from the thinnest of evidence. Wild supposition, anachronistic assertions and self-serving fantasies about humanity's origins have pandered to different contemporary vested interests. Claiming that the origins of a belief lie in the dawn of civilisation legitimises the prejudice. What is the evidence?

Urukagina was the *ensi* (ruler or governor; *patesi* or *ishakku* in early scholarship) or *lugal* (king)[2] of the Sumerian city-state of Lagash in

---

[1] Vukosavović, 2009; King, L. 1910. *History of Sumer and Akkad*. London, pp. 171–211.
[2] Urukagina, in his second year, dropped the title 'ruler' (ensi) that had been used by his predecessors, and assumed the title 'king' (lugal — literally 'big man': see below). This had not been used in Lagash since the reign of Eannatum, but utilised by the rulers of Umma in their own inscriptions, so either Urukagina was seeking to adopt the mantle of

'Urukagina' in cuneiform.

Lower Mesopotamia for probably little more than a decade in the mid-24th century before the Common Era. That is, he ruled around 2350 BC, some 4500 years ago.[3] The state of Lagash was perhaps 125 miles wide stretching from Girsu through the city of Lagash to the port of Nigin, for the Persian Gulf stretched further inland than it does today. Access to the sea gave Lagash strategic influence, controlling trade with settlements around the Persian Gulf and beyond. Its population then may have been about 100,000 people.

However, almost everything else about Urukagina and Lagash is uncertain. Scholars have wondered for more than a century who he was, and why and how he came to power. One puzzle is his background. Urukagina was apparently a senior official (the 'ungal') under his predecessor Lugalanda. But it seems possible that he was not of the royal lineage, descended from Urnansche that had held power in Lagash for the previous six generations of rulers over a 150 years. He certainly never boasted of his ancestry.[4] He claimed the throne by divine will, not birth. Urukagina may have usurped the throne from Urtarsirsira, son of Lugalanda.

---

his more successful predecessors, or was claiming parity with Lugalzagesi. Under the kings of Akkad, a hierarchy evolved in which the *lugal* took precedence over the *ensi*.
[3] Klíma, J. 1957. *Urukagina, der grosse Reformer in der mesopotamischen Frühgeschichte*. Berlin. Akademie-Verlag.
[4] However Urukagina may have been the son of the Engilsa mentioned in the Maništušu obelisk who ruled Lagash prior to Enentarzi and so represented a side-branch of the dynasty. Another theory suggests that Urukagina was the son of Urutu who appears in lists of offerings for the deceased ancestors dating to Urukagina's reign: Schrakamp, I. 2015. Urukagina, Sohn des Engilsa, des Stadtfürsten von Lagaš: Zur Herkunft des Urukagina, des letzten Herrschers der 1. Dynastie von Lagaš. *Altorientalische Forschungen, 42*, 15–23.

He is therefore sometimes portrayed as a 'man of the people';[5] and as a ruler brought to power by a popular uprising in Lagash.[6] He might have been an upstart or usurper, presumably from the military. Perhaps it is significant that he did not commemorate his predecessors: in the Oval Plaque text, when he gives a brief historical summary of an earlier struggle between Lagash and Umma, he names the ruler of the latter city, but he ascribes the former's victory to Ningirsu. He does not refer to Enanatum I. and Entemena, in whose reigns the events took place.

He may have either orchestrated the overthrow of his predecessor or deposed Urtarsirsira, Lugalanda's son and heir presumptive. Alternatively, he could have been placed on the throne by other power brokers who saw him as a malleable 'front man'. Whatever the case, because Urtarsirsira was still alive in the first year of Urukagina's reign, it seems that if it was a *coup d'état* that brought Urukagina to power, it was bloodless. Furthermore, in the second year of Urukagina's reign, Lugalanda's widow Baranamtarra was given a dignified burial. The ancestor cult continued, making it unlikely that Urukagina was unrelated.[7]

The exact years and length of his reign is not known.[8] Even his name is not certain: alternative transcriptions of it include Uru-KA-gina, Uru'inimgina, Irikagina, or Iri'inimgina; and in French, Ourou-Kagina.[9] Four cuneiform signs comprise the ruler's name (URU.KA.GI.NA). The reading of the first sign (uru/iri) and of the second one (ka or inim) is contested. This gives four possible versions of his name. Some scholars who accept the original version even insist on the spelling as 'UruKAgina'.[10]

---

[5] This is because, in the surviving records, he never signed himself as dumu, 'son of', which seems to indicate his father was neither royal nor a high-ranking nobleman with a title worth mentioning.

[6] Nemirovsky, A. 2008. *Ancient Mesopotamia*, p. 204.

[7] Bauer, J. 1998. Der Vorsargonische Abschnitt der Mesopotamischen Geschichte. In Bauer, J., Englund, R. and Krebernik, M. 1998. *Mesopotamien. Späturuk-Zeit und frühdynastische Zeit*. Freiburg: Universitätsverlag Freiburg, pp. 431–585. Orbis Biblicus et Orientalis 160/1. Attinger, P. and Wäfler, M. (eds.) *Göttingen*, p. 477.

[8] Urukagina's last documented year of rule is his 11th, on a clay tag found at Girsu recording a donation he made to a sanctuary.

[9] Lambert, W. 1970. The Reading of the Name Uru.ka.gi.na. *Orientalia, 39*(3), 419.

[10] For example, Lambert, W. 1970. *op. cit.* Lambert, W. 1992. The Reading of Uru-KA-gi-na Again. *Aula Orientalis, 10*, 256–258.

Vukosavovic (2009) suggests that the correct reading is 'Uruinimgina'.[11] This means 'city of the just/proper laws/norms' and was the regnal name that he adopted upon ascension to power, reflecting his intention from the start of his rule to implement reforms. But it is debated whether Urukagina's reforms were decreed at the beginning of his reign.[12]

It could be that his wife Sasa (Shasha, or Shagshag) was also a commoner because her brother was merely a 'chief herdsman', although this title was sometimes held by members of the minor nobility. This was, of course, also one of the posts that the 'Reform' tablets declared had become mired in corruption, and from which Urukagina dismissed the incumbents. However, her appointment as the administrator of the temple of the Goddess Bau (or Baba), overseeing a workforce numbering more than 1000 employees, may suggest she was educated, and thus a member of the nobility.

She certainly was successful in expanding her royal 'Household of Goddess Bau' (formerly the 'Household of Women') from its original size of only about 50 females, gained ownership of vast amounts of land and, in the second (or third) year of her husband's reign, presided over the lavish funeral of his predecessor's queen, Baranamtarra, who had also been an important personage in her own right.[13] She clearly defended her husband's interests for many tablets attest to Bau's divine backing for Urukagina;[14] as well as Ningirsu's support.[15]

Little else is known about the royal couple. Their daughter Amattarsirsirra dedicated to the God Mesandu, eight male and three female slaves 'for the duration of the days'.[16] A letter survives from the high priest

---

[11] Vukosavović, F. 2009. *Reforms of Uruinimgina*. Unpublished dissertation. Hebrew State University Jerusalem.

[12] Hruška, B. 1973. Die innere Struktur der Reformtexte Urukaginas von Lagaš. *ArOr, 41*, 4–13 and 104–132; Hruška, B. 1974. Die Reformtexte Urukaginas. Der verspätete Versuch einer Konsolidierung des Stadtstaates von Lagaš. In *Le Palais et la Royauté* (Archéologie et Civilisation), edited by P. Garelli. Paris: XIX RAI, pp. 151–161.

[13] Evans, J. 2012. *The Lives of Sumerian Sculpture: An Archaeology of the Early Dynastic Temple*. Cambridge University Press, pp. 132–134.

[14] For example, P222654; P222653 where he is the shepherd of the nation; p. 222643–52.

[15] P222640–3.

[16] Mendelsohn, I. 1949. *Slavery in the Ancient Near East: A Comparative Study Of Slavery in Babylonia, Assyria, Syria, and Palestine from the Middle of the Third Millennium to the End of the First Millennium*. New York: Oxford University Press.

Lu-enna addressed to the king of Lagash, believed to be Urukagina, informing him that his son had been killed in combat.[17]

Urukagina was the last Old Sumerian ruler of Lagash before its conquest by Lugalzagesi, king of Umma, and the subsequent Sargonic period after Sargon of Akkad defeated Lugalzagesi and conquered all of Mesopotamia. His reign witnessed a shrinking sphere of influence under continuous threat from Lugalzagesi who conquered Uruk and forced him to abandon the city of Lagash and move his capital to Girsu, changing his title from 'king of Lagash' to 'king of Girsu'.[18] Urukagina had earlier upgraded his title from 'ruler' (*ensi*) to 'king' (*lugal*) of Lagash early on in his reign perhaps when he also changed the political dynamic by issuing his 'reforms'. He seems to have issued them again when he was forced to retreat to Girsu so the reforms do seem to have been an attempt to win popular support and rally the people to stand firm against the invaders.

Hitherto in the border wars with Lagash, Umma had always been defeated, or at any rate halted, and expelled. For generations, Lagash and Umma had contested the possession and agricultural usufruct of the fertile region of Gu'edena. Two generations before Ur-Nanshe, Mesilim (another 'king of Kish') had intervened as arbiter and possibly overlord in dictating to both states the course of the boundary between them, but this was not effective for long.

Some administrative texts attest to repeated attacks by Lugalzagesi on the Lagash state: for instance, mentions a siege by 'the man of Uruk',[19] apparently an ironic epithet for Lualzagesi. Another administrative text is dated to the 'month that the man of Uruk came a third time'.[20]

These attacks demonstrate the widening scope of military campaigns in southern Mesopotamia and the political entities that grew out of them. Already before Lugalzagesi and Sargon, Enshagkushana of Uruk had claimed the titles 'lord of Sumer' (*en ki-en-gi*) and 'king of the land' (*lugal kalam-ma*), having conquered Kish and Akshak, and even besieging Akkad.

---

[17] Louvre AO 4238: excavations supervised by Gaston Cros, 1903–1909.
[18] P222640 He was 'king [lugal] of Girsu' in 'year 10'.
[19] P221195.
[20] P221996.

Lugalzagesi dealt the crippling blow to the Lagash state in the seventh year of Urukagina's reign. One text describes in dramatic fashion how Umma destroyed many public works and pillaged many sacred sites of the state.[21] At that point administrative documents end, although Urukagina survived for at least another four years. Other administrative texts give a more subdued account of the waning of Lagash's power, as they indicate a general reduction in the economic vitality and manpower of the state.[22]

The document describing the sack of Lagash closely resembles in shape and writing the tablets of household accounts from the archive but the text inscribed upon it consists of an indictment of Umma. A series of short, almost staccato sentences describe the deeds of sacrilege committed. It is not a royal nor an official inscription, for it was not stored in any regular archive or depository. The 'Lament' would appear to have been the work of some priest, or scribe, who had formerly been in Urukagina's service, and was written shortly after the fall of Lagash, explaining the absence of any introduction. The city's destruction had so recently taken place that the writer has no need to explain the circumstances.

The repetition of phrases and the recurrent use of the same formulæ serve only to heighten the cumulative effect of the charges he brings against the destroyers of his city. The text concludes: 'The men of Umma, by the despoiling of Lagash, have committed a sin against the God Ningirsu! The power that is come unto them, from them shall be taken away! Of sin on the part of Urukagina, king of Girsu, there is none. But as for Lugal-zaggisi, patesi of Umma, may his Goddess Nidaba bear this sin upon her head!' No blame is attached to Urukagina.

Urukagina's own interest was not in foreign conquest (was he the world's first pacifist? Or, he had no opportunity), but in internal reform. He devoted his energies to modernising the administration of his own land and to stamping out corruption. 'That he benefited the land as a whole, and earned the gratitude of his poorer subjects, there can be no

---

[21] P222618, FAOS 05/1, Ukg. 16. Antasura is a town on the Umma border.

[22] See, for instance, P221396 dating to the end of Urukagina's 5th year, and P221826, from the beginning of the 6th.

The Stele of Vultures: fragment of the victory stele of the king Eannatum of Lagash over Umma c. 2450 BC (Louvre, AO2344, 180 × 130 cm: Creative Commons license).

doubt; but it is to his reforms themselves that we may trace the immediate cause of the downfall of his kingdom'.[23]

But there is doubt. Were the reforms all rhetoric and no action? Had his reforms undermined the hegemony of Lagash? Or did his reforming zeal help win popular support to stave off impending military collapse, at least for a while?

In stressing his popular support, perhaps he was appealing to memories of a half-remembered Lagashite tradition from earlier times as a democracy with a citizen army. This may be indicated by the imagery of the Stele of the Vultures, erected by one of his predecessors, Eannatum. It depicts serried ranks of Lagashite warriors armed with spears and equipped with full-length shields, in a disciplined phalanx formation.

Eannatum was the most militarily successful ruler of the first dynasty of Lagash. He conducted many campaigns abroad, including ones against

---

[23] King, L. W. 1923. *A History of Sumer and Akkad. An Account of the Early Races of Babylonia from Prehistoric Times to the Foundation of the Babylonian Monarchy*. London: Chatton & Windus.

the southern cities of Ur, Uruk and Kiutu, as well as states further afield such as Kish, Mari, Akshak and Susa. He was able to claim the title 'King of Kish', a title associated with the unity of the Mesopotamian city-states under a single ruler.[24] After a prolonged struggle, Eannatum vanquished the ruler of Umma, celebrated on the Stele of Vultures that stressed the legitimacy of royal power. This message was doubtless repeated by every subsequent ruler. The Stele of the Vultures is important evidence on the ideology of kingship. Eannatum is the first Lagash king to explicitly claim divine birth by a God, Ningirsu.

The struggle, however, continued under Eannatum's successors, in particular Entemena, until Urukagina was defeated by Lugalzagesi, who was vanquished in turn by Sargon of Akkad.

The first ruler of Lagash, Ur-Nanshe, depicted as the 'big man' dominating the city-state c. 2400 BC (Louvre, AO2344, 46 × 39 cm: Creative Commons license).

The Musée du Louvre houses a limestone relief commemorating the construction in Girsu of a religious building, probably the temple of Ningirsu, the divine protector of the state of Lagash. The story on the

---

[24] Kish played a major role almost from the beginning. After 2500, southern rulers, such as Mesannepada of Ur and Eannatum of Lagash, frequently called themselves king of Kish when laying claim to sovereignty over northern Babylonia.

relief is told in two scenes. Both are dominated by Ur-Nanshe, founder of the first dynasty of Lagash, thanks to the artistic license of his much taller stature and larger size (perhaps also reflecting that 'Lugal', the Sumerian word for king, literally means 'Big Man'). The upper image shows Ur-Nanshe carrying a hod of bricks on his head to help build the temple of Ningirsu. Clothed in a kaunakes (a tufted woollen skirt), the king is accompanied by his wife, sons and high functionaries, all identified by name written on their garments. In the lower image, sitting with a goblet in his hand, Ur-Nanshe is presiding over a banquet, which commemorates the building of the temple. The iconography of the king's role as the builder and protector of the foundations of society is underscored by the carved inscription: 'Ur-Nanshe, king of Lagash, son of Gunidu, built the temple of Ningirsu; he built the temple of Nanshe; he built Apsubanda'.

The relief of Ur-Nanshe suggested that any prosperity granted by the Gods was due to the king and that such material well-being was proof of his divine support. This was a powerful political message. The ruler was divinely anointed so the Gods expected the people to support him. His success was proof of his special bond with the Gods.

But this success of earlier kings of Lagash in establishing the credibility of their divine status perhaps led, before Urukagina, to oppression of the citizenry by the monarchy and the priesthood. The argument, therefore, in the 'Reform Cones' that the ancient institutions of state had long been corrupt and that, from time immemorial, a bloated and corrupt bureaucracy was present across the whole country, was extraordinary. Urukagina was claiming not simply to be restoring the status quo before the abuses of Lugal-anda, but was addressing inherent failings in governance that stretched back perhaps to the time of the foundation of Lagash's greatness by Ur-Nanshe. The legitimacy of the state was challenged.

Until Urukagina took political leadership to correct the problem, abuse of office had been accepted with fatalism: *As the traditions were, it was.* Such a forthright condemnation was risky. It seems to discredit all the great rulers of Lagash and to undermine the institution of kingship — on which his own power also relied. His action may have been popular and/or populist. Yet Urukagina regards his reforms as due to the direct intervention of Ningirsu. It was not with his people but with the state God Ningirsu that he drew up the agreement to observe the political transformation.

While the former ruler is roundly condemned, the whole system was to blame if these abuses had been going on since time immemorial. The temple officials and state bureaucracy were greedy and corrupt. The comment, *no {corrupt?} persons shall serve as public officials,* echoes the earlier criticism that *Public officials were present across the whole country.* An alternative translation suggests all public officials were dismissed. If so, these disgruntled former civil servants would have constituted a powerful opposition.[25] Perhaps this was why Urukagina regime fell some years later that it had lost the support of both the elites of Lagash and its public administration.

His enigmatic reputation has inspired not only historical descriptions but also novels, like Michael Aulfinger's fictional account of *Urukagina — der gerechte König.*[26] Perhaps Urukagina was indeed a good, honest, God-fearing ruler who curbed corruption, righted wrongs, ended unjust treatment of the poor, protected the vulnerable, reduced taxation, re-established the separation of state and religion, offered criminals a second chance through a general amnesty, and above all, gave his people freedom — but who was unlucky with confronting a more powerful enemy.

Immediately on coming to power, the new ruler declared that he had ended rampant corruption in public office and proclaimed how he has restored social harmony. Social justice was the explicit aim of public policy for the first recorded time: the oppressed of the poor by the rich was rectified. These efforts to assist common people have seen him widely acclaimed as the first social reformer in history. Perhaps Mesopotamia was indeed the biblical 'Garden of Eden' where 'he established freedom'.[27]

But there is at least as strong a case that he was a disastrous ruler whose exaggerated rhetoric undermined the state's legitimacy and military power that for centuries had always kept its rivals in check. Was Urukagina a Mesopotamian Donald Trump, a populist reactionary who degraded the status of women and ended earlier efforts to curb the

---

[25] A similar error to the Bush administration's decision in May 2003, soon after the overthrow of Saddam Hussein in Iraq, to disband his army, putting 250,000 young Iraqi men out of a job and on the streets, angry and armed — all but guaranteeing the violent chaos that ensued.

[26] Aulfinger, M. 2007. *Urukagina, der gerechte König.* Edition Nove, Neckenmarkt.

[27] http://history-world.org/reforms_of_urukagina.htm.

excesses of religious oppression, irresponsibly released thieves and murderers back into society (or exiled them), sacked all his experienced officials and destroyed the tax system on which the state relied to fund its ability to run prisons and organise its defence?

In all the modern enthusiasm for his 'Reforms' as 'freedom', insufficient attention has been paid as to whether he thereby weakened the authority and administrative capacity of the state — as so conceived then. He confiscated the estates of the previous *ensi* and placed them under the jurisdiction of the Gods (i.e., the temples). This possibly resulted in weakening the fiscal stability of government, although it seems likely that, as the representatives of the Gods on earth, the *ensi* and his family retained actual control of these assets.

Confronted by such generalised attack on the professionalism of top officials, morale and public service motivation would have collapsed. Furthermore, by removing the country's key administrative leadership, a power vacuum would have been created, administrative capacity weakened, and the public authority and prestige of the state undermined. Urukagina may have dismissed all serving officials tainted by corruption. Yet, if such a drastic act seems unlikely, even sacking the most outrageous perpetrators of corrupt practices would probably have gravely weakened his regime.[28]

The sacked leadership and other allegedly corrupt would thereafter have formed the backbone of a powerful domestic opposition to the regime. They could have united with the disgruntled followers of the previous Lugalanda regime in a common cause to oppose Urukagina.

There is always a reason why someone devotes time and effort to write. Writing bridges space, time and social distance. Why did a scribe over 4000 years ago inscribe the cone-shaped clay tablets, created in the city-state of Lagash during what is now classified in Assyriology as the Early Dynastic IIIb period (c. 2540–2350 BC, at the end of the Pre-Sargonic era, in the years before Sargon of Akkad founded the Old Akkadian empire) now preserved in museums around the world? Presumably Urukagina paid him to do so. Why?

---

[28] Perhaps similar to the disaster of the Iraq occupation administration in 2003 sacking all members of the Ba'ath Party.

There may be a naïve tendency, at least among some historians, to interpret the written evidence as reality, when uncontested by the survival of alternative sources. It seems certain that Urukagina was image-conscious and media savvy. For example, he was the first Mesopotamian ruler to deploy the powerful and lasting imagery of the king as 'Shepherd' benignly guiding the citizens of Lagash as his 'flock'.[29]

Possibly the cones were written under the influence of Gilgamesh's search for everlasting fame, or a shared tradition of political philosophy that influenced both. Sumerian rulers sought to intimidate their rivals and achieve future immortality through diplomatic successes,[30] military adventures, steles, public works, (temple) buildings, canal construction,[31] and hymns of praise. Did Urukagina devise the 'Reform Cones' as his manifesto to the people — and in addition to posterity? Were these the first 'political memoirs', designed to shape how history would judge him? Winston Churchill once noted that 'History will be kind to me for I intend to write it'.

The evidence for this is that Urukagina had multiple copies of the reform cones made. The aim of that was to ensure at least one tablet would survive the vicissitudes of wars and political upheavals, then and since. The Epic of Gilgamesh and public monuments like the Stele of the Vultures reveal that Sumerian rulers were indeed preoccupied by how they would be remembered. And if Ukg. 6 is indeed not from Urukagina's reign but was written for an earlier ruler, then reforming the public service was another route by which the kings of Lagash hoped that their fame would last for all eternity.

The Epic of Gilgamesh (c. 2700 BC, but first recorded c. 2100 BC) relates how the eponymous hero learns through his adventures that the human ambition for immortality is an impossible dream. Death cannot be cheated. Permanence can only be gained through leaving a legacy of good works, recorded on tablets. Gilgamesh, accepting the inevitable, transforms

---

[29] Franke, S. 1992. 'Kings of Akkad'. In *Civilizations of the Ancient Near East*, edited by Jack M. Sasson, vol. 2. New York: Scribner, p. 833.

[30] For example, P469959 records how *Enmetena the ruler of Lagash, and Lugalkinešdudu the ruler of Uruk, established brotherhood.*

[31] For example, P431161: *Urukagina, king of Lagash, built for Ningirsu, the dam of the canal going to Nigin, with 432,000 baked bricks and 1820 standard gur of bitumen.* These closely resemble similar tablets from previous reigns, e.g. P431149 of King Enannatum.

himself into a righteous king whose good deeds will be remembered in perpetuity. His name would last for ever not by discovering the secret of eternal life but in his accomplishments on behalf of his people and his God. Were Urukagina's reform cones written for posterity, similarly influenced by the belief that eternal fame rested on one's actions? This approach certainly worked: both Gilgamesh and Urukagina have found lasting renown.

Yet what is incontestable is that the first recorded reform of public administration in human history, undertaken by Urukagina in the city-state of Lagash in Mesopotamia some 4500 years ago, ended in catastrophic failure. At some point after the city-state of Lagash was sacked by its long-time rival, the neighbouring city-state of Umma, Lagash's ruler and reformer, named Urukagina, disappears from the historical record. His city-state was absorbed into Lugalzagesi's realm and then soon thereafter into the kingdom of Akkad, to form part of the world's first empire under King Sargon.

King Gudea of Lagash c. 2144–2124 BC as the source of water and, therefore, prosperity and life. (CC, Metropolitan Museum, New York).

Chapter 5

Revolutionary or Reactionary? Urukagina in the 20th Century

First accounts of the 'Reforms' in the early years after their discovery presented a balanced view. For example, Leonard King, Assistant Keeper of the Department of Egyptian and Assyrian Antiquities at the British Museum, in his monumental work, *A History of Sumer and Akkad* of 1910 argued that the priests grew rich by plundering the people with impunity, but public officials were thoroughly complicit. Urukagina dismissed officials who had accepted bribes from the priests. The priests were deprived of their privileges, and burial fees were cut by more than half. Urukagina put an end to the extortions of officials, imposed drastic penalties for theft, and sought to protect by law the humbler classes of his subjects, including the *muskenum* (serf/villein) and the *awilum* (free man) or *mar awllim* (son of a (free) man) from oppression by their wealthier and more powerful neighbours.

During the 5th century BC, Nehemiah's reforms promoted the welfare of the populace of Yehud (Neh 2:10) and posed a threat to the interests of the nobility (Neh 6:18). He removed a prominent priest (Neh 13:7–9), ensured provisions for the Levites (Neh 13:11–12), appointed certain priests as treasurers of the storehouses, banished a son of the high priest (Neh 13:28) and generally 'cleansed the temple' (Neh 13:30).

Leonard King put considerable emphasis on the damage that Urukagina's reforms inflicted on the capability to function. This important

Votive statue of Eannatum (Creative Commons).

point has been largely lost in subsequent analysis, so it is worth quoting King at length:

> ... his zeal had led him to destroy the long-established methods of government, and, though he thereby put an end to corruption, he failed to provide an adequate substitute to take their place. The host of officials he abolished or dispossessed of office had belonged to a military administration, which had made the name of Lagash feared, and they had doubtless been organised with a view to ensuring the stability and protection of the state. Their disappearance mattered little in times of peace; though, even so, Urukagina must have had trouble with the various powerful sections of the population whom he had estranged. When war threatened he must have found himself without an army and without the means of raising one. To this cause we may probably trace the completeness of Umma's victory. .... The struggle for the throne, which appears to have preceded Urukagina's accession, must have weakened still further the military organisation of the state; and when Urukagina himself, actuated by the best of motives, attempted to reform

and remodel its entire constitution, he rendered it still more defenceless before the attack of any resolute foe.[1]

Although they apparently laid the foundation of the cuneiform legal genre that most famously flourished six centuries later with the Code of Hammurabi (c. 1792–1750 BC) in Babylon, the tablets were not written, however, to codify legal judgement or to deliver social justice by reversing the growing power of the state. Their evident purpose was to stake a political claim through public administrative reform.

Interpreting such limited evidence is to reveal pre-conceived beliefs as to the nature of statehood, its administration, the institution of religion, the structure of society and the characteristics of the private sector (attested by surviving cuneiform tablets recording commercial transactions).

Comparing translations of the 'Reform Cones' shows how much the texts can be translated, and therefore interpreted, in radically different ways.[2] Some translations are based on a preconception that the 'Reforms' are inherently legal, while other translators perceive that their purpose was political ('Liberty Cones'), or assume that Urukagina was a reformer pursuing social justice.

In seizing power, Urukagina justified his *coup d'état* by claiming that he acted in defence of the common people. But why is that accepted uncritically? Were the boats seized, sheep appropriated and fish stores confiscated by public officials? Was this corruption and exploitation?

Or is it possible, indeed probable, that the boats were unsafe and posed a safety hazard to travellers, the sheep were overgrazing the commons, over-fishing was depleting the shared asset, while the trees of the poor had been illegally planted? Perhaps official functionaries realised that the people needed to work, not just scrounge off the state, but should be steered into competitive and productive sectors. Perhaps the previous ruler had sensibly nationalised land and oxen to plough it, in order to put the state on a war-footing, able to deal with the growing threat from Umma. If so, then it is possible that Urukagina was, like Neville

---

[1] King, *op. cit.*, pp. 187–188.
[2] e.g. Thureau-Dangin. 1907. Sumerischen und akkadischen Königsinschriften.; Kramer, *Sumerians*, pp. 79 ff. and 316 ff; Cooper, 1986; and Frayne, D. 2008. *Royal Inscriptions of Mesopotamia: Pre-Sargonic Period 2700–2350 B.C.*

Chamberlain 200 generations later, pursuing a policy of appeasement doomed to fail.

Then Urukagina took popular, if not populist, policies. He set limits on the amount that the priests could collect for their religious rituals and their fees for burying the dead. He cancelled debt slavery and declared a universal amnesty for convicted criminals, even for those convicted of the most serious crimes including murder ('their prison he cleared out'). Last but not least, he provided charity for the poor and the elderly.

The general pardon for all imprisoned criminals to mark a new start and to advertise the magnanimous power of the new ruler is important as evidence of Urukagina's eye for progressive yet populist ideals. No other ruler in Mesopotamian history ever even proposed such an action.[3] The idea was revived over 2000 years later in world history by two other usurpers: in 44 BC at the end of the Roman Republic, by Julius Caesar, and in China by the Emperor Yuan Ziyou (元子攸) in 503 AD.

Urukagina justified his actions in seizing power. According to the new regime, the previous ruler, Lugalanda, had seized the best fields to grow his food (garlic and cucumber) and inappropriately used the temple oxen to plough his own farmland. Moreover, Lugalanda had appropriated land in the name of his wife and children, even though, in Lagash tradition, land title could only be held by adult male heads of household, not by women and children. Lugalanda had seized control of the most important temples, those of the Gods Ningirsu and Shulshagana and the Goddess Bau. He placed them under the administration of an official who was not, as formerly the case, a priest. Lugalanda also appointed himself, his wife Baranamtarra and other members of his family as administrators of the temples which he then referred to as the private property of the ruler. He no longer mentioned the name of the deities in temple documents and he levied taxes on the priesthood (who may, therefore, have supported Urukagina's *coup d'état*, if that is how he came to power). Lugalanda and his wife had become the largest landholders in the region.

Changing the narrative is important for getting reform accepted. Blaming the previous regime is a staple justification for any new

---

[3] Steinkeller, P. 1991. The Reforms of UruKAgina and an Early Sumerian Term for 'Prison'. *Aula Orientalis, 9*, 227–233.

government. But attacking the whole fabric of Lagash political tradition 'from time immemorial' was risky. Rulers exploit the past, adapting it to their purposes. Contexts differ and circumstances change but even most revolutionary leaders quickly come to value the legitimation conferred by respect for tradition. Yet if the past serves to sustain power, it also restrains it. In claiming the legitimation conferred by the old ways, a ruler implicitly, and often explicitly, affirms the duties of leaders to their followers. An ancient mystique surrounding the 'God's annointed' bestows not only rights but responsibilities on both ruler and ruled. The privileges of power are matched by the responsibilities that come with it — to provide prosperity and righteousness.

Ashurbanipal (668 BC–c. 627 BC; also spelled Assurbanipal or Ashshurbanipal) was an Assyrian king who amassed a significant library of cuneiform documents at his royal palace at Nineveh. In this collection, now housed at the British Museum, is a tablet believed to date from c. 737 BC, that declares:

> If a king does not heed justice, his people will be thrown into chaos and his land will be devastated. ... If he does not heed his nobles, his life will be cut short. If he does not heed his adviser, his land will rebel against him.

The text goes on to warn that the Gods would punish unjust and corrupt rulers and officials:

> ... the wind will carry away their remains and their achievements will be given over to the storm wind.

One of the reform tablets refers to Urukagina as 'king of Girsu'. This presumably means it was written towards the end of his reign, at some point after he had lost control of the city of Lagash to Lugalzagesi. So the tablets were not just the product of his inauguration and immediate justification. He maintained this same propaganda message throughout his rule.

Urukagina may have been determined to right social wrongs. Equally his main aim may have been to smear the reputation of the previous regime. Either way, it was clearly also ideological — perhaps populist or anti-clerical. This seems to explain why Urukagina sought to secure widespread support by his social policy. He reduced burial costs by more than half, and fixed the pay of *the persons (in charge) of the levy by the lamentation singers of Lagash* and elsewhere. He provided welfare for the poor and elderly: bread and beer *for the old wailing women ... the old men of Nigin* and the sagbur-priest.

He revoked the ferry toll and stopped officials from cutting down the trees of the poor for firewood. He decreed that people could not be forced to sell their property or valued possessions like donkeys to officials. He issued a general amnesty for all imprisoned criminals, even thieves and murderers, and swore under oath that the state would protect the weak and vulnerable, namely orphans and widows, against exploitation by the powerful.[4] He eliminated the abuse of the judicial process to extract money from citizens and prefigured 'habeas corpus' by ensuring the public nature of legal proceedings.

Was he writing out of conviction he was doing the right thing, or was he writing to win political support, that he was the world's first political self-publicist or spin doctor? The evidence for that includes one interesting technical point: that some of the copies of the cones seem to have been written on drinking vessels or jars.[5]

Lagash, the Mirror of Modern Times?

Three great Assyriologists dominated research into and analysis of Urukagina in the 20th century. Ideologically, they were in perfect counterpoise to each other. First, Anton Deimel (1865–1954), a German Jesuit father who was based for most of his working life in the Vatican. There he conjured up a *Tempelwirtschaft*, a benign religious government with the interests of the people at heart, but forever subverted by secular authority.[6]

---

[4] Two hundred years later, Gudea would make a similar decree: 'To provide protection for the orphan against the rich, and to provide protection for the widow against the powerful'.

[5] Cooper, J. 1985. *Medium and Message: Inscribed Clay Cones and Vessels from Presargonic Sumer. Revue D'Assyriologie Et D'archéologie Orientale*, 79(2), 97–114.

[6] The leading critique of this interpretation is: Foster, B. 1981. A New Look at the Sumerian Temple State. *Journal of the Economic and Social History of the Orient*, 24, 224–241.

Revolutionary or Reactionary? Urukagina in the 20th Century

Painted specially for this work.
THE REFORMS OF URUKAGINA.

Corrupt officials being punished, from: Hutchinson's Story of the Nations, containing the Egyptians, the Chinese, Indians, the Babylonian nation, the Hittites, the Assyrians, the Phoenicians and the Carthaginians, the Phrygians, the Lydians, and other nations of Asia Minor. London, [no date, c. 1910] p. 242.

The second was Samuel Noah Kramer (1897–1990), professor of Assyriology at the University of Pennsylvania and a vigorous populariser of ancient history. As a child, he had emigrated with his parents to the United States from Tzarist Russia to escape anti-Jewish pogroms that erupted in 1905 in response to the attempted revolution that year. Like other Jewish refugees from oppression, such as the Nobel Laureate Milton Friedman, he cherished the freedoms of opportunity and personal choice in America. Kramer declared that the word and concept of 'liberty' occurs for the first time in human history in the Reform cones.[7] He argued that Urukagina expressed 'profound conviction in the rightness of his cause and his faith in the ultimate triumph of divine justice'.[8]

The third highly influential scholar was Igor Diakonoff (1914–1999), a Soviet academic concerned to track the rise of the 'despotic state' in the class exploitation of the masses by both priests and kings. Even during the Stalin era of terror, Diakonoff was accorded by the authorities in the USSR a remarkable degree of freedom. He was permitted to work abroad (including as a visiting professor at the University of Chicago in 1963), publish in western academic journals and engage with foreign scholars. He was clearly ideologically trusted.

The three offered competing answers to the basic question: why had Urukagina repeatedly declared that he had acted on behalf of the common people? Had the citizens of Lagash hitherto been exploited, over-taxed or illegally taxed? How far, at this early stage in Sumerian history, were Urukagina and his administrators 'servants' of the people? Later, administrative officials were referred to as slaves of the king, analogous to Aristotle's 'despot'. Had the temples been oppressing or coerced? Were the priesthood the main beneficiary of his rule?

Ideas about the temple-state or the palace-totalitarian state or community assemblies cannot be separated from the creation myth of Mesopotamia that explained that Gods created men to do the work. Even among the Gods, inequality was pronounced and the more powerful of their number [such as An, sky God; Enlil, God of earth; Enki, of water] had divine servants. Ningirsu, God of war and patron city God of Lagash, was served by lesser Gods acting as heavenly counterparts to public officials on earth — like the 'inspector of fishermen'. So when some earthly equivalents like that post were accused of corruption, what was the divine response? Or more concretely, were the reforms promoting one set of interests against another — butlers, doorkeepers, armourers and stewards, perhaps, in loose coalition against the officials condemned on the 'reform' tablets?

---

[7] In the term 'amagi' or 'amargi', which literally means 'returning to mother'.
[8] Kramer, S. N. 1988. *History begins at Sumer: Thirty-nine firsts in recorded History.* University of Pennsylvania Press.

Especially on account of P222607 (Cone D), Urukagina has been heralded by historians as a 'reformer'. He is credited with curtailing the state's encroachment over the traditional power of the temples. He obtained popular support by tackling the scourge of 'big government' through promoting the world's first 'rightsizing' reform of the public sector.

> Urukagina ... proudly records that he restored justice and freedom to the long-suffering citizens, did away with ubiquitous and oppressive officials, put a stop to injustice and exploitation, protected the widow and the orphan.[9]

Much less consideration has been given as to whether, by undermining state capacity, he failed to match the rival city-states that were building their competitive advantage by improving administrative and military capabilities. Perhaps his reforming zeal and belief in justice for all alienated oligarchs in Lagash. When he was threatened with an invasion seven years later, the powerful did little to support him. Urukagina, 'ever the pious reformer', proved unable to translate civil justice into military strength. The support of the Gods to vindicate his cause failed to materialise. Passively awaiting for the hand of divine providence to destroy Lugalzagesi (2340–2316 BC), a conqueror who had recently vanquished Umma, Urukagina fell victim to the ruthless ambitions of his rival. Divine salvation never came. Urukagina and Lagash were destroyed instead.

But there is precious little evidence for any interpretation. Urukagina 'talked a good game', but what did he deliver? Little is really known about power structures, social divides or the shape of the economy in pre-Sargonic Lagash.

But this simple point, while Assyriology's loss, is our gain. For one consequence is that Urukagina's actions invariably provide a mirror for the interpreter's times. It is always difficult if not impossible to avoid projecting the present on the past. The historian's own concerns are

---

[9] Kramer, S. N. 1956. Sumerian Theology and Ethics. *The Harvard Theological Review, 49*(1), 45–62.

projected, occasionally overtly but usually subconsciously, onto the canvas of third millennium BC.

Seeing the Present in the Past is always tempting. The dangers of subjectivity and bias are inevitably even greater when considering how far Bronze Age government could be responsive to citizens, concerned for gender equity, committed to protecting the weak and vulnerable. Every wishful fantasy can take wing, unimpeded by irritating evidence from the real world.

The cones have rightly been described as 'an obstinately difficult source'.[10] The obscurity of most cuneiform text allows translations that drive or are driven by differing or often wildly contradictory interpretations. In the name of accuracy and exact faith to the original, the tablets are also rendered into gibberish English — much as Latin used to be badly taught by the use of Loeb literal translations. This lamentable obscurantism seems to be because the academics either lack faith in their own guesswork as to the real meaning of the original, or fear the scorn of their peers.[11] Meanwhile popularisers, freely modern concepts like 'property', 'kingship' or 'temple', impose anachronistic connotations.

Furthermore, interpretations of the 'widely discussed but philologically obscure reforms'[12] may often depend on the preoccupations, both academic and political, of the present. Political fragmentation of Iraq after the invasion of 2003, for instance, has renewed interest in the independent-minded localism of the Sumerian city-state.

The result has been that Assyriologists and general historians have put forward a bewildering kaleidoscope of varying and shifting interpretations of the 'Reforms' of Urukagina. In the aftermath of the French archaeologists' finds, awareness of the Reform Cones filtered out at a time of political upheaval before WWI. In the United States, government was taking reform efforts to control the distorting political influence and economic might of the 'robber baron' industrialists. Meanwhile Britain witnessed the 'People's Budget' crisis in 1911 over the power of the House of Lords.

---

[10] Steinkeller, 1991. *op. cit.*

[11] Foster, B. 1981. 'A New Look at the Sumerian Temple State'. *Journal of the Economic and Social History of the Orient, 24*(3). Brill, 225–41.

[12] Silver, M. 1983. Karl Polanyi and Markets in the Ancient Near East: The Challenge of the Evidence. *Journal of Economic History, 43*(4), 795–829.

So Urukagina was celebrated as the leader of a popular revolt to overthrow a 'legalized aristocracy entrenched in power and oppressing the lower classes'.[13] But the uncertainty of the time resulted in a worryingly problematic conclusion:

> Unhappily for Urukagina, he met the fate of most reformers. In seeking to rescue his people from suffering he plunged them into disaster. He must have alienated, possibly he exterminated, the host of aristocrats who had lived upon the taxation of the people. The loss of this upper class left the state weak; presumably they had been its chief fighting force, a sort of unorganized army supported by the peasantry. At any rate, under the reforming king, Lagash failed to uphold her previous military supremacy. ... Evidently men had already begun to dream of good deeds as deserving repayment in worldly success; and now they heard Life's grim answer to the dream — that the Gods shield not their own, that earth moves not by any practical law of poetic justice.

After the Bolshevik Revolution, Urukagina was cast in the role of 'the leader of a peasants' revolution'. The Finnish Assyriologist Knut Tallqvist, writing *Konungen med Guds nåde* (1920) on Mesopotamian Kingship under the heavy influence of the overthrow of the Tsar three years earlier in Finland's former imperial master, was pre-occupied by the fragility of public authority.[14] Like the failed Stolipin efforts at modernising Russia in the years after the 1905 Revolution, Urukagina's ultimate failure showed the danger of falling victim to any reform attempt.

Some celebrated his rule as the victory for a popular almost 'democratic' movement attempting to redress social and economic iniquities and end political oppression. The Epic of Gilgamesh refers to a political assembly with an upper and lower house.[15] Urukagina also began a massive programme of public works at the start of his reign, so it seems that Keynesian economics too was invented in Mesopotamia over 4300 years

---

[13] Ellis, E. and Horne, C. 1913. *The Story of the Greatest Nations and the World's Famous Events*, vol. 1. New York.
[14] Tallqvist, K. 1920. *Konungen med Guds nåde: skisser öfver härskarkult och imperialistisk symbolik*. Söderstrom.
[15] Kramer, *History Begins at Sumer*, pp. 66–67.

before. 'The Economic Consequences of the Peace' was published. Equally, in the United States, his 'reforms' were seen in the 1930s as a 'New Deal' to boost aggregate demand at a time of profound uncertainty.[16]

The ultramontanist Jesuit Father Anton Deimel (1865–1954) spent most of his scholarly career at the Pontifical Biblical Institute in Rome. Deimel wrote prolifically on Lagash. But even admirers of his industrious research admit that he developed his grand interpretations first and then searched the cuneiform tablets for supporting evidence. Influenced by the 1870 papal infallibility and the uncertain status of the Holy See in a unified Italy until the Accords of 1929 signed with Mussolini, he never doubted that Lagash was a Sumerian Vatican City, a theocracy or 'temple-state'. Nevertheless, Deimel declared that Urukagina was an immoral atheist who had murdered his predecessor — perhaps reflecting the murder by Mussolini's thugs of the socialist leader Giacomo Matteotti in 1924 that triggered the *Duce* to dispense with the last vestiges of genuine democracy.

Most other Catholic interpretations have argued the reverse, namely that Urukagina sought to preserve the theocratic structure of Sumerian society.[17] Indeed Deimel's articles of the 1920s and 1930s echo negotiations leading up to the Lateran Pact of 1929 by which Mussolini settled the constitutional position of the Vatican and recognised that 'the Catholic, Apostolic and Roman Religion is the only religion of the State'.

In reality, the structure of Lagash society and its economy remain speculation. Whether the *sanga-gar* was a senior administrator or a priest (Deimel) or both is unknown. The extent of citizen rights or the obligations of servitude is not well enough documented to be more than conjecture. It is not clear whether the soldier/farmers (*sub-lugal*) were independent citizens with private property or mere followers of chiefs (*ugula*) and team-workers (*ru-lugal*) under foremen. Nor do we know the extent of the authority invested in the priestly class (*abgal* or *apkallu*).

---

[16] For example, World's Oldest Peace Treaty Carried a Curse. (1934). *The Science Newsletter*, 25(690), 403–404.

[17] For example, Pettit, J. 2007. The Spoil of the Poor Is in Your Houses: Profits and Prophets in a Disrupted Society. *Journal of the Society of Christian Ethics*, 27(1), 33–55.

Giuseppe Visicato in *Power and the Writing* (2000) argues for the might of the pen, or at least scribe's cuneiform writing implement. He suggests 'the pen was mightier than the sword' from an early stage in Mesopotamia because of the authority of the written record. It is, however, interesting that by Ur III, the order of seniority ranked the *saga* or *sadu* (the 'cadaster' official) and the *dub-sar* ('scribe') ahead of the general (*sagin*). Bureaucratic power lay not just in inventories and agreements; then, as now, it defined the problem and its solution.

In 1931 Deimel put forward his *Tempelwirtschaft* ('Temple Economy') theory in his book, *Sumerische Tempelwirtschaft zur Zeit Urukaginas und seiner Vorgänger* (*Sumerian Temple Economy at the Time of Urukagina and his Predecessors*), arguing that the priesthood controlled all agricultural production and commercial activity, through 'redistribution'. In the modern secular era, however, Urukagina's reforms are seen as merging the two established sources of public authority in Sumerian cities, the temple and kingship, resulting in state-controlled religion — and a religion-controlled state.[18]

In the 1930s all Assyrian peoples were classified as Semitic. The non-Semitic source of the Sumerian language had been established in the late 19th century by Henry Rawlinson. In *Aryan Origin of the Alphabet* and *Sumer-Aryan Dictionary* (1927), Lieutenant Colonel Laurence Waddell attempted to show that world civilisation had a common origin in ancient Near Eastern cultures, linking Hittite, Sumerian and Babylonian religious practices, symbols, stories and their Gods and heroes[19] but also based on archaeological findings.

Urukagina, therefore, was viewed in Nazi Germany through a racist interpretation as Indo-Aryan, the ruler of a proto-Germanic people, upholding the political legitimisation of *Volksehre*, the honour of the Lagashite people.[20]

---

[18] Van de Mieroop, M. 1997. *The Ancient Mesopotamian City*. Clarendon Press.
[19] Rawlinson, L. A. 1927. *Aryan Origin of the Alphabet and Sumer-Aryan Dictionary*. London: Luzac & Co.
[20] Cooper, J. 1991. Posing the Sumerian Question: Race and Scholarship in early History of Assyriology. *Aula Orientalis, 9,* 47–66; Arnold, B. 1990. The past as propaganda: Totalitarian archaeology in Nazi Germany. *Antiquity, 64,* 464–478; also Goodrick-Clarke, N. 2001. *Black Sun: Aryan Cults, Esoteric Nazism, and the Politics of Identity*. NYU Press.

Then after WWII, Urukagina's reforms were increasingly trumpeted as the origins of private sector enterprise, political freedom and individual liberty.[21] During the 1960s Civil Rights Era in the United States, Urukagina's 'radical political and social change' were claimed to be the result of a nascent democracy promoted by a popular assembly.[22] More a president than a king, Urukagina was accountable to a popular assembly of the common people, both peasantry and an emerging middle class, holding in check the executive branch of government just as, in the Epic of Gilgamesh, the nobles of Uruk had curtailed the regal arrogance of the eponymous hero.

Europeans of the post-WW2 Welfare State era saw Urukagina as a social reformer. He now appeared to be the first ruler in history with a social conscience, tackling the 'antagonistic division of labour in Sumerian society'.[23] By the 1970s, Bronze Age Lagash had become a mixed socialist and capitalist system.[24] Urukagina now emerged as a mild-mannered do-gooder, *the Jimmy Carter of the ancient Middle East*.[25]

But internationally, scholarship on Lagash fell victim to the Cold War. Arnold Toynbee, writing in the first volume of his magisterial overview 'A Study of History' in 1934, had talked of 'class warfare' between Urukagina and the priesthood; and in the early 1950s the Marxist archaeologist V. Gordon Childe could write 'the State, personified in the ensi, Urukagina'.[26] Soviet Assyriology interpreted Urukagina from a materialist stance as a proto-bourgeois slave-owning usurper who curbed progressive state authority. By restoring the oppressive order of the *ancien regime* and by exploiting the antagonistic labour relations in Sumerian society, he had sought to benefit from the reactionary interests of the temples. Urukagina

---

[21] Kramer, S. 1956. *From the Tablets of Sumer: Twenty-Five Firsts in Man's Recorded History*. Indian Hills; Kramer, *Sumerians*, pp. 317–322.

[22] Kramer, S. 1964. 'Vox Populi' and the Sumerian Literary Documents. *Revue D'assyriologie Et D'archéologie Orientale, 58*(4), 149–156.

[23] Fensham, F. C. 1962. Widow, Orphan, and the Poor in Ancient Near Eastern Legal and Wisdom Literature. *Journal of Near Eastern Studies, 21*(2), 129–139; Irani, K. and Silver, M. (eds). 1995. *Social Justice in the Ancient World*. New York.

[24] Kramer, S. 1979. The First Case of Tax Reduction. *Challenge, 22*(1), 3–5.

[25] http://erenow.com/ancient/susanhistory/14.html.

[26] Childe, V. G. 1952. The Birth of Civilisation. *Past & Present, 2*, 1–10.

with his proto-'palace-totalitarian fascist state' at Lagash was in the end inevitably defeated by progressive economic forces and class struggle.

Karl Wittfogel's classic study of 'Oriental Despotism',[27] written under the influence of Marx and Stalin, portrayed Urukagina as exploiting the 'Asiatic means of production': 'The reform of the priest-king, Urukagina, of Lagash indicates that as early as the third millennium b.c. leading priestly families tried to secularize the temple land'.[28] By controlling the large and complex bureaucracy of competent and literate officials who held the real power of the 'hydraulic State' over irrigation, he was able to integrate military, religious and agricultural administrative authority for his own benefit. Primitive communism collapsed. He failed to implement efficient and effective planning run on behalf of the toiling masses — like the Soviet GOSPLAN system.[29] Presumably remarkably like a kolkhoz in the USSR, *the main means of production, viz. the land, was communal property ... [inhabited by] large extended family communes among the agricultural population outside of the state sector.*[30]

Stalin would have readily identified a system of administration based on vertical hierarchy dominated by a political elite from the inner circles of the Court, securing influence through flattery of the despot and palace intrigue. Doubtless proto-Stakhanovite enthusiasm fitted into this interpretation too.

Moreover, Diakonoff interpreted Urukagina as a reactionary who had sought to reverse the secularisation of the state.[31] Sargon was the Stalin of Ancient Mesopotamia, who suppressed the temple-based economy and

---

[27] Wittfogel, K. A. 1957. *Oriental Despotism: A Comparative Study of Total Power.* New Haven and London: Yale University Press.
[28] *Op. cit.*, p. 89.
[29] Diakonoff, I. 1969. *Ancient Mesopotamia.* Moscow, pp. 173–203 on the rise of the despotic state.
[30] Diakonoff, I. 1972. *Socio-Economic Classes in Babylonia and the Babylonian Concept of Social Stratification.* In *Gesellschaft im Alten Zweistromland und in den angrenzenden Gebiete (XVIII. Rencontre assyriologique internationale)* edited by D. O. Edzard. Munich: Verlag der Bayerischen Akademie der Wissenschaften, pp. 41–52.
[31] Diakonoff, I. 1969. *The Rise of the Despotic State in Ancient Mesopotamia.* In *Ancient Mesopotamia*, edited by I. M. Diakonoff. Moscow: Nauka Publishing House, pp. 173–203; Gelb, I. 1979. Household and Family in Early Mesopotamia. In *State and Temple Economy in the Ancient Near East*, edited by E. Lipinski, Leuven: Department

society (*Tempelstadt*) in favour of royal power (*Staatstadt*). Diakonoff suggested that the Akkadian empire, doubtless like the USSR, could only have been established and maintained by a ruthless despot. He regarded Sargon as an effective ruler for killing off most of the old ruling class, a view that seems clearly redolent of the justification by all Stalin's willing executioners and gulag guards for the Moscow show trials of the 1930s. According to Diakonoff, class antagonism in Mesopotamia was most intense in the Akkadian period — just as it had been under Stalin's culture of fear.[32]

But if Urukagina had foreshadowed FDR, he also seemingly had inspired Ronald Reagan's inaugural speech in January 1981:

> In this present crisis, government is not the solution to our problem; government is the problem. .... Our government has no power except that granted it by the people. It is time to check and reverse the growth of government, which shows signs of having grown beyond the consent of the governed.
>
> Now, so there will be no misunderstanding, it's not my intention to do away with government. It is rather to make it work — work with us, not over us; to stand by our side, not ride on our back. Government can and must provide opportunity, not smother it; foster productivity, not stifle it. It is no coincidence that our present troubles parallel and are proportionate to the intervention and intrusion in our lives that result from unnecessary and excessive growth of government.

This was surely almost nothing more than an unattributed re-writing in modern terms of the clay tablet cones in the Louvre. Samuel Kramer wrote a letter published in *The New York Times* the week President Ronald Reagan took office in 1981, urging the president-elect to emulate Urukagina and cut taxes. Professor Kramer added:

> During the rule of Urukagina's predecessor, the document states, there had developed in Lagash an oppressive and ubiquitous bureaucracy that

---

Orientalistiek, pp. 1–97; Yoffee, N. 2005. *Myths of the Archaic State: Evolution of the Earliest Cities, States, and Civilizations*. Cambridge University Press.

[32] I. M. Diakonoff. 1959. *Sumer*. Moscow: Vostocnoj Literatury, pp. 227–228.

devised and levied a multifarious assortment of taxes upon the citizens. "From one end of the state to the other", the ancient chronicler wrote bitterly, "there was the tax collector". But when Urukagina came to power, the document continues, he removed the more oppressive bureaucrats, inspectors and overseers and reduced taxes so much that the same historian recorded happily: "From one end of the state to the other, there was no tax collector".[33]

So, in France, as ever contrarian, Urukagina was declared to be *Le Reagan de Mésopotamie*.[34] The 'rolling back of the state' under Urukagina saw government involvement in Lagashite society and economy abandoned, not only in garlic and cucumbers, but also in divorce proceedings and perfume-making. Urukagina even rectified the *unnecessary and excessive growth of government* by restoring to the temples the land and property taken by his predecessor.

Kramer for three decades had been interpreting Urukagina's attack on the 'obnoxious and ubiquitous bureaucracy' he had inherited on becoming ruler of Lagash as a blow for freedom. This was Milton Friedman gone into Assyriology. Urukagina's reforms were articulating a popular reaction against an increasingly overbearing state. His revolutionary reforms seemed a prescient precursor to the American Revolution 4000 years later. Property rights became secure, the weight of oppressive public administration was lifted, and the tax burden lifted from the private sector: where previously 'From the borders of Ningirsu to the sea, there was the [tax collector]'.

Yet, if the tax inspectors were 'right-sized', presumably either the state drastically cut expenditure to fit a much lower tax-take, or compliance rates soared. Urukagina then further reduced the revenue base by returning the confiscated property to the temples. So this was the world's first experimentation with supply-side economics, but his public finances had been gravely weakened.

Reaction to such claims has resulted in increasing scepticism developing about Urukagina's self-created or heavily assisted reputation.

---

[33] *Op. cit.*, 30 January 1981.
[34] https://www.contrepoints.org/2013/04/04/120520-le-reagan-de-mesopotamie-ou-la-premiere-baisse-dimpot-de-lhistoire.

Totalitarian dictatorships in Fascist Italy, Nazi Germany and Stalin's USSR made historians in the second half of the 20th century more conscious of propaganda.[35] Some historians argue that Urukagina was simply exaggerating;[36] others doubt whether any widespread reform really occurred during his reign. Sumerian society was radically altered less by his actions and more through the ending of his reign. His defeat ushered in the Sargonic era — the start of the era of Assyrian nation-building and the Akkadian empire.[37] Furthermore, evidence of actual change under Urukagina is lacking. Perhaps it was even Urukagina who precipitated the end of the pre-Sargonic Early Dynastic IIIb Era by allying with Sargon.

Thus, Urukagina has been all things to all people — from an emancipating hero to a populist rabble-rouser. Some historians portray Urukagina as a leader of a revolution in which freemen battled against the aristocracy and wealthy landowning priests. Others argue that Urukagina's reforms tried to correct the worst abuses of power, but assert that he was a moderate, not trying to overturn the basic structures of society.

Much excitement was generated by the claim that the 'reform' tablet contains the first written reference to the concept of liberty (*amagi* or *amargi*, literally, 'return to the mother' which in a matrilineal society indicated restoration of social status, not individualism). Used in reference to the reform, this conjured up the idea that the cone tablets were a 'Sumerian Bill of Rights'.[38]

More broadly, some historians even find evidence, in these supposedly radical or progressive social policies outlined in the texts of the reform tablets, for 'the uniquely humane character' of early Sumerian institutions.[39] Yet does this stand up to scrutiny, if women were punished for speaking to a man by having her mouth crushed with burnt bricks?

---

[35] Finkelstein, J. J. 1979. 'Early Mesopotamia, 2500–1000 B.C.'. In *Propaganda and Communication in World History*, edited by H. D. Lasswell, D. Lerner and H. Spier, vol. I: The Symbolic Instrument in Early Times, Oxford, pp. 60–63.
[36] E.g. Cooper, J. 1986. *Presargonic Inscriptions*. New Haven, pp. 70–74.
[37] Knapp, A. 1988. *The History and Culture of Ancient Western Asia and Egypt*. Wadsworth Publishing Company, pp. 66–77.
[38] McGuire, J. T. 1994. *The Sumerian Roots of the American Preamble*. Lough Erne Press. 280p.; Snell, D. 2001. *Flight and Freedom in the Ancient Near East*. Brill.
[39] Steinkeller, P. 1991. *The Reforms of Urukagina and an Early Sumerian Term for 'Prison'*, pp. 227–233.

Both Enmetena and Urukagina instituted reforms using the term *Ama-ar-gi*, literally meaning 'return to the mother'. In one inscription, Entemena of Lagash boasts of having 'allowed the sons of Uruk, Larsa, and Bad-tibira to return to their mothers' and of having 'restored them into the hands' of the respective city God or Goddess. 'Mother', therefore signified the *status quo ante*, the 'golden age' of matriarchy, gender harmony and 'freedom'. But what form of freedom?

Read in the light of similar but more explicit statements of later date, this laconic formula represents the oldest known evidence of the fact that the ruler occasionally endeavoured to mitigate social injustice or postpone forced modernisation by royal command. The American professor of Assyriology Samuel Kramer interpreted *Ama-ar-gi* as signifying freedom, a restoration of 'liberty' particularly expressed by economic opportunity and reduced tax burden, carefully recorded on Urukagina's 'Liberty Cones'.[40]

The Soviet academic Igor Diakonoff (1991), however, suggested that *Ama-ar-gi* meant relief from debt, arising from a primitive form of capitalist exploitation. Such decrees might refer to the suspension or complete cancellation of debts or to exemption from public works.[41]

Scholars nowadays admit that the meaning of this term is not clear. But some then decide that it signifies that the reforms were attempting a restitution of the original freedom and liberty decreed by the Gods, which is apparently a benign 'state of nature' envisaged by John Locke and Jean-Jacques Rousseau, not the 'nasty, brutish and short' of Thomas Hobbes.[42]

Nevertheless, American lawyers are taught that the Western emphasis on individual rights originated with Urukagina, although the 'Reform Cones' are not a formal legal code.[43] Urukagina and his predecessors used divine contract theory of government: he made a 'covenant' with Ningirsu, patron God of Lagash, and he carried out Ningirsu's instructions. Biblical scholars and theologians wonder as to whether the Old Testament covenant with the faithful imitated that with Urukagina some 300 years earlier.

---

[40] Kramer, *Sumerians*, p. 79.
[41] Stephens, F. J. 1955. Notes on Some Economic Texts of the Time of Urukagina, *RA, 49*, 129–136.
[42] Kramer, *From the Tablets of Sumer*; Kramer, Sumerians, pp. 317–322.
[43] E.g. George Mason University Law School.

God told Abraham to leave Mesopotamia and to his son Isaac, in Genesis 26:3 promised: 'To you and to your descendants I will give all these lands, and I will fulfil the oath which I swore to Abraham your father'. God then appeared at Bethel to Isaac's son, Jacob (Genesis 28:13–15) and confirmed the covenant: 'I am the Lord, the God of Abraham your father and the God of Isaac; the land on which you lie I will give to you and to your descendants; and your descendants shall be like the dust of the earth ... and by you and your descendants shall all the families of the earth be blessed. Behold, I am with you and will keep you wherever you go'. God confirmed it afresh with Moses.

The reforms were the world's first documented effort to establish a public administration based on the trust of citizens. Again this built on precedent in Lagash. Some 50 years earlier, Enmetena had made important efforts at reform.[44]

The P222610 (Ukg. 6) tablet, however, should perhaps be re-assessed as a product of the reign of Enmetena.[45] It describes the continuing border wars between Enmetena's city of Lagash and the neighbouring city of Umma. Perhaps Urukagina's reforms, although apparently more comprehensive — some argue that there was nothing else like them in ancient history, which the Enmetena example would then confound.[46]

Detail, such as abuse by the previous ruler and excessive fees for religious rites, may in fact have formed part of every ruler's assertion of public authority in Lagash, but perhaps have so far only been discovered for these two reigns.

Modernising the state and state-building transition the Sumerians from a 'temple administration', with the administration of government in the hands of priests, to a 'modern' secular state — just as Henry VIII executed Cardinal Wolsey and appointed Thomas Cromwell to church and state. But Urukagina wasn't an anti-religious revolutionary or an iconoclast. The estates that he confiscated from the ruler, himself, he gave to the temples, probably also under his control.

---

[44] Cooper, pp. 66–67.
[45] Edzard, D. 2004. *Geschichte Mesopotamiens.* München.
[46] Gadd, C. J. 1971. In Edwards, I. E. S.; Gadd, C. J.; Hammond, N. G. L. *The Cambridge Ancient History Volume 1, Part 2: Early History of the Middle East.* Cambridge University Press, pp. 141ff.

Was Urukagina strengthening civil society? It is not known whether or not Urukagina enacted his reforms into law or if he was just paying lip service to social reform as a way to increase his popularity with his subjects. Many rulers announced high-minded reforms at the beginning of their reigns, only to proceed with 'business as usual'. If Urukagina was a usurper, perhaps he needed support and more justification so he repeated his 'reforms' on other foundation cones. Kingship did not mean unconditional authority but required the public backing of powerful interests to guarantee that the reforms were enacted. Social reforms were unlikely to have been Urukagina's concern, although he ruled during a period of political instability and war between the Sumerian city-states. So was it all empty rhetoric?

Statue of Eannatum, ruler of Lagash c. 2500 BC.

Chapter 6

Lugalzagesi and the Legitimacy of 'Reform'

The world's first 'Reformer' had a fine counterpoint. Urukagina's main antagonist was Lugalzagesi, the king of Umma, who was seeking to establish dominance over southern Sumeria.[1]

When Urukagina came to power, Umma and Lagash had been at war for more than a century, battling for control of the Guedena, the fertile land between the two cities. Under the leadership of Ur-Nanshe, Eannatum, and Enmetena, Lagash had always been either victorious, or held its own. One tablet states:

> Enanatum, governor of Lagaš, in the field Ugiga, the field of Ningirsu, had (previously) fought with him, but Enmetena, the beloved son of Enanatum, defeated him. Urlumma fled into the middle of Umma and was killed.[2]

The later Sumerian poem, 'Gilgamesh and Agga of Kish', describes the siege of Uruk by Agga, son of Enmebaragesi. The armed conflict between two Mesopotamian cities would hardly have been unusual in a country whose energies were consumed, almost without interruption for a

---

[1] Although there is little evidence for an 'empire': Powell, M. 1996. *The Sin of Lugalzagesi. Wiener Zeitschrift für die Kunde des Morgenlandes*, vol. 86, Festschrift für Hans Hirsch zum 65. Geburtstag gewidmet von seinen Freunden, Kollegen und Schülern, pp. 307–314.
[2] P431117.

A Sumerian couple in the Louvre.

millennium, from 2500 to 1500 BC, by clashes between imperialist, separatist and irredentist tendencies.

Lugalzagesi, originally the king of Umma, had conquered the neighbouring city-state of Uruk and perhaps moved his capital there, so 'the man of Umma', as he is called on another tablet, and 'the man of Uruk', both refer to Lugalzagesi.

Lugalzagesi made several attacks on the kingdom of Lagash that are documented in administrative tablets from this period. Numerous administrative texts record repeated attacks by 'the man of Uruk' (e.g. P221996, NIK 1, 227 is dated to the 'month that the man of Uruk came a third time'; P221195, DP 545).

The city of Lagash was besieged for the first time in the fourth year of Urukagina's reign, again in the following year, and for the third time in the sixth year of his rule.[3] Muster Lists show military preparation early in the reign. Foreign trade ceased, and in the sixth year of his reign barley rations were reduced, pigs disappeared, the flocks of sheep shrank and the population was displaced.[4] The gloominess of Urukagina's situation can be sensed in a fragment from a heavily damaged foundation cone (CDLI P222617) and a tablet (P431157):

> 'For my part, what did I have of it?' I said to him: 'I did not do any violent act, but the dogs {the enemy} today are ... in my city (?)' ... Girsu was surrounded by it {the enemy army}, and Urukagina exchanged blows with it with weapons. A wall of it he {Lugalzagesi} made grow there, and dogs he made live there. He went away to his city, but a second time he came ...

The 'wall' is probably a poetic reference to the enemy army surrounding the city. It might, however, have been literal. It is possible that a siege wall was constructed by the invaders to trap the civilians and defenders inside the city, cut off from outside food supplies, in order to starve them into submission. The prolonged siege of the city caused the enemy 'dogs' (soldiers) to live there for a while. Lugalzagesi sacked the city of Lagash, as if to avenge a century of humiliating defeats. Lugalzagesi of Umma who was clearly determined to prevent any revival of Lagash by destroying its principal landmark buildings and pillaging its sacred sites.[5]

Lugalzagesi dealt the crippling blow to the Lagash state when, in the seventh year of his reign Urukagina was forced to abandon the city of Lagash and move his capital to the smaller neighbouring city of Girsu. Lugalzagesi pursued him to Girsu and twice besieged that city too. The result was a decline in the economic dynamism and strength of the state.[6]

---

[3] Lambert, M. 1960. La naissance de la bureaucratie. *Revue Historique*, 224(1), 1–26, p. 25.
[4] A chronology of the war appears in Bauer, J., Englund, R. and Krebernik, M. 1998. Mesopotamien. Späturuk-Zeit und frühdynastische Zeit. Freiburg: Universitätsverlag Freiburg, pp. 479–493.
[5] Bauer, J. 1998. Der Vorsargonische Abschnitt, and P222618 (FAOS 05/1, Ukg. 16). The public works and sacred sites that were attacked included the Antasura, the Tirash temple of Ningirsu, the Ebabbar, the Ibgal of Inana, and the temple of Gatumdug.
[6] E.g. P221936, TSA 35, dating to the end of Urukagina's 5th year and P221826, NIK 1, 57, dating to the beginning of the 6th; also see Bauer, *op. cit.*, p. 481.

A few years later, Urukagina disappears from the historic record; and Lugalzagesi established the first reliably documented kingdom to encompass all of Sumer.

After generations of conflict, Lagash had lost the war with Umma. In response, Urukagina therefore had incised a 'lament' tablet (now in the Musée du Louvre) to condemn the aggression. Urukagina details the looting and destruction of sacred places in Lagash and curses his opponent. This extraordinary narrative (P431158, Ukg. 16) is unique in the history of Mesopotamia, otherwise known by the inscriptions of the winners.

> The Man of Umma to the levee of the boundary territory set fire. To the Antasura he set fire, and its silver and lapis lazuli he bundled off. The palace of Tiraš he plundered (?), the Smaller Abzu he plundered, the dais of Enlil and the dais of Utu he plundered, the Aḫuš he plundered, and its silver and lapis lazuli he bundled off. The Ebabbar he plundered, and its silver and lapis lazuli he bundled off. The temple terrace of Ninmah of the sacred grove he plundered, and its silver and lapis lazuli he bundled off. In the fields of Ningirsu, as many as were cultivated, their barley he uprooted.

The 'Lagash Lament' or 'Urukagina's Lament' or P431158 (Ukg. 16). (Louvre, CC).

Bringing God in is always politically helpful: *The Man of Umma after Lagaš he has sacked, it is a sin against Ningirsu that he has committed. The hand he brought against him he (Ningirsu) will cut off!*

Then make sure where the blame lies: *A sin of URU-KA-gina, 'lugal' (king) of Girsu, it is not!*

And finish with a bit more divine retribution: *Lugalzagesi, ensi (ruler) of Umma, may his Goddess Nisaba that sin let be borne on his neck!*

Soviet historians interpreted this as typical of a foreign power and imperialist aggressor, intervening in a socialist revolution to stop liberating ideas from spreading. But they also portrayed Urukagina as a reactionary who reversed the process of secularisation that they argued had been going on under his predecessors.

Lugalzagesi is commemorated as a great king on various stone bowl fragments from Nippur for creating peace and stability. Lugalzagesi was subsequently defeated by Sargon of Akkad who creates the first recorded Empire and, by bringing together, for more than a century, South and North Semitic Sumerian language, transforms Mesopotamian history. What is uncertain is to what extent defeat was the result of the leadership of Urukagina's reforms that might have alienated the military leadership from his disgruntled administration.

Revolutionaries in the heat of revolution, such as in Paris in 1789 or St. Petersburg in 1917, often reject the binding weight of history. Yet rulers usually seek the legitimation conferred by the past. In narrating the shifting observance of tradition to changing circumstances and purposes, the habits of olden days serve to sustain power, but also restrain it. In claiming the legitimation conferred by tradition, a ruler implicitly, and often explicitly, affirms the duties of the leadership to provide prosperity and justice to citizens or subjects.

Urukagina was the first to reverse that logic. He is the first ruler to claim legitimacy by reform, a revolutionary by rejecting the legacy of history — in which, as a usurper, he had no stake. He was the new self-made man in a hurry, introducing sweeping reform because he had nothing inherited to lose. Planning trumped tradition.

James C. Scott's classic work *Seeing Like a State* exposes the hubris of state planning everywhere: 'The utopian, immanent, and continually frustrated goal of the modern state is to reduce the chaotic, disorderly, constantly changing social reality beneath it to something more closely resembling the administrative grid of its observations'.[7] One example is how the British Raj (sometimes called the 'anthropological state' due to the obsessive effort to document pre-colonial India) turned the original complex but functional reality of caste into a rigid system, by attempting to make it legible and governable.[8]

There is, of course, a gender dimension to Urukagina's reign. Lugalanda's wife had shared in the ensi's power, managing her own private estates and those of the temple Bau. She sent diplomatic missions to neighbouring states and she bought and sold slaves. So, while not a champion of human rights, she and Urukagina's wife Shagshag were strong, independent females.

Two other decrees undermine any ahistorical suggestions that Urukagina was a socially progressive reformer. The downfall of women's equality perhaps dates from his gaining control over his wife's estate. He abolished polyandry by imposing monogamy on women, and with that established patrilineal society.[9] Women taking multiple husbands would be stoned with rocks upon which details of the crime were written.[10]

Second is a statute stating that 'if a woman says [text illegible...] to a man, her mouth is crushed with burnt bricks'. No comparable laws from Urukagina addressing men's behaviour or penalties for adultery by men have survived. The discovery of these fragments has led some modern critics to assert that they provide 'the first written evidence of the degradation of women'.[11] But he did add a high priestess to the list of funeral officials to be paid; and divorce could no longer be obtained by bribery.

Perhaps Urukagina was a traditional male who disliked the threat to patriarchal values that had been posed by Lugalanda's wife. She had shared in the *ensi*'s power, buying and selling slaves, and generally managing her own private estates and those of the temple Bau. Perhaps the last

---

[7] Scott, J. 1998. *Seeing Like a State: How Certain Schemes to Improve the Human Condition Have Failed.* Yale.
[8] Dirks, N. 2001. *Castes of Mind: Colonialism and the Making of Modern India.* Princeton.
[9] Rohrlich, R. 1980. State Formation in Sumer and the Subjugation of Women. *Feminist Studies,* 6(1), 76–102; Lerner, G. 1987. *The Creation of Patriarchy.* Oxford.
[10] Tetlow, E. 2004. *Women, Crime and Punishment in Ancient Law and Society.* New York, pp. 8–10.
[11] French, M. 2008. *From Eve to Dawn: A History of Women.* New York, p. 100.

straw for the Chauvinist clique was when she started sending diplomatic missions to neighbouring states.

Was Urukagina naïve, manipulated into seizing power at the behest of the priests because his predecessor tried to rein in their exploitation of the people? Did he fall for their line that the *ensi* Lugalanda, being greedy and corrupt, had seized control of the most important temples, and appointed himself, his wife Baranamtarra, and other members of his family as administrators and sacrilegiously tried to claim these temples as his private property?

Was Urukagina a realist? Did he recognise that Lugalanda's seizure of control over the temples had not worked, that running these temples as the private property of the *ensi* and taxing the priesthood had proved counter-productive to the needs of the state? As Urukagina required the support of its most important elite, the priests and temple administrators, what better than justifying his unconstitutional seizure of power by condemning his immediate predecessor, the *ensi* Lugalanda, as not only greedy and corrupt but even sacrilegious, for no longer mentioning the deities in temple documents?

Was Urukagina's regime in Lagash the first 'limited access order', in the terminology of the Nobel Prize winning founder of new institutional economics, Douglas North?

Was Urukagina the world's first Machiavellian, more than 3000 years before 'The Prince' was published? Was Urukagina genuine in his sympathy for the poor, or merely feigning empathy with the weak, sick, elderly and vulnerable? Was his social policy based on real concern, or no more than a ploy, like Bismarck's initiation of the welfare state, in order to shore up the privileged priestly classes — be they late 19th century Prussian Junkers or Lagash priests of 2350 BC? Perhaps Urukagina had merely sought to secure the throne in order to weaken the party of Lugalanda by claiming to reform.

Urukagina's rule focused on consolidating his own authority. One example for this is found in the second year of his reign, when Urukagina upgraded his title from *ensi,* which the rulers of Lagash had usually called themselves, to the loftier term *lugal,* meaning 'king'. His predecessor's son Urtarsirsira is heard of no more, but the fact that he had survived into Urukagina's reign showed there had been no violent coup, and perhaps that the 'reforms' were a literary device rather than a political platform for public service reform.

Yet, while Urukagina was promoting himself, the power and prestige of Lagash seemed already to be in decline. This decline may have been either cause or effect of Urukagina's seizure of power, who may have been encouraged to stage a coup by powerful interests worried that the previous regime had become too self-satisfied and inward-looking. Urukagina's insecurity may have been in response to the external threat from the process of state consolidation that was by then under way in southern Mesopotamia. Urukagina was to be the last Old Sumerian ruler of Lagash before the subsequent Sargonic period (after c. 2370 BC, when Sargon of Akkad founded the Old Akkadian Empire).

Yet we know almost nothing about the nature of the political settlement, 'the expression of a common understanding, usually forged between elites, about how power is organised and exercised. They include formal institutions for political and economic relations [...]. But they also include informal, often unarticulated agreements that underpin a political system...'. The underlying purpose is to restrain violence. Where it fails, the state collapses into civil war.

Government and religion were intimately inter-twined for their mutual legitimacy of divine sanction. Public authority descends from heaven. The king and the priest vied to be the link between the Gods and the people, in compliance with the will of the Gods and participation in ritual. Yet if political authority was tied to religion, it was also rendered responsible by that same association. The king's duty, as the minister of the Gods, was to ensure the just ordering of the city, to protect the widow and the orphan, to curb the abuses of the powerful, to 'establish justice in the land'.

There is little evidence for how that authority was delegated to temple administrators and whether the sacerdotal and public service function were separated by formal rules or informally joined by kinship networks in Lagash in the Early Dynastic IIIb period.

Why, if such abuses had been going on, as Urukagina claimed, 'since time immemorial', had the God waited so long before deciding to rectify the 'bad' governance at Lagash? No explanation is offered — although by the time Urukagina came to power, the city had managed to thwart its main adversary, the city of Uruk, for over 100 years. Yet, within seven years of Urukagina acting to enforce the divine will, Lagash was disastrously defeated. Was this, then, the world's first political hyperbole?

The passage in the so-called reform texts states 'on the field of the *ensi* [or his wife and the crown prince], the city God Ningirsu [or the city Goddess Baba and the divine couple's son]' had been 'reinstated as owner' is difficult to interpret. Our knowledge of the period derives from the archives of the temple of Baba in Girsu, dating from Lugalanda and Urukagina's administration, directed by the spouse of the *ensi* or by a *sangu* (head steward of a temple). Every economic activity and commerce seems to involve the temple: agriculture, vegetable gardening, tree farming, cattle raising and the processing of animal products, fishing, and the payment in merchandise of workers and employees. But the archives of the temple of Baba provide information about only a portion of the total temple administration and limited in time, and the separation of 'church and state' is unclear.

The private sector, documented by bills of sale, written in Sumerian as well as in Akkadian, for land purchases in various localities during the pre-Sargonic period, 'prove' the existence of private land ownership. But what form that took, lands predominantly held as undivided family property. Although a substantial part of the population was forced to work for the temple and drew its pay and board from it, it is not yet known whether it was year-round work.

The government could mobilise the populace for the performance of public works. The construction of monumental buildings or the excavation of long and deep canals could be carried out only by such means. Some historians condemn this as near slavery; others recognise in this a job creation scheme. Urukagina was clearly well aware that high-profile measures were desperately needed to combat the curse of unemployment, if he had come to power on the back of anger and despair caused by unemployed, and unrecorded, or under-employed in part-time work. Tackling this was an essential requirement for the regime's legitimacy. Male slavery is rare before Ur III. According to one document, the temple of Baba employed 188 female slaves; the temple of the Goddess Nanshe employed 180, chiefly in grinding flour and in the textile industry, and this continued to be the case in later times. The term slave was however only clarified about

2000 BC and later, designating persons in bondage who were bought and sold and who could not acquire personal property through their labour. A distinction was made between captured slaves (prisoners of war and kidnapped persons) and others who had been sold.

Yet the designation 'reform texts' is only partly justified. Political tensions must have influenced the reform agenda, but where the contestation arose — between the 'palace', the ruler and his administrative staff, the 'clergy', that is, the stewards and priests of the temples, or 'nobles' and the 'common people' — remains unclear.

In apparent defiance of his own interests, Urukagina seemed to defend the clergy, whose plight he describes somewhat emotionally. The passage about restoring the ensi's fields to the divinity may suggest that the situation of the temple was ameliorated and that palace lands were assigned to the priests. These reforms resemble the policies of a politically weak newcomer forced to lean on a specific 'party'.

Other measures, however, addressed social injustices — for instance, the granting of delays in the payment of debts or their outright cancellation and the setting up of prohibitions to keep the economically or socially more powerful from forcing his inferior to sell his house or donkey. New regulations sought to promote fairness, such as in the scale of fees for weddings and burials, as well as the food rations of workers.

These conditions may well have been paralleled elsewhere. But it is equally possible that archives in other cities of pre-Sargonic southern Mesopotamia may reveal different power structures to Lagash. The cities of Sumer, however, undoubtedly shared a sense of a common identity. Southern Mesopotamia shortly before the rise of the Akkadian empire was reaching out and, under Lugalzagesi, the 'upper sea' (the Mediterranean) is mentioned for the first time. The inscriptions of Ur-Nanshe name the isle of Dilmun (modern Bahrain), the Oman coast and the Indus region. Trade with Anatolia and Afghanistan was nothing new in the third millennium, but the 'public' and the 'private' spheres differed. What is meant by 'private' sector is a population group with land of its own and with revenues not directly granted by a temple or a 'palace', such as by the king's or an ensi's household.

The traditional picture is derived from the state archives of Puzrish-Dagan, a gigantic 'stockyard' situated outside the gates of Nippur, which supplied the city's temples with sacrificial animals but inevitably also comprised a major wool and leather industry; other such archives are those of Umma, Girsu, Nippur and Ur. All these activities were overseen by a finely honed bureaucracy that stressed the use of official channels, efficient administration and precise accounting. The various administrative organs communicated with one another by means of a smoothly functioning network of messengers. Although almost 24,000 documents referring to the economy of Ur III have so far been published, the majority of them are still waiting to be properly evaluated. The economic system of Ur III represented in the main by contracts (loans, leases of temple land, the purchase of slaves, and the like), the 'private' sector makes up only a small part of this mass of textual material. Until the Ur III period, the only archives so far recovered dealt with temples or the palace.

The 'reforms' are also debatable when control over the state is the principal means of accumulating wealth. Then legitimacy is not achieved through appeal to the populace through a long-term vision of a more prosperous tomorrow. Rather, power secures control over scarce resources. Patronage buys legitimacy and support, resulting in a zero-sum political process. There is no separation of the public and private spheres results in leaders depending on their networks of religious, regional, tribal and family ties. The greater the potential wealth to be acquired, the greater stakes raise the temperature of the politics.

Such patrimonial *political economy restricts long-term sustainable growth and development. Access to and maintenance of power together with broad-based rent-seeking for personal wealth and patronage networks tend to take precedence over growth policies in the common interest.*[12]

Power is centred on the ruler. The logic requires this person to be a charismatic 'big man'. Without formal institutions of legal-rational process, relations with the population stems from fear, largesse and subsidy.[13]

---

[12] Koch, C. 2015. *Political Economy Analysis of Malawi*. Donors, p. 5.
[13] *Op. cit.*, p. 6; Chinsinga, B. 2010. Resurrecting the developmental state in Malawi: Reflections and lessons from the 2005/2006 fertiliser subsidy programme. In *Reforming the Malawian Public Sector*, 69.

The process of government, therefore, is as an ever-shifting kaleidoscope of power relations.[14]

Promoting the public interest is irrelevant, other than to provide personalised power with a veneer of respectability. Formulating sensible policy and delivering results are, at best, a by-product of the elite political game. Competitors must apparently adopt similar strategies, and at sub-national levels, local elites similarly jostle for power and advantage over rivals.

The politics of informality and patronage play out in the myriad networks vying for access to the largesse controlled by the *ensi*. Qualifications needed for public office are never spelt out. Jobs do not depend on delivery and performance.

Patrimonial politics renders the public service ineffectual. This seems to explain why, for instance, performance management for the Civil Service fails because of the complex nature of the public service, absence of follow up and management support, lack of consultation and low motivation.[15]

Accepting the written justification given by a reforming government is naive. The paucity of evidence has tempted scholars, but the results are 'hazardous in the extreme'.[16] Some scholars assert that despite the difficult circumstances of his reign, Urukagina did effect a number of legislative reforms aimed at social justice and shoring up the temple institution against the growing power of the *ensi*. Why at a difficult time the *ensi* would wish to reduce his own power is assumed to be either he was by temperament a 'reformer', or that he believed that by making concessions he would attract popular and temple support. But whether governing worked along such 'democratic' lines seems open to doubt. Few were literate so the 'reforms' were presumably proclaimed at some assembly. But was Lagash really a proto-Athens?

---

[14] Hoffenberg, A. *et al.* 2013. *The Role of Elites in Economic Development.* Oxford, pp. 204–222.

[15] Chidwala, J. 2013. *Implementation of the Performance Management Policy for the Malawi Civil Service.* Witwatersrand.

[16] Foster, B. 1981. A New Look at the Sumerian Temple State. *Journal of the Economic and Social History of the Orient,* 24(3), 225–241.

The current preoccupation in Assyriology is with proving that Urukagina was pursuing a three-prong strategy of promoting the private sector, tackling corruption, and restoring state legitimacy. Some claim evidence of public-private partnerships, by privatising the temples and, while communal labour and military activities remained the direct responsibility of the state, the palace contracted out the supervision of many of its other activities, who looked after its interests in return for a share in the proceeds from the palace's estates and flocks. Modern scholars present the technical complexity of interpreting the vastly greater amount of information from later periods. But is also determined to find the private sector — without explaining what that concept really signifies in an era without property rights and contract enforcement mechanisms.

Seeing the mess that, for example, the British government got into over Metronet Rail in 2003 to 2008 through convoluted contracts and moral hazard, no one has yet been able to explain how the City of Lagash and Urukagina's officials could achieve something that defeated the City of London and the best brains of the UK Treasury 4000 years later. Indeed, with no secure private property rights nor any known enforcement mechanism for upholding contracts, what is the real significance of Lugalanda, Urukagina's immediate predecessor as the ensi, apparently 'seizing control' of the most important temples, appointing himself and his family as their administrators and regarding these temples as the 'private property' of the ensi? Can there really have been a constitutional settlement, as with the British monarchy today, between the private wealth and public assets entrusted to the ruler?

Much more is known about the extreme bureaucratisation during the third dynasty of Ur, 'when the death of a single sheep appears three times in the government archives, the bureaucratic encumbrance contributed to the state's inability to respond to internal and external threats'.[17]

---

[17] Postgate, *Bronze Age Bureaucracy*, p. 42.

Chapter 7

What Can Urukagina Teach the 21st Century?

Development nowadays is hampered by the lack of the sort of divine guidance in which Urukagina placed his faith — or what nowadays is called a credible theory of change to explain how or why an impartial, ethical, fair and merit-based public service emerges, and how it can be promoted and fostered.

About 4500 years ago, bureaucracy had already developed key 'modern' features: specialist, hierarchical officialdom was undertaking a range of tasks, recorded and documented on clay tablets. It penetrated deep into Lageshite society. The state existed as a distinct entity from the private household of the ruler. Officials were employed in the public interest. The effectiveness of public officials, if only in their abuses of office, can be vouched for by the reforms that were designed to rally support for the regime.

The world's first recorded public service reform initiative was apparently a dismal failure. That outcome is far from uncommon — either now some 4500 years later, or indeed during the interim period.

That adventure in urban civilisation continues to this day. Indeed in 2007 humanity passed a key milestone in this path when, for the first time in history, more people were dwelling in towns and cities than in the countryside. In 2015, humanity then took another step forward when the countries of the world gathered at the UN, agreed on the SDGs for 2030. The penultimate goal, Goal 16, declared that effective, accountable and inclusive institutions were the basis for good governance. Mankind's eternal quest for peaceful and inclusive societies places institutions at the centre of state-building. Institutions develop slowly. History becomes central to development.

Lagash was one of the city-states to emerge at the 'cradle of civilisation' on the great alluvial plain of southern Mesopotamia in the third millennium BC. Its prosperity was largely due to its strategic location. Lagash then, like Singapore or Dubai today, was a highly innovative small state that can lay claim to important 'firsts' — for example, the first recorded treaty is an agreement between Lagash and Umma on water supplies along the Euphrates drainage in the second millennium BC.

So few 'facts', however, exist about the life of Urukagina and the government of Lagash in the 'Early Dynastic IIIb period' that almost any interpretation is possible if not necessarily plausible.

Nevertheless, there is much to learn from the Reform episode. That shaky start over 4000 years ago to public sector reform suggests lessons for current efforts at improving public service. At the same time, experiences of our own times may illuminate an otherwise obscure yet important event: the first recorded governance reform in history. But who defines 'reform'? Whose interests does it advance? Is it simply restoring efficiency or pursuing an ideal?

The political tensions in Lagash 4500 years ago about the public service ended in collapse and conquest. This outcome raises questions about the nature of its polity. The success of small states (by population) like Switzerland, small island states like Malta, and city-states like Singapore may suggest that larger states could be on the decline. The 20th century experiments with the 'nation state' built on unifying concepts of loyalty and patriotism, and the 'market state' driven by personal profit and factional interests, were not always successful.

The fate of Urukagina's reforms provides stark evidence as the challenges confronting efforts to improve public service. That history might help us to understand better how the state's bureaucracy can develop and maintain the capacity to deliver core services to the public while leading and implementing change to meet the vision of progress laid out by political leaders. Lessons may be generic because, while much has changed, the basic functions of government — defence, taxation, law and order — and the characteristics of the people who administer it remain remarkably the same.

Written records allow a sophisticated bureaucracy to develop. The archives of cuneiform tablets structured government, city life and commerce. Public administration under Urukagina witnessed its first known anti-corruption initiative and first restructuring: 'right-sizing' results in the dismissal of many tax collectors, and those lacking 'customer-centred' skills were also let go. The problem in Lagash was not just corrupt officials. Many taxpayers were also complicit in corrupt practices.

The Political Drama of Reform

The appeal of public sector reform has also been 'big bang' political drama — taking on the corrupt, lazy pen-pushers on behalf of the 'little man', the Charlie Chaplin of Lagash, 'Mr Smith Comes to Mesopotamia'.

Predating Athenian democracy by 2000 years, Urukagina was seeking to win popular opinion, and future generations, to his side. His cones therefore suggest that the opinion of the people, or some section of them, did matter. The creative relationship between writing and political identity in our era has been reduced to Presidents using Twitter to develop public policy. But Urukagina's reforms, if not empty rhetoric, would have alienated the elites and the power structures of the state needed for support in mobilising the defence of the realm.

The first lesson, therefore, is that political context is critical to public administration. Urukagina claimed he was acting on behalf of the Gods to right the wrongs of society. This self-justifying assertion of the divine right of Kings had already been routinely deployed by his predecessors, including for instance, Eannatum and Enmetena.

Political Vision

The second lesson is that political vision matters. In Urukagina's case, that vision was made all the more powerful by the divine origins and sanction of it. Urukagina's covenant with Ningirsu was to carry out the God's wish to 'clean up' Lagash.

Lagash today.

Political Leadership

The third lesson is the importance of charismatic and inspirational leadership able to articulate a vision for change, and then put that vision into effect. Academic and management guru Peter Senge suggests truly transformative leaders need three core attributes: the ability to 'see the larger system'; second, the skill to foster reflection and 'generative conversations'; and the third, the capacity to shift from being reactive to 'co-creating the future'.

Effective Interface of Political and Administrative Leadership

The fourth lesson is that implementation of the political vision requires the interface of political and administrative leadership to be effective, to turn ideas into action. Public sector reform may seek to correct another 'problem' widely declared to exist: the need to adopt an entrepreneurial

Statue of Ur-Ningirsu, son of Gudea, c. 2080 BC. (CC, Metropolitan Museum).

spirit from the private sector. This, of course, had evidently not been a problem in ancient Babylonia. There the head boatman, the livestock official, and the fisheries inspector had, on the contrary, proved themselves only too enterprising in appropriating boats, donkeys and sheep, and the fish catch. Such private sector drive has not waned over the last four and a half millennia.

Morale and Motivation Matter

The fifth lesson is that motivation matters: strengthen the morale of officials. Here arises a tension, between the need to collaborate effectively, and the temptation for politicians to blame public officials for failure. If officials believe that 'public service reform' is a demagogic scapegoat, failure is inevitable as passive resistance and caution turns to paralysis.

Strengthen Legitimacy

The sixth lesson is that the state needs public authority legitimised by the impartiality of public officials. The 'deep state' of conspiracy theory conjures up the idea of career intelligence and military officers and bureaucrats abusing the institutional power they have spent decades mastering to advance their goals regardless of elected public officials or the people at large.

But more likely in too many countries is 'the shallow state': government that eschews accumulated experience, expert knowledge, professional relationships, hard-earned insight, the craft of good drafting, special skills, deep tradition and shared values. Instead the 'ahistoric state' celebrates its ignorance of and disdain for those bureaucratic attributes and focuses on Twitter and fake news.

Strategic Communications

The seventh lesson is that a reform programme needs to be explained if it is to overcome resistance to change. The greater the likely resistance, the more important the communication strategy becomes. The support that Urukagina enjoyed at the start of his reign seems to have been due to his 'reforms' being worded in such a way to appeal to the temples — the city's priests and state administrators (the sukkal, abgal, nimgir, sag-sug and maskim-gi).

Avoid Big Bang Revolution in Government

The final lesson derives from the probability that the 'reforms' carried within them the seed of their own destruction. Urukagina weakened the state causing Lagash to collapse. Public officials instinctively realise that markets are 'embedded' in their societies — a point that Adam Smith had made, opposing the characterisation by Hobbes, of people as 'disembedded maximizers'. Building on Max Weber's notion of *verstehen*, the understanding of meaning in societies, Polanyi argued that material exchange has always meant more than simply individual wants being satisfied. Trade affirms and strengthens the social values of the larger community. In the 18th century Adam Smith himself, in his 'other' book, had

Enannatum, king or ruler of Lagash, with hands folded apparently in worship.

pointed out that human beings were as, or more concerned about social status than they were for any profit motive.[1] Public bureaucracy is the spiritual heart of the state. The final conclusion, therefore, is avoid 'big bang' destruction of state institutions.

A cynic might wonder why career advisors and unemployment agencies don't recommend Sumerology more widely. It is clearly as an amiable field of quiet scholarship where sometimes it seems that anything goes.

Seven 'lessons' about how public administration must achieve this vision are these:

1. Public service excellence is a key competitive edge. Foster it.
2. Reform of public administration has been politically tempting for over 4000 years: be cautious in accepting at face value any claim that justifies the rationale for improvement.

---

[1] Smith, A. 1761. *Theory of Moral Sentiments*. 2nd ed. Strand & Edinburgh: A. Millar; A. Kincaid and J. Bell. Retrieved 26 May 2014.

3. Nevertheless grab the 'reform moment', especially to reverse declining trust in government.
4. Strengthen the morale and motivation of officials.
5. Communicate a clear vision, with a whole-of-government perspective.
6. Pursue 'best fit' not 'best practice' reforms.
7. The quality of leadership is critical if reform is to succeed.

A distinguished Assyriologist concluded: 'our knowledge of the political history of the Pre-Sargonic period is still virtually non-existent'.[2] Another cautions about the 'Reforms' narrative that 'any use of it as a basis for historical or social reconstruction is hazardous in the extreme'.[3]

A fragment of Urukagina's Reform Tablet (in the Ancient Orient Museum, Istanbul. Creative Commons).

---

[2] Steinkeller, quoted in Frayne, *op. cit.*, p. 15.
[3] Foster, B. 1981. A New Look at the Sumerian Temple State. *Journal of the Economic and Social History of the Orient,* 24(3), 225–241.

As one of the 'big names' in Sumerology, Professor Samuel Kramer of the University of Pennsylvania warned long ago, however, given the 'fragmentary, obscure and elusive' evidence, 'there is bound to be considerable difference of views' about Sumerian history reflecting the authors' 'prejudices, conceits and shortcomings'.[4]

True, but we know a great deal about public service reform. From that perhaps we can make more sense of Urukagina's 'reforms'. Foresight methodologies help the present imagine scenarios of potential futures. But it is time now to consider how Urukagina in the 21st century, some 4500 years later, might view public service for the 21st century.

---

[4] Kramer, Sumerians, p. 39.

Part B
Discontent and Failure

Chapter 8

Discontent With Bureaucracy

> It is always a silly thing to give advice, but to give good advice is absolutely fatal.
>
> Oscar Wilde

The Nobel prize-winning economist Sir Arthur Lewis once noted that the secret of development was really quite simple: 'sensible politics and good public administration'.[1] Those two requirements have all too often proved so remarkably elusive.

They remain so. In 1983, the *Times of Swaziland* had commented on the state of the country:

> ... the most pressing issues are the state of the economy and the chaotic state of the civil service ... The treasury is in chaos ... misappropriation of funds continues unabated... Civil servants are taking it easy; permanent secretaries make expensive overseas trips and the taxpayer gets no feed-back as to why these trips are necessary ... A depressed economy needs tight and efficient management. It cannot afford a chaotic civil service. These are pressing issues which the government will have to tackle. The civil service needs a tough and efficient hand if it is to retain the necessary discipline that is required of any public service.

---

[1] Lewis, W. A. 1966. *Development Planning: The Essentials of Economic Policy*. London: Allen & Unwin Ltd., p. xiv.

Unfortunately, in the Swazi capital Mbabane little progress has been made in the last 35 years on the problem. To many people, no doubt, that is unsurprising. Surely bureaucrats are 'grey' characterless officials who lack energy, enthusiasm and ambition?

The role of the state is to maintain peace and security; uphold the constitution and the rule of law, ensuring fair, accessible and affordable justice for all, and respect for human rights; provide essential services; and build trust in the legitimacy of state institutions, based on a vision for the country's development efforts focused on the well-being of the people.

Bureaucracy is the instrument through which governments exercise authority, penetrate society, regulate social relationships, extract and use resources. Government employees perform a wide range of vital roles — The civil service protects its population by creating stability, predictability, cohesion, continuity and trust — from national security to environmental sustainability. Officials regulate markets to ensure fair competition, oversee financial institutions to guarantee stability in banking, provide a framework for ensuring a healthy and educated population and conduct diplomacy around the globe. Viewed in this way, bureaucracy has a positive image, of a rational, efficient method for applying hierarchical authority and functional specialisation, to make possible the efficient undertaking of complex tasks. Administration reflects the political context, either replacing the arbitrary exercise of power or being used by it: the appearance of meticulous efficiency can hide 'laxity, procrastination, ineptitude, corruption, and petty brutality', as Samuel Finer, in his magisterial 3-volume 'The History of Government from the Earliest Times', describes bureaucracy in Ancient Egypt.[2]

Three strong traditions of bureaucracy emerged from 18th-century Prussian militarism, the French Revolution of 1789 and the 'Mandarin' in East Asia, where the bureaucrat is the guiding hand of the nation. In Vietnam people make offerings in Buddhist temples and monasteries in the belief that this will help their children pass exams and secure jobs in the bureaucracy. Government as a potential source of good expresses

---

[2] Finer, S. E. 1997. *The History of Government from the Earliest Times: The Intermediate Ages*, vol. I. Oxford University Press, p. 199.

the Confucian ideal of benevolent government (*ren zheng*) attained through public service operating by meritocratic elitism. Rulers have often been figureheads: bureaucrats take the key decisions. In Japan, elaborate ritual constrained both the Emperor and the 'Shogun': officials determined their daily routine. The power of Japan's bureaucracy is in part a legacy of a Confucian tradition that glorified the idea of scholars serving the emperor. In an echo of that tradition, each year 45,000 of Japan's brightest young people apply for just 780 positions in the elite ranks of the civil service. Those who pass are Japan's philosopher-kings, respected because they won their places through merit and admired for rising above pedestrian taints like politics and money. The very best of them eventually exercise more power over daily Japanese life than some fleeting politician like a prime minister.

The term 'civil service' was first used in designating the British administration of India and linked to the establishment of the East India Company College to train and examine administrators of the Company's territories. The college and its examinations for the Indian Civil Service were influenced by the meritocratic principles underlying the examination system of imperial China.

Public service is important for upholding societal values, the public good and the inter-generational interests of future generations, thereby building trust and legitimacy through fairness. In the long run, bureaucratic ritual built state legitimacy. The border guard's rubber stamp in a passport permitting entry, the Mandarin's chop recognising the transaction, the notary's seal of approval: these are the universal symbols of power and authority. The birth certificate confers the state's legitimacy on the citizen, just as the citizen, in accepting it, accedes to the legitimacy of the state. Bureaucratic process enables the social contract.

The strict routine of a government department once reflected or perfected the nature of its employees as 'faceless' administrators, petty-minded, hide-bound by the rulebook. The work was inevitably dehumanising and alienating. Management monopolised the right to participation in decision-making. Work became dull and unsatisfying.

Government bureaucracy has viewed the world as ordered, rational and mechanistic, scientific, a system to eliminate feelings. Human quirks of absurdity, meaninglessness, complexity, ambiguity, uncertainty and incoherence, empathy and compassion challenged the grand narrative of state bureaucracy. Ideals of justice and liberty were disciplined, neat and tidy; the aim was a country where 'trains run on time'. This ambition drove the state-building motivation of bureaucrats to create the state, construct its infrastructure, and apply other human and material resources to the common good as an imagined community of neatly organised suburban gardeners. Hierarchy and discipline was the only method to create uniformity.

In contrast, the public have often perceived this as a Potemkin village. Behind the façade, indolent functionaries are concerned for apparently needless procedures and unnecessary 'red tape' because it is easier than really addressing the variation in people's 'real' needs or the requirements of the wealth-creating private sector. The hard work of the taxpaying citizen and business maintain idle mandarins to aimlessly observe rules and regulations regardless of circumstance. Public servants servilely follow orders from above because this sheltered them from criticism. 'Bureaucratic' implies slow processes, time-wasting paperwork, laborious inefficiencies, rigid hierarchies occupying labyrinthine corridors of colourless offices. Soul-less, heartless and faceless, bureaucracy can be a machine or system, also be unchecked power. Officials are out of control, serve no-one but themselves and for ever feathering their own nests. These cunning and conniving apparatchiks need to be endlessly monitored to prevent them from abusing their powers.

Government involves power. This can be centralised or decentralised, accountable and able to take decisions. These are executed by public administration, which confronts the multiple challenges of turning policy into action. Yet 'administration is policy' — what actually gets done decides the outcomes. That disconnect and resulting dissatisfaction about how lofty ambition fails to be realised on the ground has driven the quickening pace of 'civil service reform' and 'deliver' agendas — modernising, measuring and managing; and governance, the broader political setting.

Attitudes towards 'bureaucrats', 'bureaucratic methods' and 'the bureaucracy' are a product of how, in different places at different times, the social contract between citizen and state is conceived, the legitimacy of the state is embraced, its public authority regarded and the government of the day accepted.

Civil service reform tackles not only inefficiency, confusion and apathy, but also the emerging from a legacy of fear. Under paranoid, ruthless rulers like the 19th-century Ottoman Sultan Abdul Hamid II or Stalin in the USSR, officials were paralysed by terror. The East German secret police, the Stasi, is the best documented system of mass surveillance. The Stasi employed 90,000 full-time staff assisted by 170,000 full-time unofficial collaborators; together with a much larger number of occasional informers they made up nearly 15% of the entire East German population. Officials reported on their colleagues. But the lack of legitimacy in the eyes of the population and the rudimentary computer technology, incapable of handling the vast amounts of information collected, led to the collapse of the regime.

How the e-legitimacy and e-social contract develop, time will tell.[3]

Action breeds inconsistencies; however, hard the rules are updated and rigorously applied. Overlapping responsibilities adds confusion. Different departments develop fierce internal loyalty that creates friction and 'turf battles' with other government agencies. Processes become fossilised. Professional disagreements become personalised and naked ambition drives inter-departmental rivalries: the Byzantine official John the Lydian (490–565 AD) wrote an account of Roman bureaucracy, *De Magistratibus reipublicae Romanae*, as a vehicle for taking revenge on his former boss, whom he depicted as not only incompetent but as an avaricious glutton, cruel, sexually depraved and physically deformed.

Since the Enlightenment, however, public officials have taken pride in their posts and the public prestige of having a handle on power and an influence on shaping history. In past times and still in a few countries today, 'bureaucratic' implies professional in manner, being reasoned, rational, sensibly cautious, fair and impartial. Bureaucrats were respected for working on behalf of the common good or, like doctors, trying to assist individuals for the welfare of all.

To capture civil servants' pride in working for the national good, the long-term perspective must look back with respect but without awe ('we stand on the shoulders of giants') in order to look forward. Indeed,

---

[3] Everest-Phillips. 2018. Ethos.

the scale of the challenges facing humanity and our planet means that, in the 21st century, public officials may be giants standing on the shoulders of pygmies.

People are Never Satisfied

To achieve that ambition, the spirit of public service must focus on the whole being greater than the sum of its parts. Rather than striving to build better components, the focus of the civil service should be on outcomes, not just outputs. Sectors such as health and education will become less 'siloed'. Instead, 'whole of government' clarity will emphasise that the purpose of government is the security and well-being of its citizens. But, to transform itself, government bureaucracy needs a human face.

Merit-based hiring and promotion are associated with faster growth. Economic history shows that the most crucial requirements of social transformation can only be delivered by the public authority. A government that does not pay for skilled personnel to deliver education, health and land reform is one that condemns its people to under-development.

What drives successful reform of public administration? The answer is simple: humanity's perpetual dissatisfaction with the present. Grumbling about the here and now has been with us 'since time immemorial'. That is unsurprising. Grumbling is vague, general, easy and fun. Everyone likes to let off steam over life's frustrations and irritations. This is usually directed at a vague 'other' in the third person plural 'they', or at an amorphous entity like 'government'.

Humour, however, can threaten the state. Earnest bureaucrats and po-faced ideologues fear nothing more than being laughed at. Under Ceausescu's communist dictatorship in Romania between 1965 and 1989, the dreaded secret police, the Securitate, was dedicated to suppressing subversive jokes.

An unpredictable incident can trigger street protests. At first usually peaceful, events can turn violent, with unexpected consequences. Fascism finally collapsed in Portugal with the Carnation Revolution of 1974. Confrontation led to the collapse of Communist regimes in Eastern Europe in 1989 and in the USSR in 1991, yet Communist rule had survived the 1956 Uprisings in Hungary, in 1968 in Prague, and in China at Tiananmen Square in 1989.

In all these events, the interface between the country's political and administrative leadership was a critical factor for the regime's survival or collapse. In October 1795 the royal coach was attacked in London as King George III was travelling to the state opening of parliament. Britain had been at war with revolutionary France for two years and the resulting economic strain had triggered food shortages across the country. The protesters called for 'peace' and 'bread', shouted 'No King!', and threw stones and rubbish at the gilded carriage. James Gilray's brilliant cartoon of the event, entitled 'The Republican Attack' published a few days later, seems to suggest revolutionary sentiment had spread from Paris. Why did a repeat of the execution of the monarch there not occur in Britain? Public officials at all levels around the country remained committed and kept their nerve. Public authority survived.

Sometimes, however, mankind has the temerity to imagine a better future. Then public service reform becomes a morality play: at the close, good will triumph. 'Yes we can'. Creativity, a vision of Utopia achieved through invention and innovation, is an essential human attribute. Without it, and the hard work of a true believer in its potential, progress would be impossible. But other characteristics hold the creative impulse in check. Jealousy, one of the nastier sides to human nature, can encourage experimentation for the wrong reasons. Ambition can foster progress or unchecked dissatisfaction.

The most debilitating dimension to human nature, however, is fear. Pessimists look to a glorified past, believing in the Fall, mankind's traumatic expulsion from the Garden of Eden. Life can only get worse. The end of the world is nigh. There is no hope. Human suffering is inevitable. Pray for a swift end.

Optimists dream of a better world. 'Old men in a hurry' seek to leave a legacy. 'Young Turks' hope to make their name. Incumbents try to reform themselves while they still can, new rulers seek to reassure within the first 100 days that things really are going to change.

Risk abounds. Political and administrative leaders delegate the task of actual policymaking to the 'street-level bureaucrats' (such as doctors, teachers, social workers and policemen) to exercise professional discretion and responsibility for 'squaring the circle' on multiple and often conflicting organisational goals. Mid-level bureaucrats reinterpret their duties to more easily deliver results, while the outcome of lower level bureaucrats' creative engagement with their everyday tasks remains uncontrollable.

Constructive discontent identifies problems and suggests solutions. This is the process known in psychotherapy as 'fight or flight',[4] and in international development as 'voice or exit'[5] — either confront a problem head on or flee from it. This choice may be triggered by experience. Or discontent can be ideological, driven by ideas and eternal faith in renewal and humanity's infinite potential. Creative dissatisfaction can arise externally, as citizens complain and their leaders seek improvements, or internally as public officials realise that they could 'make a difference' and have a greater impact.

Meanwhile, the world can change around us, often due to new technologies. Indeed, in the 21st century, technological innovation is the new divine intervention, the *deus ex machina* that alone can save humanity from the mess it is making of the planet. The creative state is an essential requirement to tackle the 2030 Agenda of the SDGs.

The civil service is shaped by the ideology of its 'founding fathers' (e.g. 'the pursuit of happiness'), the nature of the state (such as whether it is federal or centralised), the constitutional powers of the executive government, the rival sources of policy advice, the minister–civil servant relationship, and administrative culture. The size, cost, tax base are other factors that fashion how a country's civil service performs. For example, budget allocation to implement reform is likely to influence the willingness of other parts of government to listen to reform proposals.

The need to unlock that secret formula of the right mix of 'sensible politics and good public administration' has never been more pressing.

The Theory of Constant Dissatisfaction

The private sector has one aim: to be efficient, that is, to make a profit. If firms fail in that, they cease to exist. Some businesses seek to burnish their image through corporate social responsibility; a few companies like Bosch are foundations, and big family-owned corporations like

---

[4] Cannon, W. B. 1929. *Bodily Changes in Pain, Hunger, Fear, and Rage.* D. New York: Appleton and Company.

[5] Hirschman, A. O. 1970. *Exit, Voice and Loyalty: Responses to Decline in Firms, Organizations, and States.* Harvard University Press.

Mars can also take a longer-term, philanthropic view. But in the end, companies exist to make money.

By contrast, the public sector has three aims: (i) efficiency: this has a technocratic meaning, but also a political one: of eliminating distortions created by *governments* (solved by *decreasing* government involvement) or the distortions created by *markets* (reduced by *increasing* government action, for example, through effective competition policy); (ii) effectiveness: purpose is achieved, without regard for cost. This again can be technocratic, but also political, depending on the purpose; and (iii) equitable: the ultimate aim, philosophically and in practice in the view of citizens of government being fairness.

Public administration needs to demonstrate justice (including through even-handedly enforcing citizens' obligations, or 'contributive justice', and ensuring their entitlements, namely 'distributive justice'), the paramount virtue in political life. Justice even trumps liberty. Libertarians might disagree, but freedoms without fairness are of limited value, as rising inequality demonstrates. Firms become bankrupt and are wound up. States in the 21st century no longer are found wanting and taken over by imperialist rivals; rather, they collapse into zones of misrule, where terrorism thrives.

Ever since Urukagina, reform of public administration has usually tackled one or more of four areas: its purpose, in the quality of policy-making; its efficiency, delivery in relation to its size, structure, and functions; its effectiveness, aided by new processes; and staffing, skills and capability. Hidden within these aims are contradictions: the search for efficiency may undermine democratic accountability.[6]

These objectives are always in tension if not conflict. Public service can strive to be efficient, or effective, or equitable; it can also combine any two of the three aims: it can be efficient and effective, efficient and equitable, or equitable and effective. But efficiency, effectiveness and equity are inherently incompatible, so difficult political choices must be made.

---

[6] Ospina, S., Grau Cunill-Grau, N. and, Zaltsman, A. 2004. Performance Evaluation, Public Management Improvement and Democratic Accountability. *Public Management Review*, 6(2), 123–134.

The last 50 years of public sector reform in the United Kingdom neatly demonstrates this. In 1968 the Fulton Report prioritised effectiveness, reflecting the faith in experts of the 'white heat of technology' era. Thatcher's reforms started in the early 1980s with Lord Rayner's Scrutiny of efficiency. Between 1986 and 1997, this morphed into the 'Next Steps' reforms that moved 85% of civil servants into agencies. The aim was to combine efficiency with effectiveness, by giving 'managers' more control of inputs, staffing, resourcing so they could make the best choices about how to improve service delivery and make efficiencies. Similarly, 1991–1997 Citizens Charter enhanced the strong focus on efficiency with effectiveness in public services and the civil service through customer service standards and 'Chartermarks' awards for the best services. Then between 1999 and 2003 the 'Bringing in and Bringing on Talent' initiative focused on fairness and effectiveness by opening up recruitment into the civil service and improving the diversity of the civil service. In the period 2001–2010 The Prime Minister's Delivery Unit was promoting efficiency and effectiveness, in delivering the Prime Minister's priorities. The tools, methods and way of working were globally marketed without self-doubt, and much copied but with little evaluation of lasting impact. The 2005–2012 Capability Reviews prioritised effectiveness and equity by looking beyond delivery at the wider challenges to leadership and change in the civil service.

Yet The UK Parliament Public Administration committee September 2013 report, *Truth to power: how Civil Service reform can succeed*, highlighted tensions between ministers and civil servants. Ministers felt that their decisions were being deliberately blocked or frustrated by a lack of openness and trust, failure to learn from mistakes and a tendency to look for individuals to blame. The Government lacked the analysis, policies and leadership to address these problems. Ministers and senior civil servants were still somewhat in denial about their respective accountabilities. The committee concluded that fundamental change was required and that the independent evidence in favour of a comprehensive strategic review of the nature, role and purpose of the civil service was overwhelming. In other words, 45 years after the Fulton Review, the tensions between the three objectives — efficiency, effectiveness and equity — had grown starker even as the pace of reform had become more relentless.

The manner in which these policy choices are made is the social contract between citizens and the state. Hence, policy choices on the priorities of public administration have profound effects on the type of state that develops. The practical result of this social contract is significant. An African state accepted as politically legitimate by its citizens is estimated to have annual growth rates up to 2.5% higher than if the state's legitimacy does not command popular support.[7]

There is never a perfect civil service. Urukagina declared that the problems in Lagash reached back to 'time immemorial'. Compromises between citizens and state leave both sides dissatisfied with the intermediary, public officials. What is the priority: more expertise, better management or greater trust? Reform of such a complex and politically important institution is always a work in progress. No public administration ever finishes improving its capability: 'Reform is always necessary in the Civil Service — nothing is ever totally solved so it's always the same topics that come up again and again'.[8] And some beneficial impacts of reforms undoubtedly ended up being undermined by subsequent changes. Reforms which start brightly can soon tail off, and those that start poorly can be electrified to deliver significant benefits. One study neatly notes that that success in reform is a 'delicate and complex alchemy'.[9]

No international consensus exists around the 'right' civil service and, without a recognised conceptual framework for civil service, reforms often lack a credible or explicit theory of change.[10]

As a result, there are either too many public officials, when public service is a job creation scheme, or too few, when control of cost dominates over building legitimacy. The Han Empire in China had four times as many officials per capita as the late Roman Empire; ancient Sumeria more than 18th-century France.

---

[7] Englebert, P. 2000. *State Legitimacy and Development in Africa*. Lynne Rienner Publishers. Cambridge.
[8] Panchamia, N. and Thomas, P. 2014. *Civil Service Reform in the Real World*. Patterns of success in UK civil service reform. Institute for Government, p. 78.
[9] *Ibid.*, p. 76.
[10] World Bank Independent Evaluation Group. 2008. *Review of Development Effectiveness*. Washington, DC.

Contrary to expectation, there is no growing uniformity of form and commonality in function among public administrations tackling similar challenges. Rather, although public service is evolving fast everywhere, the outcome is not convergence around some neo-Weberian principles and organisational structures, but increasing divergence — just as appeared in the late 19th century between the countries of then industrialising world.

Action is needed to create 'anti-fragility'. Such political resilience requires that every citizen has a stake in long-term stability, and that public administration stewards the long-term interests of society, its institutions and the environment. In this, the objective is well-being, not GDP growth. The focus must shift from creating public value to upholding public values. A narrow focus on efficiency cuts out the capacity cushion of built-in redundancy, the spare capacity to act in a crisis.

Chapter 9

The Failure of Technocratic Tinkering

> The atmosphere of officialdom would kill anything that breathes the air of human endeavour, would extinguish hope and fear alike in the supremacy of paper and ink.
>
> Joseph Conrad

Failure has proved endemic in public sector reform, not just in developing countries.[1] Public sector reform has a long history of failure,[2] and lack of evidence that outcomes have improved.[3] Such reforms are indeed rarely successful.[4] Successive civil service reforms did not substantially improve

---

[1] The World Bank Independent Evaluation Group, 2008, and 2011. Turner, J. 2013. *Summary Report of the Public Sector Governance Reform Evaluation*. London: DfID, SIDA and IrishAid confirms the poor track record for recent external support for reform.

[2] Kiggundu, M. 1998. Civil Service Reforms: Limping into the Twenty-First Century, in Minogue, M., Polidano, C. and Hulme, D. (eds.). *Beyond the New Public Management: Changing Ideas and Practices in Governance*. Cheltenham: Edward Elgar, pp. 155–171.

[3] Evans, A. 2008. *Civil Service and Administrative Reform: Thematic Paper*. Background paper to Public Sector Reform: What Works and Why? Washington, DC: World Bank.

[4] Alonso, J., Clifton, J. and D. Díaz-Fuentes. 2011. *Did New Public Management Matter? An Empirical Analysis of the Outsourcing Decentralization Effects on Public Sector Size*. COCOPS Working Paper Series; Van Dooren, W., Lonti, Z., Sterck, M. and Bouckaert, G.

efficiency or reduce corruption.[5] Fewer than 9% of reforms across the EU showed plausible outcomes.[6] In the United States, reforms to the federal government between 1945 and 1995 rarely achieved their goals.[7]

For example, a study of public sector reform in the United Kingdom over the last 30 or 40 years summed it up as 'erratic, episodic, incoherent … and wasteful'.[8] Another suggests that the 'Civil Service reform syndrome' creates 'initiatives [that] come and go, overlap and ignore each other, leaving behind residues of varying size and style'.[9] The syndrome persists 'because the assumptions behind reforms are not fit for public sector purpose'.[10]

In developing countries, these problems are often more serious because the need for an effective public sector and, therefore, for public service reform, is greater. Such is the degree of failure generally, and continued weaknesses of governments after reform interventions are supposedly completed,[11] that one professor at Harvard categorises success as the 'positive deviant' of public sector reform.[12]

The managerial revolution in the UK public sector during the 1980s and 1990s failed to deliver the promised efficiency results.[13] In the

---

2007. *Institutional Drivers of Efficiency in the Public Sector*. OECD, Public Governance Committee.

[5] McCourt, W. 2013. *Models of Public Service Reform: A Problem-Solving Approach*. World Bank Policy Research Working Paper No. 6428.

[6] Pollitt, C. and Dan, S. 2011. The Impacts of the New Public Management in Europe: A Meta-analysis, paper to be presented at the European group for Public Administration Conference, Bucharest, September.

[7] Light, P. 1996. *The Tides of Reform: Making Government Work 1945–1995*. Yale University Press.

[8] Panchamia and Thomas, *op. cit.*, p. 172.

[9] Hood, C. and Lodge, M. 2006. *The Politics of Public Service Bargains: Reward, Competency, Loyalty — and Blame*. Oxford University Press, Oxford, UK.

[10] Rhodes, R. 2014. *So You Want to Reform the Civil Service. Reform Online Publication*. http://www.reform.uk/publication/a-civil-service-fit-for-the-future/.

[11] Pritchett, L., Woolcock, M. and Andrews, M. 2013. Looking Like a State: Techniques of Persistent Failure in State Capability for Implementation. *The Journal of Development Studies, 49*(1), 1–18.

[12] Andrews, M. 2013. *Explaining Positive Deviance in Public Sector Reforms in Development*. HKS Faculty Research Working Paper Series. Harvard.

[13] Hood, C. and Dixon, R. 2012. *A Model of Cost-cutting in Government? The Great Management Revolution in UK Central Government*. Public Administration. Panchamia and Thomas, *op. cit.*, pp. 7–8.

United Kingdom, Margaret Thatcher's 11 years in Downing Street left the level of public spending only marginally different from what she had found when she came to power in 1979. President Reagan bequeathed a huge public sector deficit and a federal civil service little altered in size by his eight years in the Oval Office. G.W. Bush, another president who was elected on an ideology of fiscal prudence and small government, presided over the transformation of a federal surplus into a big deficit and left an enlarged federal workforce.

The problem is widespread: In 2014, Pope Francis accused the Vatican Curia, the administration of the Holy See, of resisting reform due to the 'spiritual ailments' afflicting its members, including using their careers to grab power and wealth, of living 'hypocritical' double lives and of forgetting that they are supposed to be men of God.

Key reasons for failure include the complexity of human institutions, lack of clarity on the aims, and practitioners failing to reflect on the evidence that, all too often, grand reform design squashes local innovation and experimentation. The history of public sector reform is littered with overambitious 'root and branch' reform degenerating into underwhelming tinkering at the margins, wishful thinking, fallacious theories, unintended consequences.

Externally led public sector reform programmes encourage the adoption of technical practices developed elsewhere, which do not address underlying problems, and so fail to achieve significant behavioural change. This 'isomorphic mimicry', whereby beneficiary governments adopt organisational forms, which are considered international best practice, but do not work.[14]

Public sector reform is inherently a political process, largely endogenous, shaped by changing regional and global circumstances, not determined by a universal sequence of change but of 'learning by doing' complexity in which how change will happen cannot be reliably predicted.

---

[14] Pritchett, L., Woolcock, M. and Andrews, M. 2010. *Capability Traps? The Mechanisms of Persistent Implementation Failure*. Center for Global Development. Working Paper No. 234. Washington, DC. Andrews, M., Woolcock, M. and Pritchett, L. 2012. *Escaping Capability-traps Through Problem-Driven Iterative Adaptation (PDIA)*. HKS Faculty Research Working Paper.

Failure in public service reform is variously attributed to the complexity of the system, the conflicting interests of stakeholders, the political sensitivities involved, ambiguous evidence on which reform is both planned and then judged, the failure to evaluate reform systematically and then disseminate the results, political posturing,[15] and the absence of a theoretical model to guide reform that, as a result, have been *ad hoc* at best and misguided at worst. The bureaucratic toolkit to frustrate the provisions of even the best law is almost endless.

The Anti-Politics Machine: Development, Depoliticization, and Bureaucratic Power in Lesotho (1990) by James Ferguson describes a 'failed' development project in Lesotho.[16] This book has been highly influential. Ferguson emphasised the dangers in reducing political choices to technical issues, ignoring what development projects accomplish rather than what they fail to achieve, and noting that '..."failure"...does not mean doing nothing; it means doing something else'. The project did not bring about the expected development in livestock farming, yet was instrumental in building roads, post offices, health-care clinics and numerous local bureaucratic influence.

Other research unfortunately confirms that most 'mechanistic' efforts to improve the 'machinery' of government fails. The 2011 independent annual report of the performance of the World Bank Group in public sector reforms showed how success in implementing the projects did not translate into progress, suggesting that while reform programmes are initiated they often do not result in transformative change.[17]

Tinkering with the technical aspects such as remuneration, human resources, downsizing public financial management, leadership and policymaking, and service delivery may seem straight forward. The technical approach focuses on ways to improve formal (*de jure*) structures and processes, such as financial management systems in central government,

---

[15] Taylor, M. 2008. Why Public Service Reform Hasn't Worked. *Public Policy Review*. Institute for Public Policy Research, *15*(3), 137–141.

[16] Ferguson, J. 1990. *The Anti-politics Machine: 'Development', Depoliticization, and Bureaucratic Power in Lesotho*. Cambridge: Cambridge University Press, p. 320.

[17] IEG. 2008. *Public Sector Reform: What Works and Why?: An IEG Evaluation of World Bank Support*. The World Bank; IEG. 2011. *IEG Annual Report 2011 Results and Performance of the World Bank Group*. Washington, DC: World Bank.

not a complex process which requires a change in the *de facto*, informal and political aspects of public sector. 'Best practice' management mechanisms imported from elsewhere through international technical assistance rarely achieve long-term improvements.

The delightful small African country of Malawi is a telling example. Heavily donor dependent, it witnessed an almost permanent revolution of endless public sector reforms. These began in the 1960s immediately after independence, and by some accounts, there have been about 79 initiatives in the following half-century, while public services progressively deteriorated. Reforms were politically untenable, poorly conceived and badly implemented. Stability was preserved at the cost of progress.

That result illustrates that attempts to solve political problems with technocratic solutions fail. In the deeply religious country that had embraced the legendary 19th-century missionary David Livingstone, reformers have been left to find solace in the words of St. Paul addressing the Galatians, '... let us not grow weary while doing good, for in due season we shall reap if we do not lose heart'.

The outcome is startling. Singapore at independence in 1965 had a per capita income 10 times that of Malawi; today its per capita income is 210 times larger.

Tuvalu Government Files

The Commonwealth, of which Malawi is a member, is a fascinating assembly of former British colonies. In the field of public administration, its membership highlights how similarity in formal procedures masks profound differences. My most vivid experience of this was visiting one of the world's smallest and most remote countries, Tuvalu in the Pacific. This was the latter half of the Gilbert and Ellice Islands, well-known to philatelists for the famously beautiful stamps issued during the reign of George VI. I was fortunate to visit Tuvalu three times in 2011 and 2012. I was fascinated to discover the civil service there was using exactly the same cardboard files and formats that colonial administrators like Sir Arthur Grimble had inculcated into public officials on the archipelago there many decades before, and with which I had started my career in Whitehall 30 years earlier.

That influence helped shape a common understanding about public administration. Yet efforts to improve government in developing countries have often ended up reproducing such formal aspects found in developed countries, but with little of the function. Civil service practices are context-specific. But, in the absence of clarity on the implications of that often repeated observation, state-building assumes a Weberian form of public administration. As a result, the heavily aid-dependent developing countries with the weakest capacity are most subjected to pressures from donor countries to adopt the normative ideas labelled as 'New Public Management'. These originated in the 1980s with the neo-liberal ideology of reducing the role of the state in the economy. Reforms to make the public sector more effective included 'down-sizing', privatisation and emulating private sector business practices. This 'managerialism' saw people not as citizens but as customers or clients of services from the government bureaucracy. But the purchaser–provider relationship demoralises public bureaucrats committed to the public interest.

That led to restructuring of civil service by adopting private sector ideas on management, performance, finance and service delivery. These civil service reforms in developing countries invariably fail because of the politics, emphasising downsizing and cost-cutting undermines the capacity of political leaders to be effective.

The search for a responsive and legitimate state capable of sustaining an effective market economy has floundered. In the absence of any better yardstick, Civil services continue to be measured against the normative ideal of a liberal constitutional democracy with an industrialised market economy.

Reform requires effective champions inside the public service in order to work;[18] often no lasting, overall productivity gains have resulted,[19] while morale has sunk to a deep all-time low.[20] A persistent lack of key

---

[18] Grindle, M. 2012. *Jobs for the Boys: Patronage and the State in Comparative Perspective.* Cambridge, Massachusetts, and London, England: Harvard University Press.
[19] Hood, C. and Dixon, R. 2015. *A Government that Worked Better and Cost Less? Evaluation Three Decades of Reform and Change in UK Central Government.* Oxford University Press.
[20] GCPSE. 2014. *Motivation of Public Service Officials. Insights for Practitioners. Global Center for Public Service Excellence.* Singapore.

skills and capabilities and an unacceptably high level of churn of lead officials; divided leadership and confused accountabilities within central government, and mistrust among civil servants in some departments, fuelled by a tendency to scapegoat individual officials rather than to learn lessons from failures hinder progress.[21]

History suggests that civil service reform should only ever be entered into with care. Changing the 'rules of the game' for public administration often brings years of turmoil and, more often than not, little real gain to show for it.

But perhaps it is less helpful to ask why do so many public service reforms fail if, as we have seen, they are bound to fail under the Theory of Constant Dissatisfaction. That failure is technical failure. But if the covert political aim is for political leaders to stop complacency, then perhaps it has often succeeded.

'An Honourable Livelihood with Little Labour, and No Risk'

A mantra, by being repeated endlessly and relentlessly for the last 30 years, has become established 'fact': public sector reform is needed to improve the supposed universal lethargy and incompetence of public officials. So public sector reform presents an ideal mechanism for ambitious new ministers to show steely determination against an easy target.

This, however, is a phenomenon of the last few decades: as late as 1966 the British Prime Minister Harold Wilson, commenting on the Fulton Review into Civil Service reform, noted:

> ... the decision to set up this committee does not mean that the Civil Service has been found lacking in any way by the Government in its current operations. On the contrary, it is the experience of Ministers — and I think that right hon. Members opposite would wish to join me in this — that the Service meets the demands put on it with flexibility and enterprise.[22]

---

[21] Public Administration Select Committee. 2013. *Eighth Report: Truth to Power: How Civil Service Reform Can Succeed*. The Stationery Office: UK Parliament.
[22] Wilson, H. *House of Commons Home Civil Service Committee Debate*. UK Parliament. 8 February 1966.

Such praise for bureaucracy would (except in Singapore) nowadays be deeply unfashionable. 'Bureaucratic' is a term of criticism or abuse, suggesting 'red tape', slow, procrastinating, irrelevant and unimaginative. Yet the paradox within the popular concept is that officials although condemned as idle and stupid, are nevertheless also accused of managing to invent ever more cunning rules and devious regulations.

This deep ambiguity has a long history. The energetic and ambitious Frederick the Great when he became King of Prussia in the mid-18th century, like so many new governments since, immediately condemned all the officials he inherited from his father as 'indolent, careless idiots, lazy and incompetent'.[23]

In Britain a century later, the Northcote-Trevelyan Report that resulted in profound reforms professionalising public administration, equally emphatically declared the British Civil Service to be full of 'the unambitious, and the indolent or incapable' and declared that: '... those whom indolence of temperament, or physical infirmities unfit for active exertions, are placed in the Civil Service, where they obtain an honourable livelihood with little labour, and no risk...'.

This view was widely shared. In his novel *Little Dorrit* written between 1855 and 1857 at the time of those reforms, Charles Dickens described the 'Circumlocution Office' to show that in the Civil Service innovation was always crushed. One of the characters in the novel terms civil servants as 'barnacles' and describes the reason for this thus:

> in England .... An appointment in the Civil Service ... confers neither status nor consideration ... Here the Civil Servant is looked upon rather in the light of an outgrowth, to be tolerated because it cannot be shaken off'.[24]

Yet the knee-jerk condemnation was often moderated by experience. The sophisticated Frederick the Great, who hated his boorish father, nevertheless came in time to realise that he had in fact inherited many able hard-working administrators from Frederick William I. By the 18th century

---

[23] Finer, S. E. 1997. *The History of Government from the Earliest Times: The Intermediate Ages*, vol. I. Oxford University Press, p. 1367.

[24] Dickens, C. 1857. *Little Dorrit*. London: Bradbury and Evans, p. 349.

Prussia had in fact already developed a disciplined, industrious yet poorly paid public service. Not for nothing is the French phrase *travailler pour le Roi de Prusse* still used to mean to work hard for a pittance. Even the highly opinionated authors of Britain's mid-19th-century Northcote-Trevelyan Report were forced to concede that there were 'numerous honourable exceptions' to their general condemnation of the supposed blanked inadequacies of the civil service in Britain. Theodore Roosevelt in 1883 pointed out the hypocrisy behind much of the political demand in the United States for civil service reform supposedly in the name of increasing efficiency.[25]

Reformers were themselves often as unconvincing as the reforms they advocated. A century later, the Fulton Report of 1968 had also been forced to acknowledge that the civil service was full of able conscientious staff, and was itself condemned by the Economist as 'an assault on the whole-time gifted amateurs of Whitehall by a part-time group of gifted amateurs ... an ad hoc investigation by a number of uncommitted gentlemen meeting about once a week for three years'.[26]

The complexity of public service has been well understood for centuries. As a senior official of the Ottoman Empire in the late 16th century noted:

> The sovereign cannot rule without troops. He has no troops without money. There is no money if the land is not prosperous. The land will not be prosperous without good and just government. Therefore one cannot rule except by justice.[27]

In other words, the public service of a despot hundreds of years ago already had a sophisticated 'whole of government' understanding of the

---

[25] Roosevelt, T. 26 January 1883. *Speech on the Duties of American Citizenship*. Delivered in Buffalo, New York.
[26] Economist cited in Lowe, R. 2011. *The Official History of the British Civil Service: Reforming the Civil Service*. Routledge.
[27] The Ottoman administrator Hasan Kafi al-Akhisari (1544–1616), quoted in: Darling, L. 1996. *Revenue-raising and Legitimacy: Tax Collection and Finance Administration in the Ottoman Empire, 1560–1660*, p. 281. The phrase originates 500 earlier. See Black, *op. cit.*, pp. 111–112.

need for an integrated strategic development plan: its 'Key Performance Indicators' required officials to provide a framework for rule of law, benchmarking predictability and fairness. The goal was to promote economic growth; indicators of success measured the capacity to justly and efficiently tax the resultant trade and enterprise, thereby being able sustainably to fund an adequate defence policy. The overall target was to reassure investors about the stability of the regime, thereby facilitating long-term peace and prosperity.

Similarly such books as *The Memoirs of Louis XIV and his Court and of the Regency* by the Duke of Saint-Simon and the *Diaries* of Samuel Pepys show that by the late 17th century both countries employed effective public servants. On 3 June 1663 Pepys wrote:

> I to my office, and there read all the morning in my statute-book, consulting among others the statute against selling of offices.

Pepys condemned rampant corruption, and introduced into the Navy examinations for officers and a small degree of promotion by merit. Although as Secretary of the Navy he had made himself a modestly rich man entirely through 'facilitation payments' from Navy suppliers and those seeking advancement, before being swept from office due to political intrigue. In an era before pensions and job security corruption was perhaps inevitable. Importantly he had delivered real public value — a strong, effective defence force.

The Political Economy of Confusionists

In Malawi under Hastings Banda, public officials were at risk of being arrested as 'Confusionists' if their loyalty to the regime was doubted.[28] Across much of Africa, colonialism in the late 19th century created administrative order but left a political mess. At independence, states with artificial borders drawn by European powers during the 'Scramble for

---

[28] Anders, G. 2005. *Civil Servants in Malawi: Cultural Dualism, Moonlighting and Corruption in the Shadow of Good Governance*, PhD thesis, Erasmus University of Rotterdam.

Africa' had no agreed constitutional or informal methods for sharing power. The tradition of political neutrality and speak 'truth to power' did not last long.

The collaborative interface of political and administrative leadership enabled public service to be more effective in the two forms of colonial rule that tended to fare better in the post-independence era: either 'direct rule' colonies, which scrapped customary rule and systematically enforced 'modern' institutions (e.g. Mauritius, Singapore); or 'hands off' protectorates, which preserved the legitimacy of their indigenous governance (e.g. Botswana).[29] Five of the top 10 for quality of public institutions in the 2017 World Competitiveness Index are the United Kingdom's former colonies that out-ranked the United Kingdom — this may be because Singapore, New Zealand, UAE, Qatar, and Hong Kong all inherited a credible system for rule of law, essential for secure property rights, investor confidence and credible commitment, but also revised their public policy and administration for effectiveness.

More attention should be paid to the poorly understood political economy of the public service. Power dynamics, political processes and the nature of public authority determine the professionalism, sense of purpose, passion and pride that, along with pay, shape the potential individual and collective motivation for striving for excellence in public service. Reforms that focus on 'client-focused' results and 'customer' satisfaction rather than on citizens and politics will fail.

Countries need agreement across politics, the military, bureaucracy, and business on how public authority is legitimised enabling the development of rules-based institutions that all sides will respect. Public service is built upon power tested over time, so the unique contingencies of history in any context create 'path-dependency'.

So in Malawi, as in many other African countries, with no agreed rules for peaceful transfer of power tested over time, regimes that came to power on the heady euphoria of independence rapidly collapsed into dictatorship. The civil service was placed under direct presidential control, leading to politicisation and de-professionalisation. Capacity collapsed.

---

[29] Lange, M. 2009. *Lineages of Despotism and Development: British Colonialism and State Power.* Chicago.

Africa post-independence political leaders abolished the impartial public service commissions, which often hastened the decline of good governance in post-colonial eras because the state, used to functioning effectively with able and impartial civil servants, lost its mechanism to mediate public authority.

In the rush to reform, the same mistakes are repeated. An ahistorical approach results in impractically short time frames being imposed on political processes. Externally dictated 'solutions' contain an overt teleology or assumed ideology that one particular form of administration is desirable. The detail components of a well-performing civil service (e.g. HR processes, such as recruitment and promotion) are presented as technical. This overlooks the fact that such processes often plays a political role: who gets recruited and promoted in the civil service influences public authority and service performance. That power in part explains why the trade in bureaucratic jobs in Indonesia is calculated at over $1 billion a year.[30]

The critical importance for development of bureaucracy, its history and politics are increasingly noted. In *Jobs for the Boys*, Professor Merilee Grindle examined how some countries in Latin America move away from patronage and towards civil services.[31] Grindle emphasised: 'All reforms take place in historical contexts that shape and constrain possibilities for change'. Politics affect civil service reform efforts because of 'the primacy of politics in the construction, deconstruction, and reconstruction of systems of appointment to public office'.[32] As a result, patronage systems were often able to resist, get around and subvert reform: 'by the 2000s, Latin American countries were not deficient in laws mandating selection

---

[30] http://www.dlprog.org/opinions/indonesia-and-the-political-settlements-trap.php.

[31] Grindle, *op. cit*. Grindle describes civil service systems, in *Jobs for the Boys*, as follows: 'Patronage systems stand in great contrast to career civil service *systems*, in which the preponderance of nonelected public sector jobs are filled through a process of credentialing based on education, examination, or some other test of merit; in which a career ladder exists and is accessed through regularized demonstration of credentials of education, examination, tenure in office, or other form of assessing merit; in which tenure is secure barring malfeasance in office; and in which movement in and out (through retirement, for example) is regulated and compensated.

[32] *Ibid*. Preface, x.

of public administrators on the basis of merit or setting up equivalents of a civil service commission to undertake recruitment and ensure fair treatment and the political neutrality of public sector workers. Yet despite the consistency of this history throughout the region, in the early years of the new century, only Costa Rica, Chile, and Brazil recruited significant numbers of public sector workers through a structured career civil service system. Indeed, the implementation of civil service legislation was extremely weak in Latin America. As concluded in the IDB study: 'It is precisely the divergence between the norms and the practices that is the greatest weakness of civil service systems in their countries'.[33]

The problem is that no roadmap exists on modernisation or 'open access orders', that is how countries evolve from power based on patronage and kin-based loyalty to a system of public authority premised on universal rules and equal access.

Nevertheless, all too often, the bureaucrat is portrayed as either cunningly exploitative or stupidly incompetent. There is nothing new in public officials being derided as indolent pen-pushers, 'red tape' loving time-wasters, and officious yet rule-bound shirkers. Stories regaling the foibles of bureaucratic tidiness and the inverse relationship between productivity and paperwork, resulting in idiotic solutions or whimsical behaviours, always delight.

Nothing is more entertaining than the irrational outcome of bureaucrats' bounded rationality. Two contrasting examples: on 25 July 1909, Louis Bleriot became the first person to fly an aircraft across the English Channel. Bureaucracy needed creativity in handling this new phenomenon. The British Customs officer who cycled up the hill at Dover to complete the arrival formalities was armed with a declaration form that required the category of Bleriot's 'vessel' be stated — so he registered it as a yacht. Officially, therefore, Bleriot sailed to England. This was a creative solution to a new problem.

In March 2018 a Romanian court ruled that a man was dead, despite his appearing alive and well in court. Constantin Reliu had asked the court in the town of Barlad to overturn a death certificate obtained by his wife after he had spent more than a decade in Turkey, during which time he was

---

[33] *Ibid.* p. 151. With footnote 22, Grindle cites 'Iacoviello 2006: 542. Author's translation'.

out of contact with his family. The court decided that his appeal was too late. Officially he would remain dead. This was an unimaginative failure.

Reform of the public service in the world's biggest but deeply corrupt democracy has been a political football for decades. The elite Indian Administrative Service (IAS) collector, district officer, or district magistrate is the senior official of India's key administrative unit, the district. They hold the country together, maintaining order and collecting revenues across India's 600 districts, each containing hundreds of villages and perhaps 2 million people, half that of New Zealand.

Including railway workers, India's central government employs around 3 million civil servants and the states another 7 million. the elite IAS numbers only 5000. Each year around 200,000 fresh university graduates compete for barely 100 places in the IAS. These top mandarins live like mini maharajahs, surrounded by armed guards, peons, gardeners and orderlies, dispensing justice in red ink to cartloads of petitioners from distant villages, the old and ragged, or blind complaining against corrupt local officials.

The IAS is unashamedly meritocratic and elitist. It is a national and permanent service, theoretically apolitical, and recruited and trained at the centre. Yet India's administration is inefficient. Much development spending fails to reach its intended recipients. Lant Pritchett, of the Kennedy School of Government at Harvard, calls India's malfunctioning public service 'one of the world's top ten biggest problems — of the order of AIDS and climate change'.[34]

Across India, the IAS commands widespread reverence. Anecdote and newspaper advertisements for arranged marriages show that IAS officers remain among India's most marketable partners. Yet many argue that the quality of IAS is falling due to declining education standards; growing competition for talent from the private sector; increasing political interference; and caste-based reservations, which now retain half of all IAS posts for outcaste and low-caste Hindus and members of tribal communities. Former mandarins believe that probity in the public service is in sharp decline. Politicians cannot sack IAS officers, but can get them

---

[34] Cited in *The Economist*. 2008. India's Civil Service: Battling the Babu Raj. Available online: https://www.economist.com/node/10804248.

transferred, so civil servants attach themselves to politicians for enrichment, advancement or just to get their jobs done.

Postings are often used by bureaucracies in emerging economies to reward or punish staff. Property tax inspectors in Pakistan chose their location, based on their performance. This scheme led inspectors to increase the growth rate of tax revenue by 44–80%. Bureaucracies have potential to improve performance by periodically using postings as an incentive, particularly when preferences over locations are a substantial component.[35]

But now, just as the world is facing profound changes requiring motivated civil servants to find and implement innovative solutions, in many countries the morale of public officials has never been lower. Low morale adversely affects not just 'productivity' and 'efficiency', but creativity, empathy and political nous. Job commitment, professional satisfaction and ethical climate in the public service are decreasing, putting at risk fairness and impartiality.[36] In the long term, this threatens citizens' trust and state legitimacy, but in the short term is resulting in increasing misconduct, disengagement and lack of commitment. This crisis within public administrations of many countries must be acknowledged as a major obstacle to the achievement of development outcomes, particularly the SDGs.

Many pre-conceived ideas about the public sector need dispelling. The evidence suggests that innovation often thrives better in the public sector than in the private;[37] there are no grounds for believing that private sector workers are inherently any more efficient than those in the public sector.

Civil servants need to believe in the power of the state to improve the well-being of citizens, otherwise morale falls apart. Rules and regulations allow bureaucrats to believe that an ideal, all perfect society can be

---

[35] Khan, A. Q., Khwaja, A., I., and Olken, B. A. 2016. Making Moves Matter: Experimental Evidence on Incentivizing Bureaucrats through Performance-Based Postings. *Stanford School of Humanities and Sciences.*

[36] Demmke, C. and Moilanen, T. 2012. Effectiveness of Ethics and Good Governance in Central Administration of EU-27: Evaluating Reform Outcomes in the Context of the Financial Crisis, p. 23.

[37] Bason, C. and Colligan, P. 2014. Look to Government — Yes, Government — for New Social Innovations. *Harvard Business Review.* Available online: https://hbr.org/2014/11/look-to-governmentyes-governmentfor-new-social-innovations.

reached by staying late in the office adding that extra paragraph to the law or statute. But in recent years, public service reforms undertaken have also added to the general discontent among public sector workers. In the UK Civil Service, for example, only 30% of staff responding to a survey in 2016 agreed that changes made were usually for the better; only 31% felt that change was managed well in their ministry; only 44% had faith in management; and only 45% believed that a strategic vision existed.

History in Action

A detailed knowledge of the past illuminates the future by inspiring the imagination of today. The accumulation of history is then not a burden but a strength, a way for each generation to question its assumptions. History can be a good nail with which to puncture pomposity. It has all been done before.[38]

Hermann Hesse once observed: *To study history means submitting to chaos yet nevertheless retaining faith in order and meaning.*[39] History will never provide the 'answers', but it offers the best guide to asking the right questions, and doubting over-simplistic or determinist answers. Every generation should interrogate for itself the historical evidence. This is important for refining our understanding of history. By asking new questions and posing old ones anew, historians add to humanity's collective and accumulative insight about how change in the human condition comes about. The interaction of past and present expands our perspective of both on context analysis, institutional memory, and a longer view on narratives and different ways of thinking.[40] Unfortunately it is rare for any government make a serious effort to learn and build on what has gone before.

The past is not merely a 'legacy constraint' from 'path dependency'. Every state needs continuity for its legitimacy. Public service is embedded in history and is evolutionary rather than revolutionary. Its curation

---

[38] Lowe, R. 2011. *The Official History of the British Civil Service: Reforming the Civil Service*. Routledge.
[39] Hesse, H. 1943. *The Glass Bead Game*. Henry Holt & Company.
[40] Institute of Government. 2015. *What Is the Value of History in Policymaking?* London. http://www.instituteforgovernment.org.uk/publications/what-value-history-policymaking.

of the past is essential to protect the future from being compromised by the short-term interests of today.

To imagine the public service of tomorrow, it is helpful to ask how the past and the present can illuminate the future. But how can countries benefit from insights about effective reform in the past? How reliable is history? Can our understanding of the past be made more useful by first considering how the present should illuminate history? We cannot frame our inquiry into the meaning hidden in clay tablets and parchments from times gone by if we do not already possess a practical feel for where the skeletons may be buried in the emails and spreadsheets of the modern world. The professional historian, like the career politician, may have insufficient relevant personal experience of tackling 'real-world' challenges.

History had a profound influence on the evolution of public administrations in developing countries. However, the historical determinants of the quality of government are poorly understood.

Yet, while awareness of the big picture would seem essential to make sense of the contrary winds of the immediate, incumbents of political and administrative office often appear 'aggressively ahistorical'. At first this might seem surprising. Surely understanding one's place in 'the great chain of being' or the organogram of history would come naturally to people schooled in the hierarchy of bureaucratic rank.

History and public administration are bound together by the written record that is essential to both. They are also linked by repeating patterns and permanent tensions. Power is centralised to overcome local 'elite capture', but then decentralised in order to bring government closer to the people. 'Co-creation' inspires local variation to suit local context, but central control seeks to ensure common standards and avoid irresponsible digression from the norm.

But, rather than embracing the historical record a fascinating kaleidoscope of past decisions and actions by fellow holders of public office, many seem to see in the past a threat. History may appear to create 'path dependency' that curtails the policy options available in the present, while also revealing what doesn't work.

The past, offers no framework or manual yet can help would-be reformers understand why something that looks relatively simple — changing the structure, nature and staffing of the public service, an organisation wholly under government control — nevertheless turns out often to be difficult to achieve. Reformers are not always benign; change is not always progress; and the causes of failure are various and many. Where successful reforms do happen, it is usually by consulting not ignoring the expertise and experience of public officials, by keeping their motivation high, and by scaling up reforms that through experimentation have been shown to work in context.

At the same time, experiences of our own times may illuminate an otherwise obscure yet important event: the first recorded governance reform in history. For the last 4500 years, when rulers have been similarly determined to improve their societies, the public service has been the engine of progress. But in recent years the lesson on the importance of a fair and effective public service has too often been forgotten, ignored or derided. The rebalancing of the public and private sectors in the early 1980s — when taxes facing entrepreneurs could create astonishingly high levels of disincentive, such as 115% tax and surtax on income[41] — was an important corrective. But it went too far.

Unfortunately, reform of the public service is too often a remarkably ahistorical enterprise.[42] Since the long-run impact of contemporary events is often uncertain and contested, the past provides invaluable insight into the complexity of change. Goals are too often pursued with the certainty afforded by ignorance. Unfortunately, there is rarely the time and, even less, any incentive to understand the past of public sector reform.

Ambitious officials, opinionated politicians and fee-seeking consultants are focused on action, publicity and advancement. Looking back is not career-enhancing, can rarely be billed to clients, and may pose an unwelcome problem: if the reform now being proposed has already been repeatedly tried and failed, and the lessons of past activity are routinely ignored, who, and what, is the problem? But there's no time to delve into that!

---

[41] Dacre, P. 1982. *The Billy Butlin Story.* Robson Books, p. 258. The Ur III state is the supreme example of a massive centralized bureaucracy under which administrative paralysis may have set in.

[42] In part because mainstream economics appears so ready to take simplistic interpretations of history seriously: See Austin, G. 2008. The 'reversal of fortune' thesis and the compression of history: perspectives from African and comparative economic history. *Journal of International Development,* 20(8), 996–1027.

Besides seeking lessons from the past to illuminate the present, it is equally possible, but rather less usual, openly to apply insights from the present to understand the problems of the past. Such an approach, however, is especially useful when, as for the first known public sector reform, so little evidence has survived. In the absence of new evidence, it is the historians' world view that changes under the influence of contemporary events.

The historical determinants of the quality of government in many developing countries, derived from the bureaucratic effectiveness of public administration and the interplay with post-independence political leadership, are poorly understood.[43] Institutions usually develop slowly. History becomes central to development.

History is not bunk. Nor is it 'just one damned thing after another'. The present has much to learn from the past. It does not provide us with answers to today's problems. But it can ensure that we are able to ask the right questions. It can tell us whether we are going round in circles, or making real progress. But it can also imprison the mind, or blind policymakers to the potential benefits of innovation.

The history of public administration has attracted growing attention, as different countries have evolved varying understanding of the role of the state. The role of public officials under the constitution, in law, in relation to politics, and in connection to civil society distinctly differs. Long traditions of administrative norms, attitudes to accountability and public policy practices can help to explain why the outcomes in different countries of similar public service reforms can vary considerably.[44]

History had a profound influence on the evolution of public administrations in generating statehood. Since even before independence, IAS officers, selected by Delhi but assigned to a state, unified government. Their career incentives are structured in such a way that while they represent state interests, they maintain a sense of commitment to Delhi. In the Democratic Republic of Congo (DRC), public officials recognise the right of the *chefferie* (traditional authority) to collect

---

[43] Rothstein, B. 2007. *Anti-Corruption: A Big Bang Theory*. Working Paper Series. The Quality of Government Institute.
[44] Painter, M. and Peters, B. G. 2010. *Tradition and Public Administration*. London.

local taxes, and report to the *mwami* (traditional leader) as well as to the ministry.

In 2015, the international community agreed on the global SDGs for the next 15 years. This highly ambitious '2030 Agenda' sets out 17 goals, 169 targets and 231 indicators covering every aspect of development. It is profoundly ahistorical, and rightly so. The unwelcome ambiguity of the past should not hold up the ambitious certainty of the optimistic present about a better future for humanity and the planet it inhabits.

But, while ahistorical, national development ambitions should not be unhistorical. They should be informed, but not constrained, by history. In no field is the past more relevant than in government and public administration that are deeply rooted in learning lessons from the past. History has repeatedly demonstrated that the quality of public service matters for progress.

If public servants have little trust in their own leadership because political/administrative leadership pacts have been undermined, then job commitment, professional satisfaction and ethical climate in the public service will decrease, putting at risk fairness and impartiality.[45] In the long term, this threatens citizens' trust and state legitimacy, but in the short term is already apparently resulting in increasing misconduct, disengagement and lack of commitment.

In many countries, post-financial crisis austerity measures undoubtedly play a large part in the overall lowering of job satisfaction.[46] A recent study found that 83% of those OECD countries facing fiscal austerity confront *lower job satisfaction* among public officials, and 84% are witnessing increasing distrust in leadership. Yet, austerity is certainly not the only cause of malaise: 36% of the non-austerity countries are also witnessing a *decrease in workplace commitment* in public service (58% for the austerity countries); 21% of the non-austerity countries observe a

---

[45] Demmke, C. and Moilanen, T. 2012. *Effectiveness of Ethics and Good Governance in Central Administration of EU-27: Evaluating Reform Outcomes in the Context of the Financial Crisis.* Frankfurt/M: Peter Lang, p. 23.

[46] Demmke, C. 2014. Public Administration Reform and reform effects in Western Europe. *Paris, France: SIGMA.*, p. 28; and Demmke, C. and Moilanen, T. 2013. Governmental Transformation and the Future of Public Employment: The Impact of Restructuring on Status Development in the Central Administration of the EU-27. Frankfurt/M: Peter Lang.

decrease of trust (73% of the austerity countries); and a *decrease of loyalty to the public service* affects 14% of the non-austerity countries (58% of all austerity countries). Moreover, theft, fraud and corruption are creeping back, and again not just in the austerity countries of the OECD's member states.[47] The public sector in Africa is witnessing a similar decline in values such as honesty, integrity, impartiality and fairness: 'these declining values have encouraged inefficiency and misappropriation of public funds'.[48]

Old is not necessarily beautiful

History is a dynamic force, as each generation re-examines the past from shifting values as well as unearthing new evidence. Old is not necessarily beautiful. The explanation of historical events should be contested and the ensuing debate casts a long and not always constructive shadow, but progress is difficult if these challenges are not resolved. The failed incorporation of north (British) and south (Italian) Somaliland into a united Somalia is an example of how colonial modes of administration continue to influence attempts at post-colonial state-building. The differences in British and Italian rule meant that the administrative structures, organisation and interests of post-colonial elites in Somaliland were different and proved irreconcilable. Following years of civil war, an autonomous Somaliland has been formed (broadly synonymous with British North Somaliland) that has re-established British administrative mechanisms and paired these with resilient local traditions such as a Council of Elders (*Guurti*).

---

[47] Revelations as part of the recent Wikileaks and FIFA scandals showed that governments and representatives of several OECD countries to be involved in corrupt activities.

[48] Ongaga, C.K. and Nkirina, S. 2017. The Influence of Employee Values on Project Success Rate in the Kenyan Public Sector Organizations: Lessons from Kenya Civil Aviation Authority. *International Journal of Entrepreneurship and Project Management*, 2(3), 14–27.

Part C
Rethinking Public Service

Chapter 10

From Lagash to Liberia

When President Ellen Johnson Sirleaf took office in January 2006, Liberia was one of the poorest nations in the world. Its economy had collapsed. Fourteen years of a bloody civil war had destroyed the country's physical infrastructure and the health-care system. The civil service had collapsed. Bloated by patronage and neglect, only poorly qualified staff remained on the government payroll. Most educated Liberians had fled abroad, and younger people who remained had missed out on regular schooling.

Sirleaf recognised that a modern public service was essential to promote economic growth and improvement in living standards. The country also needed qualified staff quickly. Lack of training and experience threatened the president's ability to translate plans into action. But paralysis threatened to trigger popular discontent and might even reignite conflict.

The challenge, therefore, was how to recruit suitably skilled people for top leadership positions and build capacity in the middle and lower ranks. Fast action was crucial, but risked increasing levels of inequality and suspicion if not managed carefully. The president persuaded three distinguished Liberians to help her attract and develop talent. Minister of Finance Antoinette Sayeh was the first to arrive, followed by C. William Allen, who became director general of the Civil Service Agency, and Harold Monger, who led the Liberia Institute of Public Administration. During the next five years, that team recruited more than 200 highly skilled professionals, trained over 1000 civil servants, and made government a more attractive place to work.

Substantial gaps remained. The Young Professionals Programme, based on the World Bank scheme with the same name with which Sirleaf was familiar from her time working there, has been recruiting talented Liberians into the civil service. Since 2010, the program me has placed 120 young leaders into 15 ministries and 10 agencies. Mentored by senior public servants, the recruits are provided with the training, skills and capacity to eventually become leaders of change. The focus of the scheme is on basic skills like how to effectively run a meeting, take notes, public speaking, as well as negotiation, leadership, managing stress in the office and how to communicate better. A Princeton University evaluation concluded that the program 'has been hugely successful in achieving its mission', of getting motivated able young people into public service.[1] They have helped to streamline government operations: one recruit, placed in the Ministry of Foreign Affairs, reduced the time it took to process a passport from about one month to three days. The Emerging Public Leaders scheme is now seeking to replicate the idea across Africa of forging a new network of highly trained young public sector leaders.[2]

An effective state depends on credible political leadership, which in turn relies on a motivated, merit-based, innovative and adaptive public administration to address the challenges facing the common interest. Yet almost everywhere, governments come to power on a mandate of reforming form not function. As a result, too many countries have witnessed a seemingly endless parade of more laws and regulations, revised structures and new systems that alter the technical form of public administration and governance generally, without addressing the deep-seated functional problems.

Politicians are rarely interested in defending public service. Self-promotion and self-interest lies in the contemporary 'cult' of denigrating the public sector on the right and, on the left, defending outdated ways of working. As one confused public sector employee put it: 'I know what my job is and I want to do it as well as I can. Indeed I would love my work if I could get one day's peace to get on with it. But I am beset at every turn by unintelligible, time wasting and fruitless management initiatives,

---

[1] Cited in Chalaby, O. 2017. *How Civil Service Reform Could Be the Secret to Africa's Development*. Apolitical Group.
[2] https://www.emergingpublicleaders.org/.

constant change, ill-judged targets, wrong-headed "commercial" exemplars and continuous and misguided restructuring. I have to watch as, instead of my "customers" (actually patients, pupils, taxpayers) getting a better deal from me, the only beneficiaries seem to be those who can lobby for special treatment'.[3]

International development agencies for decades laboured conscientiously in the field of 'capacity building' and 'technical co-operation', hiring northern experts to offer 'best practice' solutions to southern problems. But about 20 years ago the observant started to wonder why they had so little to show for their efforts. The realisation dawned that 'institutions matter'. About a decade on, however, little had changed, and with varying degrees of reluctance the uncomfortable truth was admitted: 'politics matter'. Now, with 'thinking and working politically struggling to show impact, a further insight is emerging: that 'public administration matters' — not but the old 'capacity development' but from a politically informed, institutional perspective. Getting to this point has been a painful journey of frustration and disillusion.

But failure is not predetermined. Countries where the interface between the political leadership and the administrative leadership works well, ensuring that political leaders and top officials are aligned in vision and its implementation, are more than likely to achieve success. There is no 'best practice', no toolkit of silver bullets and easy answers. Form does not equal function; informal 'rules of the game' may be just as important, if not more so, as any legislation passed or regulation approved.

Pride, Prestige and Professionalism

The Chinese philosopher Mencius argued for a natural order that elevated the status of the public official over ordinary citizens:

> There are those who use their minds and there are those who use their muscles. The former rule; the latter are ruled. Those who rule are supported by those who are ruled. This is a principle accepted by the whole world.

---

[3] Manson, J. 2012. *Public Service on the Brink*. London.

In Europe, too, the state has often been compared to the human body. The 'body politic' needs a head to plan and structure its thoughts through 'policy'; and it needs limbs to translate its ideas into action.

The origins of modern bureaucracies and the emerging civil service was to establish a monopoly of public authority. The early civil services in pre-modern Europe evolved from royal households and were closely associated with the universal church yet facilitated the growth of nation states. The civil service evolved gradually in tandem with their political development. The requirements of state and nation-building necessitated the subordination of the periphery to the centre and the predictability of the rules and bureaucratic expression of the state.

In the Middle Ages, states were the private property of kings and barons unashamedly run in their own interests. The Domesday Book of 1086, following the Norman Conquest of England, was a rare example of a pre-modern state attempt to make a society legible, to map out the wealth of the country. Reform of the administration of the royal household sought to make it more effective and efficient, but not equitable. God had created the 'great chain of being', placed the monarch at the top of this divinely approved hierarchy. The vast majority of the 'non-elite' had to wait their reward in Heaven for putting up with this 'natural order'.

The 'divine right' of kings was difficult to dispute; but the views of God needed to be interpreted. When the wealth and privileges of the Church attracted monarchical greed, the Church struck back by discovering the king's 'two bodies': the corrupt corporeal and the divine ethereal. When the monarch tried to control or tax the Church, this was a sign that the former had overwhelmed the latter: the divine legitimacy of the monarch was not permanent.

To even the playing field, kings started to claim two other forms of legitimacy: through justice and from the will of the people, in Parliaments and through the Guilds of craftsmen and merchants in towns. Through this roller-coaster of state formation, the small band of public officials played a critical part. When a king became unpopular, his top official was a convenient scapegoat: the 'good' king had been misled by 'evil' courtiers. A swift execution and abandonment of the policy usually rectified the problem.

But occasionally the king had no 'exit strategy'. Then the king had to go: Charles I or Louis XVI. Someone had to carry the can unless, like

Stalin, terror and a ruthless secret police could intimidate everyone. A 'permanent revolution' and regular executions of any possible centre of resistance (Erich Röhm in 1934 'Night of the Long Knives'; the assassination of Trotsky in Mexico; the 'Cultural Revolution') allowed Stalin and Mao Tse-tung to die in their beds.

The establishment of a functioning civil service is neither a linear nor harmonious process. In Europe, the development of a civil service has been associated with the penetration of peripheral areas, the standardisation of physical and psychological space and the accommodation of competing sources of power. A functioning civil service is considered central to the effectiveness of the state, influencing its ability to develop policy, deliver services and manage tensions.

The international community's effort to build functioning states has often involved the expansion of central government control and the development of bureaucracies that aim to replicate European models. The literature suggests a growing consensus that effective civil service and public sector reform programmes need to move away from this practice towards 'best fit'. Programmes need to be informed by a better understanding of the complex socio-economic and political realities of the countries in which they are taking place.[4] Despite increasing focus on specificity of context, many analyses fail to pay sufficient attention to colonial legacies and the socio-historical heritage of administrative structures.

The quality of government bureaucracy

Government bureaucracy has a huge influence on the well-being of citizens. In the world's better run countries, their populations are healthier, wealthier and better educated. Life expectancy is best in countries with limited natural resources like Japan (83.7 years), followed by Singapore and Iceland.[5] The richest countries by PPP per capita in 2016[6] besides oil

---

[4] Blum, J., Manning, N. and Srivastava, V. 2012. *Public Sector Management Reform: Toward a Problem-Solving Approach*. Economic Premise, vol. 100. Washington, DC: World Bank, .
[5] WHO, 2016 figures https://data.worldbank.org/indicator/SP.DYN.LE00.IN?year_high_desc=true.
[6] World Bank, 2015 figures. https://data.worldbank.org/indicator/NY.GDP.PCAP.PP.CD.

exporters like Qatar ($141,543) and Brunei ($78,369) were Luxembourg ($101,926), Singapore ($85,382), Ireland ($65,144), Norway ($61,197) and Switzerland ($61,086). The 2016 Pisa scores for reading and maths attainment by 15-year-old children are dominated by East Asia (China, Singapore, Japan, South Korea, Taiwan and Vietnam) but also Finland, Ireland, Canada and Poland. Public administration matters. But does better public administration create healthier, wealthier and more educated wiser people, or do healthier, wealthier and wiser people produce better public officials? Or perhaps all good things go together? One famous suggestion was that Northern Europe was the home of Protestant religious faith, which fostered entrepreneurship, literacy and learning. Yet, the top countries by GDP PPP (excluding oil exporters) include Ireland and Luxembourg, predominantly Roman Catholic (78% and 67%, respectively), Switzerland, with a long history of deep divide between Protestantism and Catholicism, and Singapore, which is 33% Buddhist, 18% atheist, 14% Muslim, 12% Protestant, 11% Taoist, 6% Catholic, 5% Hindu and 0.7% Zoroastrian.[7]

Societal values might nevertheless count for quality of public administration, such as the importance attached to education in its own right. Public administration has done much to shape those values, including by setting national exam standards in China.

The Thatcher/Reagan Era

As late as 1980, the British civil servants could still be characterised as the country's 'Ruling Class'. But by then the Thatcher revolution in government had begun, ushering in perhaps the sharpest reversal in the reputation of public officials ever seen in peacetime.[8]

For the last 35 years, the status and standing of government officials at all levels of seniority has been under direct attack. The election of Margaret Thatcher in 1979 as Prime Minister in Britain and of Ronald

---

[7] Government of Singapore. 2017. Available online: https://www.singstat.gov.sg/publications/publications-and-papers/cop2010/census10_stat_release1.
[8] In wartime, governments have suffered disastrous defeats triggering collapse, such as the February and October Revolutions of 1917 in Russia.

Reagan in 1981 as President of the United States catalysed a profound transformation in attitudes to government and its bureaucracy. Their time in office marked the end of the era of two world wars and the 'New Deal' in the United States during the first half of the 20th century. That period forged a liberal consensus around a welfare state and government-managed mixed economy.

By 1980, that consensus had broken down. Thatcher and Reagan had sought to redress the then perceived challenge of an apparently remorseless growth in an unproductive public sector. The 40th President of the United States had declared in his inauguration address on 20 January 1981:

> government is not the solution to our problem; government is the problem ... it's not my intention to do away with government. It is rather to make it work — work with us, not over us; to stand by our side, not ride on our back. Government can and must provide opportunity, not smother it; foster productivity, not stifle it. ... It is no coincidence that our present troubles parallel and are proportionate to the intervention and intrusion in our lives that result from unnecessary and excessive growth of government. It is time for us to realize that we're too great a nation to limit ourselves to small dreams. We're not, as some would have us believe, doomed to an inevitable decline. I do not believe in a fate that will fall on us no matter what we do. I do believe in a fate that will fall on us if we do nothing. So, with all the creative energy at our command, let us begin an era of national renewal. Let us renew our determination, our courage, and our strength. And let us renew our faith and our hope.[9]

From this messianic tone, the language, at least in English, of public service reform rapidly became revolutionary. Government would be 're-invented' and transformed', and more recently would also 'work better and cost less'. Other developments merged into this. Pragmatic efforts notably championed by New Zealand to foster greater efficiency in government created the reform label of the 1980s — New Public Management. The end of the Cold War in the dramatic years from the fall of the Berlin Wall in 1989 to the collapse of the Soviet Union in 1991 stimulated the

---

[9] Reagan, R. 1981. *Inauguration Speech*. Washington.

call by the international community for 'Good Governance' in developing countries, including in the field of public administration.

In the United Kingdom, government expenditure rose from 13% of GDP in 1910 to about 26% in the inter-War years to 40% in 1955, where it has remained, seemingly as a baseline through subsequent political battles: 48% in 1980, reined back to 40% after a decade of Thatcherism by 1988, reaching a post-War low of 36% in 2000, reverting to 41% in 2007, back up to 48% in 2010 during the Banking Crisis, then falling to 42% by 2016.[10]

But the civil service reforms of the last 30 years often proved destructive. A culture of covert bullying was the result of institutionalising 'leadership' that established a senior civil service and failed to bolster genuine employee participation in planning, consolidating managerial power and employees' subordination while pretending to encourage consultation on policies that were already decided. 'Right-sizing' (that is, cutting back) the public sector in many countries led to understaffing, a lack of resources for front line services, and limited middle management capacity.[11]

Sensible politics and good public administration

Evidence-based policymaking is a modern mantra, but political considerations will almost always trump facts ('policy-based evidence-making'). Decisions depend on what is politically feasible.

It is salutary to note that too many countries failed to the right mix of sensible politics and good public administration. Some states like Liberia collapsed into terrible civil wars. But many became resolute under-achievers.

One such is Malawi. The post-independence collapse in perceived legitimacy across Africa was reflected in tax evasion: in Malawi, for

---

[10] Hood and Dixon, *op. cit.*, p. 123.
[11] Crook, R. C. 2010. Rethinking civil service reform in Africa: 'islands of effectiveness' and organisational commitment. *Commonwealth and Comparative Politics, 48*, 37–54; Olowu, D. 2010. Civil Service Pay Reforms in Africa. *International Review of Administrative Sciences, 76*(4), 632–652.

example, tax evasion increased sevenfold between 1972 and 1990.[12] There is a strong association between effective governance and development, and between effective taxation and good governance.[13] *Revenue is the chief preoccupation of the state. Nay more, it is the state.*[14]

Making tax systems efficient, effective and equitable is difficult everywhere, in particular in countries with weak political institutions, widespread corruption and poor administrative capacities. Too often this process of 'tax as state-building' does not happen: in many developing countries the tax base remains dangerously narrow, and its administration overly ineffectual or coercive. Different histories of taxation matter: in Western Europe taxes developed as a consequence of war and national mobilisation, whereas in many developing countries central taxes began as a colonial imposition.[15] This has an important long-term influence on how people view the legitimacy of taxation and the state. Taxes both fund public goods and help to entrench political authority.[16] The political settlement for 'elites to pay taxes' is weak in many developing countries — too many politically powerful people are unwilling to pay a fair share of the tax burden to

---

[12] As a percentage of actual total tax revenue and of potential tax revenue, tax evasion declined between 1972 and 1974, thereafter rose rapidly and was about 60% of actual tax revenue and 37% of potential tax revenue in 1990, representing sevenfold and fourfold increases, respectively. Chipeta, C. 2002. The Second Economy and Tax Yield in Malawi. *African Economic Research Consortium.*

[13] See, for example, Davis, K. and Trebilcock, M. 2008. The Relationship Between Law and Development: Optimists versus Sceptics. *American Journal of Public Law*, 56; Rodrik, D., Subramanian, A. and Trebbi, F. 2002. *Institutions Rule: The Primacy of Institutions over Geography and Integration in Economic Development. Journal of Economic Growth*, 9(2), 131–165; Haber, S., Razo, A. and Maurer, N. 2003. *The Politics of Property Rights: Political Instability, Credible Commitments, and Economic Growth in Mexico, 1876–1929*. New York: Cambridge University Press; Sancak, C. and Jaramillo, L. 2007. *Growth in the Dominican Republic and Haiti: Why Has the Grass Been Greener on One Side of Hispaniola*. IMF Working Paper No. 07/63.

[14] Edmund Burke quoted in O'Brien, P. 2001. *Fiscal Exceptionalism: Great Britain and Its European Rivals. LSE Paper* 65/01, p. 21.

[15] Examples include the Hut Tax war in Sierra Leone in 1898.

[16] Besley, T. and Persson, T. 2007. *The Origins of State Capacity: Property Rights, Taxation, and Politics*. CEPR; DFID, State-building.

improve the effectiveness of the state.[17] As a result, there is little political will to address huge inequalities by taxing easily identified assets such as property. In Kenya, for instance, the 'tax gap' of uncollected potential tax revenues by the last year of the Moi presidency in 2001 had reached at least 35%, suggesting significant and increasing levels of tax evasion as taxpayer faith in the regime collapsed.[18] This lack of 'fiscal legitimacy' exacerbates the doubts of ordinary citizens about whether governments will spend tax revenues wisely. This can lead to an excessive use of coercion to raise tax, further alienating citizens from an already fragile state.[19]

'What has brought us here cannot lead us further'

The shift to the 21st-century 'Creative State' will prove a radical transformation. It requires better citizens, more efficient but also more responsible business, and government that does not only impose but can also empathise and empower. Some countries are starting to recognise the depth of the challenge. This is due not least, since the 2008 global financial crisis, to the 'disconnect' around 'reform' being a euphemism for cuts, at a time when the job of a civil servant is becoming more complex.

A growing skill will be the capacity to imagine different futures in the years ahead as the important challenges become more complex, multifaceted and long term, with no simple causes nor single solutions. A more effective Public Service can foster prosperity and political stability, but only with a renewed sense of employee well-being and contentment. A deep legacy of scepticism, cynicism and tokenism after decades of contempt, cuts and 'right-sizing' must be overcome if the organisational culture of public service is to become what it needs to be: outward-looking, creative and citizen-centric.

---

[17] Stotsky, J. and A WoldeMariam. 1997. *Tax Effort in Sub-Saharan Africa.* IMF WP/97/101. Washington, DC.

[18] Kenya Institute of Public Policy Research and Analysis. 2004. Tax Compliance Study. Tax Policy Unit, Macroeconomics Division, Nairobi. The Kenyan Revenue Authority seemed to believe it was higher, over 40% — see www.revenue.go.ke/speeches/cgspeech-tax100304.html.

[19] Juul, K. 2006. Decentralization, Local Taxation and Citizenship in Senegal. *Development and Change, 37*(4), 821–846.

The incremental, learning by doing experimental approach is crushed by over-ambitious blueprints and 'Strategic Frameworks'. Officials themselves begin to distrust government. Their political masters fall back on the easy accusation that the public service is part of the problem.

Instead, leaders now need to explain how 'the bureaucracy' is human too, and a key component of the answer to state effectiveness in the 21st century. This task must include recognising that ill-informed contempt for the efforts of the departments of government and unfounded eulogy of the private sector does not foster innovation. The organic process of progress must escape the rigidly hierarchical 'rational' Weberian, yet performance pay incentivises caution to achieve fixed objectives. Cuts over the last decade in many countries have created a dearth in public service of young people with exactly the tech-savvy skills now needed.

Older people can offer leadership — the key to everything but, if ill-defined, the answer to nothing. Schools of government were abolished only to be re-established. In the United Kingdom, the Civil Service College at Sunningdale Park in Berkshire, rebranded as the National School of Government, was closed in 2012 as part of the austerity cuts, now a Leadership Academy has been established.

Decentralisation and recentralisation similarly go round in circles. History shows how efforts to bring government closer to citizens then need to overcome local capture. In Estonia, for example, decentralisation was necessary to overcome the legacy of 50 years of Soviet occupation under the ex-USSR, but the post-independence euphoria of freedom was followed by the necessary correction of re-centralisation to address the fragmentation of state authority that was making it difficult to implement digitalisation, creativity and whole of government coordination.

Public sector reform is too often pursued as solely about 'capacity building', not about the roots of public authority and perceived legitimacy of the state actually rest. Public sector reform is, at heart, not a technical challenge but a political one: is the country's leadership really determined to make the public service effective? Or do vested interests profit from its weakness, such as to conniving in tax evasion or illicit capital flows benefiting the rich and powerful? Politics largely determines the nature of the civil service, and civil service reforms cannot succeed in isolation.

Of course, public sector reforms can and do work: to take one example, Ireland's austerity measures from 2008 up to 2012 delivered significant productivity improvements. In the prison service there, staff numbers were reduced by 8%, even while the average number of prisoners in custody increased by 23%. In the Revenue, staff numbers were cut by 13%, while the number of audit and assurance checks carried out increased by 55%. In the health sector, spend on acute hospitals was reduced by 11% yet operations were 10% higher and the cost per discharge was 20% lower. In higher education, a 14.9% increase in students occurred even while staff numbers were reduced by 7.3%.[20]

The Big Business of Selling Reform

No single determinant can provide an adequate explanation of the pattern of history, human actions and random chance. The arrogance and ignorance of 'solutions' for improving the executive arm of government all too often become painfully apparent, in retrospect. But by then a new incumbent is peddling a new 'quick fix'.

Lack of modesty is one of the dangers of the English-speaking world. It is all too easy to take itself too seriously due to linguistic dominance and the lack of competition. UK ministers and former senior officials have come to see a career after government in advising others on how to reform — despite the fact that so little reform in the United Kingdom has been effective.

The worldwide interest in reform in the United Kingdom and New Zealand has been facilitated by the English language. It is hard to market internationally ideas in other languages, even though the results in, for example, Finland and Denmark on prosperity, health, educational achievement and general citizen satisfaction with life are all notably better than the United Kingdom and somewhat better than in New Zealand.

The public sector practices of big US and UK consultancies have flourished selling support and advice on how to copy these and other much advertised reforms. In the urgent quest for quick fixes, public

---

[20] Roche, W., O'Connell, P. J. and Prothero, A. (eds.). 2017. *Austerity and Recovery in Ireland: Europe's Poster Child and the Great Recession*. Oxford University Press.

service reform has become a very large business. In Europe alone, each year governments spend around €30 billion on consulting services to improve public sector performance,[21] while donor governments spend about $4 billion on improving government performance in lower income countries.[22] This is an enormous worldwide investment in areas as diverse as civil servant pay policy and IT systems for procurement. All offer 'international best practice'; few are grounded in evidence that they work in a different context, but are often driven by strong ideals over promoting accountability, competition and transparency. These principles are all worthy in their own right, but should not be confused with solutions.

Global institutions like the World Bank as well as niche consultancies can construct frameworks and guidance notes. High-profile veterans of supposedly successful reforms like Michael Barber find a second career as senior advisers for practical help. The Prime Minister's Delivery Unit in the United Kingdom developed, at taxpayers' cost, tools, methods and way of working that were subsequently marketed globally without self-doubt, and much copied but with little evaluation of lasting impact.

Demand is heightened further by conditionality. That is the practice of major aid donors like the United States or the United Kingdom, and the international financial institutions like the IMF to require governments to adopt elements of these reforms as part of the overall package of their financial or political support.

In this febrile atmosphere, there is little incentive to question whether much touted reforms really worked, or to reflect on the poorly understood pitfalls of implanting reforms borrowed from elsewhere. Few people seem to ask what might usefully be learnt from more modest countries like Finland or Denmark, which have quietly achieved better results in making

---

[21] Poór, J., Milovecz Á. and Király, Á. 2012. Survey of the European Management Consultancy. 2011/2012. Research Center on Management and Human Resource Management, University of Pécs, Pecs, Hungary. The UK National Audit Office found that in 2006–2007 the UK public sector spent approximately £2.8 billion on management consultants.

[22] Official development assistance disbursements for 2012 were: 'Public sector policy and adm. Management' $2.6bn; 'Public finance management' $0.9bn; 'Decentralisation and support to subnational govt'. $0.6bn; 'Anti-corruption organisations and institutions' $.2 bn. DAC, OECD, Paris, 2014.

their populations healthier, wealthier, better educated and more contented. This is particularly pertinent when research shows that the United Kingdom may be good at policy, yet poor on results. Furthermore, successive reform efforts have had a patchy record.

> ... the most ambitious reform blueprints are no more than partially adopted, let alone implemented... The majority of individual reforms have limped on, tailed off, or been discarded.[23]

Despite the popularity of grand reforms that can be launched with fanfare by prime ministers and their senior officials when in office and marketed when in retirement, the reality of the process of reforming any civil service is an incremental and chaotic agglomeration of spasmodic changes:

> Typically there is no single design or designer... just lots of localised attempts at partial design cutting across one another. It is easy to exaggerate the degree of intentionality in many reforms.[24]
>
> Talk of '[reform] strategy' can be seen as an idealization or post hoc rationalisation of a set of processes that tend to be partial, reactive, and of unstable priority.[25]

Much of the effort to help improve the effectiveness of governments and reform public services has had limited impact:

> Despite vast amounts of support from the international assistance community, increased resourcing and improved policies and/or formal systems... many states and governments across the developing world have remained unable to provide adequately for the well-being of their populations at large.[26]

---

[23] Panchamia, N. and Thomas, P. 2014. *Civil Service Reform in the Real World*, Institute for Government, London, p. 57.
[24] Goodin, R. 1996. *The Theory of Institutional Design*. New York: Cambridge University Press, p. 28 cited in P&B.
[25] Pollitt, C. and Bouckaert, G. 2004. *Public Management Reform: A Comparative Analysis*. Oxford University Press. p. 196.
[26] Rocha Menocal, A. 2014. *Getting Real about Politics: From Thinking Politically to Working Differently*. London: Overseas Development Institute, p. 2.

Three Harvard professors provide a compelling summary[27]:

> The fact that the 'development community' is five decades into supporting the building of state capability and that there has been so little progress in so many places (obvious spectacular successes like South Korea notwithstanding) suggests the generic 'theory of change' on which development initiatives for building state capability are based is deeply flawed. ...reform dynamics are often characterized by the tendency to introduce reforms that enhance an entity's external legitimacy and support, even when they do not demonstrably improve performance. ...governments constantly adopt 'reforms' to ensure ongoing flows of external financing and legitimacy yet never actually improve. Countries and development partners get trapped in a cycle of reforms that fail to enhance capability (indeed, may exacerbate pre-existing constraints).

All that said, progress in the public sector pops up in odd places. One example is the Phnom Penh Water Supply Authority (PPWSA) in Cambodia. In the last decade it has quietly built steady success. Despite the fraught authoritarian regime, new management co-opted its hardworking staff, encouraged the hitherto disengaged employees and found ways to sack the corrupt. It achieved this by aligning with local politics of serving poor, unconnected households, tackling water vendors who were stealing water from the mains supply pipes at night, and raising revenues by installing meters and implementing a volume metric tariff. The World Bank and Asian Development Bank made tariff reform a conditionality for help.

Focusing on fairness in serving poor households through a petition 'signed' by 10,000 thumbprints as signatures from the illiterate poor convinced parliament and the prime minister to adopt tariff reforms. Increased revenues allowed the PPWSA to increase salaries for hardworking staff and productivity rose as they could afford to stay in their jobs and work to expand legal connections to mains supplies. This set in motion a virtuous cycle. More connections led to more revenues and more revenues led

---

[27] Andrews, M., Pritchett, L. and Woolcock, M. 2012. *Escaping Capability Traps through Problem-driven Iterative Adaptation (PDIA)*. Working Paper 299. Washington, DC: Center for Global Development, pp. 1–3.

to better services, and higher customer satisfaction, so customers readily paid their water bills. Leakage rates fell to lower than those in New York. In March 2012, the PPWSA sold 13.5% of its equity to private investors, the first stock to be listed on the Cambodia Security Exchange. In 2014, the PPWSA had revenues of about US$39 million and net profit was about US$11 million. Its managers did not take to touring the world touting their achievements. They just got on with plugging away at improving service.

The consequences of colonialism, decolonisation and state formation have often resulted in a weak sense of political community or national identity, weak state legitimacy, a dominant political elite and exclusion of other groups, language barriers, political divisions and a lack of broadly based interest groups that could challenge the private use of public power. What form independence should take and the role of public service required a 'political settlement' between power elites. In many countries like in India, the public service has played a key role in generating statehood. Since even before independence, IAS officers, for example, have unified central and state government, selected by Delhi but assigned to a state cadre. Their incentives are structured in such a way that while they represent state interests, they maintain a sense of commitment to Delhi. But elsewhere, decolonisation often involved the adoption of the forms if not always the functions of 'modern' European models of governance. The transplantation of European state institutions was often not accompanied by the development of the economic, political, social and cultural structures and capacities that had provided the basis for a functioning political order in Europe. So, when, in the decades following WWII a host of independent states claiming to be 'nation states' came into being, the political elites of the new states and the international community conflated declarations of independence with state formation. Those new states that had no history of pre-colonial unitary rule or tradition of national identification, and no common language and culture, struggled, especially if they had been ruled in an authoritarian manner with little preparation for sustainable statehood. 'Traditional' leaders were often discredited in the post-independence era because they had been co-opted to prop up colonial rule. Post-colonial political elites attempted to portray them as anachronistic and reactionary forces of the past. The re-emergence of 'traditional' elites in some post-colonial countries is indicative of their continued influence in the absence of a robust centre.

Meritocratic recruitment is closely related to bureaucratic quality.[28] Too often, however, the civil service is staffed with political hangers-on, hired for loyalty rather than merit. Competent civil servants risk being fired when a new minister or president comes in. Typically, where civil services lack clear career structures, governments have tended to respond to a dysfunctional bureaucracy by creating islands of excellence, such as central banks and finance ministries.

More recently, countries such as Chile and Peru have improved the management of public service. Civil servants are far more likely to have a university degree than in the past. Some countries have tried to go beyond such piecemeal improvements to create an integrated professional civil service, based on merit, evaluations and rewards for performance. This replaces a muddle of different contracts. But government always need strong political will and the money to implement it.

Unacknowledged crisis

An unacknowledged crisis lurks at the heart of government. It arises from the mismatch that now exists between universal aspirations for excellence in public service policies and delivery of services, and the reality in many countries of an increasingly alienated public sector workforce.

Citizens' expectations of government are rising, while the resources to fund the public sector are shrinking — the ratio of general government debt to gross domestic product for member states of the OECD now exceeds 100%. Political ambitions for more targeted public services delivery and the need to solve more complex policy problems are challenged by unsustainable debt burdens and shrinking budgets.

These aspirations also face three additional critical issues in public service. First, citizens' perceptions of ethics in public administration

---

[28] Mauro, P. 1995. Corruption and Growth. *The Quarterly Journal of Economics, 110(3)*, 681–712; Knack, S. and Keefer, P. 1995. Institutions and Economic Performance: Cross-country Tests Using Alternative Institutional Measures. *Economics & Politics, 7*, 207–227; Rauch and Evans, *op. cit.*, pp. 49–71.

shape satisfaction with services, trust in governmental institutions, and the credibility of politics and political leadership.[29] So maintaining the highest standards of ethics in public service is essential.

Second, those high levels of probity require excellent staff morale and strong intrinsic motivation. Corruption flourishes when the public ethos, the intrinsic commitment of public officials to serve the public interest, is undermined. In many countries the commitment to an apolitical civil service responsive to the government of the day has faded. Third, 'tax morale' — the inherent willingness of citizens to pay taxes — is influenced by taxpayers' perceptions not just of the quality of public services received, but also the morale and ethics of the officials delivering them.[30]

Governments must find ways to address the sharp decline in the motivation of the very public service officials expected to deliver results in the difficult circumstances prevailing today. Solutions will not be easy — but a few ideas are emerging.

In the United States, the Office of Personnel Management's Federal Employee Viewpoint Survey for 2013[31] shows all too clearly that federal government employees, the very people in the world's most influential country who address the extraordinary mix of macroeconomic uncertainty, rapid social change and technological innovation, are deeply alienated and thoroughly demoralised. In the United Kingdom, the annual Civil Service People Survey[32] year after year reveals serious morale problems. Only 40% of British officials in 2013 felt motivated in their job, and only 43% inspired to do their best. These disastrous results are however buried

---

[29] Blind: Blind, P. K. 2006. *Building Trust in Government in the Twenty-First Century: Review of Literature and Emerging Issues*. For 7th Global Forum on Reinventing Government Building Trust in Government 26–29 June 2007, Vienna, Austria. Available online: http://unpan1.un.org/intradoc/groups/public/documents/un/unpan025062.pdf.
[30] OECD. 2013. *What Drives Tax Morale?* Paris: OECD.
[31] US Office of Personnel Management. 2013. *Federal Employee Viewpoint Survey: Employees Influencing Change*. http://www.fedview.opm.gov/2013/Reports/.
[32] UK Civil Service, Civil Service People Survey. 2013. UK Civil Service website. http://www.civilservice.gov.uk/about/improving/employee-engagement-in-the-civil-service/people-survey-2013.

away in the Report that seeks to pretend all is well, rather than confront the problem.

Many developing countries face similar trends. In Africa, for example, public service reforms focused on improving the delivery of services are still premised on the assumption that services can be improved without improving the image, morale and motivation of personnel in the public service.

There are some exceptions to the global picture of despondency. High job satisfaction among government employees both at the frontline of delivering public services, and in policy formulation, has survived in a few countries, like Singapore, that have retained the commitment to the social status, motivation and morale, of their public service. Yet it has also been suggested that public sector employees become more dissatisfied at work than their private sector counterparts because the public good aims turn out to be less altruistic and more ambiguous.[33]

Elsewhere, however, efforts at improving performance, innovation and results are in jeopardy from a dispirited public sector. Why has this occurred? The origin of widespread demotivation is that, for over a generation, the intrinsic motivation of public officials — to serve the public good — and the sense of self-worth in public sector jobs have been in decline. Politicians and the media since the 1980s have often emphasised the supposed innate superiority of the efficiency and effectiveness of the private sector[34] and discounted the importance of the role of the public service in addressing equity and defending public good and national interest.

The strongest motivation at work is 'self-actualisation' — the apex of Maslow's hierarchy of needs, the intrinsic satisfaction of an important and difficult job well done. In public services this is reinforced by the sense of national purpose and public good, epitomised by the highly respected intrinsic motivation of the armed forces in countries like the United States. Yet all too often over the last 30 years public service intrinsic motivation has been undermined.

---

[33] Sørensen, P. 2014. *Reforming Public Service Provision: What Have We Learned?* Background paper at Venice International University. p. 10.
[34] For example, Hsu, J. 2010. *The Relative Efficiency of Public and Private Service Delivery.* WHO's World Health Report. Background Paper 39.

Chapter 11

Plumbers or Psychotherapists?

In the English language, institutions and organisations are 'built'. The verb subtly implies a physical, bricks-and-mortar imagery when we talk about building up the civil service and its capacities. In the building trade, the most appropriate analogy is probably plumbing. When the pipes are properly installed and the taps fitted, water flows easily and efficiently around the structure without leaks or wastage. There is usually a 'best practice', the optimal way to position the pipes in the most cost-effective manner. Reform, then, means an outsider being hired, the plumber, to come with a toolkit for finding, often from overseas, ways to adjust the pipes and taps to ensure the 'best practice' is applied.

But if we abandon the tyranny of the construction metaphor, institutions and organisations of the public service, rather than being built, simply exist. They age and evolve by learning from experience. People are not 'machines'. Public institutions are not engineered but are organic — the product of accretions over years, decades and centuries.

Reform then equates to psychotherapy. It is a largely internal process for the patient (i.e. the single ministry or entire public service). It can certainly be assisted and facilitated by the outside expertise of psychologists or psychiatrists or psychotherapists. Each of these professionals can in a different way, guide the patient. A prescription for anti-depressants may help alleviate the symptoms. But to tackle the deep root causes, only the patient can stare down her inner demons. The technical fixes, the mechanistic solutions of 'plumbing', also matter — but only when all concerned have started to come to terms with their inner demons.

Countries around the world face similar challenges from globalisation. Yet, contrary to expectation, this is not resulting in ever-growing uniformity of form and commonality in function among public administrations tackling similar challenges. Rather, although public service is evolving fast everywhere, the outcome is not convergence, but increasing divergence — just as in the 19th century between the then industrialising world. Now, in the developed world, austerity and innovation are driving change, while in developing countries, population growth and rising citizen expectations are reshaping the 'social contract'.

The historic and philosophical differences shaping the effective behaviours and actions of public bureaucracy in different countries with different traditions and cultures are, however, poorly understood. As the flattery of 'isomorphic mimicry'[1] from 'international best practice' gives way to more home-grown 'best fit' experimentation, public service is becoming ever more diverse and divergent among the OECD member states, between the developed and developing world, and within developing countries.

Public service is the product of underlying social forces and history. Reforms that focus on technical or managerial issues while ignoring historical heritage, invariably fail. That also and equally applies to international development, yet development theory and practice remains deeply — and worryingly — ahistorical.

This focus on historical parallels leads to bigger questions, while appreciating the transformative developments as 'big data' and artificial intelligence.

The immediate purpose is to help governments plan for skills and structures that they will need to put in place to make the state fit for purpose in the coming decades.

---

[1] Meaning building organisations in weak states to appear *de jure* to resemble those found in effective states, but without the *de facto* capability of functioning properly or at all: Pritchett, L., Woolcock, M. and Andrews, M. 2010. *Capability Traps? The Mechanisms of Persistent Implementation Failure*. Center for Global Development. Working Paper No. 234. Washington, DC.

There is no 'one-size-fits-all' approach. Countries must determine their own priorities and approaches in response to their unique circumstances, seeking new ways to address complex challenges and trade-offs amidst uncertainty.

As the United Nations Development Programme (UNDP) Strategic Plan for 2018 states: 'The enormity and the rapid pace of change necessitate decisive and coherent action on many fronts, with multiple actors and across different levels. Integrated responses need to be coherent not merely across sectors, but also co-ordinated across levels (international, national, subnational and local)'.

Bureaucracy, Government and the State

Bureaucracy is the expression of the public authority and legitimacy of the state. The rise of bureaucracy is closely linked to the rise of the modern state. The 'state' is a term used to refer to the government and related entities including the military, police, legal system, and the various functions run by the government such as welfare, schools and diplomacy. The foundation of the state is its monopoly over large-scale violence, within a defined territory. But senior bureaucrats can hold a large degree of unaccountable power. Discipline is authoritarian to make officials conform. Whistle-blowers who claim to speak out in the public interest are discredited: 'power tends to corrupt and absolute power corrupts absolutely'.

The challenges facing political and administrative leadership everywhere for identifying emerging strategic opportunities are already daunting and still growing. Public officials will need a new Whole of Government Approach/ multi- and inter-disciplinary mindset, learning not training and new pattern of collaboration to address unexpected consequences of our actions. Action is needed to create 'anti-fragility' or political resilience in which every citizen has a stake in long-term stability, and in which public administration takes a clear focus on stewardship — of society, its institutions and the environment. In this, the objective is well-being, not GDP growth.

To understand public bureaucracy requires unpicking the 'black box' of the state and humanising public bodies. Governance structures the process through which bargaining over the distribution of resources, rights and responsibilities takes place. Key to these bargains is the 'political settlement' around history. That agreement about the past legitimises state power, as well as social norms and bureaucratic capacity about how effectively and equitably power can be enforced. The results determine how commitment and collective action lead to particular policies and convert them into outcomes.

Max Weber feared that bureaucracy would be part of the over-rationalisation, a looming 'iron cage' that could grow too powerful. Only charismatic and powerful politicians could prevent public service becoming a major threat to modern life. The fear that the bureaucracy was vulnerable to tyrannical usurpation did not cross his mind.

Today, challenges to evidence-based reasoning, fair procedure and impartial officialdom from the menace of populist, reckless politicians, turns the 'iron cage' into the building block of some of history's most hard-won rights. Plato looks more prescient: he warned of both the charismatic but irresponsible politicians, and the insouciant, irresponsible officials who serve them, eroding the norms of office on which the values of the rule of law and liberty rest.

Any elite to stay in power needs to control the mechanisms of public authority. One of the most crucial is the bureaucracy. So why do officials work to uphold or subvert the status quo? Such people are, after all, ideally placed to use the rules to do nothing, or even to undermine the government from within. Is it just fear — of a secret police; for their jobs, status and salaries — that keeps them working? To be effective, the civil service needs to recruit on merit, that is, to be able to attract and retain some of the brightest. Such people will be motivated by not just competitive salaries, but some belief in the vision as justification of their work.

It is remarkable and surprising how little is really known about how and why an effective, efficient and equitable civil service develops. Ancient Greece made no sharp distinction between political rulers and bureaucratic officials. They considered anyone in a position of constitutional authority as the holder of an office. Political leadership and elite pressures create incentives, respond to interests and pick up ideas. Yet nothing is clear about the extent to which the East Asian development success is due to the long history of public officialdom in China, Japan and Korea. Trust in government, a disciplined workforce, and an effective interface between political and administrative leaders may all be a direct consequence.

Social contract between bureaucrats and citizens

Humanity flourishes when the state enables, the private sector responds and civil society inspires. In this complex dance, public administration provides the unsung 'important but dull' role of protecting the long-term common good through social responsibility and public duty.[2] Inadequate appreciation of the extraordinary achievements of public administration undoubtedly results from ignorance of its past.

Attitudes to government influence the prestige or contempt, trust in or scepticism with which citizens view public service employees. Differing relations between citizen/taxpayer and the state, including between politicians, the public, public services (meaning central ministries and sub-national equivalents) and the people who are employed, contracted and co-opted to deliver them, derive from ideology and historical experience.

Ideological divides result in a lack of consensus on civil service objectives. If government is regarded as tyranny, then public officials will be perceived as arrogant and wasteful. If government is thought to be meddlesome, its civil service will be inherently officious. Conversely, if government is understood as rational collective action, its public service is a scientific manager, and if the purpose of government is to liberate, then its officials empower.

In the Arab world, the public official still has the aura of 'Effendi', the honorific title for those who work for the common good, not their own interests. In Asia, the importance of government is rarely questioned, and meritocratic civil service exams have been held since 165 BC in China, the 8th century in Korea, the 9th century in Japan and the 13th century in Vietnam. The challenge is to accept humility and be willing to listen to ordinary citizens.

L'Etat, c'est Nous

Louis XIV famously declared *L'Etat, c'est Moi*. On the night of 4 August 1789, the French Revolution abolished ancient taxes and privileges.

---

[2] New Zealand's 2013 Civil Service legislation requires the CEOs of state agencies to steward the inter-generational interests of the country.

The National Constituent Assembly announced the end of feudalism. It abolished the rights of the Second Estate (the nobility), the tithes of the First Estate (the Catholic clergy) and venality of office of the Third Estate. All became equal before the officialdom of the state. Article 7 abolished the sale of offices, and Article 11 declared that all citizens, no matter what class or background, were eligible for any office in civil and military service.

By the end of the 19th century, the patrimonial state had largely disappeared apart from in colonies like the Belgian Congo. The state had become its officials, its values internalised by its employees, who in turn shaped those values by their behaviours.

Patriotism and nationalism became powerful influences, creating belief in a common good and an imagined community. History portrayed a cohesive nation and venerated the state as a source of material prosperity or political unification. The impassive, legal-rational, objective *Bürokratismus,* aloof to be fair and impartial is struggling to become passionate and creative.

Professor Zeger van der Wal of the LKY School of Public Policy, in an important book *The 21st Century Public Manager*, suggests seven growing challenges for public officials: (i) a growing multiplicity of stakeholders; (ii) 'authority turbulence', including concerned, cynical and impatient citizens; (iii) ethical complexities; (iv) long-term, inter-generational objectives; (v) cross-sectoral collaboration; (vi) the new workforce, including older employees; and (vii) innovation, including disruptive technologies. Administrative discretion will be reshaped by the balance between individual rights and collective public goods such as security.[3]

Size matters. In Malaysia, for example, the overall size of the civil service is high compared with international standards. Malaysia's civil service employs 1.6 million people, or about 11% of the labour force. Countries of similar population size and level of development usually have a lower percentage of government employment to population. For example, while high-income non-OECD UAE is at 11.5%, high-income OECD Switzerland on 5.65% and upper-middle-income Costa Rica on 5.53%.

---

[3] van der Wal, Z. 2017. *The 21st Century Public Manager*. Macmillan International Higher Education.

As a result, Malaysia's civil servants-to-population ratio appears to be the highest in the Asia-Pacific. The ratio in 2011 was 4.68% compared to Singapore's 1.4%, Indonesia's 1.79%, South Korea's 1.85% and Thailand's 2.06% — all of which have less than half the ratio in Malaysia. The World Bank Institute Governance indicators paint a somewhat contradictory picture of the resulting quality of public service in Malaysia. Their data show both government effectiveness and regulatory quality being significantly better than the average upper-middle-income country; but government effectiveness seems to have declined over the decade from 2005 to 2015, although regulatory quality marginally improved over the same period.

A new disruptive age of digital public empowerment, big data and artificial intelligence further challenges the human capacity to cope with unprecedented scale of the 'wicked problems' and cognitive dissonance that makes identifying 'unthinkables', then taking action to prevent or pre-empt them even more problematic and unlikely. Existing comfort zones are crumbling under the speed and nature of fundamental change. Political leaders and their officials are struggling with the ever-accelerating pace of technological change and digital transformation, and delivering effectively in a climate of escalating geo-political instability.

Rapid advance in technology will not simply create public services that are better, safer, smarter and more affordable. New technologies will also alter the private and the public sectors as well as civil society, power structures, relations between the state and the people, the role of politics and the civil service in mediating that change.

The background to this 'quiet revolution' is that governments are struggling with three converging global trends. The first is the rapid adoption of new technologies and the ever-accelerating pace of digital transformation. The Greek philosopher Heraclitus, 2500 years ago, noted, 'There is nothing permanent except change'. Today, the '4th Industrial Revolution' is triggering an unprecedented pace of technological change that is redefining human potential, reshaping industries and changing societies.

Against the backdrop of deep concern about the effects of this technological change, and worries in developed countries over future rise in standards of living, the second and related trend is an unprecedented sense of uncertainty. Further factors fuelling this are jobless growth, the rise of China, unprecedented levels of migration, the demographics of aging in the developed world and a youth bulge in developing countries.

The third trend is that, partly as a consequence of the first two, in many parts of the world, citizens' trust in their governments seems to be plummeting, reflected in a lack of trust in government and in institutions more broadly. This is especially the case for the poorer people in society. A recent survey found that in 18 of 28 countries there is a double-digit gap in the trust in institutions between high-income and low-income respondents.[4]

So, too, did the 'good governance' agenda evolve in the 1990s. This was reflected by the World Bank Institute Governance Indicators along six dimensions: the rule of law, control of corruption, voice and accountability, regulatory quality, government effectiveness and political stability. Yet public sector reform of central government has overwhelmed development agencies. Effective institutions are the key determinant of development;[5] and essential for a functioning and stable democracy. The administrative capability of the state is an essential dimension of the 'effective institutions' that shape the basic functions of the state. The public service influences and enforces the 'rules of the game' for economic and political interaction. The interface between officials and citizens is the state: *L'Etat, c'est Nous.*

The evidence for its importance includes a close statistical connection between the quality of public bureaucracy and economic growth, with

---

[4] Friedman, U. 2016. Trust in Government is Collapsing Around the World. *The Atlantic.* https://www.theatlantic.com/international/archive/2016/07/trust-institutions-trump-brexit/489554/.

[5] North, D. 1990. *Institutions, Institutional Change and Economic Performance.* Cambridge: Cambridge University Press; Evans, P. and Rauch, J., E. 1999. Bureaucracy and Growth: A Cross-National Analysis of the Effects of 'Weberian' State Structures on Economic Growth. *American Sociological Review, 64*(5), 748–765; Rodrik, D., Subramanian, A. and Trebbi, F. 2004. Institutions Rule: The Primacy of Institutions Over Geography and Integration in Economic Development. *Journal of Economic Growth, 9,* 131.

merit-based recruitment, promotion from within and career stability for government bureaucracies being key determinants.[6]

Politics

In 1967, a decade after independence, Malaysia's Deputy Prime Minister Tun Haji Abdul Razak bin Dato' Haji Hussein (later the country's second post-independence Prime Minister, from 1970 to 1976) told civil servants:

> I hope you will stand up to us as politicians, and not allow yourselves to be dominated by us, because in a true democracy, the civil servants have a duty to perform. To place fairly and squarely facts before the politicians, based on balanced, unbiased judgement, which the politician 'can take it or leave it' as he so wishes. After all civil servants are pensionable; you have nothing to lose…. The future of our country's democratic way of life is dependent on you…

Fifty years on, has it worked out like that, in Malaysia or indeed anywhere else? The power of any public service is in constant contention. The political settlement that sets the 'rules of the game' over state authority reflects the relationship between political leaders, senior administrators and the citizenry. In constant negotiation is the extent of bureaucratic accountability versus administrative discretion and departmental autonomy. The credibility of political commitment to respect agreed boundaries to public authority is constantly tested — in the media, in the courts, in ministerial discussion with officials over policymaking.

Public sector reform is everywhere a complex open-ended bargain balanced between contradictions, often carefully hidden in political and bureaucratic doublespeak, of the sort brilliantly parodied in the classic BBC comedy series from the 1970s, *Yes, Minister*.

My old friend the late Adrian Leftwich identified six political components of a developmental state: (i) an elite with an interest in development; (ii) the relative autonomy of the state; (iii) a powerful, competent

---

[6] Rauch and Evans, *op. cit.*

and insulated economic bureaucracy; (iv) a weak and subordinated civil society; (v) the effective management of non-state economic interests; and (vi) the legitimacy of performance justifying repression.[7]

Thinking and working in a politically informed way has always been central to the work of diplomacy and has been recognised for some time now, in development, as essential. Yet how to handle that insight remains problematic. This is particularly true in civil service reforms where an effective interface of political and administrative leadership is obviously vital. Innovation requires policy entrepreneurs inside public service, not just outside, to achieve change.

Reform involves a negotiating balance between hype and reality, a trade-off between aspiration and delusion, a struggle between ideology and evidence. Claims for reforms often ignore how little evidence really exists on what was actually achieved. The rise of NPM in the 1980s sparked global trends in reform ideas, yet reflecting local dynamics. This highlighted tensions around independent yet politically responsive expertise, creating merit-based, yet politically astute officials following due process, yet achieving 'political will', motivated by the common good, yet demoralised by staff cuts, salary freezes and bureaucracy-bashing. Cognitive dissonance in many civil services was exacerbated further by augmented pay for top officials as CEOs 'rewarded for failure' as 'Leaders', while the talk emphasised team culture. Accountability, yet loyalty to political interest or to state saw the increasing use of performance targets as levers of control.[8]

Politics often gets a bad press but is the key process by which society allocates resources and promotes innovation. Central, however, to a political system is the pact between a country's political leadership and its administrative leadership. That is the interface that defines the nature of public authority and how it is imposed, remembering the old adage that 'Administration is Policy'. For, whether politics is personalised or institutionalised, competitive or not, the grip on power requires

---

[7] Leftwich, A. 1995. Bringing Politics Back in: Towards a Model of the Developmental State. *Journal of Development Studies, 31*(3), 400–427.

[8] Horn, M. 1995. *The Political Economy of Public Administration: Institutional Choice in the Public Sector.* Cambridge University Press, Cambridge.

agreement on some basis by the civilian and military leadership to comply with political leadership.

The formal and informal agreed 'rules of the game' is an important determinant of any political/administrative leadership pact anywhere. The extent to which civil servants will be loyal to the aim and vision, shoulder responsibility and develop the competence needed will depend on their explicit and implicit expectations.

For example, Lee Kuan Yew reformatted the political settlement over the public service through the political/administrative leadership pact in Singapore soon after coming to power in 1959 when he cut salaries in the public sector to make the post-independence finances sustainable. He then reversed these 20 years later, making the country's top civil servants well-paid. He also famously turned all the garbage collectors into civil servants in order to subject them to discipline to stop communist-led strikes that then threatened the sanitation of this small island city-state.

So it may be that from peer-to-peer learning we can identify similar political/administrative leadership pacts that will enable SDGs to succeed in other contexts, by affecting the nature of the work of public officials in key central ministries as well as service delivery, through its direct impact on policies over political empowerment and inclusion, and on the resourcing of development ends.

This 'political' approach requires looking at deep-seated roots of politically salient ideas, incentives and issues, while 'thinking and working politically' seeks to identify immediate political interests.

The focus must shift from creating public value to upholding public values. A narrow focus on efficiency cuts out the capacity cushion of built in redundancy, the spare capacity to act in a crisis.

Public service is poorly understood and comparatively neglected in development, despite shaping citizens' quality of life by delivering public goods and services to citizens, for example, clean and safe food and housing. How people view and have confidence in their government is closely related to how bureaucracies work. Particularly, bad experiences with public bureaucrats are likely to engender negative feelings about the government. How and why bureaucracies vary across nations is unclear, and bureaucracy is often conflated with an abstract conceptualisation of the state. Emphasis on impartiality is important for maintaining public support for government bureaucracy and regime performance.

Economic development has depended on professional and powerful bureaucracies by securing property rights for individuals and exerting coercive power when necessary.[9] Kohli, for example, argues that for rapid industrialisation, it is crucial that the state has a competent, 'public-spirited' bureaucracy, through which the state pursues and implements cohesive and effective economic policy.[10] An effective state requires a bureaucracy that has 'the effective capacity to command, to regulate, and to extract tax revenues'.[11] Professional and trusted bureaucracies have played an important role in progressive policymaking. Studies of comparative public administration stress the great diversity of bureaucracies across nations.[12]

A meritocratic bureaucracy that balances political interests has also proved to have a stabilising effect in situations of political or social conflict.[13] Meritocracy saves money and seems to promote economic growth. Analysis of 1.4 million procurement contracts in 212 regions of the European Union finds that the regions whose own public employees rate them as meritocratic pay less for roads, bridges and the like: if every region were as meritocratic as Baden-Württemberg, in Germany, EU governments could save €13 billion to €20 billion ($14 billion to $22 billion) a year. Too many countries suffer from well-connected (but

---

[9] Evans and Rauch, *op. cit.*, pp. 748–765; Knack, S. and Keefer, P. 1997. Does Social Capital Have an Economic Payoff? A Cross-Country Investigation. *Quarterly Journal of Economics, 112*(4), 1251–1288.

[10] Kohli, A. 2004. *State-directed Development: Political Power and Industrialization in the Global Periphery*. Cambridge University Press.

[11] Linz, J. J. and Stepan, A. C. 1996. Toward Consolidated Democracies. *Journal of Democracy, 7*(2), 14–33.

[12] Painter, M. and Peters, B. G. 2010. Administrative Traditions in Comparative Perspective: Families, Groups and Hybrids. In *Tradition and Public Administration*, edited by M. Painter and B. G. Peters. London: Palgrave Macmillan; Pollitt, C. and Bouckaert, G. 2011. *Public Management Reform: A Comparative Analysis — New Public Management, Governance, and the Neo-Weberian State*. Oxford University Press.

[13] Rothstein, B. 2015. *Report for the First Ten Years of a Research Program at University of Gothenburg*. The Quality of Government Institute.

unproductive) 'tenderpreneurs', who survive on government contracts, often secured through corruption or collusion.[14]

Competent bureaucracy is necessary to allocate resources and deliver public services. Effective discretion is required, but too strong a bureaucracy could threaten democratic values and political authority. A tension therefore always has to be politically negotiated around the degree of independence but political responsiveness of the public service. This requires intrinsic bureaucratic traits, such as professionalism, impartiality and fairness,[15] or extrinsic bureaucratic traits such as political independence, representativeness and credible commitment of politicians to 'embedded autonomy' or suitable insulation from political pressure in the decision-making process, as well as in the recruitment and dismissal of bureaucrats. Independent bureaucrats are able to provide policymakers with objective advice and implement public policies, without favouring a particular political ideology, but are responsive and accountable.

Research suggests that politically independent bureaucracies promote economic growth[16] and curb corruption.[17] The political independence of bureaucracies is highly correlated with a meritocratic recruitment in developing countries,[18] and in developed and developing countries.[19]

While public servants in a neutral bureaucracy seek to keep political conflicts within the policymaking arena, in a politicised bureaucratic apparatus they have an interest in engaging in politics to enhance their career prospects. This may result in an escalation and proliferation of political conflict within state agencies and with the public interacting with

---

[14] *The Economist*, 12 March 2016. Mandarin Lessons. The Economist Group Limited. Available online: http://www.economist.com/news/international/21694553-countries-are-trying-harder-recruit-best-bureaucrats-not-hard-enough-mandarin.

[15] Rothstein, B. and Teorell, J. 2008. Impartiality as a Basic Norm for the Quality of Government: A Reply to Francisco Longo and Graham Wilson. *Governance, 21*(2), 201–204.

[16] Knack and Keefer, *op. cit.*; Evans and Rauch, *op. cit.*; Rauch and Evans, *op. cit.*

[17] Dahlström, C., Lapuente, V. and Teorell, J. 2012. The Merit of Meritocratization: Politics, Bureaucracy, and the Institutional Deterrents of Corruption. *Political Research Quarterly, 65*(3), 656–668.

[18] Rauch and Evans, *op. cit.*

[19] Dahlström, Lapuente and Teorell. *op. cit.*

them.[20] Elite groups with different interests control each other. Politicians and bureaucrats constitute two separate groups with different career incentives preventing each other from engaging in corruption and instead stimulate good and effective governance.[21]

General representation of society can prevent bureaucratic abuse of discretion. A civil service that broadly reflects the demographic characteristics of the population — by gender, race, religion and class — should also share citizens' values, which will constrain bureaucrats' behaviour. Representative bureaucracy represents the social and economic structure of society has symbolic meaning for the elimination of societal prejudices.

Impartiality matters. The procedural fairness of bureaucracy explains citizens' perceptions of governments.[22] Positive associations exist between impartiality and economic growth, institutional trust and citizens' personal happiness.[23] Bureaucracy can be unresponsive due to inefficiency.

In the face of complex challenges, constrained resources, competition for limited talent from the private sector and increasing citizen expectations, the public service needs not only to meet today's requirements, but also be primed to deliver tomorrow's needs. While other efforts to strengthen the public service are important, paying attention to the natural advantage of intrinsic motivation within the ranks of public service institutions and in potential new recruits to the public service is increasingly becoming 'necessary' rather than 'good to have'.

Leadership, Vision and Trust

The Old Testament warned of leaders like Nebuchadnezzar of Babylon who claimed to deliver their people from bondage, offered the

---

[20] Dahlström, C. and Lapuente, V. 2010. Explaining Cross-Country Differences in Performance-Related Pay in the Public Sector. *Journal of Public Administration Research and Theory, 20*(3), 577–600.

[21] Dahlström *et al., op. cit.*

[22] Rohrschneider, R. 2005. Institutional Quality and Perceptions of Representation in Advanced Industrial Democracies. *Comparative Political Studies, 38*(7), 850–874.

[23] Teorell, J. 2009. *The Impact of Quality of Government as Impartiality: Theory and Evidence.* APSA 2009 Toronto Meeting Paper.

splendour of a conqueror, and to establish justice, freedom and peace. Leaders of organisations (those in positions of authority and responsibility) can use their authority to further their own purposes ('elite capture') or to lead the organisation toward higher levels of performance.

Deeply imbued with the 17th-century Puritan tradition, famously associated with John Winthrop's 'City Upon a Hill', the 'small government', 'just get out of the way' mind-set in America has no real equivalent in history-bound Europe. The state-building process across the continent, the competition of roughly equal-sized nations, and the development of democratic institutions bestowed a deep legitimacy to the concept even if not to every manifestation of government.

The leadership of reforms must be determined and coherent. A holistic perspective is needed: clear about accountability for implementation and with the necessary implementation capacity, and commonly understood reform objectives, with a clear strategic framework that enables prioritisation of reforms and realistic planning of their implementation.

Tackling these causes is essential if an impartial and merit-based public service, like the one in Singapore, is to emerge in other countries. Such public administration is important both in itself and for the legitimacy of the state. But development is hampered by the lack of a credible theory of change to explain how or why an 'impartial, ethical, fair and merit-based public service' emerges, and how it can be promoted and fostered.

Peer-to-peer learning offers insights in this, strengthening the intellectual validity of reform if states can learn from each other how promote a political-administrative leadership interface that can ensure results.

The administrative capacity is shaped by power, the black box of how the state functions. In 1926, John Maynard Keynes said that 'everything is politics, nothing is policies'. Seventy years later, this truism was rediscovered in international development. The governance agenda evolved rapidly in the 1990s from endless training courses for 'building capacity', to identifying the 'drivers of change'. Academics like Adrian Leftwich were particularly influential in this shift. His 1995 article 'Bringing Politics Back In: Towards a Model of the Developmental State', in the *Journal of Development Studies,* followed by his book in 2000, *States of Development: On the Primacy of Politics in Development* left no-one in any doubt that the apolitical development discourse was an often convenient but essentially unsustainable fiction. That did not mean foreign donors taking sides; but it did require them to understand the political ideas, interests and incentives that would shape development outcomes.

US President Franklin D. Roosevelt said in his first Inaugural Speech of 1933:

> ... the only thing we have to fear is fear itself — nameless, unreasoning, unjustified terror which paralyzes needed efforts to convert retreat into advance. In every dark hour of our national life, a leadership of frankness and of vigor has met with that understanding and support of the people themselves which is essential to victory.

President Kennedy neatly summed up Churchill's extraordinary power of oratory in creating vision: 'He mobilised the English language and sent it into battle'. On 15 February 1942, in the early months of WWII in the Pacific and following the disastrous surrender that day of Singapore to the invading Japanese army, the British Prime Minister Winston Churchill broadcast to the British people and her Allies. On one of the darkest days of WWII, Churchill was able to offer a powerful vision as to how to respond to the military aggression of Nazi Germany, fascist Italy and imperialist Japan:

> The whole future of mankind may depend upon our action and upon our conduct. So far we have not failed. We shall not fail now. Let us move forward steadfastly together into the storm and through the storm.

Churchill's distinguished biographer Sir Martin Gilbert described Britain's great wartime leader as an accomplished storyteller who 'loved the ebb and flow of narrative'. Churchill had a deep love for writing history and was inspired by it, observing that 'the future is unknowable, but the past should give us hope'. In turn, many world leaders have been inspired by Churchill's gripping capacity to motivate and to imagine a better world.

Such capacity to inspire, as FDR and Churchill demonstrated in the battle to defeat evil and create the vision for peace through the United Nations, is still needed today to address the world war of our time, on poverty, injustice and bad governance.

Government's highest ambition is to transform people into empowered citizens, not just clients or customers satisfied with public service delivery. Innovation should be recast, from change in government processes to recognising the role of the state in transforming society. Today the ultimate purpose of technology should be not to foster smart cities or smart nations, but smart people — a more informed, more compassionate citizenry that cherishes creativity, inclusion, empowerment, participation, humility, intellectual curiosity and empathy.

Squaring that requires a vision for institutional sustainability. In Estonia, in emphasising independently-mindedness, 'things get done', and creativity, the past is also directly addressed: 'what has brought us here will not lead us any further'. But only too often, making profits today drives hostility towards the public service as curator of the past and steward of the future.

Overcoming that is the key to intrinsic motivation. The public service offers meaningful work. Commitment to the public good drives well-being, job satisfaction and the capacity to cope with change.

Foresight methodologies can help to devise a vision; then prioritised objectives should guide and co-ordinate reform implementation, realistically, sequentially and in a coherently-planned way, with a whole-of-government perspective. Be honest in recognising that public sector reform is more a political than a technical challenge; local context is more important than lessons from elsewhere, but general principles are of universal relevance. Consider the problem more one of psychotherapy than plumbing.

The 'Sustainable Singapore Blueprint 2015' outlines a national vision and plans for a more liveable and sustainable country to support the diverse needs and growing aspirations of Singaporeans. Amidst a rapidly changing society, this blueprint seeks to work together to create a better country, a better environment and a better future. With the government, people and businesses committed to working together, the country can realise a vision for *A Liveable and Endearing Home; A Vibrant and Sustainable City; and An Active and Gracious Community.* In most other countries, such a national aspiration would be drowned at birth by cynicism.

Urukagina alleged that the entire public administration, an 'obnoxious and ubiquitous bureaucracy' (as characterised by the prolific Assyriologist in the United States of the 1950s to 1970s, Samuel Kramer)[24] had 'since time immemorial' been bloated and corrupt: *From the border territory of Ningirsu to the waters of the sea ... officials were present (everywhere).* Corruption was institutionalised and endemic: *From distant times, from when the seed (of life first) came forth ... As the traditions were, it was.* This admission that these conditions had existed 'since time immemorial ... from distant days' was perhaps an attack by an upstart on the long lineage of rulers he had displaced.

Yet it also seems, however, to underscore the political aspect of all his accusations and justifications. Corruption was then, as now, the ideal populist justification for 'reform', and an easy allegation to make.

In the name of efficiency and effectiveness, NPM *de-institutionalised* civil service recruitment, making it a component of the management process and, to all intents and purposes, removed it from public scrutiny. Whether the general interest or the public purse were served in this process remains in doubt.[25] Attacks on elite career protectionism, which critics of the system consider public service to represent, pretend to advance the rights of 'customer-citizens' through 'de-bureaucratisation'.[26]

Similarly, the great 19th-century novelist Anthony Trollope applied his first-hand knowledge as surveyor of the General Post Office to critique their reforms, 'that great modern scheme for competitive examinations', suggesting that the naked ambition let loose by open competition that the Northcote–Trevelyan Report proposed would create self-serving extrinsic motivation rather than a public service ethos. In his novel *the Three Clerks* of 1858, Trollope argued that the Northcote–Trevelyan attack on the civil service was the product of the self-interest of the private sector and that it was important to counterbalance such vested interests by disinterested governance administered by well-educated gentlemen working in the national interest.

Mid-19th-century British public officials defended themselves by declaring that they were practical men of action and looked down on

---

[24] Kramer, S. 1979. Causeries: The First Case of Tax Reduction. *Challenge,* 22(1), 3–5.
[25] Hood and Dixon, *op. cit.*
[26] Dwivedi, O. P. 2001. India in a Globalised World: Transforming Bureaucracy for the Well-Being and Prosperity of All. *Indian Journal of Public Administration,* 53(4), 717–741.

'bureaucracy' as too concerned with theories, laws and ideas. Furthermore, it was a suspiciously alien concept as its French etymology implied: Thomas Carlyle, for instance, writing in 1850 condemned it as 'a foreign nuisance' with no future in England, echoing Karl Marx's observation about Prussia that 'The bureaucracy takes itself to be the ultimate purpose of the state'.

It is no surprise that, at the same time as morale and intrinsic motivation in the public sector has been on the wane, public trust in government has been collapsing. Impartial and effective public administration builds trust between the state and citizenry, and stimulates markets.

Trust in government and state legitimacy is not principally created by democracy, the rule of law, or efficiency and effectiveness. Instead, trust and legitimacy are the outcomes of 'the impartiality of institutions that exercise government authority'.[27]

Trust is primarily the outcome of whether impartial public administration is just and fair in handling relations between the state and citizenry. As Alexander Hamilton famously noted in the *Federalist* No. 27 in 1787:

> It may be laid down as a general rule, that [citizens'] confidence in and obedience to a government, will be commonly proportioned to the goodness or badness of its administration.

Procedural fairness of bureaucracy explains citizens' perceptions of governments, with positive associations between impartiality, economic growth, institutional trust and citizens' personal happiness.[28] Citizens' perceptions of procedural fairness have been shown to shape their willingness to pay tax in sub-Saharan African countries.[29] Governments in more diverse societies that promote greater transparency enjoy more trust.[30]

---

[27] Rothstein and Teorell, *op. cit.*

[28] Teorell, *op. cit.*

[29] Levi, M., Sacks, A. and Tyler, T. 2009. Conceptualizing Legitimacy, Measuring Legitimating Beliefs. *American Behavioral Scientist, 53*(3), 354–375.

[30] Grimmelikhuijsen, S. *et al.* 2013. The Effect of Transparency on Trust in Government: A Cross-National Comparative Experiment. *Public Administration Review, 73*(4), 575–586.

That impartiality arises from, and reinforces, a public service ethos that motivates officials to deliver public services in accordance with a commitment to serving the public interest. Impartiality in bureaucracies develops through competent professionalism, as well as by a merit-based recruitment and security of tenure in public service.[31] Impartiality of government institutions is linked to higher levels of well-being and promoting interpersonal trust and economic growth.

While a skilled, motivated and efficient public service with a professional ethos may be only a necessary but not sufficient, condition for good governance, an ineffective or inefficient public service is certainly sufficient to produce bad governance.[32] Corruption systematically breaches impartiality and so lowers trust in government institutions.[33]

A skilled and motivated public service is needed. By upholding impartiality, accountability and transparency, a fair and effective public administration creates economic growth, political stability and state legitimacy.

In many parts of the world, there is, however, growing uncertainty about the role of the civil service. In countries as diverse as Bangladesh, Bhutan, the Maldives and Moldova, the government has both actively supported but also sabotaged the national bureaucracy. Politicians could not decide whether civil service was their implementing arm or a competitor for power. As the 1970s BBC TV comedy series *Yes Minister* put it:

> The Opposition aren't really the opposition. They are only the Government In Exile. The Civil Service are the Opposition In Residence.

Similarly, the civil service could not make up its mind whether it was serving or running the country. A public opinion poll conducted in Russia in 2003 found that citizens have low trust in government employees, and there is a great deal of cynicism about the influence of personal and business interests on the decisions made by public servants. This was unsurprising. The INDEM (Information Science for Democracy) Fund in

---

[31] Rothstein and Teorell 2008. *op. cit.*
[32] Schiavo-Campo, S. and Sundaram, P. 2001. *To Serve and To Preserve: Improving Public Administration in the Competitive World.* Manilla: ADB.
[33] Teorell, J. (2009). *The Impact of Quality of Government as Impartiality: Theory and Evidence.* In APSA 2009 Toronto Meeting Paper.

2001 found that the total sum paid to public officials by businessmen in Russia in that year amounted to some US$33.5 billion — about the size of government revenues. So citizens did not believe that the public service was capable of providing public services effectively, nor do citizens feel they are protected from arbitrariness in administrative decisions. The survey results also indicate little faith in the ability of administrative reform initiatives to improve the quality of life in Russia.

President Vladimir Putin in his 2005 State of the Union addresses to the joint meeting of the state Duma and the Council of the Federation. President Putin described the Russian bureaucracy as a closed and haughty caste system that saw public service as a kind of business rather than as an institution responsible for serving the citizenry.[34] He did not reflect on his role in allowing this to develop.

Shifting politics can leave the public service leadership confused. Politicians, in turn, start to construct parallel bureaucratic structures if the bureaucracy fails to adapt to a new political settlement. National funds for development are channelled through MPs. This has been happening in the Papua New Guinea and across the Pacific. Politics largely determines the nature of the civil service and civil service reforms cannot succeed in isolation. But the opposite argument is also made: that non-performing administration leaves little choice to the politicians but to resort to populist rhetoric and sectarian strategies.[35]

Where bureaucracies have managed to adapt to new political settlements (e.g. inherited colonial administrations), formally, the civil service often resembles and even retains some of the old values — however, the 'political' adaptation has taken place in the huge informal realm. India might be a good example, as well as many African systems.

The purpose of the political settlement is rarely inclusive, sustainable development. Progress is not the sole, or even the most important political ambition. The reality of political interests and power create other political priorities for a regime, regardless of what head of states say at the UN in

---

[34] Barabashev, A. and Straussman, J. D. 2007. Public Service Reform in Russia, 1991–2006. *Public Administration Review,* 67(3), 373–382.

[35] Saxena, N. 2010. The IAS Officer — Predator or Victim? *Commonwealth & Comparative Politics,* 48(November), 445–456.

New York. The civil service, as a political force, will defend its own organisational interests, implement and compete, and also be a connector between the elite and society.

The economic problems of stagflation in Western countries in the second half of the 1970s and the collapse of public sector in developing countries subjected the public sector to ferocious criticisms. The welfare state went into retreat. The financial crisis of 2008 left the private sector vilified for the failures of greed. Until then, neo-classical and libertarian public choice thought had freely revived the animosity to the role of the state in society. One telling example was when the former administrator of USAID, Rajiv Shah, told *The New York Times*:

> We are never going to end hunger in Africa without private investment. There are things that only companies can do, like building silos for storage and developing seeds and fertilizers.[36]

He was utterly wrong. It had been state-funded agricultural research, supported by public institutions and public policies that had delivered the 'green revolution' in many countries in the 1960s and 1970s. The public service ethos had ended hunger then in Asia, as it had previously done in post-war Central Europe and Japan. Nothing would stop that being repeated, except political ideology.

Unfortunately, too many reforms are still implemented as 'big bang' change. These efforts often copy inappropriate models (such as from the different challenges faced by the private sector). Frequently clever, ambitious 'modernisers' implement them with more attention to advancing their own interests and only at best a token consultation with the officials affected or who have to carry them out.

Nation-Building in 'Fragile States'

Civil services have historically played a pivotal role in the development of a collective sense of belonging to a state. Nation-building requires an

---

[36] Shah, R. Cited in: Strom, S. 2012. Firms to Invest in Food Production for World's Poor. *The New York Times*. http://www.nytimes.com/2012/05/18/business/white-house-enlists-45-firms-to-give-3-billion-to-grow-food-for-worlds-poor.html.

organised commitment to construct, standardise and institutionalise particular 'national' identities, often via the enforced primacy of certain ethno-linguistic characteristics. For example, the Académie française was established in 1635 to act as the official authority on the vocabulary and grammar of the French language. The French Revolution of 1789 unified public administration across the country, with the French language acting as a symbol of national unity.

Officials from across the state need to institutionalise and represent a shared concept of national identity. The civil service has helped to establish agreed symbols of national identity. This has been achieved by the enforcement of a national currency, time, education system (including the establishment of a language of education or curricula content), delivery of services (both the mechanisms of delivery and assessment criteria) and the development of narratives of national belonging (such as common history, public holidays and commemorative events). The railways, post office and census bureau in many countries have often played more than a passive role. The civil service has used the census for managing tensions over how people are categorised.

In the early 1990s, the nation state, like religion, seemed on its last legs. The collapse of Communism was notoriously declared the 'End of History' — by a non-historian. Any historian would have known that mankind had been there before. In 1913, Norman Angell had emphatically declared that, in a rapidly globalising world, warfare was economically irrational and therefore would be seen no more. The 20th century would be a time of unparalleled peace. Within months of the book's publication, WW1 had started. Followed a generation later by WW2, the 20th century turned out to be the bloodiest era of all time.

So the state proved a dangerous institution to write off. The tolerant world of country gentlemen in 18th-century England found one solution: 'His Majesty's Loyal Opposition'. Shared concern for protecting property rights trumped the deep divides between Whig and Tory, Catholic and Protestant, politician or civil servant. Albion's fatal tree would happily hang a man for stealing a rabbit, but proclaim all to be 'free'. The able-bodied poor were either lazy or unlucky; the worthy poor were the old, handicapped and infirm. The role of the state was to 'hold the ring': the local community must take care of their own to prevent taxpayers reducing their burden by driving welfare problems away for others to pay for.

The 7% tax/GDP ratio achieved in England by about 1715 was a level of tax performance the same as in early 21st century Yemen where the culture of compliance remained weak and the tax authority was able to collect no more than 20–25% of taxes due before it collapsed into civil war. In the 20th century, the tolerant, *laisser-faire* 'holding the ring' state, like the Ottoman or Hapsburg Empires, was replaced by states created, driven and impassioned by ideology — nationalism (we are better than you), Communism (we the vanguard of the proletariat know what is right for you), Capitalism (the Free Market, as regulated by us, knows what's best for you) or religion (God, as interpreted by us, knows your failings).

The quality of government turned out to be crucial for improving human well-being. Countries vary in their quality of governance, and by almost any measure is usually worse in developing than developed countries. For instance, the World Bank's Worldwide Governance Indicators rank low-income countries substantially lower than high-income OECD countries on government effectiveness (average percentile rank of 17.3 compared to 87.9 in 2014).

Through recorded history, regular widespread famine in Finland had been fatefully accepted as a fixed fact of life. In the far north of Europe, the agricultural year is short. If the snows stayed on late or returned early, the already short harvest season was disastrously curtailed. Around the 17th century, Europe experienced a 'little Ice Age', resulting in Finland in the 'Great Cough Year' of 1580, the 'Great Frost' of 1601–1602, and the 'Autumn of the Plague' in 1710.

But the worst climatic episode occurred between 1694 and 1697. For three years in a row, the winters were unusually long, the springs particularly cold and wet, and then autumn arrived early. The result was extreme famine. In those 'years of many deaths' as contemporary chroniclers recording the episode called it, up to a third of the population died. The poor landless peasants and small subsistence farmers with no reserves or savings were most harshly affected. Many tried to survive by consuming tree bark, grass and mud. Such unwholesome and indigestible 'food' resulted in the widespread spread of disease, epidemics of diarrhoea and dysentery. There were even some cases of cannibalism. Many farms were abandoned, and towns were filled with people begging.[37]

History repeated itself some 170 years later. The last great naturally caused famine in Europe occurred between 1866 and 1868 in Finland. The period is known in Finnish as *Suuret Nälkävuodet* or 'the great hunger years', when about 15–20% of the entire population died. Like the Irish Potato Famine 20 years earlier, in which one million people (or an eighth of the population) died and another million emigrated, the government at first failed to act and what little action it took was too little too late.

The two worst famines in 19th-century Europe make an important comparison. The Irish disaster has been seared on the political mindset of the Emerald Isle. It is widely interpreted as the heart of the national consciousness and the root of the country's national identity. In the mid-1990s, the 150th anniversary of the tragedy triggered an outpouring of research and analysis.

Year 2014 as the 150th anniversary of the start of the tragedy in Finland went largely unremarked. The capacity of government in either country to prevent these occurrences was little different. But Finland, a Grand Duchy of Russia since 1809, had gained a considerable degree of autonomy. The Senate in Helsinki had powers to tax and legislate. By comparison, Ireland, part of the Union with Great Britain of 1800, had lost its separate parliament and had little political voice.

In much of Africa, decline in the public service has been ongoing for decades: by 1985 an average civil servant's real salary in Tanzania had dropped to less than one-quarter of what it had been a decade earlier. Management-level salaries eroded considerably during this period: in Zambia, for example, in 1971 an assistant director's salary was 17 times the salary of the lowest-paid employee; by 1986, it was only 4 times as much.

Tanzania is an illustration of the success of incremental reform of a civil service. Efforts were made to improve existing public sector organisations rather than create new ones. In contrast, in Uganda the civil service

---

[37] Neumann, J. and Lindgrén, S. 1979. Great Historical Events That Were Significantly Affected by the Weather: 4, The Great Famines in Finland and Estonia, 1695–1697. *Bulletin of the American Meteorological Society*, 60(7), 775–787.

became an important lever of power. Internationally supported reforms implemented in the 1980s and 1990s by President Museveni were used to purge remnants of the opposition and reward supporters. Politicisation constrained civil servants' ability to act impartially.

In September 2015, the Vice President of Nigeria, Yemi Osinbajo lamented how that country's civil service had been deteriorating since independence due to political leaders' inability to clearly articulate and implement a vision. The civil service had gained the reputation for inefficiency, low productivity, corruption and insensitivity to the needs of the public.

Similarly in Pakistan, at independence in 1947, the civil service was the dream job for the top students graduating from elite universities. Civil servants were respected, influential, well read and intellectual. Today, few people with high academic achievements are interested in a public service career.

In China in 2014, President Xi Jinping's campaign against corruption saw 232,000 officials punished, 30% more than in the previous year. That was still only about 3% of officialdom, but the publicity surrounding these cases has compounded anxieties. In the three weeks after the lunar new-year holiday in February more than 10,000 government workers quit their jobs to seek greener pastures, mainly in the finance, property and technology industries. This was an increase of nearly one-third over the same period in 2014. The State Administration of Civil Service said 1.4 million candidates signed up in 2014 to take the test it administers, 110,000 less than the previous year. About 510,000 people signed up for the exam but did not attend. In 2010, 59 people took the test for every job on offer, but the ratio in 2014 was 40:1, the lowest in nine years. The civil service is losing its appeal. Surveys by Offcn, a private agency providing courses for candidates, and Horizon Research Consultancy Group, show that some 45.5% of respondents born in the 1990s said they wanted to be a civil servant, compared to 50.7% among people born in the 1980s, 61% those born in the 1970s, and that for the 1960s was 57.1%.[38]

In the United States over the last five years, the percentage of federal workers under 30 dropped from 9.1% to 6.6%. And the number of federal workers under the age of 25 declined from 2% to just under 1% over the

---

[38] http://english.caixin.com/2014-12-02/100758194.html.

same time period, indicating the public sector could not recruit or retain young talent.[39]

The gap between worker satisfaction in the private sector and that in the public sector has nearly tripled since 2010. As morale in business improved with the end of the recession, morale among government employees continued to slide downward.[40] The annual 'Best Places to Work' rankings by the Partnership for Public Service showed in 2014 that federal employees' satisfaction and commitment were at their lowest point since the analysis began in 2003.

In the United Kingdom, optimists note the contradiction between two predominant characterisations of the British Civil Service. The first declares officialdom to be in decline, possibly terminally, overwhelmed by the challenges posed by the reforms and the changes in its policy environment; others see it as in the vanguard by adopting modernising reforms and adapting to new public service values, progressively modernised and in a progressive way — becoming less corrupt, more accountable, more pluralist, more responsive to citizens' needs — often sceptical about reform, but nevertheless moving with the times.

A typical view of bureaucratic incompetence comes from the UK Parliament's education committee that concluded in 2017: 'The system for funding new schools and new places in existing schools is increasingly incoherent and too often poor value for money... Many free schools are in inadequate premises, including many without on-site playgrounds or sports facilities…. In the context of severe financial constraints, it is vital that the department uses its funding in a more coherent and cost-effective way'. A few days later, on another UK policy (immigration), the *Financial Times* described the 'mish-mash of special deals and sectoral carve-outs' as 'costly and incoherent'.[41] 'Incoherent', 'costly' and 'poor value for money' are damning reflections of current failings, apparently the results of confusion

---

[39] The Office of Personnel Management's Federal Employee Viewpoint Survey. Available online: https://www.opm.gov/fevs/.

[40] The government-wide employee engagement score was 57 out of 100, compared with the private sector's score of 72 out of 100.

[41] *The Financial Times*. 2017. A costly and incoherent stance on UK migration. *The Financial Times Limited*. Available online: https://www.ft.com/content/ef7baa4a-29a6-11e7-bc4b-5528796fe35c.

and inadequate policy consultation, let alone co-creation. The crux of such problems is usually not deliberate stupidity or malicious obfuscation, but the political imperative that 'something must be done' driving over-optimism-infused wrong or bad decisions, which build up over time.

Small States

Public administrations in small states face challenges due to their size which brings about a number of capacity constraints, such as a narrow resource base, remoteness and heavy dependence on export markets often exacerbated by vulnerability to the effects of climate change and limited resilience to natural disasters. Such volatile context makes sustainability harder to achieve. Small states, therefore, face additional constraints when it comes to attaining development goals because of their small size. However, if public services in small island developing states learn how to leverage size as an opportunity, they might be able to achieve SDGs and make success happen due to a small size, not just in spite of it.

How far does the capacity of public administration differ according to a country's size? City-states and very small states face appear particularly difficult and intractable challenges. In the smallest states public administration requires long-term national priorities to overcome vulnerabilities. Personalised politics can exacerbate capacity limitations of public service, and the results are problematic. Yet smallness, while creating obvious resource constraints, brings benefits too in 'whole of government' coordination, democratic responsiveness and local decentralisation. Citizen participation through co-creation and collaboration, new to developed countries to increase trust and legitimacy, are already well established in the smallest states. Very small states offer the clarity of insights in miniature into the capacity constraints faced by all states with weak governance. Smallness, however, is only one dimension of statehood. Achieving public service delivery in very small states, like other countries, is primarily a political not a capacity challenge.

The 'managed intimacy' has three components:

> *Bureaupathology* on the mix of anxiety and insecurity due to alienation, limited promotion prospects, lousy pay, pessimism and sense of powerlessness that comes as a part of working in a small, poor and insufficiently skilled bureaucracy.

> *Personalisation.* That everyone knows everybody else and the rational–legal tradition of the archetypal Weberian bureaucracy is just unfeasible. Social relationships (so important in the Pacific) being much more important than bureaucratic/hierarchical ones is again resonant.
> *Informality.* Does small size by its nature, where individuals live in a number of different social and economic worlds simultaneously (church, kinship, marriage, etc.), and where the sense of self is far less defined by what you do (as in the rich west) and more by who you are and where you are from — automatically imply informality is the norm? Does it mean that public policymaking will always be based on calculating the matrix of reciprocal obligations rather than judging the 'public interest'? So size does place real limits on the feasibility of a disinterested, 'neutral' public service and thus on the limitations of the developmental potential of the small state.

How far does the capacity of public administration differ according to a country's size? Today capacity constraints in 'micro-states' appear particularly difficult and intractable in the new global context. Yet smallness, while creating obvious resource constraints, brings benefits too.

Contexts differ. Personal observation of working in Finland and Singapore, as well as empirical data also suggests that the quality of public service may be affected by country population size. The top 10 for quality of public institutions in the 2017 World Competitiveness Index are: Finland (5.5 million; $42.1 k GDP per capita at purchasing power parity); Singapore (5.7 million; $87.8 k); Switzerland (8.4 million; $59.5 k); New Zealand (4.6 million; $37.2 k) Sweden (9.9 million; $49.8 k); Norway (5.3 million; $69.2 k); United Arab Emirates (9.3 million; $67.8 k); Luxembourg (0.58 million; $104 k); Qatar (2.3 million; $127 k) and Hong Kong (7.4 million.; $58.3 k). So the biggest by population is Sweden, ranks only 90th globally; the lowest by GDP per capita is New Zealand, ranked 31st by the IMF at PPP. The top 10 for public sector performance in the 2017 World Competitiveness Index are the same countries except the entry of Rwanda (population 12.1 million.) pushes Sweden down to 11th place.[42]

---

[42] IMF 2016 figures, World Economic Outlook Database, April 2017, International Monetary Fund.

The explanation of these findings may be that informal institutions of trust, oversight and accountability may have greater strength in smaller societies. The direction of causality is, however, unclear: being small certainly does not ensure quality of formal public institutions. The evidence is also limited as the Index only looked at 138 countries so ignored smaller, mostly less affluent nations. But the bottom 10 countries included three fairly small countries by population and GDP per capita in Paraguay (6.8 million; $9.3 k), Mauritania (4.2 million; $4.3 k) and El Salvador (6.1 million; $8.9 k); but also medium-sized Bolivia (11.1 million; $7.2 k), Burundi (11.9 million; $841) and Chad (14.9 million; $2.4 k). The bottom two countries ranked by the Index for quality of public institutions were Yemen (28.1 million; $2.3 k) and Venezuela (31.9 million; $13.7 k), 43rd by population, while Nigeria was 7th by population size at 191 million people but 126th by quality of public institutions. Size is, therefore, not destiny.

Big states can learn humility from smaller countries and from big patterns in history. These have been unfashionable in academia, as too many professional historians dig ever deeper but more narrowly, shirking their obligation to explain. One such challenge is to explain the long-run role of public service in state-building. National public administration is strengthened by centralisation and unification and weakened by decentralisation and state fragmentation, caught overcoming repressive local elite capture or rejecting the coercive arrogance of an overbearing centralised state.

Park Bench Legitimacy

Big and complex problems — illicit flows of capital, guns and narcotics; climate change; mass migration; growing inequality — are global. But global solutions are in short supply. The practical solutions to more immediate problems, however, are local. Citizens benefit from the right balance between the big ambitions of grand design at the national level, and the detailed practical solutions of municipal drainage systems building 'park bench legitimacy'. Administratively well-run cities like Milan in politically dysfunctional Italy, and city-states like Singapore and Dubai are flourishing. They do not have governments posturing on the world stage nor powerful ministries defending vested interests, but public services that simply strive to serve.

Goldilocks Government?

Neither 'big' nor 'small government' is intrinsically optimal. Some 300 million people around the world, totalling no less than some 4% of humanity or 7% of the earth's working age population, directly work for government.[43] The ratio in 12th-century Song dynasty China was one bureaucrat for every 15,000 people. In 2006, the total number of public and municipal servants in Russia reached 1,462,000, or about 9 per 1000 citizens. In 2012, India had 16 public service employees at all levels of government for every 1000 residents; the United States had 76. India's central government, with 3.1 million employees, had 2.57 serving every 1000 population, against the US federal government's 8.4 — but if the 1.4 million people working for the railways, accounting for 44.81% of the entire central government workforce, are removed, there were only about 1.25 central employees serving every 1000 people.

The highest ratios of public servants to population among the Indian States are in the conflict-torn or border regions, such as Jammu and Kashmir 36 per 1000. Poor states have low numbers of public servants. Bihar, for example, has just 4.5 per 1000, but even the well-off states struggle to ensure universal primary education and eradicating poverty. At Nigeria independence in 1960, the federal civil service had a staff strength of only 30,000, this increased steadily to 45,104 in 1970, it rose

---

[43] Depending on the definition. Public Sector Employees data from ILO statistics and databases. To take a specific example, in Laos a World Bank study of 2010 calculated that the country employed 1.8 public servants per 100 citizens, or 4% of the employed population, accounting for 28% of government expenditure, and constituted around a third of the formal sector. In the OECD countries, the average public sector employment rate was 21.3% of the national workforce in 2013. As a percentage of the total population, World Bank data (2015) show this to be 10% for high-income countries, 6% for middle-income countries and 1% for low-income countries; by Freedom House data, 9% in 'free' countries, 8% in 'not free' countries and 5% for 'partially free' countries; by region, variation ranges from 10.3% in Eastern Europe and Central Asia to 1.6% in South Asia, including a significant regional, income and freedom variation too in size of SOEs.

to 98, 877 in 1974, 213,802 in 1988 and reached 273,392 in 1988 during Babangida's administration of 200,000 in the late 1990s due to political patronage. Many unqualified personnel joined the Civil Service which resulted in an over-sized workforce whose salaries absorbed about 87% of the total government revenue.

But, irrespective of their numbers, paid bureaucrats have in every context equally struggled to extend the reach of government effectively and efficiently to local level.

The 'Custodian of the imperial Inkstand'

Bureaucracy can expand productively if increasing specialisation and expertise, but also unproductively by ever more layers of hierarchy. With the latter, job titles often grow more abstruse. One example is the 'Custodian of the Imperial Inkstand' at Constantinople that gave 'Byzantine' its meaning of labyrinthine bureaucratic complexity. But what defines is useful or excessive 'hierarchy'? 'Red tape' exists because public authorities have over decades and centuries evolved due process, codes of ethics and governance that protect the public purse from fraud and corruption. This masks the lack of objectives, strategy or leadership when politicians fail to provide these but then seek a scapegoat in the civil service. As the UK government's adviser on applying private sector thinking to the public sector, Lord Browne, noted in 2013: *'Whitehall is failing not because civil servants are lazy or incompetent, but because in the current outdated structure no one could succeed'*.

In Nigeria, for example, allegations against some civil servants on grand corruption have been staple fare. In 2001, a permanent secretary of the ministry of defence was accused of embezzling funds amounting to N450 million. The chairperson of the Educational Tax Fund (ETF) and the Accountant General of the Federation, a former chairman of the Inland Revenue Services, were alleged to have embezzled funds of the ETF to the tune of N40 billion between 1993 and 2000. In 2003, Chief Vincent Azie was appointed in Acting Auditor General of the Federation. He found that most of the accounts audited in 2002 were inaccurate and showed irregularities. His report of 2003 itemised over-invoicing, non-retirement of cash advances, lack of audit inspection, payment for jobs not done, double-debiting, contract inflation, lack of receipts, brazen violation of financial regulations and releasing funds without the involvement of the approving authorities. The report indicted all federal ministries for gross financial indiscipline in ignoring financial regulations. Little was done.

How politics shapes the effectiveness of public administration can be seen in the state of Oaxaca, in Mexico. In 1995, indigenous communities were allowed to choose their forms of governance. The reform gave full legal standing to the local tradition of indigenous customary governance called *usos y costumbres*. Under this, leaders are chosen in non-partisan elections, decisions are arrived at through participatory democracy and compliance enforced through a primarily informal system of community justice.

A decade later, comparison between the two systems showed that the provision of education, sewerage and electricity was notably better in those municipalities governed by traditional governance. One explanation is that public officials are more social embedded, giving them credible social obligation to provide services for poor communities to be more accountable, prevent elite capture, and monitor and sanction non-cooperative behaviour.[44]

The 2015 UK Civil Service 'People Survey' showed that the overwhelming majority of its personnel felt that they knew their jobs and wanted to do it as well as possible. But they often felt beset at every turn by what often seemed unintelligible, time wasting and fruitless management initiatives, constant change, ill-judged targets, wrong-headed 'commercial' exemplars and continuous and misguided restructuring: 'I have to watch as, instead of my "customers" (actually patients, pupils, taxpayers) getting a better deal from me, the only beneficiaries seem to be those who can lobby for special treatment'.[45]

Had they been consulted and bought in to the process? The same survey showed that only a quarter of these officials thought that 'When changes are made they are usually for the better' (and, indeed, only 57% of top managers thought that either); and only slightly more (28%) thought that they had

---

[44] Diaz-Cayeros, A., Magaloni, B. and Ruiz-Euler, A. 2013. Traditional Governance, Citizen Engagement, and Local Public Goods: Evidence from Mexico. *World Development*, 53, 80–93.

[45] Manson, J. 2012. *Public Service on the Brink*. London.

the opportunity to contribute their views before decisions are made that affect them. That is a telling indictment of a change management culture. innovative ideas to tackle these problems are emerging. The evidence indicates that, for instance, motivation in the UK public service is less affected despite budgetary constraints.[46] For example, while austerity measures decimated job security and pensions (rated as important or very important to 88% and 86% of UK employees, respectively[47]), many employees stayed on because of their passion for what they did (72% believed that providing a public service is an important or very important motivation for staying in the civil service, and 51% felt that being a civil servant was important), even though only 24% felt fairly paid. In fact, although 53% wanted to quit in the next year or so, 89% remained interested in their work. Public services need to stop scorning and start embracing the sense of passion for their mission felt by Non-Governmental Organisations (NGOs). The skill-sets needed in public service are evolving into something more currently associated with the NGO employee — empathy and compassion. Similarly, public service offers intellectually interesting work that creates a sense of contribution to the greater good and conveys a caring image.

Embracing *Government by Design* can inspire that sense of passion, while better decision making by 'co-creation' offers a methodology not simply to improve delivery.[48] It is also a likely way to resurrect the social status and job satisfaction of public service officials.

A 'New Public Passion' can replace 'New Public Management' as necessary to nurture high job satisfaction by ensuring that all civil servants feel directly engaged in improving the lives of their fellow citizens ... [and] that the UNDP's work can help instill and renew such a sense of passion for development in public officials around the world.[49]

---

[46] OECD. 2015. 'The Impact of Budgetary Constraints on HRM — Report on Survey Results'. OECD doc GOV/PGC/PEM(2015)11/REV1, p. 34.

[47] Cornerstone OnDemand, Civil Service World surveyed 4,196 public sector workers to find out what motivates people to join and stay in the civil service.

[48] Alford, J. 2009. *Engaging Public Sector Clients From Service Delivery to Co-production.* Houndmills, Hamps and New York: Palgrave Macmillan.

[49] Clark, H. Modernizing Civil Services for the New Sustainable Development Agenda, speech delivered at the Astana Economic Forum on Meritocracy and Professional Ethics as Key Factors of Civil Service Effectiveness, 21 May 2015.

While continuous disruptive change in an unprecedented complex environment requires ever more sophisticated policy responses, the public officials responsible for tackling these challenges on behalf of citizens and state remain deeply disenchanted. The disconnect between the expectations of public service capacities to manage a context of ever-growing complexity and the ever-deepening despondency of public service officials about their sense of self-worth is rarely acknowledged, let alone honestly addressed. Political leaders fail to promote the status of public servants in society. So the very civil servants delivering essential services and implementing the processes of reform that politicians introduce feel deep discontent, not so much with pay and conditions as with job satisfaction.

Street-level bureaucrats and front-line workers (policemen, teachers, doctors, nurses, regulators, tax collectors) can choose to either act out of self-interest (including absenteeism, corruption, abuse of power, laxity, inattention) or perform in the best interests of the organisation and go beyond mere compliance with formal policies and procedures.

The fundamental drive of all organisations is survival and perceived legitimacy, where the perception of legitimacy is integral to attracting human and financial resources.

High-performing organisations focus on demonstrated success, their leaders strive for value creation, and workers are performance oriented; low-performing organisations stress compliance.

Public sector organisations have a monopoly on the provision of services or on the receipt of public resources. The deployment of state power to impose obligations is by its nature a monopoly: a given jurisdiction can only have one army or one police force or one tax authority or one arbiter of property rights or one regulator of air polluters' emissions or one court of final appeal.

All public sector organisations struggle with encouraging, recognising and rewarding innovation because a monopoly in the utilisation of state authority and resources can seem to lead inevitably to apathy and indolence.

NPM reforms led to the fragmentation of the civil service system and a decrease in coordination and monitoring of the service, since central personnel agencies were abolished in Australia, New Zealand, the

United Kingdom and other developed countries.[50] The NPM model of HRM in the public sector dismantled recruitment to an internal labour market and reduced career employment security the reduction of public sector employment created fear, tension and feelings of job insecurity among public servants. One of the limitations of the NPM model reforms is the possibility of undermining the values of the public domain through emphasising commercial culture.[51]

State-building and bureaucracy

The state needs authority and that requires public officials. The complaint is that excessive power and oppression develops, although matched, in contradictory fashion, by incompetence.

Governance is facing a crisis in many parts of the world. Trust in government appears on the decline, for complex reasons.[52] This matters both intrinsically (if the state is not regarded by its citizens as representing the common interest of the population) and instrumentally, for example, low trust in government undermines quasi-voluntary tax compliance, the willingness to fund public service, and decreases morale of officials.

> Most reforms in government fail. They do not fail because, once implemented, they yield unsatisfactory outcomes. They fail because they never get past the implementation stage at all. They are blocked outright or put into effect only in tokenistic, half-hearted fashion.[53]

---

[50] Colley, L., McCourt, W. and Waterhouse, J. 2012, Hybrids and Contradictions: Human Resource Management in the Contemporary Public Sector. *International Journal of Public Administration*, 35(8), 507–512; Colley, L. and Price, R. 2010. Where Have All The Workers Gone? Exploring Public Sector Workforce Planning. *Australian Journal of Public Administration*, 69, 202–213.

[51] Stewart, J. and Walsh, K. 1992. Change in the Management of Public Services. *Public Administration*, 70, 499–518.

[52] Nye, J. S., Zelikow, P. D. and King, D. C. 1997. *Why People Don't Trust Government*. Harvard University Press, Cambridge, MA.

[53] Polidano, C. 2001. *Why Civil Service Reforms Fail*. IDPM Public Policy Working Paper no.16.

Another suggests that the 'Civil Service reform syndrome' creates 'initiatives [that] come and go, overlap and ignore each other, leaving behind residues of varying size and style'.[54] The syndrome persists 'because the assumptions behind reforms are not fit for public sector purpose'.[55]

In developing countries, these problems are often more serious because the need for an effective public sector and, therefore, for public service reform is greater. Such is the degree of failure generally, and continued weaknesses of governments after reform interventions are complete,[56] that three professors at Harvard categorise success as the 'positive deviant' of public sector reform.[57] Many major bilateral donor agencies have retreated from the field, as all too difficult.

---

[54] Hood and Lodge, *op. cit.*
[55] Rhodes, R. 2014. *So You Want to Reform the Civil Service.* London.
[56] Pritchett, L., Woolcock, M. and Andrews, M. 2013. Looking Like a State: Techniques of Persistent Failure in State Capability for Implementation. *Journal of Development Studies,* 49(1), 1–18.
[57] Andrews, M. 2013. *Explaining Positive Deviance in Public Sector Reforms in Development.* Working papers, Center for International Development. Harvard.

Chapter 12

Pour Encourager Les Autres

The naval battle off Minorca in May 1756 in the Mediterranean at the start of the Seven Years' War resulted in the court-martial and execution of the British commander, Admiral John Byng, for 'failure to do his utmost' to hold the island of Minorca. The French philosopher Voltaire, in his novel *Candide* (published in 1759), famously commented on this with the one-line quip: *il est bon de tuer de temps en temps un amiral pour encourager les autres* — 'it is wise to kill an admiral from time to time to encourage the others'. Presumably for the same reason in 2016 Kim Jong-Un, the leader of North Korea, ordered the execution of Ri Yong-jin, a senior official in the education ministry, for falling asleep at a meeting chaired by Kim.

Attitudes towards public officials have varied greatly between cultures. In 1870, a century before Public Choice Theory argued the same more didactically, a lawyer in London named Thomas Baker wrote a lengthy diatribe entitled 'The Insidious Red-Tape System of Government in England'. In this pamphlet attacking government bureaucracy or 'jobbery', he suggested that officials were as idle as possible in performing their official duties while devoting their efforts to working out 'how to fleece the taxpaying community in the handsomest manner'.[1] A self-employed barrister of Inner Temple personified the self-righteous indignation of the small businessman, pitting virtuous 'entrepreneurship' of hard

---

[1] *Op. cit.*, p. 4.

work and risk-taking against pen-pushing sloth. Margaret Thatcher frequently cited the influence of her father running a grocery shop in Grantham as a model of the spirit of liberty and free market. The 'land of small shopkeepers' lacked a sense of the state's, and therefore public officials' importance.

The quality of government and the trust and confidence people have in their public officials contribute to well-being. An effective state requires an effective bureaucracy. The fundamental purpose of the public service is to enable a government to rule, not manage. This means that the values that maintain and strengthen trust in public sector organisations are critical, and support the morale and motivation of officials. So do not ape the private sector search for a better bottom line by pursuing 'public value' as a tepid compromise, but proudly assert the ethics of working for the common good, and uphold public service values. A meritocratic civil service system usually deprives the top political leadership of using public service to reward political supporters.

It is important to recognise the dignity of work in the public sector as motivation and morale, built on pride, prestige and pragmatism. Plug the gap between the vision and reality through motivation surveys. The first challenge is to admit that the motivation problem exists. Employee commitment depends on: (i) personal discretion at work; (ii) opportunities to master new knowledge and skills; (iii) tasks with a higher purpose; (iv) fair and respectful treatment in the workplace; and (v) a sense of inclusion within the work group and organisation.

Stress is on the rise where budgetary cuts cause a reduction in salaries and promotion opportunities,[2] and perceptions exist of increasing organisational and procedural injustice, such as unprofessional performance assessments and unfair recruitment decisions.[3] In Zimbabwe, for instance, gains in public health coinciding with the increased availability of medical equipment and drugs have been eroded by low morale of public workers caused by poor salaries and inadequate infrastructure. This has, in turn,

---

[2] Demmke, C. and Moilanen, T. (n.d.). *Effectiveness of Public-Service Ethics and Good Governance in the Central Administration of the EU-27*. Bern, Suisse: Peter Lang D, p. 23. Retrieved 12 March 2018, from http://www.peterlang.com/view/product/17577.
[3] *Op. cit.*, p. 95.

resulted in absenteeism and moonlighting, and in more extreme cases, corruption and unauthorised sales of free medicine.[4] A study of public sector employees in Ghana confirms that dissatisfaction with pay (83%) and working conditions (64%) are among the leading factors for a demotivated and unproductive public workforce in Sub-Saharan Africa.[5]

Austerity measures have undoubtedly played a large part in the overall lowering of job satisfaction in recent years.[6] A recent study found that 83% of those OECD countries facing fiscal austerity confront *lower job satisfaction* among public officials, and 84% are witnessing increasing distrust in leadership. Yet, austerity is not the only cause of malaise: 36% of the non-austerity countries are also witnessing a *decrease in workplace commitment* in public service (58% for the austerity countries); 21% of the non-austerity countries observe a *decrease of trust* (73% of the austerity countries); and a *decrease of loyalty to the public service* affects 14% of the non-austerity countries (58% of all austerity countries).

In reality, the evidence on collapse in morale and public service motivation (PSM) is more complex than simply the result of austerity. Some believe that Singapore manages to retain high intrinsic motivation because it pays its officials well. Yet, the public service of Switzerland, one of Europe's most prosperous countries, is surprisingly among those most affected by negative workplace behaviour and a general collapse in morale. All OECD states have witnessed serious decreases in key attributes of public service: 58% of the austerity countries and 36% of the non-austerity countries reported a decrease in workplace commitment. Seventy-three per cent of the austerity countries and 21% of the non-austerity countries observe a decrease of trust; and of loyalty to the

---

[4] IRIN, Zimbabwe: Low Morale Erodes Public Health Gains. IRIN website, 3 December 2010, http://www.irinnews.org/report/91283/zimbabwe-low-morale-erodes-public-health-gains.

[5] Abugre, J. 2014. Job Satisfaction of Public Sector Employees in Sub-Saharan Africa: Testing the Minnesota Satisfaction Questionnaire in Ghana. *International Journal of Public Administration,* 37(10), 655–665.

[6] Demmke, C. 2014. *Public Administration Reform and Reform Effects in Western Europe.* Paris, France: SIGMA, p. 28; and Demmke, C. and Moilanen, T. 2013. *Governmental Transformation and the Future of Public Employment: The Impact of Restructuring on Status Development in the Central Administration of the EU-27.* Frankfurt/M: Peter Lang.

public service in 58% of all austerity countries and 14% of the non-austerity countries. About 83% of OECD austerity countries have lowering of job satisfaction, and 84% increasing distrust in leadership. *Yet the evidence is more complex than simply austerity versus non-austerity. Prosperous Switzerland, along with Portugal and the Czech Republic seem most affected; the UK, along with Finland and Sweden least affected.*

Similarly, although South Africa's GDP is roughly seven times larger than Tanzania's, a survey found that only 52.1% of South African health workers are satisfied with their jobs compared to 82.3% of their Tanzanian counterparts.[7] More alarmingly however, a review of public sector reforms in Africa identifies the decline in social values such as honesty, integrity, impartiality and fairness as a major challenge for successful public sector reforms. The review suggests that 'these declining values have encouraged inefficiency and misappropriation of public funds'.[8]

Levels of PSM can vary by seniority within an organisational hierarchy. For instance, India's *State of Civil Services Survey* showed that motivation among ordinary public servants is a challenge (34.9% of staff did not think the appraisal system was objective or fair), although motivation among the IAS and other elite officials remains relatively high.[9] Moreover, motivation can also vary across sectors in a country. A World Bank survey in the Philippines found that, with the exception of teachers, the primary motivation for nearly 80% of other public sector workers was job security.[10]

Job satisfaction (morale) among government employees includes both happiness in the job and level of individual productivity the person attains.

---

[7] Blaauw, D. *et al.* 2013. Comparing the Job Satisfaction and Intention to Leave of Different Categories of Health Workers in Tanzania, Malawi, and South Africa. *Global Health Action, 6*, 68–87.

[8] Kilelo, H. 2015. Public Sector Reform in Africa: Focus, Challenges and Lessons Learnt. *International Journal of Humanities and Social Science Invention, 4*(7), 19–27.

[9] Government of India, Department of Administrative Reforms & Public Grievances. State of Civil Services Survey 2010.

[10] World Bank. Philippines: Improving Bureaucratic Performance Assessment of the Performance-based Bonus Scheme. World Bank Working Paper AUS3494, 1 June 2014.

Quality management studies consistently show a 'virtuous circle' that happy people have higher productivity, and their high achievement encourages them to improve continuously. It is imperative to offer optimal organisational climate to stimulate the best employees' performance. How does the government encourage, recognise and reward performance improvement and productivity among employees? According to the 2017 World Competitiveness Index Singapore is the second most competitive country in the world yet in the World Happiness Index it only ranked in 26th place. Bhutan is in 97th place in both rankings, more educated people in Bhutan are happier than less educated.

Motivation and Risk Taking

Different ideas seek to explain motivation. 'Expectancy Theory', sees motivation in terms of 'instrumentality' and 'valence' or in plain English, that an individual feels motivated if they feel that their effort will result in an intended goal (expectancy), that this goal will achieve an outcome (instrumentality) and that this outcome is worthwhile (valence). So an individual must want the final outcome to be achieved and believe that their action contributes to achieving it.

'Self Determination Theory' suggests that people have a natural tendency to want to perform better, to have a greater sense of belonging and to feel in control of their behaviour and goals. This theory argues that if these intrinsic motivational factors are present, extrinsic rewards, such as money may undermine intrinsic motivation as this uses external rewards to control behaviour. Praise and encouragement, on the other hand, may make a person feel more competent, thus increasing their intrinsic motivation. An individual's performance is improved by three key factors: autonomy over their work; the ability to improve at what they do; and if they have a sense of purpose.[11] Common to all theories is 'self-actualisation', the importance of having control and responsibility over one's work. This allows an individual the freedom to work entrepreneurially, test new ideas and learn from them.

---

[11] Pink, D. 2009. *The Surprising Truth About What Motivates Us.* New York: Riverhead Books.

Research suggests that, for public sector workers, intrinsic motivation is often more important than external rewards.[12] While higher pay may be a way of recruiting skilled staff, it may put off 'pro-social' workers who have an innate a sense of social purpose and are personally committed to working for the benefit of society. The outsourcing of public services imitating the private sector's emphasis on extrinsic motivation may not work;[13] crowding out intrinsic motivation).[14]

Autonomy appears to be an especially important factor in motivating, and enabling, success in public sector work. For example, devolving decision-making power to bureaucrats has a positive impact on the quality of their work. Increased flexibility does not appear to result in bureaucrats pursuing their own objectives at the expense of social interests.[15]

Similarly, a quantitative study that examined 4700 public sector projects in Nigeria delivered by 63 different Nigerian civil service organisations found that greater autonomy in the responsible delivery organisation was a critical factor in success.[16] This is also evident in a case study of people who worked entrepreneurially to bring about legislative reform in the Philippines.[17] Motivation was personal rather than external (the reformers worked even at times when they were not paid), enjoying considerable autonomy over how they worked to achieve the reform.

---

[12] Perry, J. L. and Wise, L. R. 1990. The Motivational Bases of Public Service. *Public Administration Review, 50*(3), 367–373; Bénabou, R. and Tirole, J. 2006. Incentives and Prosocial Behavior. *American Economic Review, 96*; Francois, P. and Vlassopoulos, M. 2008. Pro-Social Motivation and the Delivery of Social Services. *CESifo Economic Studies, 54*(1), 22–54.

[13] Frey, B., Homberg, F. and Osterloh, M. 2013. *Organizational Control Systems and Pay-for-Performance in the Public Service*. Working Paper Series 2013–2011, Center for Research in Economics, Management and the Arts (CREMA).

[14] Jensen, P. and Stonecash, R. 2005. Incentives and the Efficiency of Public Sector-outsourcing Contracts. *Journal of Economic Surveys, 19*(5), 767–787.

[15] Simon, W. 1983. Legality, Bureaucracy, and Class in the Welfare System. *Yale Law Journal, 92*, 1198–1269.

[16] Rasul, I. and Roggery, D. 2013. *Management of Bureaucrats and Public Service Delivery: Evidence from the Nigerian Civil Service*. International Growth Center.

[17] Faustino, J. and Booth, D. 2014. *Development Entrepreneurship: How Donors and Leaders Can Foster Institutional Change*. The Asia Foundation 2014 and the Overseas Development Institute.

The significance of having autonomy over one's work to be able to pursue a goal in the way one thinks best is particularly salient in the public sector where hierarchy has traditional approach to handling political risk. Risk-taking entrepreneurial spirit may be tolerated so long as things go right. In politically highly charged and bitterly divided contexts, however, organisational structure and management practice will tightly limit autonomy, thereby demotivating public sector workers to be experimental in achieving public service goals.

This view, strongly propagated in the United States and reflected in some developing states, has been in the ascendancy for three decades. It is the product of British political philosophy and American 18th-century politics and 19th-century historical experience. In other countries and at other periods this view would be greeted with quiet puzzlement or hoots of derision. For hasn't the public official always been at the heart of state-building? What prosperous country today does not owe its current good fortune to its administration 50 or 100 years ago or longer back still, when the institutions or 'rules of the game' were painstakingly put in place?

Unrestrained free market capitalism produced the South Sea Bubble in 18th-century England or the 'robber barons' of 19th-century America. The 'Just Get out of the way' approach to government is the product of either ignorance or malign self-interest. The Mandarin selected by rigorous examination from among the brightest minds to advance the common interests of all, to restrain the greed of the private sector and the exploitation of the poor and powerless for the greater good.

Research does not uphold the supposed superior efficiency of business. In refuse collection, utilities, public transport and hospital administration, publicly owned enterprise is often more efficient.[18] For half a century from FDR's launch of the New Deal, the *visible* hand of the State and its public service, both as a profession and as a field of study, training and research contributed immensely to the success of decolonisation, social development and shared prosperity.

---

[18] Goodsell, C. 2004. *The Case for Bureaucracy: A Public Administration Polemic.* 4th ed. CQ Press, Washington, DC.

But the election of Margaret Thatcher in 1979 and Ronald Reagan a year later triggered the *Withering away of the State* of the *Washington Consensus*.[19] Economists had all the answers. History was reduced to 'path dependency'.

The collapse of communism a decade later seemed to vindicate this approach. It led to the abandonment of all the evidence that successful development has always required an effective state, not just a small one. Instead, private enterprise led the quest for efficiency. While disastrous experiments in free market solutions across the former USSR and ex-Warsaw Pact countries resulted in oligarchies capturing state assets, and foreign advisers enriching themselves too, public administration was reduced to the monotonous beat of public management by cost-benefit analysis. Effectiveness was devoid of social concern (Pope Francis, 2015, pp. 115, 121). New Public Management (NPM)[20] justified this new approach to government under a mantra of *downsize, deregulate* and *de-centralise*. Others knew better.

The public service profession was undermined by Public Choice Theory that claimed it was wholly self-serving. The concept of it as a career was attacked as privileged protectionism. The search for *best practices* ignored history and local context. Accountants replaced humanists at the top levels of government. The citizen became merely a consumer or customer of public goods. National identity and culture could not be measured, and only the measurable mattered.

The ultimate hubris came when the 'End of History' was declared. Now there was nothing left to debate. Politics had been reduced to the search for efficiency.

---

[19] The Washington Consensus was a set of 10 economic policies promoted as the 'standard' reform package for developing countries, irrespective of local context, by the Washington, DC–based international institutions, the International Monetary Fund (IMF) and World Bank.

[20] New Public Management (NPM) is a term that was coined in the later 1980s to denote the importance of market-oriented management of the public sector that would lead to greater cost-efficiency for governments, with the introduction into public services of the three 'M's: Markets, Managers and Measurement, or of the three 'E's: Economy, Efficiency and Effectiveness.

In 1989 the world-renowned political scientist Francis Fukuyama made his professional name (at the modest price of becoming the laughing stock of historians, and indeed anyone else with common sense) by declaring the passing of the Cold War marked the 'End of History'.[21] Media fame and academic glory blossomed even as his prediction of Western liberal democracy 'as the final form of human government' grew ever more questionable.

The philosophy behind outsourcing and privatisation seemed to dismiss the idea that serving the public was 'different' in kind and ethos from shopping. 'Institutional memory' was no longer a valuable asset and the rule of law was not essential for democratic governance, merely a technical addendum, subordinated to management and expert direction. In NPM, management came first. Economists knew best. Other considerations, including human rights, the law and an understanding of history were certainly useful but only so far as they promoted efficiency and effectiveness judged in economic terms. Concern for equity faded. NPM stripped Law and Political Science out of Public Administration. Government became Applied Economics in a new guise.

Thirty years on, the rise of international terrorism and the Great Recession of 2008 revealed that the state was not withering away. It was clear that the market model of governance and NPM had not produced a government that worked better or cost less. Instead, what it had yielded was serious *collateral damage* to traditions and institutions of democratic governance and public service professionalism.[22]

Rather, public officials working for the common good had suffered the 'Great Demoralisation', undermined on seven fronts:[23]

1. *Ideological* — An assertion, regardless of evidence and repeated often enough that it became accepted as a truism, that the public service is

---

[21] Fukuyama, F. 1992. *The End of History and the Last Man*. Stamford, an expansion of the 1989 essay *The End of History* published in *National Interest*.

[22] Hood, C. and Dixon, R. 2015. *A Government that Worked Better and Cost Less? Evaluation Three Decades of Reform and Change in UK Central Government*. Oxford University Press.

[23] Baimenov, A. and Everest-Phillips, M. 2016. A Shared Perspective on Public Administration and International Development. *Public Administration Review,* 76, 389–390.

inherently incompetent, indolent and unresponsive by its nature — rather than, if those characteristics were true, it is because political leaders allow this (contrast this with post-independence Singapore: political determination for building a highly disciplined and motivated public service has transformed the city-state).
2. *Intellectual* — A 'Catch 22' conundrum has developed:
   - Public Choice Theory posits the idea that the public service is inherently self-serving and needed to be constrained.
   - NPM propagates the exact opposite view that public service is inherently apathetic and needed to be incentivised into being effective.
3. *Commercial* — Big profits for consultants and business are created by the belief that was fostered by the ideas of NPM, of running government more like a business, outsourcing services and promoting public–private partnerships.
4. *Political* — Blaming the public service for failure offers a tempting scapegoat for politicians to deflect criticism of their own inadequate leadership and direction.
5. *Financial* — Pay levels in professional posts in the public service have lagged behind those of the private sector, so that either many high-skilled vacancies could not be filled or special pay arrangements were required.
6. *Institutional* — There has been enough (selected) truth in some imagery of obstructive public service unions and unhelpful 'street level bureaucrats' to drown out the much more positive images of devotion to public good, such as was famously demonstrated by the unstinting self-sacrifice of officers of the New York fire service on and after 9/11.
7. *Organisational* — Both elected leaders and senior administrators benefit from creating a 'permanent revolution' of ceaseless reforms and reorganisation of the public service. Despite the mounting evidence over the years that many reforms achieve almost no lasting improvements but greatly demoralise staff, the temptation to appear to be shaking up supposedly lazy and incompetent bureaucrats is all too great.

What is the problem?

Ethics in Public Service

Almost everywhere, public service is in crisis. Citizens' perceptions of ethics in public administration shape satisfaction with services, trust in governmental institutions, and the credibility of politics and political leadership. Maintaining the highest standards of ethics in public service is essential.[24]

The evidence from Anglophone Africa is disturbing. Any impetus for development collapsed when public sector wages declined 80% in real terms between the early 1970s and 1980s (in parallel to the general decline in per capita GDP).[25] In Eritrea, a desperately poor country of 5 million people, during the mid-1990s, public service morale collapsed as a result of 'restructuring', 'right-sizing', 'streamlining' and other euphemisms for cuts. The civil service shrank by 34%, with over 11,500 people losing their jobs.[26]

In one tradition, public administration is synonymous with massive waste, mindless rules, useless forms. Inefficiency abounds, poor service is guaranteed, but the number of bureaucrats — lazy, overpaid, yet inflexible — is ever growing. This view, strongly propagated in the United States and reflected in some developing states, has been in the ascendancy for three decades. The public's distrust of politicians and of the media creates a downward spiral of cynicism sapping the morale of public officials. But it is very much the product of the American 18th-century politics and 19th-century historical experience.

However, in other countries and at other periods this view would be greeted with quiet puzzlement. For isn't the mandarin selected by rigorous examination from among the very brightest minds to advance the common

---

[24] See for instance Blind, *op. cit.* http://unpan1.un.org/intradoc/groups/public/documents/un/unpan025062.pdf.

[25] Van de Walle, N. 2001. *African Economies and the Politics Permanent Crisis.* Cambridge University Press, New York, p. 134.

[26] See Tessema, M. 2005. *Practices, Challenges and Prospects of HRM Developing Countries: The Case of Eritrea.* PhD thesis, Tilburg University; Tessema, M. and Soeters, J. 2006. Challenges and Prospects of HRM Developing Countries: Testing the HRM–Performance Link in Eritrean Civil Service. *International Journal of Human Resource Management, 17*(1), 86–105.

interests of all, to restrain the greed of the private sector and the exploitation of the poor and powerless for the greater good?

> Native-born of high family, influential, well trained in arts, possessed of foresight, wise, of strong memory, bold, eloquent, skillful, intelligent, possessed of enthusiasm, dignity, and endurance, pure in character, affable, firm in loyal devotion, endowed with excellent conduct, strength, health and bravery, free from procrastination and ficklemindedness, affectionate, and free from such qualities as excite hatred and enmity.

The recruitment process would work as follows:

> Of these qualifications, native birth and influential position shall be ascertained from reliable persons; educational qualifications (silpa) from professors of equal learning; theoretical and practical knowledge, foresight, retentive memory, and affability shall be tested from successful, application in works; eloquence, skillfulness and flashing intelligence from power shown in narrating stories (katháyogeshu, i.e., in conversation); endurance, enthusiasm, and bravery in troubles; purity of life, friendly disposition, and loyal devotion by frequent association; conduct, strength, health, dignity, and freedom from indolence and ficklemindedness shall be ascertained from their intimate friends; and affectionate and philanthrophic nature by personal experience.[27]

The *Amatyah*, states Arthashastra, must be: well trained, with foresight, with strong memory, bold, well spoken, excellence in their field of expertise, learned in theoretical and practical knowledge, pure of character, of good health, kind and philanthropic, free from procrastination, fickleness, hate, enmity, free from anger, and dedicated to dharma, or upholding duties, rights, laws, conduct, virtues and 'right way of living' or righteousness. Those who lack such characteristics can only be employed in middle or lower positions in the administration. Officials who lack integrity must be arrested. The highest level ministers must have

---

[27] *Op. cit.*, Book 1, Chapters 5 and 6.

been tested and have successfully demonstrated integrity in all situations.

Loyalty to the party in power, rather than neutrality in the wider interest, has been increasingly demanded.[28]

'Bureaucracy' is an easy target for short-term, populist and narrow political interests, this too can negatively affect the morale and motivation of public employees.

Bangladesh has been undertaking administrative reform initiatives almost continuously since independence in 1971. The constant flow of reform studies and proposals produced little evidence of real change. In the first 30 odd years, 19 reform commissions or committees sought to reorganise/reform civil service and public sector. More than 20 reports on public administration reform were prepared by these commissions and committees and some at the initiative of important development partners, particularly the World Bank, the UNDP, the Asian Development Bank (ADB), the Department for International Development (DFID) and the US Agency for International Development (USAID).[29]

The result was change-without-change politics, the turmoil of the talk of change without producing its benefits. This suited the bureaucracy that became remarkably skilled in adapting to views of political rulers. Politicians lacked political will to break away from a highly centralised administrative system, inherited from the colonial era.

Bangladesh civil service reform actions were merely cosmetic. The needed radical change to the structure and composition of the public service and the work attitudes of the civil servants did not happen. The public bureaucracy suffers from outside interference in administrative decision-making and is deeply politicised. Nepotism and favouritism are endemic. The lack of delegated authority for initiative from mid-level and local level public officials is matched by a lack of public scrutiny of public administration and a paucity of citizen demand for improvements in public administration.

---

[28] Rhodes, R. 2015. *Recovering the 'Craft' of Public Administration in Westminster Government*. Paper presented at the Political Studies Association 65th Annual International Conference, 30 March–1 April 2015, Sheffield City Hall and Town Hall, UK.

[29] http://unpan1.un.org/intradoc/groups/public/documents/apcity/unpan035761.pdf.

Public administration in Bangladesh remains largely centralised, excessively reliant on hierarchy and multiple layers of decision-making. Human resource planning is hardly existent and although frequent changes arrive in postings, inter-departmental mobility is rare. There are no incentives currently in place that encourage initiative and award excellence. The performance management system is obsolete and subjective. Training is neither linked to career planning, nor related to other dimensions of personnel management. Career opportunities are generally confined within a cadre.

Muddling Through

In 1959 — coincidentally, in the same year Singapore attained self-government — an American professor of public administration called Charles Lindblom published his now-classic paper, 'The science of "muddling through"' in the journal *Public Administration Review*. This paper presciently expressed the pragmatism that has become characteristic of Singapore's public service. The art of Singapore's governance is frequent, incremental improvements. This ability and capacity in public officials for continuous change appears to have become institutionalised in Singapore, as in Toyota car manufacturing KAIZEN approach in Japan.

Public Service Excellence in the 'Singapore Story' is the principles that have driven public service excellence in Singapore, such as integrity, meritocracy, results orientation, a fair share of talent for the public sector, delegating operational authority to Boards and autonomous agencies, budgetary reforms to maximise the public sector value proposition, instiling a culture of ownership, pride and continuous improvement in the public service, measuring and rewarding organisational performance, continuous innovation and a culture of leadership by example,

Rather than prescribe what public bureaucracies should do, it is necessary to know what they actually do. This is especially important in the context of developing countries, for 'reform' is never just a technocratic issue. One reason for that is that changes to the nature of public sector change the nature of the state, and state–citizen relations. For example, altering human resource management (HRM) of the civil service affects governance by amending the profile of administration. Pragmatic incrementalism driven by public officials recruited on the basis of merit. Finally, one insight from the present is particularly pertinent: trying to modernise the civil service indicates that caution is needed in accepting at face value any political claim for reforming public administration. Carefully spell out the ambition.

Today, the quality of public service is the most decisive factor determining national competitiveness in the 21st century. This is exemplified by city-states like Monaco, small states like Finland, small island states like Malta, and the only small island city-state, Singapore. Like Urukagina, Lee Kuan Yew was determined to stamp out corruption, which enabled him to foster the politics of practical pragmatism and encourage merit-based bureaucracy.

Small states in particular must be concerned for the welfare of all their people because social inequalities are more visible, so Urukagina too worried about boatmen, fishermen, and so forth.

But the modern city-state frets about its survival.[30]

Happy Citizens

The inter-war fascist dictator of Italy, Benito Mussolini, dismissed democracy as:

> The absurd conventional untruth of political equality dressed out in the garb of collective irresponsibility, and the myth of 'happiness' and indefinite progress.[31]

---

[30] The fate of the Hanseatic League or of the great Renaissance entrepôts like Genoa or Venice suggests that great trading port cities become targets of international rivalries or national state-building ambitions. Goa and Macao were swept away by resurgent India and China, intolerant of colonial era quirks. Most of Europe's surviving city-states like San Marino, Andorra, Mount Athos or Lichtenstein are mountain redoubts. Monaco's blockade by France in 1962–1963 prefigured today's concerns over tax havens, mostly island vestiges of empire like the Caymans or BVI, where international investors benefit from the security of high quality 'rule of law' and administrative institutions without having to pay the tax to secure them.

[31] *1932 Mussolini with Giovanni Gentile Entry for the Italian Encyclopedia on the Definition of Fascism.*

Governments are struggling to address citizen well-being, not just by sector. In the Age of Anxiety, social cohesion and equality of opportunity confront high economic vulnerability, unequal political capital and limited social mobility. The Happiness Index, first published in 2012, suggests contentment rather than wealth is the proper goal of public policy.

Collectively, wealth does not buy happiness. Bhutan's 2015 GNH Index showed that, while the overall population becoming 'happier', the level of contentment of civil servants had declined from 2010.[32]

Singapore is under-performing in a public sector to citizen contentment ratio by comparison with the Nordic countries, Switzerland and New Zealand, on a rough par with the UAE, and well ahead of Qatar and Hong Kong.

His Highness Sheikh Mohammed Bin Rashid Al Maktoum, Vice-President and Prime Minister of the UAE and The Emir of Dubai, is grimly determined to make the citizens of Dubai happy. The goal of his Smart Dubai initiative is to make Dubai the happiest city on earth. Launched in March of 2014, it embarked the city-state on transformation including legal, governance, infrastructure and public services, driven by the vision that the city-state's most valued asset is its people. Their happiness is the future.

Context matters

Improving pay reduces corruption. That is obvious. But think again. In one of the most ambitious public sector reform experiments in Africa, the Ghana government doubled its police officer salaries in 2010 in part to mitigate petty corruption on its roads, while leaving salaries for other officials unchanged. Researchers used unique data on bribes paid from over 2100 truck trips in West Africa and representing over 45,000 bribe opportunities. Even to their own astonishment, the researchers found that, far from decreasing petty corruption, the salary policy significantly increased the police efforts to collect bribes, the value of bribes and the

---

[32] Tshiteem, K. and Everest-Phillips, M. 2016. Public Service Happiness and Morale in the Context of Development: The Case of Bhutan. *Asia Pacific Journal of Public Administration, 38*, 168–185.

amounts given by truck drivers to policemen in total. The results show that raised salaries for Ghanaian police officers caused the police to increase the effort they put forth to get bribes by 19%, the value of bribes taken at each individual stop by between 25% and 28% and increased the total amount taken on the road, even while they reduced the number of times they received a bribe. So raising salaries of corrupt officials can have the consequence of worsening petty corruption, in contrast to many cross-country and lab-based studies that have appeared to show that higher salaries or payments reduce corruption. Since the Ghanaian salary increase experiment took place without an equivalent increase in enforcement of anti-corruption laws, the results here suggest that fighting corruption cannot be done by salary policies alone.[33]

In Pakistan research is showing the motorway police is the least corrupt force in that country, apparently due to pride in the job.

Such examples raise doubts about 'Pay for Success' schemes that focus on outcomes (e.g. ex-offenders do not re-offend) rather than endlessly paying to lock up criminals in prisons. Singapore's success with prisons came from the initiative of warders.

In a complex interconnected and rapidly changing world, the quality of civil service that a country has is still largely under the control of the citizens and their leaders. Take Papua New Guinea. Papua New Guinea is 158th on the Human Development Index.[34] It is a land of great opportunity and challenge and has not been able to deliver on any of its Millennium Development Goals.[35] It is one of the most linguistically diverse countries in the world with 840 languages[36] spoken by a

---

[33] Foltz, J. and Opoku-Agyemang, K. 2016. *Do Higher Salaries Lower Petty Corruption? A Policy Experiment on West Africa's Highways*. International Growth Centre.

[34] Of 188 countries measured in 2015. UNDP. 2015. *Human Development Report 2015, Briefing note for countries on the 2015 Human Development Report*, Papua New Guinea. http://hdr.undp.org/sites/all/themes/hdr_theme/country-notes/PNG.pdf.

[35] Inter Press Service. 2015. *Papua New Guinea Reckons with Unmet Development Goals*. 27 May. http://www.pg.undp.org/content/papua_new_guinea/en/home/presscenter/pressreleases/2015/05/27/papua-new-guinea-reckons-with-unmet-development-goals.html.

[36] http://www.ethnologue.com/country/PG.

population of more than 7 million people.[37] It is rich in natural resources but has high levels of exposure to movements in international resource prices.[38] With a significant reliance on subsistence farming many Papua New Guineans are at the mercy of the weather as seen in the drought from December 2015.[39]

Papua New Guinea cannot control its cultural context, global resource prices or the weather. It can largely control the quality of its civil service within these constraints and can leverage civil servants to support the decisions and implement the actions needed to improve Papua New Guinea's development and mitigate its exposure to social, economic and environmental risks over time.

The challenge is that the goalposts keep shifting — for the public, private and non-profit sector. The rate of change is accelerating in an increasingly complex globalised and interconnected world.

In public management, Peter Ho has been a clear voice on this challenge. As Head of the Singaporean Civil Service in 2007 he spoke of the need for increasingly networked and experimental government to better cope with uncertainty and the speed of change for Singapore to 'thrive in a turbulent world'.[40] This idea has underpinned most recent thinking on public management systems — under the collective heading of New Public Governance. A leading example of this is the New Synthesis of Public Administration work led by Jocelyne Bourgon.[41]

'Morale and motivation in the public sector have collapsed in many countries across both the developed and developing worlds… [which]

---

[37] The 2011 census records the population as 7,275,324. http://www.nso.gov.pg/index.php/population-and-social/other-indicators.

[38] UNDP, *op. cit.*

[39] ReliefWeb. 2015. *Papua New Guinea: Drought and Frost — Information Bulletin.* 5 September. http://reliefweb.int/report/papua-new-guinea/papua-new-guinea-drought-and-frost-information-bulletin.

[40] Ho, P. 2007. *Thriving in a Turbulent World.* Opening Address at the Public Service Staff Conference, 18 September. In Low, D. and Kwok, A. (eds.). 2009. *In Time for The Future: Singapore's Heads of Civil Service on Change, Complexity and Networked Government.* Civil Service College.

[41] Bourgon, J. 2011. *A New Synthesis of Public Administration: Serving in the 21st Century.* Queen's Policy Studies.

represents a major obstacle to the achievement of the SDGs'.[42] The OECD[43] shows that this is a 'systemic problem, not just reflecting fiscal austerity, for while 58% of OECD countries undertaking strict austerity measures reported a decrease in workplace commitment, so, too, did 36% of "non-austerity" countries'.[44]

For many civil servants the world of increasing complexity and change is not a welcoming place if they feel devalued, disempowered and buffeted by contradictory 'winds of change'. Yet there is a pressing need for civil services that can deliver trust, responsiveness and dynamism in a world of change and complexity often while cutting costs and from a base of low morale. The SDGs cannot be achieved without overcoming this challenge.

The values established by public administration remain the lifeblood of effective civil service. Integrity, professionalism, merit-based appointment and political neutrality take different forms in different contexts but any jurisdiction that does not have a clear and consistent approach to these issues is in trouble. New Zealand is able to draw on 100 years of largely fulsome and consistent application of these values and as a result is the only non-Scandinavian country consistently in the top four countries with the lowest perceived corruption.[45]

Public administration relied on the power of intrinsic motivation from the start — seeking an alignment with these values in its appointments and largely relying on voluntary compliance with codes of conduct in a pre-digital world where actions were harder to audit. But that passion for service was, and is, often channelled into routine compliance activities where the enforcement of rules and the tyranny of process supersede real service to citizens.

---

[42] Everest-Phillips, Max. 2015. The Power of 'New Public Passion'. *The Strait Times*, November 5. http://www.straitstimes.com/opinion/the-power-of-new-public-passion.

[43] Demmke, C. 2014. *Public Administration Reform and Reform Effects in Western Europe*. SIGMA. http://www.slideshare.net/SIGMA2013/presentation-by-dr-christoph-demmke-oecd; and Demmke, C., and Moilanen, T. 2013. *Governmental Transformation and the Future of Public Employment: The Impact of Restructuring on Status Development in the Central Administration of the EU-27*. Peter Lang.

[44] Everest-Phillips, *op. cit.*

[45] Transparency International, *Corruption Perceptions Index*, http://www.transparency.org/research/cpi/overview.

So the primary motivation becomes one of compliance — or even worse of self-preservation in the face of the forces of change. If change is accelerating and the civil service is rigid rather than adaptable then responsiveness is bound to suffer. Without responsiveness — to political decision-makers and citizens — the civil service is not serving.

Enter NPM. NPM addresses shortcomings in responsiveness through a central focus on accountability. What gets measured gets done and if accountability for delivery is clearly assigned and incentives for performance aligned then responsiveness will follow. As a result NPM tends to favour competition and clarity of focus over collaboration and joint responsibility. New Zealand is a classic example of its implementation where sharp accountability have driven high levels of responsiveness on complicated issues but not the stewardship and dynamism required to ensure long-term delivery on complex issues where sole accountability cannot be assigned.[46] Extrinsic motivation is king with performance incentives aligned to clear accountabilities and key performance indicators.

NPM is a powerful tool for improving performance but it struggles to provide a framework for effectively addressing rapid change in a complex interdependent environment. New Public Governance seeks to address this shortcoming by harnessing networks inside and outside of government to enable dynamic responses to complex issues. New Public Governance emphasises an outcomes focus with a reduced compliance burden, the integration of citizen services and citizen engagement in the coproduction of services.[47]

New Public Governance recognises a greater role for intrinsic motivation as a force for enhancing public value,[48] strengthening coproduction[49]

---

[46] New Zealand Government. 2011. *Better Public Services Advisory Group Report*. November. https://www.ssc.govt.nz/sites/all/files/bps-report-nov2011_0.pdf.

[47] Osborne, S. P. 2009. *The New Public Governance? Emerging Perspectives on the Theory and Practice of Public Governance*. Routledge.

[48] Bryson, J. M., Crosby, B. C. and Bloomberg, L. 2014. Public Value Governance: Moving Beyond Traditional Public Administration and the New Public Management. *Public Administration Review*, 74(4), 445–456. Doi: 10.1111/puar.12238.

[49] Pestoff, V., Brandsen, T. and Verschuere, B. (eds.). 2011. *New Public Governance, the Third Sector and Co-production*. Routledge.

and triggering innovation.[50] There remains, however, a significant risk of underplaying the critical role of intrinsic motivation in achieving adaptability. Particularly in environments where the public discourse on public bureaucracy is focussed on waste and cost-cutting, reforms may continue to exclusively rely on extrinsic incentives and measures to drive change. In New Zealand, re-centralisation is underway as the public service has become too fragmented to harness intrinsic motivation. 'New Public Passion' is an attempt to motivate in a complex and rapidly changing environment of the 'Age of Anxiety'.

The role of intrinsic motivation in framing the need for reform is standard and often taken for granted. Civil servant disengagement, apathy and low morale are pointed to as a driver of the need for change. The former UNDP Administrator, Helen Clark, in her Keynote Speech on *Modernizing Civil Services for the New Sustainable Development Agenda* at the VIII Astana Economic Forum in Kazakhstan on 21 May 2015, remarked:

> I welcome the idea launched by the Astana Regional Hub and our Global Policy Centre in Singapore to advocate for what they call a 'New Public Passion'. This builds on the concept of 'New Public Management', an influential reform approach closely associated with my own country, New Zealand. The 'New Public Passion' emphasizes that officials need to be empowered, and to feel empowered, to do what they joined the public service for in the first place, namely to serve citizens. This 'New Public Passion' seeks to nurture high job satisfaction by ensuring that all civil servants feel directly engaged in improving the lives of their fellow citizens. ... Surprisingly little is known about what could drive civil servants to go the extra mile to serve disadvantaged groups. I hope that our contributions can help instil and renew such a sense of passion for development in public officials around the world.[51]

---

[50] Daglio, M., Gerson, D. and Kitchen, H. 2014. *Building Organisational Capacity for Public Sector Innovation*. Background Paper prepared for the OECD Conference 'Innovating the Public Sector: from Ideas to Impact'. Paris, 12–13 November.

[51] Ryan Orange (Deputy Commissioner, New Zealand State Services Commission) first coined the phrase 'New Public Passion' in 2014.

Chapter 13

That Shrinking Feeling

In 2015, Singapore commemorated a half century of independence. It was something worth celebrating. Since splitting away from Malaysia in 1965, the small island city-state has enjoyed sustained economic growth, achieved long-term political stability and maintained honest government. The country's success can, however, be all too easily taken for granted. The early days of the newly independent city-state were challenging. In 1967, Singapore's political and administrative leadership unexpectedly confronted a 'pre-modern' public health scare that threatened their still fragile aspirations for national development. The newly independent city-state briefly suffered a mass psychogenic illness or collective anxiety neurosis.

Hundreds of people suddenly became overwhelmed by intense alarm. A cultural epidemic of public anxiety was triggered across Singapore by a deeply private neurosis.[1] Sufferers (mostly men, but sometimes women; almost entirely ethnically Chinese) suddenly believed that their genitals were disappearing. This medical condition, known as *Koro*, was sparked by a false rumour among residents of Singapore that eating pork from pigs vaccinated against swine fever caused genital

---

[1] Tseng, W.-S. and McDermott, J. 1981. *Epidemic Mental Disorders*, in *Culture, Mind and Therapy: An Introduction to Cultural Psychiatry*. New York; Atalay, H. 2007. Two Cases of Koro Syndrome or Anxiety Disorder Associated with Genital Retraction Fear. *Turk Psikiyatri Dergisi, 18*(3), 282–285.

shrinkage. This ailment was widely believed not only to threaten their sexuality, but also to put their lives at risk.[2]

Half a century on, in modern Singapore, this strange episode has two well-established interpretations. The medical literature suggests that it was an acute hysterical panic syndrome.[3] Ethnographic accounts describe a cultural, non-psychopathological phenomenon of social psychology.[4] Both explanations accept that excessive, disproportionate anxiety not only expresses an individual's acute personal worries but also, as an epidemic, reflects collective neurosis. Such mass hysteria transmits shared culturally specific delusions through rumours and fear. It often causes people to believe that they are suffering from the same disease and manifest similar symptoms. Although the phenomenology and nosology remain unclear, these occurrences all appear to articulate deep anxiety when people feel vulnerable during a time of rapid social and economic change. That suggests a third explanatory factor: politics.

This account of the '*Koro* Crisis' of 1967 offers the first from a political perspective. The episode is examined for its political significance, reflected in the handling by its public administration of the government's response to socio-economic transformation in Singapore. The incident presented the then Prime Minister Lee Kuan Yew (LKY) with undoubtedly the oddest, yet potentially serious, problem to arise concerning public health during the early years of Singapore's independence. The event provides a bizarre, yet revealing, vignette of the challenges faced by the country's officials in seeking to modernise national institutions. It highlights the importance of political trust for effective public administration, and of co-ordination between the different arms of a government. Furthermore, 50 years later some of the political issues remain salient. Since the comparatively poor election results in 2011, the authorities have again sought to allay the anxieties of citizens troubled by the rapid pace of change.

---

[2] Mun, C. 1968. Epidemic Koro in Singapore. *British Medical Journal, 1*, 640–641; Ngui, R. 1969. The Koro Epidemic in Singapore. *Australian and New Zealand Journal of Psychiatry, 3*, 263–266.

[3] Ng, B. 1997. History of Koro in Singapore. *Singapore Medical Journal, 38*(8), 356.

[4] Adeniran, R. and Jones, J. 1994. Koro: Culture-Bound Disorder or Universal Symptom? *British Journal of Psychiatry, 164*(4), 559–561; Bartholomew, R. 1994. The Social Psychology of 'Epidemic' Koro. *International Journal of Social Psychiatry, 40*(1), 46–60.

Anxious Times

The *Koro* mass hysteria began in Singapore around the middle of 1967. The immediate trigger for the delusion was alarm generated over rumours concerning unspecified health risks of eating pork from pigs inoculated with anti-swine fever vaccine. Why this worry arose at that time is unclear. Popular anxiety over the transmission of the swine fever virus from pigs to humans was first reported in medical literature in 1958. The first case of swine fever in Singapore had been detected on 8 July 1967. Within seven weeks, 57 cases involving 680 pigs were confirmed. The government responded with a mass vaccination campaign, covering about 113,000 pigs at 1485 farms. Publicity in the press and over the radio and television advised farmers to have their pigs vaccinated as early as possible. The scientific evidence was, however, clear. Meat from vaccinated pigs posed no health hazard, so pork from such animals remained on sale.

In 1967, there were still about 10,000 pig farms (with more than 715,000 pigs) dotted around the island. The $120 million industry was sufficient to meet the domestic demand for pork. But the Primary Production Department (now the Agri-Food and Veterinary Authority) of the Ministry for National Development (MND) was concerned that pig farming required too much intensive use of land and water — increasingly scarce resources as Singapore sought to industrialise. This policy position may explain why, in the ensuing weeks and months, the 'urban legend' (believed to have started, however, in rural areas) took hold that the government was hiding another threat to the existing way of life.

Before the swine fever epidemic, up to 3000 pigs a day were being slaughtered in the state-run abattoirs. After the epidemic began, rumours about the supposed danger of eating pork from vaccinated pigs took hold. Bland assurances from the government that 'pork is safe' failed to convince the public. By early September, the number of pigs slaughtered daily had dropped to barely 100. Butchers could not sell the meat. Farmers did not want to sell their pigs, only to receive heavily discounted prices for the carcasses. Some pig producers, clearly hoping to save on vaccination costs, ignored government advice and accepted the risk that any pig that died as a result of the disease could not be sold.

When the impact of the swine fever outbreak was raised in Parliament on 7 September 1967, the government revealed that compulsory pig vaccination was being considered but during October, sales of pork still remained unusually depressed. These events came together and resulted in an open public health crisis on 29 October. That morning, local newspapers broke the news that many Singaporean men had become convinced that their genitals were at risk of withering away, due to eating pork from pigs vaccinated against swine fever — and that this would eventually lead to its permanent disappearance. Sufferers from the 'genital retraction syndrome' often sought to prevent further shrinkage by securing their private parts with red string or wooden clamps until medical assistance could be sought.

With the fear publicly surfacing, victims of the condition rushed in growing numbers to seek medical advice. An unrecorded number of patients consulted traditional healers in Chinese medicinal dispensaries or private doctors. In addition, over 500 sufferers sought treatment at public hospitals. The records from Accident and Emergency (A&E) departments show that patients suffering from a disappearing manhood panic attack usually recovered within hours or at most a few days, either after being sedated or persuaded that the 'illness' was over or had never existed. The only lasting medical damage occurred in those few cases where the wooden clamps, rubber bands, chopsticks or red string that patients had tied around the *membrum virile* to prevent shrinkage had unduly restricted normal blood circulation.[5]

This physical risk was not the only threat. The country's rapid urbanisation and economic transformation was also imperilled. Pig waste caused considerable pollution and was expensive to treat. By the 1980s, improved technology for safely importing live pigs and frozen pork would allow pig farming to be phased out, but in 1967 a core component of the staple Chinese diet was under threat without a policy solution. In addition, swine fever, believed by then to have been eradicated in the United Kingdom, could still only be controlled in Singapore by rapid diagnosis, temporary bans on the import of pigs and slaughter.

The MND imposed strict controls and required any pigs who died as a result of swine fever to be buried on the spot. As a result, consumers had

---

[5] Gwee, A. & The Koro Study Team. 1969. The Koro 'epidemic' in Singapore. *Singapore Medical Journal, 10*, 234–242.

no legitimate reason to fear that the pork that they were consuming was infected by swine fever and were also informed that meat from vaccinated pigs was safe to eat. On 3 November 1967, the MND declared that 'no one in Singapore need worry over the safety of pork from pigs slaughtered at the government abattoir where every carcass is carefully examined and stamped as fit for human consumption before they are released to the market'.

The general public was, however, evidently not convinced. Far from alleviating the problem of public concern over the safety of meat from vaccinated pigs, the initial intervention by the authorities seemed to intensify public panic. Newspapers added to the scepticism, under such headlines as in the *Eastern Sun* on 1 November 1967: 'Contaminated pork rumours strongly denied'. The minister for the MND handling the crisis then was Edmund Barker, a Cambridge-educated lawyer. He was a close personal friend of LKY and had worked for the Lee & Lee law firm before becoming the People's Action Party (PAP) Member of Parliament for Tanglin. Criticism of the MND was therefore particularly unwelcome to LKY. He arrived back in Singapore on 2 November to find the next day that the *Koro* crisis was vying for attention on the front page of the *Straits Times* with coverage of his five-week mission abroad.

The reported *Koro* caseload peaked in the first week of November. On 2 November, Thomson Road General Hospital recorded 11 cases, and the following day at the Singapore General Hospital 97 patients turned up. Worried parents brought their sons, and anxious mothers carried in their baby boys.[6] In one incident, a driver stopped for speeding by the police was supposedly given an escort to a hospital A&E department when the officers discovered the cause of his hurry. Female cases now also appeared, albeit in much smaller numbers.

The doctors on duty had been counselling their patients and, if unable to allay their fears, administered mild Valium tranquilisers and sedatives such as chlordiazepoxide. The spike in the number of cases and the rapidity of its spread across the island, however, now alarmed the medical profession and the Ministry of Health (MOH). The concentration of cases pointed to epidemic proportions. On 3 November 1967, newspapers ran

---

[6] Chong, T. 1968. Epidemic Koro in Singapore. *British Medical Journal*, 5592, 640–641.

on their front pages the MND instruction, *Pork: Ignore rumours*. This uninformative order did nothing to alleviate public concern.

On 4 November, the Singapore Medical Association (SMA) announced that its experts had reviewed all the scientific evidence. The panel it had set up a few days earlier was spearheaded by Dr Ah Leng Gwee, then Senior Physician at Singapore General Hospital and Honorary Editor of the *Singapore Medical Journal*, who had already published a study on the cultural characteristics of the *Koro* phenomenon.

The SMA's statement was simple and its message was clear: the physicians had reviewed all the evidence and had unanimously concluded that there was no threat to humans from the current strain of swine fever, the vaccine against it, or from consuming the pork produced from inoculated pigs.[7] Despite this re-assurance, some alarmist newspaper reporting continued. Under the headline 'Koro hits Tampoi', the *Eastern Sun* on 5 November 1967 stated that the condition had spread across the border to Johor Bahru in Malaysia.

Over the next few days, the MOH repeated the message, which was widely covered in the national newspapers and on television. Public respect for the medical profession seemed to have been the decisive factor in calming anxiety and quelling rumours. From then on, A&E visitor numbers rapidly declined. The Singapore General Hospital caseload fell from 38 *Koro* patients on 5 November, the day after the first SMA announcement, to 17 by 7 November. That day, the *Straits Times* prominently declared that *Koro* was a delusion due to psychological worries and reported on another MOH press conference in which a panel of experts headed by MOH permanent secretary, Dr Ho Guan Lim, repeated the message that *Koro* was purely a psychological ailment caused by mass hysteria. The next day, however, the story appeared in the foreign press. The *Canberra Times*, under the headline KORO 'NOT THREAT TO MANHOOD' reported that the Singapore government was seeking to calm thousands of men who feared that their manhood was being threatened by a mysterious ailment sweeping the city.

---

[7] Gwee, A. 1963. Koro — A Cultural Disease. *Singapore Medical Journal*, 4(3), 119–122; Gwee, A. 1968. Koro-Its Origin and Nature as a Disease Entity. *Singapore Medical Journal*, 9, 3–6.

The epidemic scare faded away as rapidly as it had appeared. The price of pork had returned to normal by mid-November and public concern had completely disappeared by the end of the month, though occasional individual cases were reported over the following years.[8]

Culture Politics?

In China, the condition of genital retraction (*suo-yang*) has a long history.[9] Traditional Chinese medicine sees the cause as sexual anxiety arising from a dangerous disturbance of the Taoist *yin-yang* equilibrium between the heart and the kidneys. This is often due to mischievous female fox spirits, and it is treated it by acupuncture.[10] *Koro* was almost unknown among other races in the Malay Peninsula. Ethnic-Chinese sufferers treated by public hospitals were distributed between Chinese language (133) and English language-educated (82) roughly in proportion to the overall population, further suggesting that at that stage in development, at least, culture trumped schooling.[11] So, in 1967, Chinese-speaking doctors in Singapore declared it to be a 'culture-bound' ailment.[12] The medical profession risked being aligned with language politics.

---

[8] Ng, *op. cit.*

[9] Tseng, W.-S. 1973. The Development of Psychiatric Concepts in Traditional Chinese Medicine. *Archives of General Psychiatry,* 29, 569–575; Tseng, W. S., Kan-Ming, M., Hsu, J., Li-Shuen, L. and Li-Wah, O. 1988. A Sociocultural Study of Koro Epidemics in Guangdong, China. *American Journal of Psychiatry,* 145(12), 1538–1543.

[10] Prince, R. 1992. Koro and the Fox Spirit on Hainan Island (China). *Transcultural Psychiatric Research Review,* 29(2), 119–132.

[11] Gwee & The Koro Study Team, *op. cit.*

[12] Gwee, *op. cit.*; Simons, R. and Hughes, C. (eds.). 1985. *The Culture-Bound Syndromes: Folk Illnesses of Psychiatric and Anthropological Interest.* Dordrecht; Tseng et al., *op. cit.*; Ng, B. and Kua, E. 1996. Koro in Ancient Chinese History. *History of Psychiatry,* 7(28), 563–570; Chowdhury, A. N. 1998. Hundred Years of Koro the History of a Culture-bound Syndrome. *International Journal of Social Psychiatry,* 44(3), 181–188. Garlipp, P. 2008. Koro — A Culture-bound Phenomenon Intercultural Psychiatric Implications. *German Journal of Psychiatry,* 11, 21–28; Wing, F. 2013. Singapore — Chinese Culture and Mental Health, in Tseng, W. and Wu, D. H. (eds.). 2013. *Chinese Culture and Mental Health.* Academic Press.

However, the *Koro* phenomenon has been observed in other places and in other eras. The condition was already known in the Middle Ages in Europe, where it was widely believed that a man could lose his *membrum virile* through magic spells cast by witches. The late medieval study on witchcraft, the *Malleus Maleficarum* by Heinrich Kramer and Jacob Sprenger, warned of sorceresses who 'take away male members' and keep them in birds' nests. The end of such superstition, according to Oxford historian Sir Keith Thomas in *Religion and the Decline of Magic: Studies in Popular Beliefs in Sixteenth and Seventeenth Century England* (1971), was the product of the intellectual spirit of scientific enquiry that came to characterise education in Europe through the Enlightenment, and which spurred the Industrial Revolution. Many non-European states, however, achieved industrialisation without the scientific and philosophical transformation that preceded 'modernisation' in Europe. This left their populations still superstitious and, perhaps, less politically able to exercise critical judgement on collective anxieties.[13]

Sir Philip Manson-Bahr, in his medical textbook *Tropical Diseases: A Manual of The Diseases of Warm Climates* (1960 edition), suggested that the condition, known as *Koro* in Malay, had first been recorded in the region at the end of the 19th century.[14] The Dutch ethnographers Nicolaüs Adriani and Albert Kruyt encountered the phenomenon in the Dutch East Indies and in 1912 proposed that the name derived from a tribe in Sulawesi bearing the name *Koro*.[15] The Dutch professor of psychiatry and neurology, Pieter van Wulfften Palthe, believed that the term derived from the Malayan *kura* (head of the tortoise) because both the Chinese and the Malays used the expression 'head of a turtle' for the *glans penis*.[16]

---

[13] Gabrielpillai, M. 1997. *Orientalizing Singapore: Psychoanalyzing the Discourse of 'Non-Western Modernity'*. Unpublished PhD thesis, University of British Colombia, Vancouver.

[14] Blonk, J. C. 1895. *Geneeskundig Tijdschrift voor Nederlandsch-Indie*. Batavia.

[15] Adriani, N. and Kruyt, A. 1912. *De Baree-sprekende Toradjas van Midden-Celebes*. Batavia: Landsdrukkerij.

[16] van Wulfften Palthe, P. M. 1934. Koro, een eigenaardige angstneurose. *Geneeskundig Tijdschrift voor Nederlandsch-Indie, 74*, 1713–1720; 1936. Psychiatry and Neurology in the Tropics. In *A Clinical Textbook of Tropical Medicine*, edited by C. de Langen and A. Lichtenstein. G. Kolff and Companie, Batavia, pp. 325–347.

Dr Gwee thought that the etymology of the term came from the word *keruk* ('to shrink' in the Malay language).

Incidents of individual cases have been recorded in contexts as varied as Britain, Ireland, Jamaica, Ethiopia, Haiti and Israel.[17] Anthropologists have interpreted the phenomenon to be an important example of the influence of culture on medical conditions.[18] The psychological disappearance of genitalia may be a universal syndrome of an obsessive-compulsive disorder and treated with psychoanalysis.[19] As a result, the *Koro* phenomenon has been reported elsewhere since the 1967 Singapore incident in other societies experiencing sudden political shocks or undergoing rapid change.[20] In Thailand, for instance, *Koro* epidemics during the 1970s supposedly caused by pollution appear to have reflected anxiety over industrialisation;[21] in Assam and West Bengal in India during the 1980s, the malady affected the middle classes, worried by rapid social upheaval and its influence on their political power.[22]

Nowadays, the most frequent occurrences happen on the African continent. In recent decades, claims of genital theft accredited to sorcery have become a widespread phenomenon.[23] Among diverse ethnic and religious groups, popular delusions still command widespread respect. A study

---

[17] For example, Durst, R. and Rosca-Rebaudengo, P. 1991. The Disorder Named Koro. *Behavioural Neurology*, 4, 1–14; Garg, B. K. 1968. Koro in Britain. *British Medical Journal*, 2(5606), 700; Modai, I., Munitz, H. and Aizenberg, D. 1986. Koro in an Israeli Male. *British Journal of Psychiatry*, 149(4), 503–505.

[18] Ahmed, K. and Bhugra, D. 2007. The Role of Culture in Sexual Dysfunction. *Psychiatry*, 6(3), 115–120.

[19] Davis, D., Steever, A., Terwilliger, J. and Williams, M. 2012. The Relationship between the Culture-bound Syndrome Koro and Obsessive-Compulsive Disorder. In *Psychology of Culture*, New York, Chapter 13, pp. 213–238.

[20] Dan, A., Mandal, T., Chakrabarty, K., Chowdhury, A. and Biswas, A. 2016. Clinical Course and Treatment Outcome of Koro: A Follow Up Study from a Koro Epidemic Reported from West Bengal, India. *Asian Journal of Psychiatry*; Al-Sinawi, H., Al-Adawi, S. and Al-Guenedi, A. 2008. Ramadan Fasting Triggering Koro-like Symptoms during Acute Alcohol Withdrawal: A Case Report from Oman. *Transcultural Psychiatry*, 45(4), 695–704.

[21] Suwanlert, S. and Coates, D. 1979. Epidemic Koro in Thailand — Clinical and Social Aspects. *Transcultural Psychiatric Research Review*, 16, 64–66.

[22] Dan *et al.*, *op. cit.*

[23] Ilechukwu, S. 1992. Magical Penis Loss in Nigeria: Report of a Recent Epidemic of a Koro-like Syndrome. *Transcultural Psychiatric Research Review*, 29(2), 91–108.

published in 2005 in the journal *Culture, Medicine and Psychiatry* noted that at least 56 separate cases of genital shrinking, disappearance and snatching had been reported in the media in the past seven years across West Africa.[24] In places as diverse as Nigeria (in 1990), Ghana (in 1997), Benin (in 2001), Sudan and the Gambia (in 2003), the Congo (in 2008) and the Central African Republic (in 2013), for instance, periodic episodes of collective '*Koro* panic' have occurred in the aftermath of political turmoil. The delusion is facilitated by the underlying common belief in witchcraft. A 2010 Gallup poll found that faith in black magic is widespread throughout sub-Saharan Africa: on average, 55% of the people polled believed in witchcraft, and people from minorities and other politically powerless groups are regularly accused of causing penises, breasts and vaginas to shrink or disappear.[25]

In Africa, the fear can be ascribed to the collective anxieties caused by rapid urbanisation. In vast and growing cities like Lagos in Nigeria often illiterate erstwhile village inhabitants suddenly found themselves rootless, living among unfamiliar cultures and suffering economic insecurity.[26] *Koro*-type beliefs thrive where political systems fail to articulate the concerns of rapidly changing societies and address their needs. This can have deadly consequences, when the supposed perpetrators of genital thefts are lynched on the spot by 'street justice'.

The Politics of Modernity

Managing modernisation effectively, therefore, is a profoundly political process.[27] While the *Koro* phenomenon itself was not unknown in 1967,

---

[24] Dzokoto, V. and Adams, G. 2005. Understanding Genital-shrinking Epidemics in West Africa: Koro, Juju, or Mass Psychogenic Illness? *Culture, Medicine and Psychiatry, 29*(1), 53–78.

[25] Geschiere, P. 1997. *The Modernity of Witchcraft: Politics and the Occult in Postcolonial Africa*. Charlottesville: University of Virginia Press; Meyer, B. 1998. The Power of Money: Politics, Occult Forces, and Pentecostalism in Ghana. *African Studies Review, 41*(3), 15–37.

[26] Ndjio, B. 2016. Sex and the Transnational City: Chinese Sex Workers in the West African city of Douala. *Urban Studies*, 123–144.

[27] Piot, C. 1999. *Remotely Global: Village Modernity in West Africa*. University of Chicago Press.

the Singapore episode was significant as the first reported epidemic of the disease. An article in the *Singapore Medical Journal* published in December 1969 by local doctors reviewing the epidemiology of the outbreak two years earlier described it as a disease characterised by psycho-dynamics. Subsequent research has demonstrated that outbreaks highlight the complex interplay between the psychic and the cultural aspects of symptomatology.[28] The ailment seems to occur at times of political tension, accompanied by socio-cultural, psychological-psychiatric and organic-neurological triggers, such as improving gender equality.[29] Some even argue that LKY's paternalistic politics deliberately fostered crises. The alleged aim was to generate a widespread psychosis that strengthened the PAP ideology of 'survivalism'.[30]

This incident, however, potentially posed a threat to LKY's ambitious plans for modernising the country — he had been overseas seeking to attract foreign investment when the *Koro* crisis erupted. Singapore in 1967 was at a significant stage of development. Partly 'modern', especially in the widespread use of English as the language of Western education, many in the country nevertheless also remained 'pre-modern', reflected in the use of colloquial Chinese and vernacular Malay, as well as the prevalence of popular folk beliefs and traditional cultural attitudes. The potential impact of the *Koro* episode on the country's long-term development strategy was serious. A bizarre 'pre-modern' culture-bound ethno-psychiatric syndrome could imperil Singapore's political ambition to attract foreign investment and tourism. The idea that the Singaporean labour force was subject to such beliefs would contradict the image of modernisation which depended on government efforts to attract American and European multi-national companies. Foreign investments were then needed to create the jobs required to tackle unemployment and foster political stability. Mass hysteria in factories, within a few years, did indeed affect Singapore.

---

[28] Crozier, I. 2011. Making Up Koro: Multiplicity, Psychiatry, Culture, and Penis-shrinking Anxieties. *Journal of the History of Medicine and Allied Sciences*, 9, 11–18.

[29] Tan, K. P. 2010. Pontianaks, Ghosts and the Possessed: Female Monstrosity and National Anxiety in Singapore Cinema. *Asian Studies Review*, 34(2), 151–170; Bures, F. 2016. *The Geography of Madness: Penis Thieves, Voodoo Death, and the Search for the Meaning of the World's Strangest Syndromes*. New York.

[30] Ortmann, S. 2009. Singapore: The Politics of Inventing National Identity. *Journal of Current Southeast Asian Affairs*, 28(4), 23–46.

In January 1973, the General Electric factory in the Kallang Industrial Estate suffered a disruption to its TV assembly lines from mass hysteria among Malay female employees troubled by ghosts.

Today, the traditional local community 'kampong' life of the 1960s is often described in nostalgic terms. The reality was less benign. Rigid conformity, entrenched social hierarchy and the comparative isolation of village life often fostered divisive politics. While some three-quarters of Singapore's population were of Chinese descent, the rest of Malaysia had a majority of Malays, with ethnic Chinese comprising about 37% of the population and ethnic Indians another 10% (according to the 1971 Census). In such a context, rumours spread rapidly in Singapore about Malay atrocities planned against the ethnic Chinese population in Malaysia, and in Malaysia of imminent Chinese rioting that required Malays to strike first.[31]

Such rumours are most liable to spread and appear credible at a time of international or domestic tension, and their political dynamics deserve more attention.[32] In August 1964 for example, LKY presciently warned against rumours of ethnic threats as a significant cause of 'pre-emptive' or revenge violence in the fraught racial politics of Singapore. Just a few weeks later, when a Malay trishaw rider was stabbed to death at Geylang in September 1964, rumours that the murder was the racially motivated work of the Chinese secret societies triggered five days of communal rioting that left 12 dead and over 100 people seriously injured.

The Malay minority in Singapore had been urged by the United Malays National Organisation (UMNO) to demand special political rights in Singapore, in opposition to the ideology of a Malaysian Malaysia or that of racial equality as espoused by LKY's government. An inflammatory 'urban legend' developed, fostered by the Chinese-language press speculation that Malay butchers in Singapore were covertly killing off Chinese males. As a result, racial attacks and apparently at least one murder occurred. That the delusion of emasculation in Singapore in 1967 was ascribed to eating pork, and that 98.2% of patients recorded were ethnic

---

[31] Conceicao, J. 2007. *Singapore and the Many-Headed Monster*. Singapore.
[32] Kapferer, J.-N. 2013. *Rumors: Uses, Interpretations, and Images*. New Brunswick; Coast, D. and Fox, J. 2015. Rumour and Politics. *History Compass, 13*(5), 222–234.

Chinese (95% males and 3.2% females), further suggested a politically contentious connection to religious divides and racial tensions. Only three years earlier, serious race riots had broken out in Singapore. 36 people were killed and over 500 seriously injured. The government clamped down hard: thousands were arrested, including many members of Chinese secret societies, and curfews were imposed. The fear of further racially motivated violence remained a deep concern in 1967. Barely 18 months after the *Koro* crisis, a race riot in Malaysia against ethnic Chinese triggered a reaction in Singapore against Malays. Four people were killed and 80 wounded. LKY believed the violence to have been politically motivated and blamed the UMNO Secretary-General, Syed Jaafar Albar, and the Malay language nationalist newspaper, *Utusan Melayu*.

Lessons for Public Administration

What insights, then, can be derived from the events of 1967 for public administration and development? The first lesson from the *Koro* episode is the importance of 'whole of government' co-ordination. The vaccination campaign against swine fever was implemented by the Primary Production Department of the MND. The director of the department, Cheng Tong Fatt, despite (or on account of) being a trained veterinarian, evidently struggled to win the trust of pig farmers. He had brought swine fever under control but was clearly frustrated that its complete eradication was thwarted by ignorant farmers adopting a 'wait-and-see' attitude to the epidemiology, instead of following the scientific advice and getting their pigs vaccinated as soon as possible. Such pig-breeders were mainly people with either no or limited education who felt their small-scale livelihood was under threat.

The subsequent *Koro* epidemic and the public's trust in the SMA and MOH ultimately resolved the resistance to the vaccination campaign. In 1967, the MND's veterinary experts from the Primary Production Department were regarded with suspicion by some pig farmers, and thus apparently lacked credibility with the citizens. As a result, official efforts to halt the swine fever vaccination rumours through public education using scientific evidence failed. By contrast, the SMA and MOH doctors had evidently established the trust of their patients, and their factual non-emotive guidance was believed. People evaluated individual and collective risk against the perceived reliability of public institutions and evidently trusted Western medicine even while the threat was premised on traditional Chinese beliefs that the penis could shrink under certain conditions of ill health. The medical authorities were able to build on the trust that the public had in doctors, in order to bring the epidemic under control. The government learnt the importance of clear messages. One possible source for the crisis may have been inadvertent comments by an official at the MND about the anti-swine fever vaccine.

A second lesson from the episode is that any immunisation campaign — an essential 'public good' to reduce the collective threat posed by communicable diseases — requires public trust in both the government and science. The early efforts at building trust in public health in Singapore have implications for public administration everywhere. Such trust is strongest within social groups, while distrust often prevails across different social divides. As society becomes more complex, people are increasingly reliant on the quality of public administration. On the basis of trust and common values, societies learn to delegate their collective protection to public authority. Technical solutions can only work in context, even during a public health crisis.

Since 1967, the government of Singapore has improved its approach to public fears about health crises. But the political context has also sheltered public health administration from public criticism. One example was the outbreak of severe acute respiratory syndrome (SARS) in Singapore that occurred in February 2003; 33 people died before the country was removed from the World Health Organization's list of SARS-affected areas on 31 May 2003. The strategy involved educating the public on the disease while the MOH invoked the Infectious Diseases Act on 24 March 2003 to quarantine and monitor all SARS patients. The use of infra-red scanners and home quarantine surveillance cameras was an important technological breakthrough. Airlines operating flights to Singapore were required to screen passengers. Visitor arrivals and hotel occupancy rates plunged, revenues at shops and restaurants dived, taxi drivers reported fewer passengers, the stock market fell, and some people lost their jobs. At the height of the outbreak in mid-April, the government cut Singapore's economic growth forecast for 2003 from 2–5% to

0.5–2.5%. During the April–June quarter, when the full impact was felt, the economy contracted sharply, by 4.2%. The government announced a S$230 million relief package on 17 April, specifically to help affected sectors.

The politics of trust influences policy effectiveness. When politics and science get badly intermingled, public trust in the authorities can quickly evaporate in ways that do not help improve public policy. Tan Tock Seng Hospital held its Annual Dinner and Dance as scheduled on 14 March 2003, even though the World Health Organisation had issued a global alert, and the hospital had alerted the MOH to a rare infection not responding to antibiotics. The landmark research papers published in the world's premier medical journals such as *The Lancet* came from Hong Kong, not Singapore, even though the outbreaks occurred in both places at about the same time. In other political contexts, there might have been more media criticism of such limitations.

A parallel can be drawn with two other politically sensitive public health scares shaping and shaped by citizens' trust elsewhere in government, both of which occurred in the United Kingdom. First, in the 1980s, was the fact that officials sought to hide the public health implications of the outbreak of Bovine Spongiform Encephalopathy (BSE) (popularly named 'Mad Cow Disease'). When the dangers became known, public confidence in ministers and public servants plummeted.

Then, in 1998, the influential medical journal *The Lancet* published research that seemed to suggest that autism in children was linked to the combined measles, mumps and rubella (MMR) vaccine. Although the research was soon discredited, serious damage was again done to public confidence in the government's stewardship of public health. Sceptical parents thought the Government's approach to be 'defensive' and too heavy-handed. Many parents perceived the MMR debate to be a political issue, and they did not trust politicians. British ministers' earlier mishandling of the BSE crisis seriously undermined parents' confidence in 'political' pronouncements related to health. As a result, the government's emphatic support for the MMR vaccine apparently diminished, rather than restored, UK public confidence. Broader politics also shaped citizens' trust. The widespread perception that the prime minister had lied about the justification for the war in Iraq undermined belief in the integrity of his government.[33] Official strategies that were perceived as emotional manipulation into immunising proved damaging to the credibility of the medical authorities.

The third lesson is the role of education. An informed citizenry is essential to an effective polity. With the adult literacy rate having improved from 73% in 1965 to almost 100% in Singapore today, it seems that *kong-tow*, or the traditional Chinese belief in magic, has waned. This makes it inconceivable that a similar outbreak of mass hysteria could happen today. But education itself is not sufficient to 'modernise'. Indeed, in the episode in Singapore, only 5% of those patients who agreed to a follow-up interview (some 236 out of the 469 treated) were uneducated. Today, a better educated population might be more sceptical of the government and the media. In 1967, television underpinned the credibility of the public health message. Although televisions were still new (service began in 1963), it was widely trusted and seen as speaking directly to every viewer, thereby helping forge national identity.[34]

The *Koro* hysteria reflected potentially explosive racial aggravations and religious sensitivities at a politically difficult moment, both domestically and internationally. In July 1967, Britain had announced the withdrawal of its military presence in Singapore, threatening both the country's security and its economy, with 20% of national income being derived from the military bases. Although Indonesia's *Konfrontasi* campaign had started to ease in 1966, the politics in Jakarta remained uncertain. Singapore's small size, its lack of natural resources and its location as a predominantly ethnic Chinese enclave surrounded by Malaysia and Indonesia posed threats from which Singapore's post-colonial leaders constructed a national identity and so legitimated the ideology of 'survival'.[35]

The collective neurosis that the episode revealed reflected disempowerment and the lack of adequate political 'voice' or influence at a

---

[33] Critcher, C. 2007. 'Trust Me, I'm a Doctor': MMR and the Politics of Suspicion. In *Communication in the Age of Suspicion*, edited by V. Bakir, Chicago, pp. 88–101.

[34] Lewis, T. and Martin, F. 2010. Learning Modernity: Lifestyle Advice Television in Australia, Taiwan and Singapore. *Asian Journal of Communication*, 20(3), 318–336.

[35] Ortmann, S. 2009. Singapore: The Politics of Inventing National Identity. *Journal of Current Southeast Asian Affairs*, 28(4), 23–46.

time of political instability. When the hysteria appeared to be growing, with the authorities uncertain on how to respond, the political credibility of the government was threatened. Even if the PAP intuitively fostered crises to generate a widespread collective psychosis, nevertheless, an effective interface between a country's political and administrative leadership proved critical to address public concerns at a time of upheaval and transformation. The challenge was not of medical science but, at a time of deep concern over rapid social change, of public trust in the authority of the state.[36]

Politics of Change and Unchanging Politics

The early days of independence were politically anxious times. Singapore then was a country plagued by existential doubt. Small and insecure, it had been suddenly expelled from the Malaysian Federation. The Communist threat, the 'confrontation' with Indonesia and the ongoing Vietnam War meant that national survival in the 1960s was not guaranteed.

That climate of existential anxiety triggered the 'Great Singapore Penis Panic' of 1967. The fact that this mass hysteria was prompted by a veterinary vaccination policy and focused around public health also suggests a fear of modernity and, at least in the farming community, an evident ambivalence to public authority in the immediate post-colonial era. The root causes were, therefore, at once psychological, socio-economic and cultural, all of which were well covered in the burgeoning literature on the episode, but above all political. This chapter offers the first analysis of the 1967 *Koro* epidemic as an early test of the newly independent state's political responsiveness to public concern.

Singapore's capacity to embrace constant change is nowadays regarded as an essential characteristic if the country is to survive and thrive in the 21st century. Today's Singapore, constantly encouraged by the government to embrace innovation, can perhaps laugh at the events of 50 years ago. In retrospect, even LKY might have been amused. Thirty years later, Dr Gwee remembered the episode as the oddest moment in his

---

[36] Gwee & The Koro Study Team, *op. cit.*

distinguished medical career. He recalled how a touch of humour about the effect of cold weather on the male organ had helped to dissipate his patients' anxiety around the shrinking Singaporean penis.[37] Indeed, for cheap laughs, the 1967 incident in Singapore has periodically also attracted international prurient curiosity. The episode was the subject of a 2011 book written by US psychiatrist Scott Mendelson with the low-key title, *The Great Singapore Penis Panic and the Future of American Mass Hysteria*. Perhaps unsurprisingly, this publication was shortlisted for the Diagram Prize for Oddest Book Title of the Year.

The cause of '*Koro* epidemics' is ultimately political — and serious. The disease reflects the worry that citizens of a country can feel at being powerless in the face of rapid social change and economic transformation. Although clinicians diagnosed sexual and bio-cultural causes arising from interpersonal difficulties and intra-psychic conflicts, the political context of 1967 could hardly have seemed worse. Modernisation was resisted, and urbanisation resented; domestic and international anxieties were profoundly troubling. As a result, the '*Koro* Crisis' posed a potential challenge not just to the credibility of LKY's PAP government but also to the competence of its public administration.

Some two generations later, public disquiet about the speed of the country's transformation resulted in a comparatively marked decline in electoral support for the ruling PAP government in the 2011 general election. In response, the government launched the 'Singapore Conversation'.

One significant political worry then was, and remains, the country's declining birth rate, the subject of an unusually contentious White Paper in 2013. Half a century on from the panic, to the strategic planners in the Prime Minister's Office, the 'black swan' existential threat of another '*Koro* epidemic' in Singapore is probably no laughing matter.

---

[37] Singapore National Archives. 13 January 1997, Medical Services in Singapore 新加坡医药服务, Accession Number 001996, Reel/Disc 6. He later served as President of the SMA.

Part D
The Passionate Bureaucrats of the 21st Century

Ur-Nanshe: (Louvre CC).

Chapter 14

The Fourth Bureaucratic Revolution

Dramatic change happens in public administration when political discontent and disruptive technologies merge. Technology advances in giant leaps, not incremental steps. To change habits, new technology cannot just offer marginal improvement. It must be enormously better — as a rule of thumb, at least 10 times better — than the technology that it replaces. Electric light was far cheaper, safer and more convenient than burning candles. The car was much more convenient than a horse.

Disruptive technologies foster societal change and revolutions in government administration that have similarly progressed by quantum leaps. Each bureaucratic revolution has been triggered by technological progress.

The first, over 4000 years ago, in Sumerian cities like Lagash, established 1-dimensional order, by developing hierarchy, written records and fixed process. Civilisation meant order; chaos and uncertainty equated to barbarity.

The second bureaucratic revolution in the 18th century was 2-dimensional order with purpose. Triggered by the military ambitions of Prussia, the enlightenment and the French Revolution, the state embraced the Industrial Revolution, democracy and nationalism, with bureaucracy as an ideology of national ambition. The *fonctionnaire* bathed in the reflected *Gloire* of the state as the Will of the People.

The third bureaucratic revolution was triggered by WW1 that led to the 'total state'. Officials represented the common good and the greater reach needed to impose the state's vision, from 'Fabian socialist earnestness' in the United Kingdom to the more conservative *Staatslehre* in Weimar Germany. The 'total' state, whether big or little, run by communist planners or free-market entrepreneurs, created a vision with officialdom at its centre. This was 3-dimensional order (through discipline and hierarchy), purpose to mobilise the whole resources of the state, and 'scientific', because the state created a world according to the data it could collect. Reality was made to fit the model of the world that officialdom could construct from tax returns, census surveys, statistics and so forth. Planning required the invention of categories. The world had to fit the rational, logical, scientific taxonomy in order that planners could record, count, analyse, apply, implement and monitor. The 'black swan', wild card, irrational, illogical, random and complex had no place in the plan. Simplification was essential as the complex or unpredictable could not be made to fit the framework.

The disconnect between the bureaucratic world and the real world infuriated but, for the most part, inspired only resigned fatalism. The informal, irrational and organic could never precisely match the formal structures and regulations required by scientific management, the 'best practice' and rational efficiency of business process re-engineering, logistics, log-frames that all processes can be defined, measured, analysed, improved and controlled. The assumptions needed to translate unknown uncertainties into known risks empowered the officials who decided on the precedent, similarity, definition or categorisation.

People were those who lived in harmony with nature, rather than sought to exploit the natural world according to their own vision, were 'backward' and 'primitive'. Theory trumped practical experience and drove out common sense. Abstract concepts ('the poor', 'development', 'government') stripped the human face from individual people. Authoritarian efficiency (memorably expressed by the justification for fascism in Italy, that Mussolini made 'the trains run on time') trumps messy democratic deliberation. Meanwhile the 'Nobel science' of economics[1] assumed self-interested profit-maximising individualism — despite all the

---

[1] While the Nobel Prize is careful to avoid equating economics with the other award areas like physics, the award inevitably strengthens the misleading impression that economics is a 'science'.

'real-world' evidence that people are social animals concerned for social recognition and prestige. The rise of 'behavioural economics' that has belatedly acknowledged this still suggests that there are other kinds. A neat theorem tidies away messy contingency.

Planners 'will to improve' is a mentality that defines 'government' as 'the attempt to shape human conduct by calculated means'. It identifies deficiencies that need to be rectified, then renders problems as 'technical' by defining boundaries, making them visible through selected data, then mobilising the state to alter the 'facts'.

From New Deal to New Zeal

Now, piecemeal and incoherently, the realisation is dawning that the successful states of the 21st century will be those that can foster a new revolution in public administration. The objective of this 'New Zeal' will be to develop creativity in public service. To achieve this requires reimagining the role of the state in transforming society. Only government has the legitimacy to attempt such experiments through collaboration or coercion. By radically improving their administrative capacity, these countries will overcome the divisive fallacy that the private sector is inherently more innovative and efficient and will achieve three things: (i) they will unlock national drive for excellence, to cope with an increasingly complex world; (ii) they will maximise the potential of the Fourth Industrial Revolution; and (iii) they will foster societies that are perceived by their citizens as fair, including by rewarding creative flair. The second point reinforces the first; and the third is the root of political stability without which no society can thrive and prosper.

Saint-Simon in the late 18th/early 19th century, Marx in 19th century and Lenin in the 20th century had emphasised the need for rational planning by bureaucracy. Rationality gave 'Bureaucracy' in English a negative connotation of centralised power governed by formal rules and hierarchical structures suppressing individual liberty of home-grown amateurish decentralised administration. The tone of the thinking appears from publications with such self-explanatory titles as *Bureaucracy v. Liberty* published by The National Anti-Vaccination League in 1896, or the Lord Chief Justice Gordon Hewart's *The New Despotism: An Essay on Bureaucracy*, published in London in 1929.

After the USSR's apparent social and economic achievements and military success through administration under Stalin, 'bureaucracy' was accepted by many as the way of the future, for both totalitarian/authoritarian and pluralist, democratic political systems in modern industrial and urban societies.

In 1944, Ludwig von Mises published *Bureaucracy* in which he argued that state-building derives from the ambition of bureaucracy. 'Rule from the office' organised society through the written record: maps, tax returns, conscription papers and census forms. Civilisation required fixed urban settlements, where power could be made manifest by paperwork: the manifest as manifesto and manifestation. Anarchy and lack of documentation therefore go hand in hand. Geographical anarchy derived from the oddities of rivers and mountain ranges, dense jungle and arid desert 'naturally' creates political contestation over frontiers. Technology played a key role and has immeasurably strengthened the power and reach of the state.

In the 1950s a positive connotation had taken root, aided by the death of Stalin and the rise to power in Moscow of the more convivial Khrushchev. 'Bureaucracy' was used to describe the apparently successful 'modern' form of governance in the USSR (e.g. John Armstrong's *The Soviet Bureaucratic Elite. A Case Study of the Ukrainian Apparatus*, of 1959). However, its seductive appeal was also recognised as a concern. British sociologist called Michael Young wrote a book in 1958 called *The Rise of the Meritocracy*. In this, Young warned that a new elite class was emerging that was out of touch with ordinary people. Young invented the term 'meritocratic' as a warning that it could create a new nomenklatura.[2]

Nevertheless, through the 1960s (e.g. Michel Crozier's *The Bureaucratic Phenomenon* of 1964) and 1970s, the bureaucracy retained its modern appeal and was adopted in the United States to explain the growth of large corporations as well as government (e.g. Warren G. Bennis's *American Bureaucracy*, of 1970) and the influence of 'scientific' socialism in Europe (e.g. Antony Jay's *The householder's guide to community defence against bureaucratic aggression: a report on Britain's*

---

[2] Elman, B. 2000. *A Cultural History of Civil Examinations in Late Imperial China*. University of California Press, Berkeley.

government machine, presented to the British taxpayer, 1972). The term described administrative modernisation in former colonies (e.g. Lloyd Fallers' *Bantu Bureaucracy* of 1956; David Apter's *The Political Kingdom in Uganda. A Study in Bureaucratic Nationalism* of 1961; or Anna Weinrich's *Chiefs and Councils in Rhodesia. Transition from Patriarchal to Bureaucratic Power* of 1971).

Fine distinctions in hierarchy loomed large in workplace conflicts. In the British Civil Service of the mid-1970s, there were 8500 different grades across the administrative, executive and clerical classes and 1400 occupational groups. All were distinguished by different job titles, pay bands and varying patterns of merit progression, upgrading and promotion. Many saw such bureaucracy institutionalised 'petty-bourgeois moral poverty' through employees' subordination to mid-level managerial or trades union power, sharply contrasted to the entrepreneurial independence of the self-employed.

By the late 1970s an ever-expanding bureaucratic state seemed inevitable everywhere. 'Bureaucracy' was 'an institution or caste, a mode of operation, an ideology, a way of viewing and organising society or a way of life'.[3] A national council of officials could set equitable pay differentials to ensconce distributive justice.

In Britain, the civil servant was a stereotype: bowler hat-wearing, carrying a furled umbrella, classics-educated generalists, indolent and wasteful dilettantes, cocooned by secure jobs and inflation-linked pensions, usurping the power of parliament or ministers.

The BBC Radio classic comedy 'Men from the Ministry' ran between 1962 and 1977. It was light-hearted humour, relating the escapades of lazy, incompetent civil servants from the 'General Assistance Department' in Whitehall. The main characters were affectionate stereotypes. 'Number One' (played by Wilfrid Hyde-White; later by Deryck Guyler), 'Number Two' (by Richard Murdoch), their dim, typo-prone young secretary, Mildred Murfin (Norma Ronald). Their boss was the lecherous, pompous, self-seeking Permanent Under-Secretary Sir Gregory Pitkin (Roy Dotrice and later Ronald Baddiley), worried about his reputation and pension.

---

[3] Kamenka, E. and Krygier, M. 1979. *Bureaucracy: The Career of a Concept.* Saint-Martin's Press, New York.

The mix-ups and misunderstandings that the officials caused by luck rather than design in the end turned out for the good. The civil service was portrayed as a benign if bungling institution, rigidly hierarchical. 'Men from the Ministry' was New Public Management in covert philosophy. It presented public service as inherently apathetic and needed to be incentivised into being effective.

In contrast, the BBC TV series *Yes Minister* between 1980 and 1984, and its sequel, *Yes, Prime Minister*, from 1986 to 1988, was Public Choice Theory conveyed through more trenchant humour ('I don't want the truth, I want something I can tell Parliament'). The cutting edge of the jokes conveyed a consistent message: that the apparently dutiful public service was inherently self-serving and should be constrained from manipulating ministers and the public.

The Creative State

The 21st century is witnessing 'the re-invention of history'. Technological and other disruptions will change society, the economy and Public Service more over the next 20 years than in the past 4500 years. Year 2007 marked the beginning of an 'Age of Acceleration' in which new technologies combined forces.[4] Year 2008 marked the start of the 'Great Recession' financial crisis that relaunched the importance of government, forcing politics to catch up with private sector greed (reward for failure) and growing inequality: the richest 1% own half the world's wealth, increasing from 42.5% at the height of the 2008 financial crisis to 50.1% in 2017, or $140tn (£106tn).[5]

This period of unparalleled change will mean that the successful states of the 21st century will be those that are innovative and develop a civil service capable of addressing unparalleled complexities and harnessing new technologies. A poorly articulated yet fundamental revolution in government is already under way. The civil service everywhere

---

[4] Friedman, T. 2017. *Thank You for Being Late: An Optimist's Guide to Thriving in the Age of Accelerations.* Farrar, Straus and Giroux.
[5] Credit Suisse's global wealth report published in November 2017.

is being re-created. This is happening in a fragmented fashion to varying degrees around the world.

The historic parallel is with the 'Gilded Age' in the last few decades of the 19th century, when many of the greatest names in corporate America were widely regarded as using ruthless and immoral business practices to enrich themselves and promote their own political influence, regardless of wider societal interests. Andrew Carnegie, Henry Clay Frick and Charles M. Schwab all of Pittsburgh and New York cornered the market in steel; James Buchanan Duke monopolised tobacco production from Durham, North Carolina; George Hearst and his son William Randolph Hearst of California, in mining and then newspapers; Andrew W. Mellon of Pittsburgh and J. P. Morgan of New York ruled in finance; John D. Rockefeller of Cleveland controlled the oil industry; and Edward Henry Harriman and Cornelius Vanderbilt of New York dominated the railroads.

By the end of the 19th century democracy seemed at risk: inequality of both income and political influence grew so extreme that finally the US government felt forced to act: the anti-trust legislation of 1890 eventually led in 1911, under the Presidency of Theodore Roosevelt, to the break-up of Standard Oil, controlled by John D. Rockefeller. The wicked capitalists had finally been subdued.

The challenge now is 'transformative leadership': how can civil servants keep the long-term interests of the country in mind while addressing the problems of today. Politicians have notably short time horizons — to get re-elected. Only public service can attempt to confront inconvenient truths, keep the moral high-ground and forge strategic coherence around the vision for a better future.

Now the fourth industrial revolution is fostering the Creative State. This is the startling opposite of the Weberian traits that characterised 2-dimensional bureaucracy, 4-dimensional order (through co-creation with citizens), purpose (to mobilise not only the resources of the state but also beyond through e-legitimacy on the Internet), 'scientific' but also imaginative. Big data will enable unquantifiable uncertainty to be converted into quantifiable risk.

As with the first three revolutions, the fourth bureaucratic revolution is driven by and made possible by technological progress combined with societal change. Big data, robotics and artificial intelligence (AI) are revolutionising both the knowledge base of government and also its use. Public anxiety over complex, volatile, unpredictable issues calls for public administration that is able to offer creative and imaginative solutions. Social media and the fourth industrial revolution are fuelling an extraordinary period of social, economic and political transformation, making creativity possible, through the combination of a technological revolution and societal change. Only the creative mindset will be able adequately to accept and embrace the tensions inherent in the complexity of 21st century public life: public service leaders of the future will be blending what today seem like contradictions: the ability to be entrepreneurs in spirit but committed to public sector ethics and focus on the common good; the capacity to balance short-term tactics with long-term strategic objectives; the intellectual strength to have professional expertise combined with an informed generalist's ability to inspire genuinely multi-disciplinary thinking; and will act as well-rounded, individualistic team players.

Public servants of the future will combine the more esoteric aptitudes of intelligence analysts, secret agents and diplomats. They will need the skills required to understand and interpret the evidence, win over potential adversaries and collaborate with a wide range of stakeholders through strength of personality as well as professional persuasion. 'Excellence' in public administration will mean the capacity to adopt and adapt the technologies and incorporate the transformation in society.

The fourth industrial revolution, like its predecessors, will also alter government. This will happen in three ways. First, it will change the information basis on which government is structured, the volume of information which government can absorb, and the variety of information on which can government rely. Rapid advance in technology will create public services that are better, safer, smarter and more affordable. Yet a profound disconnects can already be anticipated, not least between the need for knowledge, and the requirements to re-interpret privacy.

Second, it will change the capacity within government to analyse that information and to take decisions based on that analysis. The politics of creativity will overcome the infinite capacity of bureaucratic caution to stifle originality. Polarised and bitterly adversarial politics, normally a cause of public sector paralysis, will need to change.

Third, it will alter the potential and expected speed, reliability and quality of government and the government's capacity to learn from its action. In response, much attention is devoted to how government agencies can square the circle of overcoming silos to create 'whole of government' approaches. These require sharing sufficient access to each participating agency's data to make such collaboration workable. Better policy requires improved evidence. That will be based on 'big data', the huge quantities of information that drives AI, the analysis that can provide unprecedented insight into human behaviour, collectively and individually, with predictive potential.

But the need for effective institutions, trustworthy government and good governance will remain, premised on and, in many ways synonymous with a fair, efficient and effective public service. This fundamental element of state-building establishes the enabling environment for social, political and economic development, by giving governments the capability to plan for the long term, and formulate and implement policies, strategies and programmes that deliver public goods and services, predictable control of public expenditure and revenue, sustainable management of the environment, as well as institutional development to entrench better ways of working.[6]

Everywhere around the world bureaucrats are proving that they are not averse to innovation. What has been lacking, only too often, is an effort to respect their public service ethos, harness their intrinsic motivation and boost their morale.

Government officials are not all paragons. In 1843, an extraordinary squabble among British colonial customs officers in Kingston, Jamaica came to the notice of their supervisors in London. It appears that the trouble started in the custom-house. Several of the participants (Messrs. Elliott, Evans, Davis and Murphy) had come to blows. Their immediate boss, the Collector, admonished the officials concerned, but did not apprise the Board.

---

[6] A parallel argument is made with regards to Human Resource Management (HRM) and its impact on organisational performance McCourt, W. 2006. *The Human Factor in Governance: Managing Public Employees in Africa and Asia*. Palgrave Macmillan, UK.

Then a few weeks later, on June 12, 1843, Davis and Murphy were at a club in Kingston, when Elliott and Evans entered. Elliott observed in staccato tones to his friend, 'Who introduced these blackguards here? Who brought the snobs into this place?' Murphy at once struck him with a cane, and a melee ensued. Elliott shouted, as he attacked Murphy, 'You scoundrel! I'll knock out your brains!' and then, as he bestowed similar favours on Davis, who was a mulatto, 'You brute beast, you woolly-headed scoundrel, I can find no brains to knock out in you!'

Davis replied, while defending himself, to the effect that Elliott's mother had been a camp-follower, and that Elliott's position in the Service was the result of Elliott's sister's good looks and extreme complaisance. Several members of the club intervened and parted the enraged officials.

Later in the evening Elliott and Evans, armed with stout canes, placed themselves in ambush on the Parade. Perhaps the wine of the island had obscured their faculties, for they fell upon an inoffensive stranger, and gave him an unmerciful drubbing. On discovering their mistake, they begged a thousand pardons and explained that the attack was intended for Murphy.

This quarrel, at first carried out with wood, was soon transferred to paper. Elliott reported Davis to the Board of H.M. Customs in London for casting aspersions upon the female branch of the Elliott family. The Board directed the Collector to censure all concerned.[7]

But thinking and working politically in development, working 'with the grain' of existing institutions without imposing external norms and expectations, still eludes most development practice.

Creative, Collaborative Communicators for the Complex 21st Century

Policymakers are dealing with increasingly complex, multi-dimensional issues that are frequently interconnected and interdependent. Globalisation and technological innovation are accelerating change on all fronts. Events

---

[7] Atton, H. and Holland, H. 1910. *The King's Customs*, vol. II, London, pp. 216–217. The authors added a laconic note: *Undoubtedly the Board made allowance for temperature, and the potency of the cooling drinks used so freely in the West Indies at that time.*

and trends interact with one another in complex, often mystifying ways. Small changes may have big effects; big changes surprisingly small effects; and the unanticipated defies precise prediction. Government plans confront people and human institutions that interact in a nonlinear fashion. Toolkits and frameworks that seek to squeeze the wide variety of governance contexts into fixed problems with the same formulaic solutions, such as promoting accountability, competition and transparency, confuse principles that all worthy in their own right, with solutions to institutional complexity.

The 'systems' approach of complexity science, not just respect for complexity, can offer significant insights on institutions. It can enable building resilience by tackling 'risk dumping' and inequality, and 'sowing diversity'. The evidence shows the nonlinear nature of development; there are no simple answers. A variety of possible factors are involved in applying ideas from complexity theory to reforming public service and tackling related development problems. Better planning and foresight capabilities, rooted in effective political economy analysis, may be needed.

Public service can translate complexity approaches into practical steps. These activities can improve their capabilities to respond to complex interdependencies that are inexplicable, emergent and difficult to predict. The evidence also shows that combining foresight and 'complexity theory' from adaptive systems science can promote anticipatory and agile planning a complexity-based theory approach to governance and development.[8]

Complexity is nothing new. The ancient Chinese philosopher, Lao Tzu over 2500 years ago had observed that 'everything is connected, and every matter relates to every other'. Central government departments are

---

[8] Duit, A. and Galaz, V. 2008. Governance and Complexity — Emerging Issues for Governance Theory. *Governance — An International Journal of Policy Administration and Institutions, 21*(3), 311–335. Fuerth, L. 2009. Foresight and Anticipatory Governance. *Foresight, 11*(4), 14; Morçöl, G. 2010. Issues in Reconceptualizing Public Policy from the Perspective of Complexity Theory. *Emergence: Complexity and Organization, 12*(1), 52–60; Jeroen, R. 2012. Fit-for-Purpose Governance: A Framework to Make Adaptive Governance Operational. *Environmental Science and Policy, 22*, 73–84.

estimated to be 30% more complex than private companies.[9] Public sector complexity is caused by the mechanisms of democracy, constitutions and politics. While private companies pursue revenues, profits and market share, public sector organisations confront the ambiguity of politics. 'Deliverology' confuses 'results' with subjective measures of service quality. Perceived fairness and the importance of the process of delivery matter as much or more than just results.

Where the answer to 'complicated' problems has all too often been to impose the technocratic 'certainty' of Log-frame Linear Logic (LLL), 'Complexity' theory and thinking recognises that 'real life' is much more — er — well yes, complex. It offers a 'systems' approach that not only avoids the trap of LLL, but can also embrace the importance of political economy analysis. That has become fashionable in international development discourse.

Complex networks decision-making is fragmented but interdependent leading to unpredictability and rapid change as 'patterns arise out of a vast array of interactions and seemingly out of nowhere'.[10]

Modernising the state

The state is to find viable solutions to complex issues and seemingly intractable problems. 'Bureaucraft' is the professional techniques of public officials to balance the competing pressures and interests on them in policymaking.[11] These derive in four ways: (i) *organisational*: this can be either formal (the organisational rules and structures which guide public officials' everyday activities), or informal (the values, beliefs and networks that shape how they behave within their organisations); (ii) *professional*: pressures from professional bodies and communities of practice (e.g. doctors, teachers, engineers, managers) with expert knowledge;

---

[9] Methodology to measure the level of complexity in an organisation the Global Simplicity Index.

[10] Bourgon, J. 2009. *New Governance and Public Administration: Towards a Dynamic Synthesis*. Public lecture hosted by the Australian Department of the Prime Minister and Cabinet, Canberra, Australia, 24 February.

[11] Joshi, A. and McCluskey, R. 2018. *The Art of 'Bureaucraft': Why and How Bureaucrats Respond to Citizen Voice*. IDS.

(iii) *elites*: political pressures to allocate resources to specific groups (as patronage), to implement rules and regulations that benefit powerful interests; and (iv) *citizens*: pressures through citizen action that seeks responsiveness from public officials. The extent to which pressure is effective depends upon the strength of the demand and the influence of formal and informal mechanisms.

In a growing number of countries, both developed and developing, innovation teams, foresight departments and delivery units are changing the public policymaking process and abilities to anticipate, intervene, innovate and adapt, by strategic foresight, planning, prioritising, coordinating and monitoring implementation.

In Armenia, for instance, the civil service is developing a systematic problem-solving mentality *experimenting with pop-up labs* allowing staff to share ideas on improving processes and prototyping services and since 2016 has held Public Sector Innovation week. Across Central Asia, governments are suddenly opening up. Since independence in 1991 on the collapse of the former USSR, these countries kept their Soviet ways. But now in Uzbekistan, Kazakhstan and Kyrgyzstan public sector effectiveness and efficiency, decision-making based on evidence is suddenly in demand. The Kyrgyz Government mid-term strategy 2018–2022 'Kyrk Kadam' ('Forty Steps') outlines wide-ranging reforms. Its digital transformation programme 'Taza Koom' ('honest nation') under the Prime Minister takes a whole-of-a-government approach informed by a social innovation lab.

Singapore and Dubai: Thrive or Don't Survive

As globalisation results in international competition between nations heating up on every front, the capacity of the state to think creatively about how to tackle the escalating challenges it faces will be its main comparative advantage. That capacity will depend on the morale, motivation and effort of its employees — the much derided 'bureaucrat'. Their impact on the quality of public institutions will be the key edge in the global race for state effectiveness of the 21st century.

Singapore and Dubai are setting the pace in this undeclared competition. Small and largely unencumbered by competitive politics, the two city-states benefit from municipal pragmatism. The aim is impact driven by evidence, not ideology. City-states tend not to last. The great urban settings of Renaissance Italy, the trading ports of the Hanseatic League and the earliest centres of civilisation in Mesopotamia all succumbed to their own success: attractive thriving city-states through history have always been swallowed up.

An effective public service is at the heart of development. Nowhere can this be seen better than in Singapore. Its people are rightly proud of their nation's remarkable success. In barely the space of two generations, this small island has progressed from being little more than a fishing village, to its current status as one of the most dynamic cities on earth.

This extraordinary achievement of the 'Singapore Story' since independence in 1965 has complex causes, but central to it is the importance of excellence in public service. A defining characteristic that the country's government wisely nurtured was the strong intrinsic motivation of public officials to deliver in the public interest. Yet the nature of how that motivation developed deserves more attention. The topic is in general a poorly studied or understood subject.[12]

Drawing out the lessons for today's developing countries is a significant contribution to the UN's 2030 Agenda of SDGs.

Since independence in 1965, Singapore's leadership has been unremittingly focused on survival. Prime Minister Lee Kuan Yew so dominant a figure in his country's history that he is known in Singapore simply as 'LKY', battled against communist insurgents seeking to destabilise the country. Neighbouring Indonesia waged a 'confrontation', the undeclared war to thwart Malaysian independence. Race relations were dire: Indeed for Singapore, with a then fragmented multi-ethnic society, a shared narrative to shape its 'imagined community' was essential.[13] This imperative was keenly felt following the race riots of July 1964, which had starkly exposed Singapore as 'a transient and disunited society, a simmering cauldron of emotions which was all too

---

[12] From an unpublished strategic review of key studies on Public Service Motivation commissioned by GCPSE.

[13] Hobsbawn, E. and Ranger, T. 1992. *The Invention of Tradition*. Oxford, passim.

easily stoked up by demagogues, chauvinists, racists, extremists and fanatics'.[14]

LKY, although a formidable intellect, needed to keep the support of the population. He therefore focused the country's civil service not on crafting high-sounding policies but on delivering the basics: jobs, housing, schools, health clinics, street lighting and pleasant public amenities. LKY argued: 'If you want Singapore to succeed … you must have a system that enables the best man and the most suitable to go into the job that needs them…'.[15] In 1965, the city-state was a military base and trading port with an unemployment rate was 14%. Fifty years later, its unemployment rate had dropped to 1.9%. In 1959 Singapore's GDP per capita was $510. Fifty years later it is 100 times bigger. His success is exemplified by the fact that Singapore's per capita income is now far higher that of its former colonial master, Great Britain.

LKY himself cited meritocracy, anti-corruption and pragmatism as key to his achievements in office. When he died just a few months before the SG50 celebrations, almost every obituary around the world consistently agreed on one thing: that he had been pragmatic, and that this attribute had proved to be a significant causal factor in Singapore's rapid leap not just in economic prosperity but also in human development.[16] In the West, the 'Guardian' of Britain described him as 'leaving a legacy of authoritarian pragmatism' used to justify one party rule. *The Economist* stated that 'Singapore owes much of its prosperity to a record of honest and pragmatic government'. In Asia, *The China Daily* highlighted his 'diplomatic pragmatism', while *The Times of India* argued that he had forged his country in his own image as 'efficient, inventive, forward-looking and pragmatic'.

At home, the semi-official *Straits Times* argued that the key lesson of his premiership was that *Pragmatism can serve as a trustworthy compass when all agree that the good of the nation is what really counts*.[17]

---

[14] Yap, S., Lim, R. and Kam, L. 2009. *Men in White: The Untold Story of Singapore's Ruling Political Party*, p. 593, Marshall Cavendish, Singapore.
[15] Quah, J. 2010. *Public Administration Singapore-Style*. London, p. 71.
[16] UNDP. 2015. *Human Development Index*.
[17] Editorial of 30 March 2015. The newspaper is owned by Singapore Press Holdings whose former executive president ran the Internal Security Department from 1986 to 1993. S. R. Nathan, director of the Ministry of Defence's Security and Intelligence Division and then president of Singapore, had served there as a senior editor.

The supposedly fundamental tenet of the national narrative is pragmatism, a non-ideological search for optimal results. This builds on pride in hard-headed realism and the flexibility of adapting and innovating while 'learning by doing'. What distinguishes this approach from simply 'muddling through'[18] is the idealised belief that merit-based public service, liberated from the messiness of democratic debate or concern for popularity, can best advance rational and realistic policies.[19] Effective government requires painstaking collecting data and weighing the potentially unpopular but essential implications of policy. Here 'Bureaucratic' means professional, impersonal, hierarchical, technical and procedural, with the moral legitimacy conveyed by a rational approach, thoughtful process, carefully acting in the collective, long-term interest, fairly judged, logical and thorough.[20]

Interestingly, the idea is not only a key component of Singapore's successful political ideology;[21] it also forms part of the country's 'state-building' myth. Newly independent states prosper with a founding mythology that forges a shared identity and common purpose among disparate groups in a new nation.[22] Most such political legends are inspired by liberation struggles. But for countries that amicably achieve independence, like Singapore, inventing unifying myths and traditions is less easy — but no less important. Development built on the accepted legitimacy of public institutions needs an inclusive myth.

Yet how credible is this narrative? For, when asked in 1965 whether the answer to overcoming communism and colonialism was purely pragmatic, in the provision of housing, social welfare, higher standards of living, education — or required a positive ideology and political philosophy, LKY had emphatically rejected the idea, declaring: *You have got to believe in something ... you have got to have the ideological basis.*[23]

---

[18] Lindblom, C. 1959. The Science of 'Muddling Through'. *Public Administration Review,* 19(2), 79–88.

[19] Koh, T. 1998. *The Quest for World Order: Perspectives of a Pragmatic Idealist.* Institute of Policy Studies.

[20] Rohr, J. 1986. *To Run a Constitution: the Legitimacy of the Administrative State.* Kansas.

[21] Tan, K. 2012. The Ideology of Pragmatism: Neo-liberal Globalisation and Political Authoritarianism in Singapore. *Journal of Contemporary Asia,* 42(1), 67–92.

[22] Smith, A. 1999. *Myths and Memories of the Nation.* Oxford University Press.

[23] 5 March 1965: Singapore National Archives lky19650305.

LKY's son, the current Prime Minister Lee Hsien Loong, has inherited a mindset of tangible results over rhetoric. But the failure to think about ideological principles caused the biggest upset to date of his period in office. In 2011, his government suffered its biggest setback at the polls. This was the result of advancing rational arguments for mass immigration without considering the human dimensions of mass social upheaval.

In Dubai, the government has been facing a different existential crisis — fast dwindling oil revenues. Its answer has been to embrace a new nation vision, built on public service excellence. As Sheikh Hamdan bin Mohammed bin Rashid Al Maktoum, then Crown Prince of the city-state, said in 2010: 'Excellence encompasses effort, benevolence, innovation and achievement. By adopting and applying this approach at every level of service, our government entities have become centres of knowledge, professional leadership and schools of advanced administrative thought and practice'. Excellence in public service is effective and efficient. But it has to be more than that in the 21st century. As Tancredi says in Tomasi di Lampedusa's great novel *The Leopard*, 'If we want things to stay as they are, things will have to change'.

'Excellence' and 'Innovation'

Cures for the perceived ills of the public sector are sought in business management tools such as privatisation, market solutions, reinventing government, total quality management (TQM) and its associated concepts. Hence the two terms excellence and innovation become catchword for both public and private sectors reformers.

The concept of excellence in the public sector emphasises the expectations and needs of the client. The client determines excellence. Service excellence means exceeding clients' expectations by paying close attention to client needs. Public service excellence is concerned with the quality of services and their delivery.

Innovation is related to the creative ability of the public sector to look for new ways and design new services that exceed client expectations.

'Innovation' the Buzzword of the Moment

The need to square the circle on 'doing more with less' and achieving economic growth while preventing damage to the environment calls for humanity to be rescued from its own folly through its creativity.

The urge to tinker with, or radically restructure the public sector has become a constant fact of modern life. This is due to various political aims, from improving the efficiency and effectiveness of the state, to an ideology of 'bureaucracy-bashing'. Is there genuine innovation in principles of justice, tolerance and the dignity of all human beings, or are these concepts pretty much the same as Socrates and Plato would have conceived of them?

Reading the burgeoning literature on innovation, one might think that no-one ever thought of thinking for themselves at all until around March 2011. The current wave of thinking builds on a recycling of ideas: 'open innovation' from the 1960s; 'user innovation' from the 1980s; 'distributed innovation' from the 1990s, and on 'social innovation' in the 2000s. All these insights were themselves elaborations of the same observation that as knowledge becomes more widely distributed, ideas become more permeable between governments, citizens, rival companies and academic institutions.[24]

Edmund Burke warned: 'A spirit of innovation is generally the result of a selfish temper and confined views. People will not look forward to posterity, who never look backward to their ancestors'.

But the anthropologist Margaret Mead once said: 'Never doubt that a small group of thoughtful, committed citizens can change the world; indeed, it's the only thing that ever has'.

President John F. Kennedy understood it well when he noted: 'Change is the law of life. And those who look only to the past or present are certain to miss the future'. Now that's an innovative thought!

Change, experimentation, invention and innovation are not exactly new ideas. Washing one's hands and not defecating in drinking water supplies is modern hygienic practice. However, this was taken up years ago in Ancient Greece, explaining why inhabitants of Athens and Sparta

---

[24] Mulgan, G. and Albury, D. 2003. *Innovations in the Public Sector*. London: Cabinet Office.

often lived to a ripe old age with a life expectancy not much different from that of today. Stealing, adapting and adopting ideas from others has always been and easier and more reliable process. Ha-Joon Chang has provided many examples in the book *Kicking Away the Ladder*.[25] Indeed three-quarters of innovations in government are actually copied from elsewhere.[26] This is nothing new either: Peter the Great of Russia (1682–1725) tried to borrow 'best practice' in public administration from Sweden.

In Bangladesh, the Prime Minister's Office has come up with a nice definition of innovation. it must demonstrably make life easier for the citizens in terms of their time, inconvenience and money. Innovation becomes an easily quantifiable concept — reduction of time, cost or number of visits for the citizens to get a service. ICT is used to simplify steps for delivering a service, by 'service process simplification'. The results have proved impressive. Service delivery through the digital centres has reduced time by 85%, cost by 63% and number of visits by 40%. Bangladeshi bureaucrats are proving that they are not averse to innovation.[27]

The Tyranny of the Practical

'There is nothing so practical as a good theory'. At first, breakthrough innovations appear impractical — if not, they would probably have already been invented. Bureaucrats may declare new ideas impractical in order to kill them off, without piloting a test to find out.

---

[25] Chang, H. 2002. *Kicking Away the Ladder*. Anthem Press, London.
[26] 'Innovations Barometer' report published by the National Centre for Public Sector Innovation of Denmark in 2016.
[27] http://www.huffingtonpost.in/anir-chowdhury/innovative-bureaucracy-in-bangladesh-an-untold-story/?utm_hp_ref=in-blog.

Chapter 15

Pen-Pushers With Passion?

The 'passionate bureaucrat' sounds like a contradiction in terms, or possibly the title for a particularly uninspired Mills and Boon 'romantic' novel. Yet in the third century BC, the ancient Indian political philosopher Kautilya, in the *Arthashastra*, advised that the qualifications (*amátyasampat*) to be a senior official (*amátya*) should include *possessed of enthusiasm*. Other attributes that he regarded as essential included being well-trained, possessed of foresight and a good memory. Public officials also needed to be bold, well spoken, excellent in their field of expertise, learned in theoretical and practical knowledge, pure of character, of good health, kind and philanthropic, free from procrastination, fickle-mindedness, hate, enmity, and anger. Bureaucrats should be dedicated to dharma, or righteousness, by upholding duties, rights, laws, conduct, virtues and the "right way of living".

The ancient world had a pithy saying: *Everything changes but everything stays the same.* Many long-established ideas get recycled, as academics and consultants are in ceaseless search for the competitive advantage: *Old wine in new bottles.* A cognitive bias towards novelty is perhaps a driver of innovation, but also an incitement to plagiarism and intellectual property theft. But as we will see, copying others rather than inventing new things or thoughts is how most progress happens.

Ideology and history weigh heavily on perceptions of public administration. Deeply influenced by his background in Prussia, Max Weber defined bureaucracy as efficient and rational government structured by systematic process and hierarchy that ensured order, efficiency and eliminated corruption and patronage. To others, however, bureaucracy signifies inefficient and oppressive administration, imposing unnecessary procedures and arcane red tape for its own interests, not the common good.

The successful states of the 21st century will be those that develop competitive advantage in public administration. Excellence in 21st century public administration requires M.I.A.M.I. This means Motivated — Impartial — Adaptive — Merit-based (yet empathetic, not 'meritocratic' implying superior and aloof) — and Imaginative: Public service that is impartial (treats all equitably and fairly, essential for building citizens' trust in government); based on ability; and is motivated, including to promote continuous learning and incremental change.

By enhancing the excellence of their capacity to shape the common good, they will achieve five things: (i) unlock the creativity needed to solve complex problems; (ii) overcome the disempowering fallacy that the private sector is inherently more innovative and efficient than the public service; (iii) create societies that are perceived by their citizens as fair; (iv) foster trust between citizens and their governments; and (v) bolster the effectiveness and legitimacy of the state.

These five aims interconnect: the second point reinforces the first; the third is the root of political stability without which no society can thrive and prosper; the fourth derives from the third and builds the fifth. The skills needed to achieve these aims will include not just empathy and grasp of digital data, but also an awareness of the big picture.

While civil services at the political level articulate the authority of government, they also challenge ideological beliefs with evidence. Furthermore, research dispels the supposed efficiency of business. In refuse collection, utilities, public transport and hospital administration, publicly owned enterprise is often more efficient.[1]

---

[1] Goodsell, C. 2004. *The Case for Bureaucracy: A Public Administration Polemic.* 4th ed. CQ Press, Washington, DC.

Passionate Bureaucrats, from Oxymoron to National Advantage

> Theory is when you know everything and nothing works. Practice is when everything works and nobody knows why. We have put together theory and practice: nothing is working ... and nobody knows why!
>
> Attributed to Albert Einstein

The negative image of public bureaucracy has always been highly marketable. This has been true even when the state and its officials have undoubtedly played a vital role. This was never more apparent than in the 1930s. The 'New Deal' reforms enacted by President Franklin Delano Roosevelt to address the Great Depression triggered by the 1929 Wall Street Crash, and the looming prospect of war did nothing to abate some critics of public officialdom.

In 1940 a Washington-based journalist called Lawrence Sullivan wrote a book called *The Dead Hand of Bureaucracy*. Expanding an article that he had originally written when FDR was first elected in 1933, Sullivan warned that an expansion in the size and remit of the federal government would result in terror, censorship and a 'planned economy' that would quickly degenerate into 'planned confusion'. Muddled government would foster inefficiency and divided authority in food, manpower, housing, printing, war contracts, labour, transportation, and so forth. Sullivan argued that the inevitable result would be uncontrollable national debt, rampant inflation and widespread bankruptcy. Sullivan's main evidence for these risks arising from a more active federal government was that, since 1800 the federal payroll had increased 1780 times faster than the growth in the size of the US population.

Four years later, the D-Day landings marked the beginning of the end to WWII. The Allied victory a year later had been due to the unparalleled effort of government to mobilise the full resources of the state to defeat Nazi Germany, fascist Italy and militaristic Japan. Sullivan was still not convinced and in 1944 could write a sequel to his attack. *Bureaucracy Runs Amuck,* published three weeks after the Normandy Landings, is a populist diatribe of over 300 pages against the government effort.

This was nothing new. In the Roman Empire under the emperor Diocletian (ruled 284–305 AD) at the start of the 4th century, the number of employees in the imperial civil service of the probably doubled from 15,000 to 30,000 bureaucrats for an empire of 50–65 million inhabitants (approximately 1667 to 2167 inhabitants per imperial official empire wide). Diocletian sought to professionalise public service by creating separate departments to handle the different tasks of government — dealing with petitions, requests, correspondence, legal affairs and foreign embassies. The result was a large increase in the number of bureaucrats. The early Christian writer Lactantius (c. 250–325 AD), in predicting the second coming of Christ when the wicked would be destroyed, the devil bound and the righteous dead would rise again, confidently asserted that the beginning of the end world would coincide with the imminent fall of the Roman Empire. His evidence that this was at hand was Diocletian's persecution of the Christians, when there were more public servants spending tax money than there were taxpayers paying for the emperor's reforms of public administration.[2]

In contrast, during the 'Progressive Era' of the 1890s and 1900s in the US government, imagery of technocratic, professional public administration inspired a generation. Francis Rolt-Wheeler's many-volume US service books inculcated the career ambition to pursue government job opportunities freed from political patronage and offering an idealised image of meritocracy. The Progressive Era administrative state understood the importance of creating a fantasy for future government agents.

People like Sullivan have, of course, been grumbling ever since government was invented about 'red tape' idle bureaucrats abusing their positions of public authority. Probably few reformers or public service officials, however, are aware that this relentless 'bureaucracy-bashing' phenomenon explains the first-ever reform of the civil service, over 4000 years ago.

Urukagina, ruler of the Sumerian city-state of Lagash, apparently in response to 'civil society' dismissed allegedly corrupt officials, who supposedly demanded excessive fees for performing their duties. (Was this, however, perhaps the first recorded example of blaming the public

---

[2] *De opificio Dei* ('The Works of God').

administration as a populist gesture?) That this first recorded reform of public administration ended in catastrophic failure requires an explanation. This is especially the case since so many subsequent reforms have also failed. In searching for explanations, perhaps bureaucrats, politicians and citizens would all be equally surprised to discover how relevant that episode still is today.

Attempts to reverse the tide of ill-informed tirades against public officialdom have rarely enjoyed much success. In Britain in 1927, a book titled *The Romance of the Civil Service* had valiantly tried to 're-brand' public administration as a fascinating career choice offering the opportunity to shape the nation. The book sought to show how, although steeped in history and tradition, the civil service nevertheless embraced the future. Today's 'innovation agenda' is nothing new.

Year 1939 was not an optimistic or auspicious time in Europe for launching new ventures. Nevertheless that year the French government established a museum of public works in the centre of Paris and, to mark its opening, the authorities issued a commemorative bronze 68-mm medal. It was designed by a distinguished sculptor, Édouard-Pierre Blin (1877–1946). The obverse features a standing figure of Marianne surrounded by symbolic vignettes illustrating highways, waterways, mines and the electricity grid. The reverse shows the museum building, with the legend above: MUSÉE PERMANENT DES TRAVAUX PUBLICS.

Commemorative bronze 68-mm medal designed by Édouard-Pierre Blin (1877–1946).

The nation's pride in the achievements of its public sector, as expressed by the medal, is palpable. The idea for the institution and its exhibits had derived from the success of the International Exhibition of Technology in Modern Life (*Exposition internationale des Arts et des Techniques appliqués à la Vie moderne*) that had also been staged in Paris two years earlier. There the French pavilion had proudly presented innovations in the country's public works. The first section explained the functioning of sea-ports including Dunkirk, Calais, La Rochelle and Bordeaux; inland ports such as Rouen on the Seine, and *Nantes on the Loire*; and ways toforecast the threat of flooding in Paris. The second section on the country's road network explained the advances made in highway construction. On the second floor of the pavilion, the visitor encountered dioramas and models explaining the extraction and uses of liquid fuels, including synthetic gasoline made by the hydrogenation of coal. The room on mining came next, showing. a geological map of France identifying the nation's mineral wealth in oil, potash, salts, coal, cement, lime, and plaster, iron, copper, lead, zinc, aluminium, gold, silver, etc.). The next room on electricity showed the controls of a power station, and stressed how consumer demand influenced energy prices. The Public Works Pavilion had a library, which supplied books by modern automatic means, a congress hall and a cinema.

The success of the pavilion with visitors to the exhibition led to the establishment of the museum. It offered a clear message. Its aim was to convey the impression that France was technologically advanced, with a dynamic public service pioneering the country's development.

But the initial enthusiasm waned rapidly. In a rare moment of decisiveness, one of the 21 governments during the 12 years of the French Fourth Republic between 1946 and 1958 closed the museum in 1955. It had lasted only 16 years, including the dark days of German wartime occupation. Opinions differed as to why the closure happened: some claimed that its political message no longer accorded with the post-war need to foster private sector growth. Others asserted the closure was simply due to poor visitor numbers.

In 1982, the city of Baltimore in the United States opened a Public Works Museum. Its objective was to explain how a large city provides vital but unfashionable services to its citizens, such as street lighting, phone lines, drains, drinking water, gas and electricity, road maintenance, garbage collection and sewage disposal. In 2010, citing budget constraints, the municipal authorities closed the museum.[3]

The pride that public officials have in promoting the long-term interest of the state, the passion many have for defending the needs of citizens and the environment, the upkeep of its traditions and the sense of continuity, a sense of history and respect for the greater good not just a concern for naked self-interest, those are the attributes that mark out a good public official of any era.

Pride and discipline meant that in many countries during the 19th and early 20th centuries, public servants wore uniforms. Around 1800, many European countries introduced occupational uniforms for state employees as an important part of extensive administrative reforms that most countries issued as a response to the French Revolution and Napoleonic wars. The new reforms broke down the privileges of the aristocracy and the church, and prepared the ground for the development of a modern civil service. The governmental officials' uniforms were intended to serve as symbols for the new ideal of a nation state run by an efficient and just administration. Inspired by those of the military, the uniforms' shape, colours and decorations signified the function and rank of the officer.

The uniforms worked on two levels. From within, they enhanced the new bureaucratic structure and lent new confidence and pride to the state employees. From without, the uniforms represented acceptance of the new state and its regulations as well as elicit new respect for its employees.

> The King's uniform, which every Civil Servant had to wear when on duty, kept the feeling alive among them that they were the King's servants and had to represent the King's interests. The power of the officials and their independence, in case they were opposed by strong social influences, was increased by the fact that the officials were strangers in

---

[3] In October 2012, the School of Public Affairs and Administration at Rutgers University opened the Virtual Museum of Public Service. It aims to explain the importance of the public sector in promoting the Public Good, to inspire the best and brightest to careers that are socially responsible but largely unrecognized and poorly paid.

the districts in which they were employed, for Frederick William continued the policy of appointing only strangers to the district to official positions...[4]

Gradually most employees of governmental departments were clad in uniforms, for the police services, fire departments, postal services, state-run mining and metalworking industries, forestry and transportation departments, as well as the departments of finance, interior, justice and foreign affairs. The small dukedom of Brunswick had a bewildering array of uniforms in different colours and embroidery designs for each department. The large state of Prussia emphasised unity and efficiency by restricting their uniforms to one colour, dark blue ('Prussian blue'). Trimmings and signs identified different departments and ranks. The Prussian postal services wore their blue uniforms with orange-coloured collars, cuffs and pocket flaps. The richness and width of embroidery on the chest, collar, cuff and pocket flaps were meticulously prescribed and varied according to the rank of the officer within the administrative hierarchy.

If the civil uniform symbolised the new administrational structures of modern states early in the 19th century, by the end of the century the civil uniform was regarded as a sign of stultifying bureaucracy. At the end of WWI, when most monarchies in Europe were abolished, most civil uniforms for state employees disappeared. After the two world wars, only law-enforcement (police, immigration, or prison wards) as well as certain public services (postal services, railways, fire fighters, or foresters) continued to wear uniforms. Public officials in Bhutan still wear a sword to work. Thailand, civil servants wear court uniform or ordinary office uniform.

In India, the Ambassador car, modelled on the 1948 Morris Oxford, complete with siren and flashing blue light, symbolised officialdom in India for six decades after independence. In 2016, the ministry of finance in Vietnam began a pilot scheme of providing travel allowances of VND9 million ($400) per month to officials instead of cars. Vietnam has about

---

[4]Barker, J. B. 1916. *The Foundations of Germany*. E. P. Dutton and Company, New York, pp. 11–15.

37,000 state cars, each requiring an annual maintenance cost of VND320 million (US$14,000). Reducing the vehicle fleet by 50% and offering each official a monthly allowance of VND9 million would save up to VND4.2 trillion ($185 million), not to mention salaries for drivers, according to the ministry's projections.

Public service as competitive advantage

> Public service excellence is any state's key competitive edge. Foster it.

When General Matthew B. Ridgway, the US Army Chief of Staff in the mid-1950s, was asked what he thought was his most important role as the nation's top soldier, he answered, 'To protect the mavericks'. What Ridgway meant was that a future war might be completely different from that currently envisaged on which plans were being made. The mavericks were an essential asset for challenging dominant 'group-think' orthodoxy and, by seeing the future differently and hopefully more correctly, would reduce the risk of another 'Pearl Harbor'.[5]

A perennially popular joke about two of the rare white lions in Amman Zoo evokes one way of seeing public service reform. One day, on escaping from the zoo, the two lions take different paths. One lion goes to hide in the wooded area of the King Hussein Park. He knows that he should not give himself away so he stays in hiding without eating or drinking so he becomes thin and emaciated. Finally he becomes so hungry that he can't contain himself any longer. He pounces on a passer-by and eats him, whereupon the lion is swiftly tracked down, is apprehended and returned to the zoo.

The second lion is more cunning and succeeds in remaining at large for many months. Finally captured, he is returned to the zoo looking well-fed and rather proud of himself. His companion is in awe of this achievement and inquires with great interest, 'Where did you find such a great hiding place?'

---

[5] Quoted in W. Bell. 2009. *Foundations of Futures Studies: History, Purposes, and Knowledge*, vol. 1. Transaction Publishers, New Jersey, p. 77.

'In one of the ministries' is the successful escapee's answer. 'Every day I ate a bureaucrat and nobody noticed'.

'So how did you get caught?' asks the other lion.

'I slipped up badly when I ate the man who served coffee at the morning tea break', came the sad reply. If you don't find this poignant, the BBC reported that a Spanish civil servant had been off work unnoticed for six years, according to *BBC News* in February 2016.

In July 2016, the mayor of a small town outside Naples had to shut down most municipal offices after police arrested 23 of his staff in the latest revelations of absenteeism in Italy's public sector. Staff were filmed clocking in and then leaving to go about their personal business or using multiple swipe cards to register absent colleagues. A police video showed one man trying to tamper with a security camera and then putting a cardboard box over his head to hide his identity before swiping two cards. Police arrested around half of all employees in the town hall offices of Boscotrecase following a week-long investigation that they said revealed 200 cases of absenteeism involving 30 people. 'I'll probably have to shut down the town hall', Pietro Carotenuto, elected a month ago as mayor of the town of 11,000 people, said four major town hall departments had been closed on Tuesday due to a lack of staff.

In August 2016, a spot inspection of civil service offices by Dubai's ruler resulted in embarrassing footage of Sheikh Mohammed standing awkwardly by empty desks which should have been occupied by high-ranking officials. If there ever was a day not to turn up late for work, it was Sunday morning in Dubai where Sheikh Mohammed bin Rashid carried out an early morning inspection of several civil service departments, *The Gulf News* newspaper reports. Sunday is a normal working day in the Emirate. The Sheikh began his surprise tour at 7.30 am, expecting to meet senior officials already working at their desks. But as video posted to Twitter by the government's media office showed, the Dubai ruler was the only person present, save for his own framed portrait on the wall. Nine senior officials from the Dubai Municipality were ordered to retire as a result of the sheikh's visit. According to the *Khaleej Times*, Sheikh Mohammed is known for his early-morning inspections 'to ensure government services are up Dubai's globally-admired standards', so his presence should not have come as a surprise.

Public service excellence is not a luxury. Nor can it be taken for granted but it is often contested. This first record of this happening occurred 4500 years ago, as it has often been since. This was a critical period in human history, when the state emerged, and sparked revolutionary changes in society and the structure of inequality. It is tempting to believe that this outcome was the 'hydraulic state' — a settled community of farmers depended on reliable irrigation that required canal-building and sophisticated water management. Such analysis interpreted Lagash and its rival city-states as the *Le premier triomphe de la bureaucratie,* under the 'temple-state' (by analogy to the role of the church as providing the administrative machinery of Europe in the Middle Ages). This interpretation in due course provoked a reaction, bringing in the private sector and civil society.[6]

'Good governance' including public service excellence, is necessary for development — but what exactly that means in practice remains uncertain. The standard institutional prescriptions over the last 25 years have frequently failed, often due to an overly normative approach. Copying the formal institutions in developed countries did not work. Countries that achieved high and sustained economic growth were so varied in their history and governance that it proved impossible to determine a precise formula for the institutional arrangements essential for development. Variation in state structures, political systems including the extent of political competition, and the distribution of power, all affect incentives for delivering results.[7]

---

[6] Lambert, M. 1961. Le premier triomphe de la bureaucratie. *Revue Historique, 225,* 21–46.

[7] Pritchett, L., Woolcock, M. and Andrews, M. 2010. *Capability Traps? The Mechanisms of Persistent Implementation Failure.* Center for Global Development; Leftwich, A. and Sen, K. 2010. *Beyond Institutions: Institutions and Organizations in the Politics and Economics of Poverty Reduction — Thematic Synthesis of Research Evidence.* DFID-funded Research Programme Consortium on Improving Institutions for Pro-Poor Growth (IPPG). Manchester: University of Manchester; Fukuyama, F. 2010. *Development Strategies: Integrating Governance and Growth.* Policy Research Working Paper. No. 5196. World Bank, Washington, DC.

Although the exact process of development may remain opaque, the outcomes are highly visible. In the 1960s, Southeast Asia was on average poorer than Africa. Today it is two and a half times more affluent. As a result of such disparities, it has been calculated that, on current trends, it will take Haiti today some 600 years to reach Singapore's levels of effective, non-corrupt bureaucracy.[8] In Indonesia, 60% of the population lived below the national poverty line in 1970. By 1984, this had fallen to 22%. In Malaysia this figure dropped from 49% to 18% in the same period. More recently, between 1993 and 2008, poverty rates in Vietnam fell from 58% to 14%.

Public administration not only delivered these improvements but also itself improved: for example over the past decade, nearly two-thirds of the 144 countries for which data is available were able to plan and deliver their national budgets effectively (defined as the final out-turn being within 10% of the original budget forecasts — although some may have also improved their ability to 'game' the system).[9]

Differences in the quality of public administration, mediated through political direction, policy formulation and implementation, explain sustained growth and poverty reduction. State formation requires political-administrative leadership pacts to contain existential external threats along with domestic conflict and communal tensions.

Institutions matter; indeed they are critical for growth and development. Institutions are the formal and informal rules and norms that organise social, political and economic relations. Institutions are not the same as organisations. Organisations have budgets, buildings and binoculars. In contrast, institutions can be formal (like constitutions or financial regulations) and informal (like shaking hands, using cutlery or punctuality).

Public service is both an organisation and an institution. Too often, reform treats solely the organisational challenges. Yet the state as a 'political settlement' or a 'political order' is the single most important institution for addressing the challenges of the 21st century — jobs, inequality, economic growth, redistribution, basic services, public goods,

---

[8] Pritchett, Woolcock and Andrews, *op. cit.*
[9] IMF data.

social welfare policies and enabling environment for private sector investment. The state's legitimacy did not derive from democratic accountability and open, inclusive and participatory decision-making processes. Rather, legitimacy arose from a more complex mix of emotions and needs — nationalism, charismatic leaders and cultural values drove state performance in fostering of economic growth, public-service delivery, the enforcement of law and order and the state's overall responsiveness to the people's needs.

The public service represents both a 'vested interest' in its own right and the common citizenry from among whom public officials are recruited. This dual role plays a vital but little noted role as the intermediary between power of political leaders and of corporations or individuals that have acquired extraordinary wealth and political influence. Such powers that raise concerns about monopolistic tactics that threaten democracy and disempower ordinary citizens.

A capable, autonomous bureaucracy is also embedded in society — that is, relatively independent of special interests. With the support of the political leadership, key ministries manage a mutually beneficial relationship between state and business so that policy interventions for growth were not captured or distorted by vested interests.

Such centralised 'developmental' patrimonialism presupposes effective bureaucracies with hierarchic organisation and impersonal decision-making.

The challenge now is to build strong public administrations which can manage social cohesion. That requires tackling complex cross-sectoral challenges. Those challenges include inequalities, marginalisation and discrimination, and corruption. Where present, these undermine and maintain wide gaps between states and citizens. Sustainable development requires co-ordination across economic, social and environmental policy-making. The goal must be to promote inclusive growth which doesn't exacerbate inequalities or wreck the environment that requires whole of government co-ordination.

Reform in our era is driven by a realisation that the successful states of the 21st century will be those that enhance their civil service with the aim of making it a key national competitive advantage. To achieve that, the public official of the future will need to be motivated to foster societies that are perceived by their citizens as fair, thereby enhancing the trust of citizens in their governments and bolstering the legitimacy of the state. To these ends, they will need to demonstrate the creativity and collaborative spirit required to solve complex problems. They will expose the fallacy that the private sector is inherently more innovative and efficient than the public service. This quiet revolution in the public sector will have profound implications in many countries around the world.

The challenges that confront public officials around the world today are formidable. 'Wicked problems' fall to government to handle, by 'the ways in which governments, citizens, and communities engage to design and apply policies'.[10] Despite huge progress in recent decades, across the globe, some 650 million people live in extreme poverty. Growing inequalities within and between countries affect too many men, women and children. Disparities between the advanced economies and poorer countries continue. Gender inequality and distressing levels of violence against women and girls continue to hamper humanity. Vulnerable groups are marginalised by discriminatory norms and practices.

Urbanisation, demographic change and future technologies could disrupt progress unless their positive potential can be harnessed. Climate-related disasters have increased in number and size. Over the past decade, more than 700,000 people lost their lives; over 1.4 million were injured and approximately 23 million are homeless as a result of disasters. The world is facing catastrophic loss of biodiversity and forest cover. Conflict, sectarian strife and political instability have been on the rise. More than 1.6 billion people live in fragile and conflict-affected settings, including half of the world's extreme poor. Around 244 million people are on the move, including 65 million who are forcibly displaced. The causes of crises are deeply interlinked and require multifaceted responses.

A report by McKinsey Global Institute summarised the uniqueness of change in the 21st century as follows: 'All at once, emerging economies are rapidly industrializing, populations are aging, new technologies are coming into use, and a growing web of interconnectedness is transforming geopolitics, the competitive landscape, and sustainability concerns. Not

---

[10] World Bank, *World Development Report: Governance and the Law*, 2017, p. xiii, https://www.worldbank.org/en/publication/wdr2017.

one of these disruptions, on its own, is a surprise. The unique challenge is that they are happening at the same time — and on a huge scale, creating second-, third-, and even fourth-order effects that are scarcely possible to anticipate. As they collide, they are producing change so significant that much of the management intuition that has served us in the past will become irrelevant. This is no ordinary disruption'.[11]

(i) Unlocking the creativity and collaborative spirit needed to solve complex problems

This has been a key message of this book.

(ii) Overcoming the fallacy that the private sector is inherently more innovative and efficient than the public service

The visible hand of the State is needed before the invisible hand of the market can be effective. The private sector does not compare in the complexity and often contradictory nature of the aims imposed on bureaucracy by the political leadership. This thought is not new:

> We trained hard — but it seemed that every time we were beginning to form up into teams we were reorganized. I was to learn later in life that we tend to meet any new situation by reorganizing, and what a wonderful method it can be for creating the illusion of progress while actually producing confusion, inefficiency, and demoralization.

This insight sounds like the victim of the latest fad in reform. But the quote comes from the 1950s although spuriously attributed to Petronius Arbiter in the *Satyricon*, written 2000 years ago.[12] Fake news may be in fashion, but there is nothing new in fake academic footnotes.

Just as ideological divides result in a lack of consensus on civil service, the same applies to the private sector. If business is regarded as exploitative, then public service is needed as a corrective. The civil service will be inherently oppressive if the private sector liberates and empowers. Being ideological positions, the evidence tends to be limited

---

[11] McKinsey Institute. 2016. *No Ordinary Disruption: The Four Global Forces Breaking All the Trends*. New York.

[12] Brown, D. 1978. Petronius or Ogburn. *Public Administration Review*, 38(3), 264.

and partial. Concepts like 'public value', by covertly mimicking private sector thinking, added further to the destruction of the traditional distinction of the unique attribute of public service — concern for the public good.[13]

(iii) Creating societies that are perceived by their citizens as fair

Fairness is central to the trust of citizens in government.

(iv) Fostering the trust of citizens in their governments

Effective public administration builds trust and trust is critical. Though government performance in many countries has probably been improving (based on proxy indicators such as economic growth, quality of life, level of security, and so forth), yet generally citizens' trust in the government has declined. Too many reforms in different countries have not addressed deep, systemic problems: an unacceptably high level of churn of top officials, divided leadership and confused accountabilities within government, breeding a lack of trust among civil servants. All too often that can be fuelled by 'scapegoating' individual officials rather than honestly trying to learn lessons from failures. Yet the manner in which officials behave is as, or more, important than the policy they implement for building the trust of citizens in their governments.

Declining trust in government reinforces the need to build public service that is not merely effective and efficient, but also just and inclusive has never been greater.

(v) Bolstering the legitimacy of the state

The key competitive advantage a nation can have in the 21st century is a motivated, merit-based innovative public service. The purpose of this book, by looking back to the dawn of governance and public administration, is to relay that message forwards — in order to look to a better world in the future.

Another purpose is to address the current malaise in public administration research. Only too often, writing in this field is either so theoretical

---

[13] Meynhardt, T. 2009. Public Value Inside: What is Public Value Creation? *International Journal of Public Administration, 32*(3–4), 192–219.

as to be surreal, or so bogged down in practical detail as to lack adequate conceptual underpinning and a readily applicable theory of change.

By tying together both ends of the history of public sector reform together, this work seeks to bind theory and practice to the needs of today, and with the added benefit of providing insight into the past.[14] This book will put forward seven propositions about public administration. These derive from public service reform in the city-state of Lagash nearly 4500 years ago or reflect the public service reform in recent years that illuminate the world's first recorded reform of public administration at the dawn of history.

In order for countries to thrive in the future, adopting new technology is not enough; institutional underpinning will remain critical. All regime types — authoritarian, 'illiberal democracy' and democracies — will be gathering big data on their citizens. The difference between states in its use will depend on the quality of governance. Effective institutions are the key to a functioning and stable society. States that fail to modernise their political and economic institutions to accommodate new technologies risk falling behind. Public organisations will need to manage how the collection, analysis, and use of big data creates heightened risks over the privacy and security of citizen data.

Privacy is under siege from five different directions: (i) new technologies, including big data and AI; (ii) 'Whole of Government' data sharing; (iii) social media that foster a spurious sense of intimacy and spread bias, misinformation and fake news; (iv) the digital economy; and (v) hacking, leaks and fraud, facilitated by inter-connectivity and inter-operability.

States are struggling to respond. The methods of controlling national territory cannot police a non-physical space like the Internet. Its governing body, the Internet Corporation for Assigned Names and Numbers seeks to preserve its 'operational stability, reliability, security and global interoperability' in the face of threats to the 'world-wide' ideal from government censorship. Unauthorised access to digital systems, for data manipulation, forgery or theft can originate anywhere around the globe. In response,

---

[14] Farazmand, A. 2002. Administrative Legacies of the Persian World-State Empire: Implications for Modern Public Administration. *Public Administration Quarterly,* 26(3), 280–316.

effective democratic states are evolving a digital, non-territorial fourth dimension. Authoritarian and 'illiberal' democracies will become more isolated.

The political imperative of privacy will increasingly place public administration in a contradictory tension between joined-up knowledge and confidentiality. Governments will need to allow all its data to be pooled for 'big data' analytics. Yet at the same time as linking up different data sets, the state is trying to enforce personal privacy protection by restricting access in accord with current fragmented mandates. In other words, privacy and big data/AI lie at the shifting and contested intersection of commercial profit, public policy and cultural attitudes.

When the Universal Declaration of Human Rights (UDHR) was drawn up in 1948, the threat to the inviolability of human dignity was the surveillance state. That dignity was conceived as a fundamental right in itself and as the foundation for subsequent freedoms and rights, including the rights to privacy and to the protection of personal information. The right to privacy became enshrined in international law. Article 17 of the International Covenant on Civil and Political Rights provides that 'no one shall be subjected to arbitrary or unlawful interference with his privacy, family, home or correspondence, nor to unlawful attacks on his honour and reputation'. Such privacy is central to the protection of human dignity and liberal democracy. Restrictions by the state on the right to privacy, such as surveillance and censorship, can only be justified when prescribed by law, necessary to achieve a legitimate aim, and proportionate to that aim.

Will citizens have dual identities, analogue and digital? This is already foreseen in the Estonian offer of e-residency to non-Estonians. It is aimed at attracting the digitally-independent, and perhaps amounts to a digital off-shore tax haven. Via a smart card, the e-resident status provides access to government services such as company formation, banking, payment processing, and taxation.

In retrospect, the coordinated cyberattacks on Estonia in April 2007 were the beginning of a new era of digital citizenship. After that episode, the government in Tallinn ensured that cybersecurity was rooted in perceived legitimacy. When cyberattacks are perpetrated by, or on behalf of governments in pursuit of a political agenda, the importance of citizens' consent to digital defences curtailing e-rights such as digital privacy grows exponentially, and this consent may then define privacy.

Fluid identities in an era of constant technological change will render the traditional 'right to privacy' an anachronism. Privacy is becoming more complex, negotiated and contested and is already losing out to technologies that make life easier: mobile telephones that record our every move, search engines that note our every interest. In the digital world, private space is shrinking fast as every action instantaneously generates data somewhere. The proliferation of network technologies and the unmediated communication that social media facilitates are blurring the divide between public and private life. Social media renders everyone a self-created public figure, a celebrity in their own web space. Citizens collude with this trend, wanting the algorithmically driven better customer satisfaction and user experience. Governments and citizens need to start by ensuring that the post-privacy e-state is a tolerant place, buttressed by effective institutions that build citizens' trust.

Public service excellence for 21st century

Bureaucrats cannot win. When administration works effectively, its rational impartiality is condemned as heartlessly mechanistic and a threat to personal freedom. Yet when it fails it is condemned as ineffectual, unimaginative, indecisive, self-important and bound by routine. Few celebrate its failing and incompetence as humanising a mechanistic mindset, the shortcoming of over-ambition. Few stop to ask what causes the annoying facets of the modern bureaucracy: are long queues at government offices, surly workers, and 'red tape' symptoms of long struggles to be not only effective and efficient, but also fair to all.

The author and former mandarin, Sanjoy Bagchi, describes how IAS officers become arrogant: 'Overwhelmed by the constant feed of adulatory ambrosia, the maturing entrant tends to lose his head and balance. The diffident youngster of early idealistic years, in course of time, is transformed into an arrogant senior fond of throwing his weight around; he becomes a conceited prig'.

In retrospect, these reforms could be retrofitted into a coherent package aiming to build a stronger sense of personal responsibility for delivery of policies, projects, programmes or services; the use of objectives, performance indicators and measurement to strengthen and accountability and make progress transparent. More open competition for senior roles reflects the greater value attached to leadership. A drive for greater diversity of the civil service makes for a more politically relevant organisation that is outward-facing, better at learning and adopting new ways of working.

From 2350 BC to the 2030 Agenda

One way to consider how a state-building public service may emerge is to examine the first recorded example of public service reform. This dates from around 4400 years ago. Urukagina, the ruler of the Sumerian city-state of Lagash in southern Mesopotamia (around the Tigris and the Euphrates rivers) in the third millennium BC, declared that he had instituted sweeping changes in public administration and tackled widespread deep-rooted corruption. Although the structure and size of the Lagashite public service doubtless differed from modern equivalents, its purpose — at least as conceived by the 'Reforms' — was remarkably similar: to deliver services to assist the needy and vulnerable.

Despite or because of this, his reform ended in failure. His rule apparently proved disastrous and he was ousted from power. Was Urukagina an 'Oriental Despot', a demagogic dictator exploiting the language of social reform for his own political ends? Or was he an ill-fated 'moderniser' of the new concept of the state, whose championing of social justice was lauded in Sumerian praise yet turned out to be too far ahead of his times?

The civilisation of Assyria and Babylon, long known from the Bible yet mainly myth until rediscovered by 19th-century archaeology, emerged from a still older culture. During the fifth to the second millenniums BC, the city-states of Sumer had developed around the southern stretches of Mesopotamia. The invention of cities, agriculture and state bureaucracy transformed this hot and infertile land, lying between the rivers Tigris and Euphrates in modern Iraq. The result was to set humanity off on an continuous journey into urban living and effective governance. Then the city, citizenship and civilisation co-evolved with public administration to make possible cultural, political, legal, economic and social development.

Now, in international development, the transformative 2030 Agenda must be realised in a world that is already transforming at a neck breaking speed. The 193 countries signing up to the SDGs at the United Nations all require a functioning bureaucracy to implement them.

The SDGs provide an articulation of the core development needs of countries — including eliminating poverty, protecting the environment, strengthening communities, access to work, education and health services and gender equality.[15] The SDGs cannot be achieved without effective civil services.[16]

The key practical message on the attainment of the SDGs is that that is dependent on the ability of the public services to prioritise effectively, allocate limited resources efficiently, promote participation and inclusion equitably, foster consensus and promote long-term national aims. The true 'enabling environment' for the private sector is a competent and committed public sector able to discipline as well as liberate the entrepreneurial spirit.

The 2030 Agenda is universal. It includes issues such as inequality and peace and security, democratic governance, tackling corruption, promoting participation, access to information and other human rights and institutional capacity which were not part of the MDG framework.

Goal 16 of the SDGs represents a significant social contract between state and society as it seeks to ensure a match between people's expectations of what the state will deliver and the institutional capacity available within the state to meet those expectations. Building peaceful, just and inclusive societies will take different forms adapted to culturally diverse, complex and evolving realities on the ground (an example will be the definition of national indicators for Goal 16; or the 2063 Vision of the African Union), and aims at leaving 'no one behind'.

Institutions which are effective and accountable will play a central role in achieving the SDGs. Indeed, many of the 169 SDG targets need institutional capacity.

---

[15] http://www.un.org/sustainabledevelopment/sustainable-development-goals/.
[16] Clark, H. 2015. *Achieving the Post-2015 Sustainable Development Agenda — The Role of the Public Service*, 2015 Manion Lecture. 26 May. http://www.undp.org/content/undp/en/home/presscenter/speeches/2015/05/26/achieving-the-post-2015-sustainable-development-agenda-the-role-of-the-public-service.html.

The 2030 Agenda of the SDGs is hugely ambitious. Some of the SDGs, such as combating climate change, could be undermined by the pursuit of others, particularly those focused on growth or high levels of human well-being. Developmental challenges can affect women, men, old and young differently. Differentiated responses will be needed to ensure that the great vision of our times, that 'no one is left behind' by 2030, is fulfilled.

The successful implementation of the 2030 SDGs will depend on transformative public service and public services, and not just on efficient and effective ones. The centrality of an effective public service to development outcomes is so obvious that it is simply taken for granted. Almost all of the 17 Goals, 169 proposed Targets and 231 recommended indicators rely directly or indirectly on public officials for implementation. This includes not only prioritisation of the SDG targets and indicators but also their interpretation, given that some targets are expressed in vague, qualitative language rather than being clearly measurable and time-bound.

Civil Services will also confront another challenge — that the targets are 'siloed'. This will require a 'Whole of Government' effort to link different goals together and overcome potential policy trade-offs, such as between overcoming poverty and environmental sustainability. Public officials will also need political leadership able to champion a national vision for the overall purposed of development.

Now the era of the SDGs poses new challenges for the governments around the world. Progress on the SDGs is critical to each country and 'no-one left behind' approach is enormously ambitious.

For achieving the SDGs, it is necessary not simply to make government more accountable and responsive, closer to citizens, and more efficient. It is also imperative to consider how in all our societies we can build trust and legitimacy.

But making progress in offering practical guidance through peer-to-peer learning must address the all too familiar political logic for an ineffectual public service — either unable or unwilling to make the extra effort required.

Modern development thinking in general should be better informed about the past, and in a more practical approach than seeking to address 'the rules of the game'.[17] Economists in recent decades have discovered that 'institutions matter'. This finding is perhaps surprising only to anyone who ever doubted it. But the SDGs, unanimously agreed by every nation on Earth at the United Nation in 2015, have placed this insight at the heart of the international development agenda.

In recent times, impressive progress has taken place on many fronts. Global poverty has fallen from 35% in 1990 to under 10% in 2016, reducing the number of poor people in the world by over 1 billion. The world has united to recognise and address climate change. Digital technologies and advances in artificial intelligence have transformative implications for economies and societies, offering tremendous potential for progress.

All the countries of the world, developing and developed, have committed to achieve the 17 goals of the 2030 Agenda. But countries face complex development challenges. For some (including many in special development situations), alleviating widespread poverty, meeting basic social needs and establishing the foundations of effective and inclusive government systems continue to be at the core of development policy. The need for more effective and responsive governance systems matters for building resilience to shocks and crises, and maintaining economic growth.

SDG 16, by declaring effective, accountable and inclusive institutions to be the basis for establishing peaceful and inclusive societies, represents a significant advance. It goes well beyond the normative thinking that in the past usually reduced 'governance' to technical capacity building and public administration to HRM systems.

The Gauger: A cautionary tale

Constant discontent is important to keep high standards. Public officials have not always been people of exemplary character. In 1849 the details that came to light following the murder of a middle-aged Customs 'Gauger' (minor official) employed at the Port of London provided a stark reminder of this.

---

[17] This nebulous concept of 'institutions' arising from 'new institutional economics' has successfully thwarted practical attempts to operationalise reform of 'rules of the game' in developing country contexts: see Andrews, *op. cit.*

The victim Patrick O'Connor turned out to be a scoundrel. Without morals or scruples, he was entrepreneurial and had no reservations about exploiting the poor. One of his schemes involved a conspirator approaching fellow Irishmen looking for work in the docks. The gauger would arrange permanent employment in the docks, on payment of a 'facilitation fee'. When this was paid, the labourers were taken on, but in every case the gauger soon found an excuse to dismiss them. When one disgruntled ex-docker attempted to blackmail O'Connor, the crafty gauger stationed a detective in ambush. The would-be blackmailer was arrested and sentenced to 12 months imprisonment. But the revelations during the trial were sufficiently disturbing that the Customs Board declined to promote O'Connor when his turn by seniority arose.

Meantime he had formed an illicit connection with Mrs. Manning, an attractive and buxom creature, who was married to a railway guard. Her husband appears to have tolerated his wife's behaviour on the condition that O'Connor paid for the housekeeping. Perhaps O'Connor was penurious, for in the end the Mannings laid a trap. He was going on leave to Ireland, and they induced him to deposit his trunk, containing valuable securities, at their house in Rotherhithe, and to come and dine with them before his departure.

On the Saturday they procured a fat goose and other delicacies, and dug a hole under the hearthstone in the kitchen. On the Sunday morning, while Manning basted the goose in the kitchen, his wife went upstairs and shot O'Connor through the head. They shoved his body underneath the hearthstone, and then sat down to eat the goose. Afterwards they gave up the house, and sold O'Connor's possessions. This caused them to be arrested. The authorities tried to find O'Connor and searched the empty house in Rotherhithe. During the search a stray dog entered the kitchen, and began to sniff and whine above the hearthstone. The stone was taken up, and the corpse discovered. Both the Mannings were hanged. The last trace of O'Connor was his application to the Customs Board for promotion. On this an official had written a note, dated August 20, 1849: 'Mr. P. O'Connor was found dead on the 17th inst., under circumstances that leave but little doubt he has been murdered'.[18]

---

[18] Atton and Holland, *op. cit.*, pp. 306–309.

Chapter 16

The Digital Developmental State

For governments to be perceived as legitimate requires effective institutions — which are deeply rooted in history and core principles of impartiality, meritocracy and trust needed to address the deeply rooted human desire for certainty to allay primordial fears about the future:

> ... as we know, there are known knowns; there are things we know we know. We also know there are known unknowns; that is to say we know there are some things we do not know. But there are also unknown unknowns — the ones we don't know we don't know. And if one looks throughout the history of our country and other free countries, it is the latter category that tend to be the difficult ones.[1]

The debate over digital statehood is just starting. Today, technology is evolving fast. This 'Fourth Industrial Revolution' is just beginning, but the evidence for its future impact is already clear. Technologies will disrupt the public and private sectors, to an unprecedented degree. Existing comfort zones are crumbling under the speed and nature of fundamental change.

> We hold these algorithms to be self-evident, that all Internet users are created equal, that they are endowed by their software with certain unalienable Rights, that among these are digital Life, e-Liberty and the pursuit of Internet Happiness.

---

[1] Former US Defence Secretary Donald Rumsfeld, February 2002.

Wording like that might someday be the opening of the Digital Declaration of Independence, designed to establish the legitimacy of ethereal virtual cyber e-statehood alongside the territorial analog nation. The 'inventor' of the World Wide Web, Sir Tim Berners-Lee has called for a digital Magna Carta, and in the United States similar suggestions have been put forward for a digital Bill of Rights. Such 'constitutions' would set out the fundamental principles governing the Internet. These would include a definition of equality of cyber access to information. The rights of e-citizens to communicate freely and freedom of speech would be matched with the responsibilities of anonymity. The obligations of business with regard to big data and personal information would balance the legitimate powers of governments to control it and tax e-commerce.

Politics is the process of action and ideas to shape, gain and contend power. Cyber politics is concerned with the power relations over how data is generated, collected, analysed and used in the digital realm. The state, citizens, civil society, and business all have interests and incentives to control or influence the Internet and disruptive technologies. Around the world, effective analog states are evolving a digital, non-territorial 4th dimension. This is founded on a digital social contract of citizens' consent. The resulting e-legitimacy can offset the inevitable decline of privacy, hitherto a defining characteristic of a modern effective democratic state.

The digital state will need a digital social contract with its citizenry, on which to build its e-legitimacy. This would be the basis for the consent of the on-line population. A modern-day Rousseau might observe:

> The Internet surfer is born free; and everywhere she is chained down by spam, malware, phishing, spyware, randsomware, keyloggers, worms, Trojans, backdoor viruses and hacking.

The Internet has opened a Pandora's Box of paranoia. On the political Left, companies that track attitudes using AI are cast in the role of the new evil corporations for the modern era, manipulating the weak and defenceless.

On the political Right, the Internet and new technologies threaten freedoms through censorship and authoritarian governments splintering of the world-wide web. What would 'No taxation without representation' look like in the digital age? How would e-citizen 'consent' be achieved? Can judicial oversight and search warrants work in the digital world?

The Digital States of the Future

Effective democracy	Profit centred	People centred
Weak democracy	Pornography–Populist centred	Power centred
	Weak state institutions	**Strong state institutions**

Public service will confront four broad and overlapping political visions for our digital future.

1. *The 'people-centred' Internet.* This cyber-realm reflects the idealist digital state. The educated citizenry exercise democratic participation, a 'community policing' view of upholding freedoms of expression, communication, rights to knowledge and personal development, affordable access for everyone, no-one left behind. This puts human dignity and the pursuit of 'happiness' (meaning contentment from a fulfilling life) at the centre of Internet governance. It reflects the proposal of the Global Commission on Internet in 2016 that 'social compact for Internet governance' should be based on the principles of openness, trustworthiness, inclusiveness and security.[2]

    This is the ideology of the Internet Society, a US-based NGO that promotes 'public policies that enable open access' and facilitates 'the open development of standards, protocols, administration, and the technical infrastructure of the Internet'.[3]

2. *The 'pornography-populist' Internet.* This is the crude version of all the others. Here the politics of fear, fury and fake news fosters electronic mob rule. It is a world dominated by base interests, instant gratification, a 'digital bread and circuses' to keep the population distracted. This is the daytime shopping TV channels, in which good quality news

---

[2] For more, see Global Commission on Internet Governance (21 June 2016) 'One Internet'. Available online: https://www.chathamhouse.org/sites/files/chathamhouse/publications/research/2016-06-21-global-commission-internet-governance.pdf.

[3] For more, see Internet Society webpage https://www.internetsociety.org/what-we-do.

and journalism is hidden behind paid passwords, daily e-referendums of emotive voting from the sofa in front of the TV/computer.

3. *The 'profit-centred' Internet.* This is a digital world that is dominated by the 'robber barons' of the 21st century. Just as, in the late 19th century with steel and railroads, the private sector in the last few decades has created a whole new economy through ICT and the resultant big data, AI and machine learning. With it, the major computer, telephone, Internet and web companies/corporations have acquired extraordinary wealth and political influence that raise concerns about monopolistic tactics, not least control over data that threatens democracy and disempower ordinary citizens.

In the last few decades of the 19th century, corporate America appeared ruthless and immoral. Democracy seemed at risk from inequality of both income and political influence until finally the US government felt forced to act: the break-up of Standard Oil, controlled by John D. Rockefeller showed the world that exploitative capitalism had finally been subdued.

The American self-image as the land of opportunity and democracy, however, soon led to a re-evaluation of that formative era. *John D. Rockefeller: The Heroic Age of American Enterprise* (1940) by Allan Nevins, *Triumph of American Capitalism* (1942) by Louis Hacker, and *Titan: The Life of John D. Rockefeller, Sr.* (1998) by Ron Chernow reinterpreted 'Robber Barons' like Rockefeller as 'industrial statesmen'. While admittedly ruthless in amassing tremendous power and wealth, their image now metamorphosed into successful entrepreneurs and 'captains of industry' who were portrayed as 'civic patron saints'. Their philanthropy, once seen as the cynical purchase of civic respectability and the assuaging of guilty consciences, was recast as supposedly the product of an innate sense of the social responsibility, that outweighed any alleged unscrupulous, if not outrageously corrupt business practices and political influence, most famously exposed by the 1941 film *Citizen Kane*.[4]

---

[4] Based on the life of Randolph Hearst. To try to prevent the film's release, Hearst's representatives began gathering information on the private life of the film's director, Orson Welles, while Senator Burton K. Wheeler hinted that a Congressional investigation of

In the 21st century, will the new generation of 'Robber Barons' in the current era of growing inequality,[5] be the owners of big data — the showy or shadowy Carnegies, Fricks, Schwabs, Dukes, Mellons, Morgans, Rockefellers and Vanderbilts of our day — who control the algorithms that allow companies like Apple, Google, Amazon, MySpace, Flickr, Twitter, Skype, Youtube and Facebook in the United States, along with Alibaba, JD.Com, Baidu and TenCent from China, and Yandex from Russia — to dominate the new global economy and social networks, just as once their predecessors had controlled the old industrial economy of steel, tobacco, oil and the railroads?

By 2012, 10 of the world's top 50 richest billionaires were Americans (with three from just one company), who had made their wealth from computers and Internet technology: Bill Gates, $61 billion, Steve Ballmer, $15.7 billion and Paul Allen, $14.2 billion, all of Microsoft; Larry Ellison of Oracle, $36 billion, Michael Bloomberg, $22 billion; Larry Page and Sergey Brin of Google, $18.7 billion each; Jeff Bezos of Amazon, $18.4 billion; Mark Zuckerberg of Facebook, $17.5 billion; and Michael Dell, of the eponymous computer manufacturer, $15.9 billion. By 2015, the new economy was becoming internationalised, with the world's wealthiest people including: from China, Jack Ma with $22.7 billion, derived from e-commerce, Ma Huateng with $16.1 billion from Internet media, and Robin Li owning $15.3 billion from Internet search; while from India, Azim Premji with $19.1 billion from software. Oligopoly is on the rise: 10 out of the 13 industrial sectors were more concentrated in 2007 than a decade earlier, and 41% of cash held by big US companies outside the finance sector is owned by tech corporations.

'un-American' influences in Hollywood would result. A member of the Rockefeller family acting for Hearst then convinced Louis B. Mayer of Metro-Goldwyn-Mayer (MGM) Studios to offer to buy the film from its producers, R.K.O. Pictures, so that it could be destroyed and not released. Welles, however, had White House support because of the film's overt backing for President Franklin D. Roosevelt's effort to win over public opinion to end isolationism and enter WWII, and had already privately screened it for enough influential people by that time that R.K.O. felt forced to release it: see Carringer, R. 1985. *The Making of Citizen Kane*. Berkeley and Los Angeles: University of California Press.

[5] See Picketty, T. 2014. *Capital in the 21st Century*. London, Passim.

Will the digital moguls of the 21st century be unscrupulous in exploiting the weak and vulnerable to amass even greater personal fortunes and political muscle? Or will they fear the scorn that once attached to the 'Robber Barons' and aspire to an honourable posterity built from a reputation of admiration and legacy of respect, associated with the Rockefeller Foundation, the Frick Collection, the Carnegie Endowment, or Duke University? Similarly, will 'digital philanthropists' emerge to promote 'corporate data responsibility' by setting up institutions aimed at sharing big data analytics to protect vulnerable populations and fortify democracy?

Big data and AI analytics feeds everyone what they think they want, limiting the ability to develop and change. This is the world of police profiling, in which minority and disadvantaged communities are trapped by the past performance predicting repeat offending.

New technologies are exposing that cultural attitudes to privacy vary and can often be contradictory. Privacy as the protection of personally identifiable data according to fair, moral, legal and ethical standards is a social construct. People who consent to their personal information being collected and stored by government agencies and by corporations only if it is kept confidential may then be willing to reveal the same intimate details of their lives on social media posts, blogs and profiles.

In that, the individual exercises personal choice. However, people are increasingly disclosing, and being required to disclose, personal information over the Internet in order to participate in the modern digital society and economy.

The sudden and unprecedented commercial success of Google, Amazon and related Internet-based digital media and marketing corporations both sprung from and generated big data. This had unexpected but significant consequences. The private sector has been the biggest beneficiary to date of Internet, AI and big data, and it raises issues about the legitimacy of the potential new forms of immense political influence that companies may be able to exert. Social networking sites encourage popular opinion as individuals exchange and display personal information in a distinct form of web-based interaction. The business model is predicated on the ever-expanding use of customers' information, often without their consent, or even knowledge.

So how tech companies collaborate with government will be an important dimension of public service and its future legitimacy and trustworthiness in the eyes of citizens.

While many of the major tech companies, such as Facebook, Twitter and Google release transparency reports on how much they comply with information sharing and content removal requests from governments, the process of cooperation between the company and government (much akin to information sharing between governments) itself is not inherently transparent.[6] Different companies employ different policies and criteria, most of which are vague by their nature. Moreover, users of the same platform may have different rights from their countries of origin — for example, whereas the European Union has been very strong about the rights of its citizens online, Net Neutrality is a raging debate in the United States.

In the second half of 2016 alone, Twitter suspended 377,000 accounts for posting content related to terrorism.[7] The enormity of the challenge means that companies cannot resolve this issue on their own.

4. *The 'power-centred' Internet.* This is the strong dystopian digital state, in which the citizen is kept in a Kafka-esque fog of manipulation, censorship, filter bubbles, the end of privacy, fake news and tech-savvy populism. Digital power is used to project analogue values in debates on governance (authoritarian vs. liberal, state-centric vs. multi-stakeholder, and security-first vs. rights-based).

Unprecedented state and private surveillance capacities may be misused. An article written by a member of the propaganda department committee at the University of Electronic Science and Technology in Chengdu and published in October 2015 in *Studies in Ideological Education*, a journal issued by China's education ministry, suggested using big data to track the political views of individual university

---

[6] CNN Tech (2017, April 17) 'Facebook on murder video: We know we need to do better'.
[7] CNN Tech (2017, March 21) 'Twitter suspends 377,000 accounts for pro-terrorism content'.

students. This would be done by creating a 'political ideology database' from library records, surveys, social media and other sources to collect 'quantifiable, accurate, and personalized information' and 'improve the effectiveness of ideological education'. In 2015 details of the British security service's 'Karma Police' programme became public, showing comprehensive screening of Internet use.[8]

The Snowden/NSA and 'Wiki-leaks' affairs had already intensified fears of 'Big Data for Big Brother' that totalitarian surveillance techniques of the state were becoming ever more invasive.[9] The 2015 report on big data for the European Parliament calls for strengthening the rights of digital citizens, given *the high degree of opacity of many contemporary data processing activities directly affects the right of the individuals to know what is being done with the data collected about them.*[10]

Russia has announced that its military has established military units to wage information wars.[11] 'Fake news' is becoming 'war by other means'. The Organisation for Security and Co-operation in Europe (OSCE) to establish confidence building measures in the cyber realm. The OSCE adopted the Initial Set of OSCE Confidence-Building Measures to Reduce the Risks of Conflict Stemming from the Use of Information and Communication Technologies,[12] consisting of 11 items in December 2013 and expanded this list in

---

[8] D. Helbing, B. Frey, G. Gigerenzer, E. Hafen, M. Hagner, Y. Hofstetter, J. van den Hoven, R. Zicari, A. Zwitter. 2017. Will Democracy Survive Big Data and Artificial Intelligence? *Scientific American; The Economist* 2016. Big data, meet Big Brother: China invents the digital totalitarian state. The worrying implications of its social-credit project.
[9] Edward Snowden, a contractor for the US National Security Agency, in 2013 revealed a US government global big data signals surveillance programme. In George Orwell's novel *Nineteen Eighty-Four*, Big Brother is the leader of a totalitarian state where the slogan 'Big Brother is watching you' expresses government by mass surveillance.
[10] *Op. cit*, p. 4.
[11] Russian defence minister Sergei Shoigu, February 2017.
[12] Organization for Security and Co-operation in Europe Permanent Council (2013) 'Decision No. 1106 Initial Set of OSCE Confidence-Building Measures to Reduce the Risks of Conflict Stemming from the Use of Information and Communication Technologies'.

March 2016 with five additional measures.[13] The list encompasses voluntary information sharing and cooperation among states on the threats and incidents they face, their strategies, policy measures and best practices. It foresees regular meetings among Member States, the appointment of focal points, establishment of communication channels, cooperation on national legislation and the promotion of public–private cooperation. While all cooperation is on a voluntary basis, the OSCE confidence building measures set one of the important precedents of efforts to govern international cybersecurity.

In its 2015 Antalya summit, G-20 members agreed to uphold two principles: (a) that no country should conduct or support ICT-enabled theft of intellectual property, including trade secrets or other confidential business information, with the intent of providing competitive advantages to companies or commercial sectors' and (b) that states should 'respect and protect the principles of freedom from unlawful and arbitrary interference of privacy'.[14]

Governing cyberspace is contested. Countries such as Russia and China take a statist approach, arguing that states and intergovernmental organisations should have primacy in determining the rules of cyberspace, and notions such as state sovereignty should be in the centre. One affirmation of this position are two letters that the Permanent Representatives of the Shanghai Cooperation Organisation (SCO) countries submitted to the UN Secretary-General in 2011 and 2015, respectively, that called for establishing an international code of conduct for cyberspace. The proposed code of conduct promotes negative security assurances, obliging states not to launch cyberattacks for example, reaffirms the United Nation's position in developing international legal norms, and promotes confidence building measures and assisting developing countries to close the digital divide.

---

[13] Organization for Security and Co-operation in Europe Permanent Council (2016) 'Decision No. 1202 OSCE Confidence-Building Measures to Reduce the Risks of Conflict Stemming from the Use of Information and Communication Technologies'.

[14] See G-20 Leaders' Communique, Antalya Summit, 15–16 November 2015. Available online: http://www.consilium.europa.eu/en/press/press-releases/2015/11/16-g20-summit-antalya-communique/.

The state-centric approach argues all states have rights and responsibilities in cyberspace and that 'all States must play the same role in, and carry equal responsibility for, international governance of the Internet, its security, continuity and stability of operation'.[15] It also calls for states to respect each other's sovereignty, territorial integrity and political independence online. While individual rights and freedom of expression are recognised, the SCO countries argue that such rights should be subject to restrictions stemming from the need to respect the rights and reputation of others, and 'for the protection of national security or of public order (*ordre public*), or of public health or morals'.[16]

The non-statist view argues that cyberspace is a multi-stakeholder venture, and as such, the role of states in dictating its terms should be limited, and this role should be shared with others, including the private sector, NGOs and academia. Reflecting their more liberal outlook, this tendency to favour a multi-stakeholder approach also reflects a degree of pragmatism, especially for the United States. The US and US-based entities continue to be the primary players in the cyber realm. One notable example is the Internet Corporation for Assigned Names and Numbers (ICANN), which manages, maintains and coordinates several key functions of the Internet, including the global Domain Name System which links domain names (such as .com, .org, .edu) with their unique Internet Protocol (IP) numbers. This function was given to ICANN in 1999 following a contract with the United States Department of Commerce National Telecommunications and Information Administration (NTIA), and as of October 2016, ICANN as a private and volunteer-based multi-stakeholder entity has fully assumed this function after its agreement with NTIA expired.[17] This multi-stakeholder model works for the United States,

---

[15] Letter dated 9 January 2015 from the Permanent Representatives of China, Kazakhstan, Kyrgyzstan, the Russian Federation, Tajikistan and Uzbekistan to the United Nations addressed to the Secretary-General, United Nations General Assembly 69th Session (13 January 2015) A/69/723 Art. 8.

[16] *Ibid.* Art. 7.b.

[17] ICANN.org (1 October 2016) 'Stewardship of IANA Functions Transitions to Global Internet Community as Contract with U.S. Government Ends'. Accessed on 30 August 2017. Available online: https://www.icann.org/news/announcement-2016-10-01-en.

as 'only this model has the flexibility and adaptability to ensure that the extraordinary growth of the Internet will continue along with the economic prosperity it has helped create',[18] but it has also benefited the United States directly as the country continues to have an influence over the Internet's governance through the weight that hosting and attracting technological capital, key players of the private sector, and academia brings. Some, therefore, have accused Washington of 'Internet imperialism'[19] and seek to challenge the primacy of the United States in the governance of the Internet.[20]

In the absence of international frameworks, governments have also turned to establishing bilateral agreements on more concrete matters. Examples include a bilateral cooperation agreement between Russia and China which has been dubbed a 'non-aggression pact for cyberspace'[21] by some, a framework for the United States–India Cyber Relationship established in 2016 which includes mutual commitments to shared values and bilateral cooperation,[22] as well as agreements signed by China with several partners such as the United States, United Kingdom and Canada, where the sides have pledged to refrain from conducting cyber-espionage for commercial gains, among other issues. While such agreements may in time help the creation of norms on governing cyberspace and state conduct online, they remain limited in scope.

The use of AI is starting to influence politics. In 2016, the 'Brexit' movement in the United Kingdom and the Trump presidential campaign in the United States deployed psychometric profiling tools digitally to target voters, while some governments and corporations may be creating fake social media identities to spread fake news and propaganda.

---

[18] Ulgen, S. 2016. *Governing Cyberspace: A Road Map for Transatlantic Leadership.* Carnegie Endowment for International Peace, p. 38.
[19] *Ibid.*
[20] *Ibid.*
[21] Council on Foreign Relations (20 August 2015) *The Next Level For Russia-China Cyberspace Cooperation?*
[22] For more, see Framework for the U.S.–India Cyber Relationship at https://in.usembassy.gov/framework-u-s-india-cyber-relationship/.

AI makes it easier than ever before to learn more about individuals. Recent research has suggested that AI can already guess sexual orientation based on photographs of faces more accurately than humans are able to do.[23] AI could therefore be used to classify people without their consent, and perhaps to identify other possible links between facial features and such phenomena as political views, psychological conditions or personality traits.

Governments are also being exhorted to deliver better targeted services to citizens. But that use of big data arouses concerns for privacy and ethics. Police profiling based on AI to predict people's behaviour risks reinforcing stereotypes and social exclusion, subverting individual choice and equal opportunities.

Privacy worries over national ID systems highlight a stark cultural divide. While countries like Australia and Ireland seem troubled by 'Big Brother' connotations of ID cards that can act as unique identifiers online, other countries that also consistently rank at the top of international indices measuring the quality of democratic institutions, like Finland and Sweden, issue them without political demure. Such systems can transform government capability. Perhaps the most striking example is Aadhaar, India's biometric digital identity scheme.[24] It has enrolled 1.16 billion people between 2010 and August 2017. The Indian government considers Aadhaar as a 'strategic policy tool for social and financial inclusion, public sector delivery reforms, managing fiscal budgets, increasing convenience and promoting hassle-free people-centric governance'. Aadhaar authentication is widely used by the private sector, including by banks and telecommunications companies, as well as by the National Payment Corporation of India.

Yet the Supreme Court of India observed in August 2017 that the privacy and data management implications of AI storing ever more personal information are immense. It unanimously ruled that privacy

---

[23] Kosinski, M. and Wang, Y. 2017. Deep Neural Networks Are More Accurate Than Humans at Detecting Sexual Orientation from Facial Images. *Journal of Personality and Social Psychology*, *3*, 27–48.

[24] Aadhaar is a 12-digit number issued by the Unique Identification Authority of India.

is a fundamental right, curtailing the government's effort to ensure complete enrolment by restricting access to essential public services for anyone not in the system.

Big Data is offering unprecedented opportunities and challenges to the ways citizens and governments interact, it will alter the nature of the state and the nature of government. Big data politics will therefore have the potential to reconfigure the power dynamics of elites and shift the social contract between citizen and state.

In the public sector, big data will transform the design, the delivery and the monitoring of public policies. It will dramatically transform public services into better targeted, needs-based delivery. That will increase the accessibility, reach and effectiveness of public services. By delivering to citizens the precise services that they need, big data can significantly improve public trust in political leadership. The result will be to boost the legitimacy of the state.

Big data will throw up new challenges requiring political judgment. Rapid and pervasive technological progress, including Big Data, will have many disruptive effects, on labour markets, the economy and society, as well as in government. Managing these 'disruptions' will require political skill.

The balance between privacy and the common interest will become more complex. The rights and liberties of the individual will be more constrained, while the limitations, errors and biases in data gathering and its interpretation will pose new problems. The politics of data resistance and manipulation will increase the pressure on organisations to transform their thinking and practices. The extent to which the state should regulate in the interests of the subjects of the data, the data generators or the data owners will become a further topic of political contention.

Chapter 17

'Something Must be Done!'

'Something must be done!' shrieks every politician. The ambitious local MP emerges to congratulate the government on its handling of the crisis. The opposition spokesman puts in an appearance to condemn the ruling party for allowing acts of God to happen. The high-flying political appointee in the departmental 'delivery unit' continues to adjust the data until at last the graph shows that the problem has been 'fixed'. The junior minister rushes to the scene of the disaster, looking more shaken by the bumpy ride in the shabby vehicle from the office car pool than by the incident. The Secretary of State cancels her holiday to exploit a much-needed opportunity to appeal to voters as earnest, committed and deeply motivated, at least to hang on to her job. Meanwhile her cavalcade is blocking the road, thus hampering the emergency services from dealing with the scene. The Prime Minister flies home from the Summit meeting, clutching his umbrella, waving a piece of paper and declaring 'Peace in Our Time', even as the invasion is taking place.

But, despite all the melodrama of apparent action, the government feels insecure. The reason is clear. 'Events, dear boy, events!' warned British Prime Minister Harold MacMillan, when asked to sum up the problem of governing a country.[1] He was right of course but, typically perhaps, not wholly honest: he had, after all, spent a career getting to the top of the greasy pole of national politics by turning happenstance to political advantage.

---

[1] Despite being one of the most cited quotations on politics, its origins remain uncertain.

The 'Action Bias' of Politicians

In a penalty shoot-out in football (soccer), the speed of the kick means the direction of the ball to the left, right or centre of the goal cannot be judged. The goalkeeper has to guess and then fully commit to that choice. The kicker usually aims at the farthest point away from where the goalkeeper is standing — namely far left or far right of the goal. Yet research shows that, even though the direction of the ball cannot be accurately guessed and therefore whether the goalkeeper guesses right or wrong can only be a matter of luck, goalkeepers feel more guilt about conceding a goal following inaction (staying in the centre) and are indeed more likely to be criticised for it, than following action (jumping the wrong way), even though staying in the middle covers a greater area of the goal than jumping either left or right, leading to a clear bias for action even though the results of action can be no better than inaction. The usual 'omission bias' in favour of inaction is reversed because the norm in many games is to act rather than to choose inaction.[2] So the best and most efficient solution is the appearance of action: psychologically the goalkeeper feels he did his best, his team and its supporters accept that at least he tried, but no effort was actually expended.

Events are indeed the oxygen of politics. Being a politician is about leading and, more importantly, being seen as a leader. That requires opportunities to show leadership skills: 'lights, camera, action!', or *wayang*, the Malay word used for politics as dramatic performance.

Yet the politics of prestige and panic under the spotlights has not always seemed inevitable. Over the throne in the Forbidden City hangs a piece of calligraphy designed to remind any Chinese emperor of the limits to even heavenly ordained power, and the preposterousness of political posturing. The writing captures the great insight from thousands of years of studying the art of good governance in ancient China, including how to avoid the danger of political over-reaction. In a few elegant brush strokes, the skills of a great ruler are reduced to two Chinese pictograms.

---

[2] Bar-Eli, M. *et al.* 2005. Action Bias among Elite Soccer Goalkeepers: The Case of Penalty Kicks.

Wu-wei: **Purposeful 'Non-Doing'**

The word these two Chinese characters render, *wu-wei*, literally means 'non-doing', and so can be translated simply as 'inactivity' or 'inaction'. But its true meaning is more refined, certainly does not imply 'indolence'. Rather, as a personal objective and a rule for effective and efficient government, the idea exercised many ancient Chinese philosophers, including Confucius, Mencius, Xunzi and Zhuangzi.[3] The clearest elaboration of the concept comes from Laozi, the founder of Taoism, in three pithy insights offered in the core text of this philosophy, the *Tao te Ching*. The first states: *The wise man deals with things through wu-wei and teaches through no-words. Ten thousand things flourish without interruption. They grow by themselves, and no one possesses them.*[4] The principle, then, is enigmatic, of non-action by purposeful design (the wise *deal with things*, not ignore them). This is elaborated by a second, more direct insight: *When wu-wei is done, nothing is left undone.*[5] This emphasises contrast, the union of two contradictory concepts, namely action (nothing remains undone) and no action (nothing is done). Any credible resolution of this paradox (and others related to it in the same school of thought, such as of 'trying without trying' or upholding the 'virtue of non-virtue') must somehow manage to combine both.[6] How this can be anything other than a contradiction in terms might seem impossible.

That leads to the third and final strand of Laozi's insight on the concept: 'The highest attainment is wu-wei and is purposeless'. So *wu-wei* also means avoiding a conscious effort in performing an action. Instead, through instinct or training, the action becomes second nature, without effort. Success, as in the Japanese martial art of judo, is the result of turning the force of the adversary against himself. Rather than 'doing nothing', this is Sun Tzu's 'winning without fighting': under the weight of a heavy snowfall, the branches of a tree bend until the snow falls off and, having dropped the burden, the branches spring back.

---

[3] Ames, R. 1994. *The Art of Rulership: A Study of Ancient Chinese Political Thought*. SUNY Press.
[4] Laozi. *The Tao Te Ching*. Edition. Date of edition. Chapter 2.
[5] *Ibid*. Chapter 48.
[6] Loy, D. 1985. Wei-Wu-Wei: Nondual Action. *Philosophy East and West, 35*(1), 73–86.

Some scholars have concluded that *wu-wei* represents a mystic or unresolvable contradiction. Others suggest that the paradox can be resolved by the realisation of Tao, which, like the Vedāntic revelation of Brahman and the Buddhist attainment of nirvāṇa, cannot be understood logically. A third interpretation suggests that the term was the unintentional consequence of the juxtaposition in early Taoism of its original 'contemplative' and a subsequent 'purposive' stance. However, such ambiguous responses need not be the only credible interpretations of this enigmatic concept.

The seeming contradiction of *wu-wei* can be resolved by realising that 'non-action' refers not to physical action but the mental state of the doer, in which *wu-wei* is balanced by *wu-bu-wei (nothing left undone)*. *Wu-wei*, then, is more than studied fatalism 'at the edge of chaos'. Rather it describes 'a state of personal harmony in which actions flow freely and instantly from one's spontaneous inclinations — without the need for extended deliberation or inner struggle — and yet nonetheless perfectly accord with the dictates of the situation at hand, display an almost supernatural efficacy'.[7] In modern context and parlance, this implies critical judgment, enabling strategic prioritisation where intervention can make a real difference for all.

So *wu-wei* is action that is 'natural': not controlling or micromanaging to force things artificially in a certain direction, but 'going with the flow'. In essence, *wu-wei* represents 'the culmination of knowledge manifested in an ability to move through the world and human society in a manner that is completely spontaneous and yet still fully in harmony with the normative order of the natural and human world'.[8] It is therefore, a professional skill, honing effective behaviours. If public service recruit for and inculcate *wu-wei*, officials would have a philosophical depth and an institutional consensus that would minimise politicisation, media pressure and self-promotion. Integrity would become intuitive, realism instinctive, honesty almost second-nature — the objective of any anti-corruption agency. As Zhuangzi, another early Taoist thinker explains, the best

---

[7] Slingerland, E. 2000. Effortless Action: The Chinese Spiritual Ideal of Wu-Wei. *Journal of the American Academy or Religion*, 8, 111–132.
[8] *Ibid.*

butcher is the one who has been chopping meat for so long that he does not need to think about where to cut, but carves up the meat by force of habit. If he stops to think about what he does, that perfect efficiency would be lost.

Wu-wei as the Ethics of 21st Century Public Service

Seen from this perspective, Laozi's insights imply that as the complexity (*Ten thousand things*) of events (that *grow by themselves*) cannot be 'possessed' or controlled, the public official must 'deal with' events purposefully, not by neglecting his/her duty, but nevertheless with 'non-action'. This is either through 'effortlessness', or the instinctive ability to act effectively and efficiently that is, indeed, a prized skill in public service everywhere, or on the basis of a carefully considered 'do no harm' problem diagnostic. That conclusion then must be communicated to the population ('teaches through no-words', supported by professional expertise and standards) judiciously through 'non-action that speaks louder than words'.

Since the Dwight Waldo/Herbert Simon debate 70 years ago on whether public administration is a science, it has been a concern that public service lacks an adequate philosophical and methodological underpinning. As a result, research on public administration may suffer from insufficient analytical rigor because of the absence of testable theory.[9] *Wu-wei* as a deeply rooted philosophical basis for the professional ethics of public administration posits an ideal of peace and prosperity built on effortless standards of spontaneous behaviour derived from either natural skills or cultivated habits, or both, that appear effortless.[10]

In the institutional context of public service, spontaneity to respond effectively to crisis requires constant exercise, regular drills and routine training. Public services must hire, train and retain public officials who are, by nature and training, calm and effective when a problem arises.

---

[9] Raadschelders, J. C. N. 1999. A Coherent Framework for the Study of Public Administration. *Journal of Public Administration Research and Theory, 9*(2), 281–304.
[10] Hon, T. 2006. *The Yijing and Chinese Politics: Classical Commentary and Literati Activism in the Northern Song Period, 960–1127.* SUNY Press.

This requires staff professionally trained to think and sufficiently self-confident to act by themselves and not wait for instructions for every step, but who can prioritise and keep headquarters well-informed but not overwhelmed by trivia. This, in colonial times, was described as 'character' and 'common sense',[11] but is too often lacking in modern public service.[12] Similarly, the Japanese culture of etiquette and propriety continues to contribute greatly to assisting in times of crisis, as people are still capable of behaving in a 'civilised' way, such as after the Tōhoku tsunami in 2011. This is a sharp contrast to many other parts of the world where society breaks down in the event of a crisis and looting and rioting become the norm. It is a culture of 'every man for himself' where public authority imposes a solution the problem. True bureaucratic 'non-action' is only possible when a culture of 'non-action' is also established in that society. Professional ethics in public service require an ethical political leadership and population.

Wu-wei identifies bureaucratic non-action as the essential skill of anticipating problems and tackling those that are susceptible to intervention early before they grow into major challenges. So in a well-functioning bureaucracy that acts with the professional ethics of *wu-wei*, much of their efforts will often go unnoticed. And if any, problems that are visible to the public are testament of the failure of a bureaucracy to anticipate these issues early enough. The arrogance of 'answers', 'fixes' and 'solutions' is then dangerous, when political leaders demand certainty where certainty is lacking. Instead, one can try to influence, but not pretend to control. Edmund Burke had similarly warned against the ambitions of the French Revolution to remake mankind.

By contrast, Benito Mussolini, the dictator of Italy between 1922 and 1943, coined the term 'Totalitarian' in his closing speech at the fourth Congress of the Italian National Fascist Party on 22 June 1925. His political vision advocated total state penetration of society. To achieve this, he called for radical social innovation through experimentation in which Italy

---

[11] Talib, N. S. 1999. *Administrators and Their Service: The Sarawak Administrative Service under the Brooke Rajahs and British Colonial Rule.* Kuala Lumpur.
[12] Hollingsworth, C. 2012. Reclaiming Ethics and Character for Public Service. *Public Manager,* 41(1), 60–62.

would serve as a 'pop-up lab of life'.[13] By destroying ancient laws and venerable traditions, a new 'rational' society could be created in which the individual would be totally subservient to the state. Freed of ethical values and liberated from the past, the politician would become the artist, creating the amoral beauty of a new world forged by force and liberated through violence.[14] Innovation, freed from any constraint from history, would be chiselled by the *Duce* or *Führer* from the raw material of the characterless anonymous 'masses' and informed by rigorous and systematic record-keeping like the methodical lists kept by the Gestapo of Jews gassed at Auschwitz; or by the NKVD of millions of Soviet political prisoners to be shot in gulags, all scrupulously authorised by Stalin, would be chiselled from the raw material of the characterless anonymous 'masses'.

Not for nothing, therefore, did both Hitler and Mussolini declare themselves to be artists.[15] This was not just Hitler as house-painter in pre-1914 Vienna or Mussolini as a blacksmith helping his father beat iron into shape in Predappio. The cult of leadership under Nazism and Fascism promoted the rhetorical trope of the effective leader called on to destroy the old and endlessly innovate. A new unified aesthetics and mythology of men of action informed by data and governing by ceaseless activity, backed by emotive symbols and populist spectacle, would replace the gap left in society by the decline of religion and tradition in newly industrialising societies. The artist-cum-political leader destroys in order to create. 'Moulding', 'sculpting' and 'shaping' were the terms by which Mussolini referred to his political function of transforming the masses. Politics was an art and Mussolini imagined himself as a sculptor who, armed by better information, could alone create a new society able to deal with the needs of a rapidly changing world.[16]

---

[13] Kandel, L. 1997. *Féminismes et Nazisme*. Publications de l'Université Paris.

[14] Georges Sorel's *Reflections on Violence* of 1908 posited an endless struggle between bourgeoisie and proletariat. Douglass North suggests economic growth is constrained in many countries by 'limited' access orders needed to pay off potential sources of violence.

[15] In August 1939, Hitler told the British ambassador in Berlin: 'I am an artist and not a politician. Once the Polish question is settled, I want to end my life as an artist'.

[16] Falasca-Zamponi, S. 2000. *Fascist Spectacle: The Aesthetics of Power in Mussolini's Italy*.

In contrast, non-totalitarian governments can only 'nudge' events and people. The skill, in the analogy of classical philosophers, is to imitate water sweeping around rocks and gradually wearing even granite down, rather than acting as a boulder crashing down on a river and upsetting the flow of its natural order. By training the instincts of long-term patience in an administrator or politician, behaviours become effortless or instinctive, based on universally shared professional ethics, ethos and values of public service as an institution with a lasting collective memory (systems thinking suggest the same point).

This is not surprising to the seasoned bureaucrat who, the world over, follows the universal, deep wisdom of *wu-wei* as the skill or art of 'non-action'. The collective experience from over 4000 years of organisational development suggests that the wisest path may be the pursuit of the deliberate, conscious act of either effortless action (through good preparation) or non-action.

An Ancient Philosophy for Modern Public Service

Seen from this perspective, *Wu-wei* does not reflect a lack of professional ethics, or absence of concern. The core competence of public service is the capacity to maintain calm 'common-sense' — in the face of 'something must be done' hysteria and opinion poll chasing populist politics — should therefore be regarded as an essential quality of good administration. The capacity of officials to maintain professional ethics, side-step the need for knee-jerk solution and offer decision-makers, honest and fearless advice in the tradition of speaking truth to power, should become the hallmark of 'good governance'. The public official should aspire to calm common sense, or action without desire, based instead on a higher motivation or intention.

Professional ethics as *the highest attainment being wu-wei, purposeless* and *nothing left undone,* characterised by ease and alertness by which — without even trying — experienced public officials are able to respond appropriately to whatever situation may arise. These ethics are vital if liberal democracies are to remain 'liberal' and avoid pandering to every whim of vociferous interests, public service must have the status and capacity to discern when public opinion is valid and needs to be factored into decision-making and when it is frenzied, ill-judged and guided by a mob mentality. The last few decades have exposed the dismaying failure of comprehensive reforms that claimed to drastically change how governments worked.[17] Unfortunately, rather than making make public service more 'responsive', they instead fostered short-termism often resulting in the public service blindly following and not querying and guiding public opinion. The Dangerous Dogs Acts[18] rushed through parliaments in the United Kingdom and Holland were classic examples of this.

Now, having realised, albeit late that knee-jerk yet wide-ranging reforms may not be the solution, could *wu-wei* be the universalist philosophy required for a context-specific effective public sector? *Wu-wei* indeed implies that any action should be cautious and piecemeal experimentation rather than the grand design implementing the master plan through a 'logical' framework of causality. It implies cautious incrementalism in reforms, along the lines of Lindblom's 'science of muddling through' within bureaucracies,[19] as a rational way of managing complexity and the inherent uncertainty in predicting exactly what the consequence of reforms at each stage will be. This means rejecting 'best practice' in favour of 'best fit', that is the most appropriate to context, and proceeding by reason and compromise, quiet negotiation, 'purposive muddling' and 'satisficing'. This is not 'effortless action' but the minimum appropriate action, that is, efficient within bounded rationality: *Reason must guide action in order that power may be exercised according to the intrinsic properties and natural trends of things.*[20]

---

[17] Hood, C. and Dixon, R. 2015. *A Government that Worked Better and Cost Less? Evaluation Three Decades of Reform and Change in UK Central Government*. Oxford University Press.

[18] 'In Westminster, that's the byword for a spectacular mess, specifically legislation botched through being rushed. If a minister ponders a panicked response to a news story, a wise spad, or special adviser, will be on hand to whisper: "Careful. That could end up being a bit dangerous dogs"'. Cited in: Freedland, J. 2013. Dangerous Dogs Legislation — Don't Mess It Up Again. *The Guardian*, 6 August 2013.

[19] *Op. cit.*, p. 317.

[20] Book Nine of the *Huai Nan Tzu*, compiled under the patronage of Liu An at the court of Wu Ti perhaps around 140 BC presents *wu-wei* as serving state efficiency, within the Legalist political philosophy.

This philosophy of self-generating natural order derived from a seeming contradiction assumes high relevance when confronted by 'the edge of chaos'.[21] This modern concept, in complexity science, of emergent self-order in complex systems means the search for such a sense of natural order will place a premium on calm common sense throughout the 21st century. For public service everywhere is confronting rapid change, as well as limits on funding and capacity constraints. Henry Kippin, for example, calls attention to changes evident in public service. A major one is that public service will increasingly be delivering less by itself, and doing more to create the platforms to enable others.[22]

In any society, people learn how to interact with one another, to work with one another through social etiquette, norms, or professional protocols. Public service as an organisation and institution derived from the 'political settlement' in every state, links elites to the wider population, politicians to taxpayers, government to citizens, an instrument of state but also a symbol of unity, galvanising or blocking action by careful positioning and the use of discretionary authority, creating the climate where self-order can finally emerge. The public service of the future will act less as the universal solution. Instead it will have the *wu-wei* ambition of symbolic 'non-action'. Effortless and pre-emptive, meaningful by signalling concern for problem, its main task becomes to uphold and guide a natural order, and its main skill the emotional and cultural intelligence underpinning spontaneity and intuition.[23] The more public service collaborates to co-create with society, the more it will be capable of non-action, offering direction, but leaving civil society and the private sector to act.

This concept of 'non-action' is, indeed, the central guiding insight in Taoist thought. If *wu-wei* meant ignoring complexity and rapid transformation, it would risk being irrelevant. In that, perhaps, there is another profound divide between those people who see the commonality of mankind with small albeit important differences and those who see deep differences with a weak commonality. But the 'Act of non-action' refers to

---

[21] Ramalingam, B. 2014. *Aid on the Edge of Chaos*. Oxford.

[22] Kippin, H. 2015. *Five Shifts in Public Service*. Paper presented at the UNDP Workshop 'Work in the Public Service of the Future'. Singapore, May 2015.

[23] Slingerland, E. 2014. *Trying Not to Try: The Art and Science of Spontaneity*. New York.

mastering the art of minimum effort to align public authority to create trust and the legitimacy of power. This, indeed, is the original sense of *Wu-wei* when it appears for the first time, not in Taoist texts, but in the work of Confucius.[24] His sole recorded reference to *wu-wei* relates how the philosopher–king, Shun, governed efficiently by simply occupying the throne: *If anyone could be said to have achieved proper order while remaining inactive (wu-wei), it was Shun. What was there for him to do? He simply made himself respectful and took up his position facing due South* (*Analects*, 15.5). By regulating his own conduct so that it upholds order and tradition (Emperors 'naturally' always face south), the ruler sets a positive example and thus influences his subjects without any need for coercion.[25] So, as Laozi observed, *If he acts without action, order will prevail* (Chapter 3). Competent bureaucracy requires effective political leadership, applying *wu-wei* to promote prosperity for all citizens, or, as in Singapore, an 'administrative state' constraining the 'irrationality' of politics. Thus the developmental state evolves, usually to the lyrics of nationalism.[26]

Yet, while the influence of *wu-wei* has been credited for the rise of *laissez-faire* liberal democracy in Europe in the 18th and 19th centuries,[27] Laozi posits a philosophy of government also suitable for the post-Great Recession 21st century: *The more laws and restrictions there are, The poorer people become. ... Therefore the sage says: ... I do nothing and people become rich.*[28] But this is *wu-wei*, not inaction. Markets only work when well regulated, not unregulated. The effective central bank governor or head of the competition commission/anti-trust agency is not indolent or inactive, but rather working by non-action.

The concept of 'Non-action' therefore captures the idea that informed bureaucracy everywhere undertakes considerable fact-finding, analysis and planning before concluding that, in the face of risk and uncertainty, a

---

[24] Ames, R. 1981. Wu-wei in 'The Art of Rulership' Chapter of Huai Nan Tzu. *Philosophy East and West, 31*(2), 88–123.

[25] Loy, *op. cit.*

[26] Everest-Phillips, M. 2015. The Lyrics of Public Service Excellence. *Asian Journal of Public Affairs, 8*(1), 106–109.

[27] Hobson, J. 2004. *The Eastern Origins of Western Civilization*. Cambridge.

[28] *Op. cit.*, Chapter 57.

'do no harm' caution is prudent. *Wu-wei* promotes 'learning by doing' and 'muddling through' that has been a notable attribute of effective public administration reform.[29] One reason, as the Nobel Prize winning economist Herbert Simon pointed out, is that public administration is governed by contradictory principles, similar to *Wu-wei*. As a result, public officials do not seek optimal but rather accept satisfactory and sufficient solutions. *Wu-wei* as a 'natural' and 'effortless', not 'maximising' approach, pre-empted 'satisficing' in public administration and 'problem-driven iterative adaptation' in public service reform by 2500 years.

The common understanding about how the world actually works, shared by public administrations addressing the universal needs and characteristics of humanity, is *wu-wei*. Refined by over 2000 years of practical experience, it offers insights of common value today that helps link an ever more integrated, yet divided, globalised world. While the political rhetoric of intransigence can foster a dialogue of the deaf between east and west or north and south (and, increasingly between other more refined polarities such as north-west and south-east), a common understanding of public service would ease the sense of humanity divided by its common problems. The legitimacy bestowed by a shared philosophical understanding of public administration would be invaluable, in the ever-increasing complexity of decision-making in the 21st century, for guiding officials to cope with the pressures in public service careers.

Non-action in bureaucracy requires, however, hard work and cunning, as viewers of the BBC series *Yes Minister* and *Yes Prime Minister* are aware. Cautious, risk-averse bureaucrats intuitively embrace *Wu-wei* or *not doing*, as a professional skill. The meaning is not indolence as in just the 'doing nothing' of laziness: as every seasoned public official knows, *wu-wei* requires profound knowledge of the institutional context and experience in organisational culture, so rarely does 'non-action' allow for 'inaction'. A one-page official document can often be the result of months of writing, commenting, redrafting, inter-departmental consultative meeting, inter-agency wrangling and condensing into a ministerial submission.

---

[29] Andrews, M. 2013. *The Limits of Institutions Reform in Development.* Cambridge; Levy, B. 2014. *Working with the Grain: Integrating Governance and Growth in Development Strategies.* Oxford.

The successful monarch or CEO reigns but does not rule: that is, the effective political leader, like a figurehead of state, avoids getting bogged down in trivial matters of government but influences or controls through strength of personality, breadth of political and professional networks, depth of ideas or the charismatic influence of his or her virtue (*te*). That, in modern parlance, delivers the vision that sets the direction and atmosphere.

Personal commitment is different from professional procedure: the medical doctor should feel a strong personal commitment to saving life and reducing people's suffering; but professionally must pursue calm procedures and clear rationality. As with the placebo effect, the general public may not be able to discern between purposive 'non-action' (a decision to not act as the best approach to the matter after heavily investigating the problem) and evasive 'inaction' (avoiding responsibility due to indolence, corruption or inefficiency). *Wu-wei* lay behind the Laozi's concept of government as the minimum interference conducive to the individual's quest for personal fulfilment. This is profoundly democratic,[30] but different from neo-liberal small government and free market argument for the state just to 'get out of the way'.

> Modern public administration is a never-ending merry-go-round of more or less desperate reorganisation and reform in a quest for something that 'works. ... the encouragement of public servants is much more difficult than the designing of public services. Bureaucracy is organisation; mobilisation is personal. It is psychological.[31]

One way to tackle this is for civil servants to crowd source solutions. They would continue to safeguard state interests while managing a proliferation of interest groups as citizens use new media to amplify concerns. Since 2011 the Kenyan Government, for example, through the Open Data Initiative has made statistics and data on public service delivery available on line to encourage independent developers to create

---

[30] Feldt, A. 2010. Governing Through the Dao: A Non-Anarchistic Interpretation of the Laozi. *Dao,* 9(3), 323–337.

[31] Ringen, S. 2013. *Nation of Devils: Democratic Leadership and the Problem of Obedience.* Yale, pp. 119–120.

useful tools and applications. Kenya shows that developing countries must also navigate and adapt to shifting trends.

Public servants of the future will need both technological and soft skills to listen effectively and empathise with their users, understand needs as service users themselves, co-design effective solutions, and empower citizens to shape narratives of change. Encouraging the values and attributes that enable these activities is paramount. However, inculcating and strengthening the public service ethos will require going beyond mere service guidelines or codes of conduct. In Singapore, systemic efforts have been made to ensure that operating mind-sets, practices and daily work habits throughout the organisation are kept consistent with espoused public service values. This includes an expectation that leaders will behave as organisational role models.

Wu-wei could offer the philosophical basis that is currently lacking for guiding public service in the 21st century. It eschews applying simplistic private sector principles but recognises that problems resolve themselves where political interference is more their cause than their solution. One idea of the last few decades that has overflowed all to readily to public service around the world, the often inappropriate fashion for PPP ('public–private partnerships'), should be replaced with PPPP — Prestige, Professionalism, Pride and Passion. For *Wu-wei* captures the cautious spirit of realistic ambition and officials' pro-social expectations of the added value from enhancing public welfare. It represents the public service's professional ethos of considered incremental change confronting complexity. The concept rejects the simplistic temptation of political leadership's 'vision' for sweeping reform to 'mould the masses' in the fascist manner, but recognises politics as a public spectacle and sport. People instinctively want heroes for leaders.[32] Prestige matters, while political vision is needed to drive possibility of change.

Two schools of thoughts developed for how effortless action can happen. While Confucianism advocates the discipline derived from years of practice to make a particular skill second nature, the Taoists promote freeing the natural instincts from within. The compromise approach of

---

[32] Brown, A. 2014. *The Myth of the Strong Leader: Political Leadership in the Modern Age*. Oxford.

Mencius in the 4th century BC was to combine both approaches under the epithet: *Try, but not too hard*. That doubtless includes trying to explain the Wu-Wei concept itself. By eschewing grand but unrealistic plans, *wu-bu-wei (nothing left undone)* signifies the credibility of clear commitment to feasible policies.[33] *Wu-wei* articulates realism and honesty about the limitations of public authority. Rather than forcing action and acting for the sake of it, the wisdom of *wu-wei* is to assist things to take their natural course, to work 'with the grain' — a principle only just discovered in international development. The polarity of East and West may not, after all, be so polarised: bureaucracy fulfils an important function everywhere to uphold the present and inter-generational public good.

---

[33] Krishnadas, D. 2015. *FUSE: Foresight-Driven Understanding, Strategy and Execution.* Singapore.

Conclusion: The 21st Century Race for a Creative State

From the 4500 years perspective, the current 'Age of Anxiety' is witnessing a 'Fourth Bureaucratic Revolution' that will develop into a competition among countries to become 'Creative States'.

Change might seem, indeed is, a daunting challenge. Urukagina, the ruler of the Sumerian city-state of Lagash, may have had the same thought. He claimed that he had dismissed corrupt officials — the chief boatman and head herdsman, fishery inspectors, grain tax supervisors and temple administrators, along with those priests who had demanded excessive fees for performing religious rituals and for burying the dead. He stated his intent to defend the poor and the elderly.

So was Urukagina the world's first reformer of corrupt and incompetent public officials? Did he start the 4500 year search for an effective, efficient and equitable public service to transform people's lives?

Or was he the first populist 'bureaucracy-basher'? Was the collapse of Lagash undeserved bad luck? Urukagina, like Josiah in far later times, had restored the law, had introduced humanitarian measures, had shown himself the special protégé of the national God. But just rule was unfairly rewarded by destruction: 'The men of Umma, since they have made desolate Lagash, have sinned against Ningirsu. The might that has come to them shall be taken away. Sin of Urukagina, king of Girsu, is there none'.

Yet progress does happen. Innovative ideas do emerge. Public services can embrace passion. Design thinking is beginning inspire compassion.

Better decision-making by 'co-creation' fosters empathy.[1] It will resurrect the social status and job satisfaction of public service officials. Public service will offer ever more intellectually interesting work that creates a sense of contributing to the greater good. The 'whole of government' approach will ensure that everyone in the public sector knows and is held responsible for how their jobs contribute to the wider national aims. A sense of civic duty will reinforce other important attributes. More attention will be paid to autonomy within the organisation, enjoy satisfaction in working on existential challenges, improving skills, respecting diversity, managing people fairly, while also promoting the professional development, creativity and empowerment of employees.

Repeated reorganisations cynically implemented for political reasons have generated deep disquiet in public service employees; the politicisation of once proudly neutral civil services has devastated faith in the commitment to protect the long-term national interest. Unchecked, the disconnect between rhetoric and reality will grow ever deeper. So not only must governments learn to do more with less while rebuilding trust of the public and responding to ever growing citizens' demands; they must rebuild, from an all-time low, the morale of the officials responsible for both front-line services and for central policy formulation.

Reform of public administration has been politically tempting for 4500 years: success is elusive. The world is a complicated place. It defies depiction by 'Twitter'-sized sound bites. But, by starting with a problem, not a solution, by 'muddling through' rather than 'big bang', by understanding the political context, reform can and does happen. To achieve it requires knowing the people not just the institutions: Think people not systems for the shorter term, recognising the crucial role of personality — politicians, civil servants and advisers — in the reform process. Think systems not people for the longer-term: reform leadership has too often been too personalised on heroes and not an institutionalised 'steward of the Civil Service', so fails to survive transitions of power. See the bigger 'Whole of Government' picture. Win allies, by building a coalition inside and out. Seek but adapt external advice ('How did you solve this problem?').

---

[1] Alford, J. 2009. *Engaging Public Sector Clients: From Service Delivery to Co-production*. Palgrave Macmillan, Houndmills, Hamps and New York.

Focus on a broader vision about the role of the civil service around performance and outcomes, not reorganisation and outputs. Consider yourself a psychotherapist, not a plumber. Be clear on what is needed for building citizens' trust in government in general, and specifically *in public service as fair and impartial*. Appreciate the historical context and understanding of bureaucratic heritage. Recognise the role informal institutions can play in developing an emerging civil service, and acknowledgement that hybridity is not failure. Support continuous improvements, such as developing the capacities of civil servants. Focus on 'missing middles' that manage tensions and foster dialogue between the 'formal centre' and 'informal periphery', particularly in regions where the state may be contested.

Passionate Bureaucrats, Happy Citizens

Public service will revert to its unique core task: to build and preserve fairness, trust and legitimacy. As Theodore Roosevelt, the most famous US civil service commissioner of the 19th century said:

> Civil service reform is not merely a movement to better the public service. It achieves this end too, but its main purpose is to raise the tone of public life, and it is in this direction that its efforts have been incalculable good to the whole community... Undoubtedly, after every success there comes a moment of reaction. The friends of the reform grow temporarily lukewarm, or, because it fails to secure everything they hoped, they neglect to lay proper stress upon all that it does secure. Yet, in spite of all disappointments and opposition, the growth of Civil Service Reform has been continually more rapid, and every year has taken us measurably nearer that ideal of pure and decent government which is dear to the heart of every honest American citizen.[2]

When 4500 years ago, the ruler of Lagash in Babylonia implemented the world's first recorded anti-corruption policy and public sector reform by stopping the head boatman from appropriating boats, the livestock

---

[2] Roosevelt, T. 1895. Six Years of Civil Service Reform. *Scribner's Magazine, XVIII*(2), August.

official from appropriating donkeys and sheep, and the fisheries inspector from appropriating the catch, he initiated a process that has been with us ever since.

This time is different. Yes of course. But then, didn't Urukagina of the Sumerian city-state of Lagash argue that too? Competitive advantage will fall to those that are nimble, innovative and, above all else, motivated — passionate about promoting public welfare in an ever more complex world. Neither the private sector nor civil society can substitute for an effective, efficient and equitable state, run by officials who aspire to both improve and preserve.

On reflection, therefore, that the first recorded reform of public administration ended in catastrophic failure is unsurprising. Nor is it puzzling why so many subsequent reforms have also failed. The evidence from Lagash 45 centuries ago is tantalisingly limited, but questioning the 'Reforms of Urukagina' sheds light on all public service reform.

The text of Urukagina's Cones will continue to fascinate generations to come. The power of the ideas that they record is more important than the extent or success of the specific reforms attempted in Lagash over 4000 years ago. The cones are a permanent inspiration to every generation seeking anywhere to build a fair, effective and efficient public administration. Through these dull-looking cuneiform clay tablets, Urukagina's magnificent vision of a well-run and just society lives on.

One thing, however, that we do know for certain, thanks to those non-descript clay tablets on display in the Louvre: grumbling about the civil service has remained an inherent human characteristic since the first public official to take an unpopular decision in the wider common interest was brave enough to look to society's long-term need, rather than the short-term benefit promoted by the most vocal of vested interests.

Yet, without that vital first step towards an effective state, we might still be huddled within the mud walls of Lagash praying for the divine intervention of Ningirsu, the hero of Enlil, to improve our lives.

Conclusion: The 21st Century Race for a Creative State

Gudea of Lagash. Many statues of Gudea, a ruler of Lagash two centuries after Urukagina, survive.

The inscriptions on his robe listing the temples that he built or renovated in Lagash: 'Gudea, the man who built the temple; may his life be long'.[3]

---

[3] Thureau-Dangin, F. 1924. *Statuettes de Tello: Monuments et Mémoires Publiés par l'Académie des Inscriptions et Belles-Lettres. Fondation Eugène Piot*, vol. 27. Paris; Johansen, F. 1978. *Statues of Gudea: Ancient and Modern*. Mesopotamia: Copenhagen Studies in Assyriology, 6.

Index

A

2030 Agenda, 156, 301
Aadhaar, 316
Abraham, 96
Absurdity, 127
Académie française, 203
Action bias, 320
Administrative leadership, 190
Adultery, 104
Africa, 146
Age of Acceleration, 266
Age of Anxiety, 4–5, 234, 239, 335
Agga, 99
Akkad, 75
Akurgal, 20
Alibaba, 309
Amagi or *amargi*, 94
Amattar-sirsirra, 66
Amazon, 309
Anti-swine fever vaccine, 243
Anton Deimel, 58, 82, 88
Apple, 309
Armenia, 273
Arthashastra, 230, 281
Artificial intelligence, 268

Asian Development Bank, 175, 231
Assyria, 300
Astana Civil Service Hub, xii, 239
Aulfinger, Michael, 72
Austerity, 221–222
Autumn of the Plague in 1710, 204
Avaricious glutton, 129
Azim Premji, 309

B

Baba (or Bau), Goddess, 50
Baba, 51
Babylon, 194
Baden-Württemberg, 192
Baidu, 309
Baimenov, Alikhan, Chairman, xii, xv
Baker, Thomas, 219
Baltimore, 286
Banda, Hastings President of Malawi, 146
Bangladesh, 37, 200, 231–232, 279
Bau, 36, 42
BBC Radio classic comedy 'Men from the Ministry', 265

BBC TV series *Yes Minister*, 189, 200, 266
Beer, 44
Belgian Congo, 186
Benin, 250
Berners-Lee, Sir Tim, 306
Bhutan, 200, 223, 234, 288
Big Data for Big Brother, 312
Big data, 268, 297, 317
Bihar, 211
Black elephants, 6
Black swan, 258, 262
Bolivia, 210
Botswana, 147
Bourgon, Jocelyne, 236
Bovine Spongiform Encephalopathy (BSE), 255
Brazil, 149
Brexit, 315
British Civil Service, 265
British government, 111
Brunswick, 288
Bureaucracy, 54, 263–264, 276
Bureaucracy-bashing, 278
Bureaucratic Revolution, 13
Bureaupathology, 208
Burials, 35
Burundi, 210
Bush, George W., US President, 139
Butlin, Billy, 154
Byng, John Admiral, 219

C
21st Century, 282
Cambodia, 175
Canada, 166
Canberra Times, 246
Cardinal Wolsey, 96

Carlyle, Thomas, 199
Carnegie Endowment, 310
Carnegie, Andrew, 267
Carter, Jimmy, 39th President of the USA, 90
Ceausescu, Nicolae dictator of Romania, 130
Central African Republic, 250
Chad, 210
Chamberlain, Neville, 79
Chaplin, Charlie, 115
Charles I, 164
Childe, V. Gordon, 90
Chile, 149
China, 166, 211
Chinese secret societies, 252
Churchill, Winston, 196
Citizen Kane, 308
City-states, 274
Civil service college, 171
Civil service exams, 185
Civil service reform syndrome, 217
Clark, Helen, former Prime Minister of New Zealand, 239
Code of Hammurabi, 30
Cold War, 167
Collective anxiety neurosis, 241
Collective neurosis, 242, 256
Commonwealth, 141
Complexity, 127, 271
Confucian ideal, 127
Confucius, 321, 329
Congo, 250
Corruption, 200
Costa Rica, 149, 186
Creative State, 170
Credibility, 256
Cromwell, Thomas, 96

Cucumber, 43
Cult of leadership, 325
Cuneiform, 52
Custodian of the Imperial Inkstand, 212
Cyber politics, 306
Cybersecurity, 298
Cynic, 119
Czech Republic, 222

D

Dangerous Dogs Acts, 327
Demographics, 188
Denmark, 39, 173
Department for International Development, 231
Deryck Guyler, 265
Diagram Prize for Oddest Book Title of the Year, 258
Diakonoff, Igor, 58, 84, 95
Dickens, Charles, 144
Digital Bill of Rights, 306
Digital Magna Carta, 306
Diocletian, 284
Divorce, 104
Domesday Book, 164
Douglass North, 325
Dr Ah Leng Gwee, 246
Dr Ho Guan Lim, 246
Dubai, 114, 273, 277
Duke of Saint-Simon, 146
Duke University, 310

E

Eannatum, 20, 38, 40, 53, 69
Edmund Barker, 245
Edmund Burke, 278
Édouard-Pierre Blin, 285
Education, 256

Effendi, 185
El Salvador, 210
E-legitimacy, 306
Elites, 177, 184
Employee commitment, 220
Enanatum I, 20, 65
Enanatum II c, 20
End of History, The, 227
Enentarzi, 20
England, 203
Enki, 84
Enlil, 84
Enmetena, 20, 53, 95–96
Enshagkushana, 67
Ensi, 63
Entemena, 65
Epic of Gilgamesh, 20
Erich Röhm, 165
Eritrea, 229
Estonia, 171, 298
Estonian, 298
Evidence, 295
Expectancy Theory, 223
Extreme poverty, 294

F

Facebook, 309, 311
Fairness, 133
Fake academic footnotes, 295
Fake news, 295, 315
Female fox spirits, 247
Finland, 166, 173, 204, 209, 222
Flickr, 309
Forbidden City, 320
Fourth bureaucratic revolution, 261, 267, 335
Fourth industrial revolution, 4, 187, 263, 268, 305
Francis Rolt-Wheeler, 284

Franklin D. Roosevelt, 196
Frederick the Great, 144
Frederick William I, King of Prussia, 144
French Revolution, 126, 185, 261, 287
Frick Collection, 310
Frick, Henry Clay, 267
Fukuyama, Francis, 227
Fulton Report, 134, 145

G
Gambia, 250
Garden of Eden, 131
Garlic, 43
Gates, Bill, 309
Gauger, 303
General Electric, 252
General Matthew B. Ridgway, 289
Genital retraction, 247
George III, 131
Ghana, 221, 234, 250
Giacomo Matteotti, 88
Gilbert, Sir Martin, 196
Gilgamesh, 74, 87
Girsu, 32, 50, 335
Giuseppe Visicato, 89
Global Centre for Public Service Excellence, xvi
Global Commission on Internet, 307
Global Simplicity Index, 272
Globalisation, 270
Goal 16, 301
Goat, 38
Good governance, 291
Google, 309, 311
GOSPLAN, 91
Government abattoir, 245
Grantham, 220

Great Cough Year of 1580, 204
Great Depression, 283
Great Frost of 1601–1602, 204
Great Recession, 227, 266
Great Singapore Penis Panic of 1967, 257–258
Grimble, Sir Arthur, 141
Grindle, Merilee Professor at Harvard, 148
Grumbling, 15, 130

H
H.M. Customs, 270
Haiti, 292
Ha-Joon Chang, 279
Hamilton, Alexander, 199
Hammurabi, 39, 46, 79
Hanseatic League, 274
Harriman, Edward Henry, 267
Harvard University, Kennedy School of Government, 150
Harvard, 13, 217
Helsinki, 11
Henry IV, 57
Henry Kippin, 328
Henry Rawlinson, 89
Henry VIII, of England, 57
Heraclitus, 187
Herbert Simon, 323, 330
Hermann Hesse, 152
Hewart, Lord Chief Justice Gordon, 263
History, 152, 155
Hobbes, Thomas, 95, 118
Hong Kong, 147, 209
Humour, 130
Hungary, 130
Husar, Arndt, Deputy Director GCPSE Singapore 2013-2018, xvii

Hyde-White, Wilfrid, 265
Hydraulic state, 291

I
Iceland, 165
Ideology, 276
Incoherence, 128
India, 127, 150, 211, 222, 288
Indian Administrative Service (IAS), 150
Indonesia, 256, 292
Inequality, 294
Informality, 209
Innovation, 277–278
Integrity, 237
International Covenant on Civil and Political Rights, 298
Internet Corporation for Assigned Names and Numbers, 297, 314
Intrinsic motivation, 197, 221, 237
Ireland, 166
Iri'inimgina, 65
Irikagina, 18, 65
Iron cage, 184
Ishakku, 63
Isomorphic mimicry, 182
Italian National Fascist Party, 324

J
J.P. Morgan, 267
Jack Ma, 309
Jamaica, 269
James Buchanan Duke, 267
James Gilray, 131
Jammu and Kashmir, 211
Japan, 127, 165–166, 232
Jean-Jacques Rousseau, 95
Jeff Bezos, 309
Job satisfaction, 222

Jobless growth, 188
John Locke, 95
John Maynard Keynes, 195
John the Lydian, 129
John Winthrop, 195
Julius Caesar, 80
Just get out of the way, 225
Justice, 133

K
Kallang Industrial Estate, 252
Karl Marx, 199
Karl Wittfogel, 91
Kautilya, 281
Kazakhstan, 239, 273
Kenya, 170, 331
Kenyan Revenue Authority, 35
Khrushchev, Nikita First Secretary of the Communist Party of the Soviet Union from 1953 to 1964, 264
Kim Jong-Un, 219
King of Girsu, 68
Kingston, 269
Kish, 38, 67
Koro, 241
Kramer, Samuel Noah Professor, 83, 92, 95, 121, 198
Krishnadas, Devadas, esteemed entrepreneur, lucid author, trenchant wit and profound socio-political commentator, xvii
Kyrgyzstan, 273

L
Labyrinthine corridors, 128
Lack of modesty, 172
Lactantius, 284
Lagash, 27, 29–33, 46, 50, 56, 261, 284, 297, 300, 335, 337–338
Lagos, 250

Lamentation, 44
Lao Tzu, 271
Laozi, 321, 323, 329
Larry Page, 309
Lateran Pact, 88
Latin America, 149
Leadership Academy, 171
Lee Hsien Loong, Prime Minister of Singapore, 277
Lee Kuan Yew (LKY) Prime Minister of Singapore 1959 to 1990, 16, 191, 233, 242, 251–253, 274
Leftwich, Adrian, 189, 195
Legitimacy, 293, 296
Lenin, 40, 263
Lewis, Sir Arthur, 125
Liberia, 161
Lindblom, Charles, 232
Livingstone, David 19th-century missionary, 141
Log-frame linear logic, 272
Louis Bleriot, 149
Louis XIV, 185
Louis XVI, 164
Louvre, 25, 338
Low morale, 151
Ludwig von Mises, 264
Lugal, 63
Lugalanda, 20, 37, 64, 80, 105
Lugalanda, son of Enentarzi, 20
Lugalzagesi, 57, 67, 70, 85, 99, 101–103
Luxembourg, 166

M
MacMillan, Harold, British Prime Minister, 319
Mad Cow Disease, 255
Malawi, 141, 146–147, 168

Malaysia, 186, 241, 292
Maldives, 200
Malleus Maleficarum, 248
Malta, 114, 233
Manson-Bahr, Sir Philip, 248
Mao Tse-tung, 165
Margaret Mead, 278
Marine Le Pen, 13
Mark Zuckerberg, 309
Maslow's hierarchy of needs, 179
Mass hysteria, 243, 256
Mass psychogenic illness, 241
Matriarchy, 95
Mauritania, 210
Mauritius, 147
Max Weber, 118, 184, 282
Mbabane, 126
Measles, mumps and rubella (MMR) vaccine, 255
Mencius, 163, 321, 333
Meritocracy, 192
Meritocratic recruitment, 193
Mesopotamia, 300
Mexico, 213
Michael Bloomberg, 309
Michael Dell, 309
Michael Young, 264
Milton Friedman, 83, 93
Ministry for National Development, 243
Ministry of Health, 245
Modernisation, 250
Moldova, 200
Monaco, 233
Morale, 336
Moses, 96
Motivation, 224
Muddling through, 232, 276, 327

Mussolini, Benito Dictator of Italy 1922–1943, 88, 233, 262, 324
MySpace, 309

N

National Anti-Vaccination League, 263
National School of Government, 171
Nebuchadnezzar, 194
New Deal, 225, 263, 283
New Public Governance, 238
New Public Management (NPM), 10, 167, 190, 214, 226, 238, 266
New Public Passion, 214, 239
New Zeal, 263
New Zealand, 147, 167, 209, 237–238
Nigeria, 206, 210–212, 224, 250
Nineveh, 81
Ningirsu, 27, 40–41, 50–51, 335, 338
Ninshubur, 40
Nippur, 46, 52
Non-action, 329
Non-Governmental Organisations, 214
Norma Ronald, 265
Norman Conquest, 164
North Korea, 31, 39, 219
Northcote-Trevelyan Report of 1854, 16, 144
Norway, 166, 209

O

Oligopoly, 309
Open Data Initiative, 331
Organisation for Security and Co-operation in Europe, 312
Oriental Despot, 300
Oriental Despotism, 91
Oscar Wilde, 125
Ottoman Empire, 145
Ourou-Kagina, 65
Oval Plaque, 41

P

Pakistan, 34, 206, 235
Papua New Guinea, 201, 235–236
Paraguay, 210
Passion, 332
Passionate bureaucrat, 281, 283
Patesi, 63
Patrick O'Connor, 304
Patrimonialism, 293
People's Action Party (PAP), 245, 251
Perfect swans, 6
Peter Senge, 116
Peter the Great, 279
Petronius Arbiter, 295
Philippines, 222, 224
Philosopher–king, 329
Phnom Penh Water Supply Authority, 175
Pieter van Wulfften Palthe, 248
Pig farms, 243
Pitkin, Sir Gregory, 265
Poland, 166
Polanyi, Karl, 118
Policy, 128
Political authority, 193
Political settlement, 176
Politics of modernity, 250
Polyandry, 44
Pope Francis, 139, 226
Pork, 241
Portugal, 130, 222
Power, 128
Pragmatism, 275–276

Predappio, 325
President Ellen Johnson Sirleaf, 161
President John F. Kennedy, 278
Prestige, 332
Pride, 129, 332
Primary Production Department, 243, 253
Prime Minister's Delivery Unit, 134
Privacy, 310, 317
Professionalism, 332
Professor Anastase Shyaka, xvi
Prussia, 288
Psychotherapy, 132, 181
Public administration, 128, 237, 282
Public authority, 128
Public Choice Theory, 55, 219, 226, 266
Public health, 256
Public officials, 129
Public panic, 245
Public service excellence, 299
Public service values, 220
Public service, 191, 292
Public Works Museum, 286
Purposive muddling, 327
Putin, Vladimir President of Russia, 201

Q
Qatar, 147, 166, 209, 234
Queen's College, Oxford University, xiv

R
Rajiv Shah, 202
Reagan, Ronald, US President, 92, 139, 166, 226
Red tape, 212, 219
Reform of public service, 154

Reforms of Urukagina, 338
Reforms, 109
Ri Yong-jin, 219
Richard Murdoch, 265
Rigid hierarchies, 128
Robber barons, 308
Rockefeller Foundation, 310
Rockefeller, John D., 267, 308
Romance of the Civil Service, 285
Roosevelt, Franklin Delano, 32nd President of the USA, 283
Rules of the game, 191
Rumours, 243, 252
Russia, 200, 211, 312
Rwanda, 209
Ryan Orange, xvii

S
Samuel Finer, 126
Samuel Pepys, 146
Sargon of Akkad, 20
Sargon was the Stalin of Ancient Mesopotamia, 91
Sargon, 57, 70, 73
Sasa (Shasha, or Shagshag), 66
Sasag, 55
Satisficing, 327, 330
Scapegoat, 143
Schwab, Charles M., 267
Second bureaucratic revolution, 261
Seeing Like a State, 103
Self Determination Theory, 223
Sergey Brin, 309
Seven Years War, 219
Severe acute respiratory syndrome (SARS), 254
Sexually depraved, 129
Sheikh Hamdan bin Mohammed bin Rashid Al Maktoum, 277

Shimani Aishath, xvii
Shul Shaggana, 42
Shulshaga, 50
Simplification, 262
Singapore General Hospital, 245–246
Singapore Medical Association, 246
Singapore Medical Journal, 251
Singapore, 114, 147, 165–166, 191, 209, 223, 234, 241, 273, 292
Skype, 309
Smith, Adam, 118
Social contract between citizen and state, 128
Somalia, 157
Somaliland, 157
South African, 222
South Korea, 166
South Sea Bubble, 225
Stalin, 165
Stalin, Joseph dictator of the former USSR, 129
State effectiveness, 273
Stele of the Vultures, 40, 69
Stolipin, 87
Straits Times, 246
Sub-Saharan Africa, 221, 250
Successful states, 282
Sudan, 250
Sullivan, Lawrence, 283
Sultan Abdul Hamid II, 129
Sumer, 54
Supreme Court of India, 316
Sustainable Development Goals, 8
Swaziland, 125
Sweden, 209, 222
Switzerland, 114, 166, 186, 209, 221–222
Syed Jaafar Albar, 253

T

Taiwan, 166
Tallqvist, Knut, 87
Tanzania, 205, 222
Taoism, 321
Target, 315
Taxation, 169
Technological innovation, 270
Tell Al-Hiba, 51
Telloh, 51
Temple of Baba in Girsu, 107
TenCent, 309
Thailand, 288
Thatcher, Margaret, former Prime Minister of UK, 139, 166, 220, 226
The Lancet, 255
The oxygen of politics, 320
Theodore Roosevelt, 145, 267, 337
Theory of Constant Dissatisfaction, 132
Third bureaucratic revolution, 261
Thomas, Sir Keith, 248
Thomson Road General Hospital, 245
Tinkering, 140
Tōhoku tsunami, 324
Tomasi di Lampedusa, 277
Toynbee, Arnold, 90
Toyota, 232
Trenchant humour, 266
Trollope, Anthony, 198
Trump, Donald, 45th President of the USA, 72
Trust, 184, 296
Tun Haji Abdul Razak bin Dato' Haji Hussein, 189
Tuvalu, 141
Twitter, 9, 309, 311
Tyranny of the practical, 279

U

UAE, 234
Uganda, 205
Umma, 75, 79, 102, 335
United Arab Emirates, 209
United Kingdom, 147, 168, 174, 207
United Malays National Organisation (UMNO), 252
United States, 206
Universal Declaration of Human Rights, 298
Ur III, 109
Ur, 38
Urbanisation, 294
Ur-Nammu, 46
Ur-Nanshe, 20, 67, 71, 108
Urtarsirsira, 64–65
Uruinimgina (*see* Urukagina), 18, 20, 29, 37, 40–41, 49, 53, 65, 81, 105–106, 108, 113, 115, 121, 135, 197, 233, 284, 300, 335
Uruk, 38, 107
Urukagina, *le Reagan de Mésopotamie*, 93
Urukagina's Cones, 338
US Agency for International Development, 231
USSR, 171
Utusan Melayu, 253
Uzbekistan, 273

V

2063 Vision of the African Union, 301
Values, 237
Vanderbilt, Cornelius, 267
Vatican, 139
Venezuela, 210
Vietnam, 126, 166, 288, 292
Voltaire, French enlightenment writer, historian and philosopher, 219

W

1929 Wall Street Crash, 283
Waldo, Dwight, 323
Weimar Germany, 262
Whole of government, 130, 297
Wicked ostriches, 6
Wicked problems, 294
Wiki-leaks, 312
William Randolph Hearst, 267
Wilson, Harold, British Prime Minister, 143
World Bank Institute Governance Indicators, 187–188
World Bank, 140, 175, 231
World Bank's Worldwide Governance Indicators, 204
World Competitiveness Index, 223
World Economic Forum's, 8
World Happiness Index, 223
World Health Organisation, 254–255
Wu-bu-wei, 322
Wu-wei, 321, 323, 326, 328

X

Xunzi, 321

Y

Yandex, 309
Yemen, 204, 210
Yes, Prime Minister, 266
Young Turks, 131
Youth bulge, 188
Youtube, 309

Z

Zambia, 205
Zhuangzi, 321–322
Zimbabwe, 220

Printed in the United States
By Bookmasters